Man and the State

By
JACQUES MARITAIN

———————————————————

THE UNIVERSITY OF CHICAGO PRESS

CHARLES R. WALGREEN FOUNDATION LECTURES

320.15
M33m
83671
July 1973

ISBN: 0-226-50551-0 (clothbound); 0-226-50552-9 (paperbound)

THE UNIVERSITY OF CHICAGO PRESS, CHICAGO 60637

Hollis and Carter, Limited, London, S.W. 1, England

The University of Chicago Press, Ltd., London

ACKNOWLEDGMENT

✻

IN CONNECTION with this book I am happy to express my gratitude for the assistance that was given me by four good friends of mine: Professor John U. Nef, Mr. John Hite, Msgr. Charles Journet, Professor Yves Simon. Professor Nef kindly contributed to putting the first chapter in its final shape. Msgr. Journet was good enough to pay special attention to Chapter VI. I availed myself of some valuable remarks by Professor Simon, especially with regard to Chapter V. I am particularly grateful to Mr. Hite, who generously assumed the burden of revising the entire book; thanks to him I hope that my English does not appear seasoned by too many French manners of expression.

I am also indebted to Mrs. Oskar Morgenstern and Mrs. Elbert Benton Borgerhoff, who greatly assisted me in the drafting of these pages.

The book is the outgrowth of six lectures given in December 1949 under the auspices of the Charles R. Walgreen Foundation for the Study of American Institutions. I take this opportunity to extend my heartfelt thanks to the Foundation and to its distinguished chairman, Professor Jerome G. Kerwin.

✳ ✳ ✳

For the reprint edition of this book, I have made a few minor additions and alterations.

TABLE OF CONTENTS

✻

CHAPTER I

THE PEOPLE AND THE STATE

✵

I

NATION, BODY POLITIC, AND STATE

THERE is no more thankless task than trying rationally to distinguish and to circumscribe—in other words, trying to raise to a scientific or philosophical level—common notions that have arisen from the contingent practical needs of human history and are laden with social, cultural, and historical connotations as ambiguous as they are fertile, and which nevertheless envelop a core of intelligible meaning. Such concepts are nomadic, not fixed; they are shifting and fluid. Now they are used synonymously, now in opposition to one another. Everybody is the more at ease in using them as he does not know exactly what they mean. But as soon as one tries to define them and separate them from one another, hosts of problems and difficulties arise. One runs the risk of being switched onto a wrong track while attempting to bring out the truth, and to make analytical and systematic what has been conveyed to him by confused experience and concrete life.

The preceding remarks apply strikingly to the notions of *Nation*, *Body Politic* (or Political Society), and *State*. Yet nothing is more necessary, for a sound political philosophy, than to try to *sort out* these three notions, and clearly circumscribe the genuine meaning of each.

Often, when we speak in the current, more or less vague manner, these three concepts are used, and can be legitimately used, as synonymous with one another. But when it comes to

1

their genuine sociological meaning and to political theory, they must be sharply distinguished. The confusion between, or the systematic identification of, *Nation* and *Political Society*—or *Political Society* and *State*—or *Nation* and *State*, has been a woe to modern history. A correct restatement of the three concepts in question is badly needed. The austerity of my analysis may perhaps be excused, therefore, on account of the importance of the principles in political philosophy it may make us aware of.

II

COMMUNITY AND SOCIETY

A preliminary distinction must be made—namely between *community* and *society*. Of course these two terms may licitly be used synonymously, and I myself have done so many times. But it is also licit—and proper—to assign them to two kinds of social groups which are actually different in nature. This distinction, though it has been misused in the most grievous manner by the theorists of the superiority of "life" over reason, is in itself an established sociological fact. Both community and society are ethico-social and truly human, not mere biological realities. But a community is more of a work of nature and more nearly related to the biological; a society is more of a work of reason, and more nearly related to the intellectual and spiritual properties of man. Their inner social essences and their characteristics, as well as their spheres of realization, do not coincide.[1]

1. The concept of community, as it is used here, is a generic concept, covering the three specific forms of sociability that Professor Georges Gurvitch distinguishes under the names of "masses," "community," and "communion" (cf. Georges Gurvitch, *Essais de sociologie* [Paris: Recueil Sirey, 1938]; "Masses, Community, Communion," *Philosophical Review*, August, 1941). We agree with Professor Gurvitch on the distinction between Political Society and State (*Essais de Sociologie*, p. 60) and the fact that the Political Society as well as the State are "functional," not "suprafunctional," forms of organized sociability. We dissent from him on three main points: (1) His theory deals only with communities (in the generic sense of the word), so as to miss the basic distinction between community (especially the Nation) and society

In order to understand this distinction, we must remember that social life as such brings men together by reason of a certain common *object*. In social relations there is always an object, either material or spiritual, around which the relations among human persons are interwoven. In a *community*, as J. T. Delos[2] has rightly pointed out, the object is a *fact* which precedes the determinations of human intelligence and will, and which acts independently of them to create a common unconscious psyche, common feelings and psychological structures, and common mores. But in a *society* the object is a *task* to be done or an *end* to be aimed at, which depends on the determinations of human intelligence and will and is preceded by the activity—either decision, or, at least, consent—of the reason of individuals; thus, in the case of society the objective and rational element in social life explicitly emerges and takes the leading role. A business firm, a labor union, a scientific association are *societies* as much as is the body politic. Regional, ethnic, linguistic groups, social classes are *communities*. The tribe, the clan are communities that pave the way for, and foreshadow the advent of, the political society. The *community* is a product of instinct and heredity in given circumstances and

---

(especially the Political Society), with the essential rational characteristic of the latter, and thus makes of the Political Society a mere "superstructure" of the Nation. (2) He insists that the Nation is *supra-functional* (*ibid.*, p. 58), whereas we deny the existence of any *supra-functional* social group (that is, implying "an infinite ensemble of ends and values" [*ibid.*, p. 59]). The infinity in question is merely potential, therefore cannot be a specific determination of any social group whatever. Every social group is determined by an object (which is a *fact*, not an *end*, in the case of the Nation as of any community in general). The Nation is acephalous, it is not supra-functional: it is rather *infra-functional*. (3) Professor Gurvitch, like many modern authors, defines the State by the "monopoly of unconditional constraint" (cf. Georges Gurvitch, *Sociology of Law* [New York: Philosophical Library, 1942], pp. 238 ff.). The criterion of unconditional constraint is a merely empirical note, deriving from more essential characteristics, and does not make clear the nature of the State. The true criterion is the maintenance of law and public order, as relating to the common good of the Political Society.

2. Cf. J. T. Delos, *La Nation* (Montréal: L'Arbre, 1944).

historical frameworks; the *society* a product of reason and moral strength (what the Ancients called "virtue").

In the *community*, social relations proceed from given historical situations and environments: the collective patterns of feeling—or the collective unconscious psyche—have the upper hand over personal consciousness, and man appears as a product of the social group. In *society*, personal consciousness retains priority, the social group is shaped by men, and social relations proceed from a given initiative, a given idea, and the voluntary determination of human persons.

Even in *natural* societies, such as the family society and political society—that is, in societies which are both necessarily required and spontaneously rough-hewn by nature—*society* finally springs up from human freedom. Even in communities —regional communities, for instance, or vocational communities—that grow around some particular society, like an industrial or commercial establishment, *community* springs up from nature; I mean, from the reaction and adjustment of human nature to a given historical environment, or to the factual impact of the industrial or commercial society in question upon the natural conditioning of human existence. In the *community*, social pressure derives from coercion imposing patterns of conduct on man and comes into play in a deterministic mode. In *society*, social pressure derives from law or rational regulations, or from an idea of the common aim; it calls forth personal conscience and liberty, which must obey the law freely.

A society always gives rise to communities and community feelings within or around itself. Never can a community develop into a society, though it can be the natural soil from which some societal organization springs up through reason.

III

The Nation

Now the *Nation* is a community, not a society. The Nation is one of the most important, perhaps the most complex and complete community engendered by civilized life. Modern times have been faced with a conflicting tension between the Nation and another momentous human community, the Class; yet, as a matter of fact, the dynamism of the Nation has appeared to be the stronger—because it is more deeply rooted in nature.

The word nation originates from the Latin *nasci*, that is, from the notion of *birth*, but the nation is not something biological, like the Race. It is something ethico-social: a human community based on the fact of birth and lineage, yet with all the moral connotations of those terms: birth to the life of reason and the activities of civilization, lineage in familial traditions, social and juridical formation, cultural heritage, common conceptions and manners, historical recollections, sufferings, claims, hopes, prejudices, and resentments. An ethnic community, generally speaking, can be defined as a *community of patterns of feeling* rooted in the physical soil of the origin of the group as well as in the moral soil of history; it becomes a *nation* when this factual situation enters the sphere of self-awareness, in other words when the ethnic group *becomes conscious* of the fact that it constitutes a community of patterns of feeling—or rather, has a common unconscious psyche—and possesses its own unity and individuality, its own will to endure in existence. A nation is a community of people who become aware of themselves as history has made them, who treasure their own past, and who love themselves as they know or imagine themselves to be, with a kind of inevitable introversion. This progressive awakening of national consciousness has been a characteristic feature of modern history. Though it is normal and good in itself, it finally became exacerbated and gave rise to the plague of Nationalism, while —and probably because—the concept of Nation and the concept of State were confused and mixed up in an unfortunate and explosive manner.

The Nation has, or had, a soil, a land—this does not mean, as for the State, a territorial area of power and administration, but a cradle of life, work, pain, and dreams. The Nation has a language—though the linguistic groups by no means always coincide with the national ones. The Nation thrives on institutions—the creation of which, however, depends more on the human person and mind, or the family, or particular groups in the society, or the body politic, than on the Nation itself. The Nation has rights, which are but the rights of human persons to participate in the peculiar human values of a national heritage. The Nation has a historic calling, which is not its *own* calling (as if there were primordial and predestined national monads each of which was possessed of a supreme mission), but which is only a historical and contingent particularization of man's calling to the unfolding and manifestation of his own multifarious potentialities.

Yet for all of that the Nation is not a society; it does not cross the threshold of the political realm. It is a community of communities, a self-aware network of common feelings and representations that human nature and instinct have caused to swarm around a number of physical, historical and social data. Like any other community the Nation is "acephalous"[3]: it has élites and centers of influence—no head or ruling authority; structures—no rational form or juridical organization; passions and dreams—no common good; solidarity among its members, faithfulness, honor—no civic friendship; manners and mores—no formal norms and order. It does not appeal to the freedom and responsibility of personal conscience, it instils in human persons a second nature. It is a general pattern in private life, it does not know any principle of public order. Thus it is that in reality the national group cannot *transform itself* into a political society: a political society can progressively differentiate itself within a confused social life in which political functions and community activities were first com-

3. Cf. M. Hauriou, *Principes de droit constitutionnel* (Paris, 1923), p. 29.

mingled; the idea of the body politic can arise in the bosom of a national community; but the national community can only be a propitious soil and an occasion for that blossoming. In itself the idea of the body politic belongs to another, superior order. As soon as the body politic exists, it is something other than a national community.

The preceding analysis makes us realize how serious have been for modern history the confusion between Nation and State, the myth of the National State, and the so-called principle of nationalities understood in the sense that each national group must set itself up as a separate State.[4] Such a confusion has wrenched both Nation and State out of shape. The trouble began in the democratic theater, during the XIXth century. It came to full madness in the anti-democratic reaction of the present century. Let us consider the result in the most acute cases.

Uprooted from its essential order, and therefore losing its natural limits in the course of an anti-natural growth, the Nation has become an earthly divinity whose absolute selfishness is sacred, and it has used political power to subvert any steady order among peoples. The State, when it has been identified with the Nation, or even with the Race, and when the fever of the instincts of the earth has thus invaded its own blood—the State has had its will to power exasperated; it has presumed to impose by force of law the so-called type and genius of the Nation, thus becoming a cultural, ideological, caesaro-papist, totalitarian State. At the same time, that totalitarian State has degenerated by losing the sense of the objective order of justice and law, and by swerving toward what is peculiar to tribal as well as to feudal community achievements. For the universal and objective ties of law and for the specific relationship between the individual person and the

4. Cf. René Johannet, *Le Principe des nationalités* (2d ed.; Paris: Nouvelle Librairie Nationale, 1923).

political body, have been substituted personal ties derived
from blood, or from a particular commitment of man to man
or to the clan, the party, or the chief.

I have just emphasized the distinction between that sociological reality which is a *National Community* and that other
sociological reality which is a *Political Society*. It must now be
added that, as I have previously remarked, the existence of a
given society naturally calls forth the birth of new communities within or around that societal group. Thus, when a *political society* has been formed, especially when it has a century-old
experience strengthening genuine civic friendship, it naturally
gives rise, within itself, to a *national community* of a higher
degree, either with regard to the self-awareness of such an already existing community, or with regard to the very formation of a new National Community in which various nationalities have been merged. Thus, to the exact contrary of the
so-called principle of nationalities, the Nation here depends
on the existence of the body politic, not the body politic on
the existence of the Nation. The Nation does not become a
State. The State causes the Nation to be. Thus it is that a mul-
ti-national *Federation of States*, as is the United States, is at the
same time a multinational *Nation*. A genuine principle of nationalities would be formulated as follows: the body politic
should develop both its own moral dynamism and the respect
for human freedoms to such a point that the national communities which are contained within it would both have
their natural rights fully recognized, and tend spontaneously
to merge in a single higher and more complex National Community.

Let us compare from this point of view four significant instances: Germany, the old Austro-Hungarian Empire, France,
and the United States. Germany is a complex of nations, and
has been unable to bring about a genuine body politic; it has
made up for that frustration by an unnatural exaltation of the

national feeling and an unnatural Nation-State. The Austro-Hungarian double crown created a State but was unable to produce a Nation. France and the United States enjoyed particularly favorable circumstances,—as well as a sense of freedom and of the basic role of free choice or consent by people in political life; in each case this helped to produce a single Nation centered on the body politic— a Nation which achieved unity, as a result either of century-old trials or of a ceaseless process of self-creation. So for practical purposes we may use the expression the American Nation, the French Nation, to denote the American or French political body. Yet such a practical synonymity must not deceive us and make us forget the fundamental distinction between National Community and Political Society.

IV

THE BODY POLITIC

In contradistinction to the *Nation*, both the *Body Politic* and the *State* pertain to the order of society, even society in its highest or "perfect" form. In our modern age the two terms are used synonymously,[5] and the second tends to supersede the first. Yet if we are to avoid serious misunderstandings, we have to distinguish clearly between the State and the Body Politic. These do not belong to two diverse categories, but they differ from each other as a part differs from the whole.

5. "The State is a particular portion of mankind viewed as an organized unit" (John W. Burgess, *Political Science and Constitutional Law* [Boston: Ginn & Co., 1896], I, 50).

A similar confusion between Body Politic and State is usual among jurists. According to Story and Cooley, "a state is a body politic, or society of men, united together for the purpose of promoting their mutual safety and advantage by the joint efforts of their combined strength" (Thomas M. Cooley, *Constitutional Limitations* [Boston, 1868], p. 1; cf. Joseph Story, *Commentaries on the Constitution of the United States* [Boston, 1851], I, 142). The word "state," Story goes on to say (*ibid.*, p. 143), "means the whole people, united into one body politic; and the state, and the people of the state, are equivalent expressions."

The *Body Politic* or the *Political Society* is the whole. The *State* is a part—the topmost part—of this whole.

Political Society, required by nature and achieved by reason, is the most perfect of temporal societies. It is a concretely and wholly human reality, tending to a concretely and wholly human good—the common good. It is a work of reason, born out of the obscure efforts of reason disengaged from instinct, and implying essentially a rational order; but it is no more Pure Reason than man himself. The body politic has flesh and blood, instincts, passions, reflexes, unconscious psychological structures and dynamism—all of these subjected, if necessary by legal coercion, to the command of an Idea and rational decisions. Justice is a primary condition for the existence of the body politic, but Friendship is its very life-giving form.[6] It tends toward a really human and freely achieved communion. It lives on the devotion of the human persons and their gift of themselves. They are ready to commit their own existence, their possessions and their honor for its sake. The civic sense is made up of this sense of devotion and mutual love as well as of the sense of justice and law.

The entire man—though not by reason of his entire self and of all that he is and has—is part of the political society; and thus all his community activities, as well as his personal activities, are of consequence to the political whole. As we have pointed out, a national community of a higher human degree spontaneously takes shape by virtue of the very existence of the body politic, and in turn becomes part of the substance of the latter. Nothing matters more, in the order of material causality, to the life and preservation of the body politic than the accumulated energy and historical continuity of that national community it has itself caused to exist. This means chiefly a heritage of accepted and unquestionable structures,

6. Cf. Gerald B. Phelan, *Justice and Friendship*, in the "Maritain Volume" of the *Thomist* (New York: Sheed & Ward, 1943).

fixed customs and deep-rooted common feelings which bring into social life itself something of the determined physical data of nature, and of the vital unconscious strength proper to vegetative organisms. It is, further, common inherited experience and the moral and intellectual instincts which constitute a kind of empirical, practical wisdom, much deeper and denser and much nearer the hidden complex dynamism of human life than any artificial construction of reason.

Not only is the national community, as well as all communities of the nation, thus comprised in the superior unity of the body politic. But the body politic also contains in its superior unity the family units, whose essential rights and freedoms are anterior to itself, and a multiplicity of other particular societies which proceed from the free initiative of citizens and should be as autonomous as possible. Such is the element of pluralism inherent in every truly political society. Family, economic, cultural, educational, religious life matter as much as does political life to the very existence and prosperity of the body politic. Every kind of law, from the spontaneous, unformulated group regulations to customary law and to law in the full sense of the term, contributes to the vital order of political society. Since in political society authority comes from below, through the people, it is normal that the whole dynamism of authority in the body politic should be made up of particular and partial authorities rising in tiers above one another, up to the top authority of the State. Finally, the public welfare and the general order of law are essential parts of the common good of the body politic, but this common good has far larger and richer, more concretely human implications, for it is by nature the good human life of the multitude and is common to both the *whole* and the *parts*, the persons into whom it flows back and who must benefit from it. The common good is not only the collection of public commodities and services which the organization of common life presupposes: a sound fiscal condition, a strong military force; the body of just laws, good customs, and wise institutions which provides the political society with its structure; the heritage of its great historical remembrances, its symbols and its glories, its living traditions and cultural treasures. The common good also includes the sociological integration of all the civic conscience, political virtues and sense of law and freedom, of all the activity, material prosperity and spiritual riches, of unconsciously operating hereditary wisdom, of moral rectitude, justice, friendship, happiness, virtue and heroism in the individual lives of the members of the body politic. To the extent to which all these things are, in a certain measure, *communicable* and revert to each member, helping him to perfect his life and liberty as a person, they all constitute the good human life of the multitude.[7]

V

The State

From this enumeration of the features of the body politic, it should be evident that the body politic differs from the State. The State is only that part of the body politic especially concerned with the maintenance of law, the promotion of the common welfare and public order, and the administration of public affairs. The State is a part which *specializes* in the interests of the *whole*.[8] It is not a man or a body of men; it is a set of institutions combined into a topmost machine: this kind of work of art has been built by man and uses human brains and energies and is nothing without man, but it constitutes a superior embodiment of reason, an impersonal, lasting superstructure, the functioning of which may be said to be rational in the second degree, insofar as the reason's activity in it,

7. Cf. our book, *The Person and the Common Good* (New York: Charles Scribner's Sons, 1947).

8. Harold Laski described the State as a public service corporation (*A Grammar of Politics* [London: Allen & Unwin, 1935], p. 69).

bound by law and by a system of universal regulations, is more abstract, more sifted out from the contingencies of experience and individuality, more pitiless also, than in our individual lives.

The State is not the supreme incarnation of the Idea, as Hegel believed; the State is not a kind of collective superman; the State is but an agency entitled to use power and coercion, and made up of experts or specialists in public order and welfare, an instrument in the service of man. Putting man at the service of that instrument is political perversion. The human person as an individual is for the body politic and the body politic is for the human person as a person. But man is by no means for the State. The State is for man.

When we say that the State is the superior part in the body politic, this means that it is superior to the other organs or collective parts of this body, but it does not mean that it is superior to the body politic itself. The part as such is inferior to the whole. The State is inferior to the body politic as a whole, and is at the service of the body politic as a whole. Is the State even the *head* of the body politic? Hardly, for in the human being the head is an instrument of such spiritual powers as the intellect and the will, which the whole body has to serve; whereas the functions exercised by the State are for the body politic, and not the body politic for them.

The theory which I have just summarized, and which regards the State as a part or an instrument of the body politic, subordinate to it and endowed with topmost authority not by its own right and for its own sake, but only by virtue and to the extent of the requirements of the common good, can be described as an "instrumentalist" theory, founding the genuinely *political* notion of the State. But we are confronted with quite another notion, the *despotic* notion of the State, based on a "substantialist" or "absolutist" theory. According to this theory the State is a subject of right, i.e., a moral person, and

consequently a whole; as a result it is either superimposed on
the body politic or made to absorb the body politic entirely,
and it enjoys supreme power by virtue of its own natural, inalienable right and for its own final sake.

Of course there is for everything great and powerful an instinctive tendency—and a special temptation—to grow beyond
its own limits. Power tends to increase power, the power
machine tends ceaselessly to extend itself; the supreme legal
and administrative machine tends toward bureaucratic self-
sufficiency; it would like to consider itself an end, not a means.
Those who specialize in the affairs of the whole have a pro-
pensity to take themselves for the whole; the general staffs to
take themselves for the whole army, the Church authorities
for the whole Church; the State for the whole body politic.
By the same token, the State tends to ascribe to itself a peculiar common good—its own self-preservation and growth—
distinct both from the public order and welfare which are its
immediate end, and from the common good which is its final
end. All these misfortunes are but instances of "natural"
excess or abuse.

But there has been something much more specific and serious
in the development of the *substantialist* or *absolutist* theory of
the State. This development can be understood only in the
perspective of modern history and as a sequel to the structures
and conceptions peculiar to the Mediaeval Empire, to the absolute monarchy of the French classical age, and the absolute
government of the Stuart kings in England. Remarkably
enough, the very word *State* only appeared in the course of
modern history; the notion of the State was implicitly involved in the ancient concept of city (πόλις, *civitas*) which
meant essentially body politic, and still more in the Roman
concept of the Empire: it was never explicitly brought out in
Antiquity. According to a historical pattern unfortunately
most recurrent, both the normal development of the State—

which was in itself a sound and genuine progress—and the development of the spurious—absolutist—juridical and philosophical conception of the State took place at the same time.

An adequate explanation of that historical process would require a long and thorough analysis. Here I merely suggest that in the Middle Ages the authority of the Emperor, and in early modern times the authority of the absolute King, descended from above on the body politic, upon which it was superimposed. For centuries, political authority was the privilege of a superior "social race" which had a right—and believed it to be an innate or immediately God-given and inalienable right—to supreme power over, and leadership as well as moral guidance of, the body politic—made up, it was assumed, of people under age who were able to make requests, remonstrances, or riots, not to govern themselves. So, in the "baroque age," while the reality of the State and the sense of the State progressively took shape as great juridical achievements, the concept of the State emerged more or less confusedly as the concept of a whole—sometimes identified with the person of the king—which was superimposed on or which enveloped the body politic and enjoyed power from above by virtue of its own natural and inalienable right,—that is to say, which possessed sovereignty. For in the genuine sense of this word—which depends on the historical formation of the concept of sovereignty, prior to jurists' various definitions—sovereignty implies not only actual possession of and right to supreme power, but a right which is *natural and inalienable*, to a supreme power which is supreme *separate from* and *above* its subjects.[9]

At the time of the French Revolution that very concept of the State considered as a whole unto itself was preserved, but it shifted from the King to the Nation, mistakenly identified with the body politic; hence Nation, Body Politic and State

9. See chap. ii.

were identified.[10] And the very concept of sovereignty—as a *natural* or *innate* and *inalienable* right to supreme *transcendent* power—was preserved, but shifted from the King to the Nation. At the same time, by virtue of a voluntarist theory of law and political society, which had its acme in eighteenth-century philosophy, the State was made into a person (a so-called moral person) and a subject of right,[11] in such a way that the attribute of absolute sovereignty, ascribed to the Nation, was inevitably, as a matter of fact, to be claimed and exercised by the State.

Thus it is that in modern times the despotic or absolutist notion of the State was largely accepted among democratic

10. This confusion between State, Body Politic, and Law was to become classical. It appeared in a striking manner in the theory of A. Esmein (see his *Éléments de droit constitutionnel* [6th ed.; Paris: Recueil Sirey, 1914]), who insisted that "the State is the juridical personification of the Nation."

11. The notion of moral or collective personality—in which "personality" has a *proper analogical* value—applies to the *people* as a whole in a genuine manner: because the people as a whole (a *natural whole*) are an ensemble of real individual persons and because their unity as a social whole derives from a common will to live together which originates in these real individual persons.

Accordingly, the notion of moral or collective personality applies in a genuine manner to the *body politic*, which is the organic whole, composed of the people. As a result, both the people and the body politic are *subjects (or holders) of rights:* the people have a right to self-government; there is a mutual relationship of justice between the body politic and its individual members.

But that same notion of moral personality does not apply to the *State* (which is not a whole, but a part or a special agency of the body politic), except in a *merely metaphorical* manner and by virtue of a juridical fiction. The State is not a subject of rights, a *Rechtssubjekt*, as many modern theorists, especially Jellinek, mistakenly put it. (On the opposite side, Léon Duguit clearly realized that the State is not a subject of rights, but he went to the other extreme, and his general theory jeopardized the very notion of right.)

The rights of the people or of the body politic are not and cannot be *transferred* or given over to the State. Furthermore, in so far as the State *represents* the body politic (in the external relations of the latter with the other bodies politic), "the State" is a merely abstract entity which is neither a moral person nor a subject of rights. The rights ascribed to it are no rights of its own; they are the rights of the body politic—which is *ideally* substituted for by that abstract entity, and *really* represented by the men who have been put in charge of public affairs and invested with specific powers.

tenets by the theorists of democracy—pending the advent of Hegel, the prophet and theologian of the totalitarian, divinized State. In England, John Austin's theories only tended to tame and civilize somewhat the old Hobbesian Leviathan. This process of acceptance was favored by a symbolical property which genuinely belongs to the State, namely, the fact that, just as we say twenty head of cattle meaning twenty animals, in the same way the topmost part in the body politic naturally *represents* the political whole. Nay more, the notion of the latter is raised to a higher degree of abstraction and symbolization,[12] and the consciousness of the political society is raised to a more completely individualized idea of itself in the idea of the State. In the absolutist notion of the State, that symbol has been made a reality, has been hypostasized. According to this notion the State is a metaphysical monad, a person; it is a whole unto itself, *the* very political whole in its supreme degree of unity and individuality. So it absorbs in itself the body politic from which it emanates, as well as all the individual or particular wills which, according to Jean-Jacques Rousseau, have engendered the General Will in order mystically to die and resurge in its unity. And it enjoys absolute sovereignty as an essential property and right.

12. So it happened that a great theorist like Kelsen could make out of the State a mere juridical abstraction and identify it with Law and the legal order—a concept which uproots the State from its true sphere (that is, the political sphere) and which is all the more ambiguous as the real State (as topmost part and agency of the body politic) will in actual fact avail itself of that fictitious essence, ascribed to it as juridical *ens rationis*, to claim for itself the saintly attributes and "sovereignty" of the Law.

Be it noted, moreover, that the expression "sovereignty of the law" is a merely metaphorical expression, which relates to the rational nature of the law and its obligatory moral and juristic quality but has nothing to do with the genuine concept of sovereignty.

The concrete function of the State—its principal function—is to ensure the legal order and the enforcement of the law. But the State is not the law. And the so-called "sovereignty" of the State (see chap. ii) is in no way the moral and juridical "sovereignty" (that is, the property of binding consciences and being enforceable by coercion) of the Law (the just law).

That concept of the State, enforced in human history, has forced democracies into intolerable self-contradictions, in their domestic life and above all in international life. For this concept is no part of the authentic tenets of democracy, it does not belong to the real democratic inspiration and philosophy, it belongs to a spurious ideological heritage which has preyed upon democracy like a parasite. During the reign of individualist or "liberal" democracy the State, made into an absolute, displayed a tendency to substitute itself for the people, and so to leave the people estranged from political life to a certain extent; it also was able to launch the wars between nations which disturbed the XIXth Century. Nevertheless, after the Napoleonic era the worst implications of this process of State absolutization were restrained by the democratic philosophy and political practices which then prevailed. It is with the advent of the totalitarian régimes and philosophies that those worst implications were released. The State made into an absolute revealed its true face. Our epoch has had the privilege of contemplating the State totalitarianism of Race with German Nazism, of Nation with Italian Fascism, of Economic Community with Russian Communism.

The point which needs emphasis is this. For democracies today the most urgent endeavor is to develop social justice and improve world economic management, and to defend themselves against totalitarian threats from the outside and totalitarian expansion in the world; but the pursuit of these objectives will inevitably involve the risk of having too many functions of social life controlled by the State from above, and we shall be inevitably bound to accept this risk, as long as our notion of the State has not been restated on true and genuine democratic foundations, and as long as the body politic has not renewed its own structures and consciousness, so that the people become more effectively equipped for the exercise of freedom, and the State may be made an actual instrument for the common good of all. Then only will that very topmost agency, which is made by modern civilization more and more necessary to the human person in his political, social, moral, even intellectual and scientific progress, cease to be at the same time a threat to the freedoms of the human person as well as of intelligence and science. Then only will the highest functions of the State—to ensure the law and facilitate the free development of the body politic—be restored, and the sense of the State be regained by the citizens. Then only will the State achieve its true dignity, which comes not from power and prestige, but from the exercise of justice.

VI

Normal Growth and the Simultaneous Process of Perversion

At this point I should like not to be misunderstood. I hope that my previous remarks have made it sufficiently clear that I by no means condemn or depreciate the State and its astonishing growth in the course of modern history. That would be as blindly unreal and futile as to condemn or reject the mechanical achievements which have transformed the world, and which could and should become instruments for the liberation of man. From the last period of the XIXth Century on, state intervention has been needed to compensate for the general disregard for justice and human solidarity that prevailed during the early phases of the industrial revolution. State legislation with regard to employment and labor is in itself a requirement of the common good. And without the power of the State—the democratic State—how could a free body politic resist the pressure or the aggression of totalitarian States? The growth of the State, in modern centuries, as a rational or juridical machine and with regard to its inner constitutive system of law and power, its unity, its discipline; the growth of the State, in the present century, as a technical machine and with regard to its law-making, supervising, and organizing functions in social and economic life, are in themselves part of normal progress.

Such progress has been entirely corrupted in totalitarian States. It remains normal progress, though subject to many risks, in democratic States, especially as regards the development of social justice.

We may dislike the State machinery; I do not like it. Yet many things we do not like are necessary, not only in fact, but by right. On the one hand, the primary reason for which men, united in a political society, need the State, is the order of justice. On the other hand, social justice is the crucial need of modern societies. As a result, the primary duty of the modern State is the enforcement of social justice.

As a matter of fact, this primary duty is inevitably performed with abnormal emphasis on the power of the State to the very extent that the latter has to make up for the deficiencies of a society whose basic structures are not sufficiently up to the mark with regard to justice. Those deficiencies are the first cause of the trouble. And thus any theoretical objections or particular claims, even justified in their own particular spheres, will inevitably be considered as but minor things in the face of the vital necessity—not only factual but moral—of meeting the long-neglected wants and rights of the human person in the deepest and largest strata of the human society.

The problem, in my opinion, is to distinguish the normal progress of the State from the false notions, connected with the concept of sovereignty, which prey upon it; and also to change the backward general conditions which, by imposing a too heavy burden upon it, make it liable to become seriously vitiated. For both those backward social conditions and those false absolutist notions give rise to a process of perversion combined with and preying upon normal growth. How to describe this process of perversion? It occurs—that is apparent from all our previous remarks—when the State mistakes itself for a whole, for *the* whole of the political society, and consequently takes upon itself the exercise of the functions and the performance of the tasks which normally pertain to the body politic and its various organs. Then we have what has been labelled "the paternalist State": the State not only supervising from the political point of view of the common good (which is normal), but directly organizing, controlling, or managing, to the extent which it judges the interests of public welfare to demand, all forms—economic, commercial, industrial, cultural, or dealing with scientific research as well as with relief and security—of the body politic's life.

Let us point out in this connection that what is called "nationalization," and is in reality "statization," can be opportune or necessary in certain cases, but should by nature remain exceptional—limited to those public services so immediately concerned with the very existence, order, or internal peace of the body politic that a risk of bad management is then a lesser evil than the risk of giving the upper hand to private interests. The fact remains that the State has skill and competence in administrative, legal, and political matters, but is inevitably dull and awkward—and, as a result, easily oppressive and injudicious—in all other fields. To become a boss or a manager in business or industry or a patron of art or a leading spirit in the affairs of culture, science, and philosophy is against the nature of such an impersonal topmost agency, abstract so to speak and separated from the moving peculiarities, mutual tensions, risks, and dynamism of concrete social existence.

By virtue of a strange intermingling in human vocabulary, the word *nationalization* conveys a socialistic meaning, whereas the word *socialization,* on the contrary, if it were correctly understood, would have rather personalist and pluralist implications. For, taken in its genuine sense, it refers to that process of social integration through which association in a single enterprise extends not only to the capital invested, but also to labor and management, and all persons and various groups involved are made participants in some form or other of co-ownership and co-management. This process is not an attack on, but an expansion of private ownership. It depends on the search of free initiative for new economic modalities and adjustments, the more successful of which will be one day sanctioned by the law. It rises from the natural growth of the system of free enterprise, when common consciousness becomes aware of the social function of private property and of the necessity of giving organic and institutional forms to that law of the "common use" on which Thomas Aquinas has laid particular stress.[13]

As a result I would say that if our present social structure is to evolve along normal lines, a first step, made necessary by the requirements of public welfare, would consist in having the State start and support—as has been shown possible by the outstanding example of the Tennessee Valley Authority —large scale undertakings planned and managed *not* by the State and not from the center of the country's political administration, but on the spot, by private enterprises co-ordinated with one another and by the various communities of the very people concerned, under the leadership of independent responsible appointees. Thus the State itself would launch a movement of progressive decentralization and "destatization" of social life, tending toward the advent of some new personalist and pluralist[14] régime.

13. Cf. our book, *Freedom in the Modern World* (New York: Charles Scribner's Sons, 1936), Appendix I, "Person and Property."

14. On the notion of pluralism see my books, *Du régime temporel et de la liberté* ("Freedom in the Modern World"), chap. i, and *Humanisme intégral* ("True Humanism"), chap. v. See also Professor R. M. MacIver's observations on the "multigroup society" (*The Web of Government* [New York: Macmillan Co., 1947], pp. 421 ff.).

When I developed this theory of the pluralist principle, forging the expression for

The final step would take place, in such a new régime, when prodding by the State would no longer be necessary, and all organic forms of social and economic activity, even the largest and most comprehensive ones, would start from the bottom, I mean from the free initiative of and mutual tension between the particular groups, working communities, co-operative agencies, unions, associations, federated bodies of producers and consumers, rising in tiers and institutionally recognized. Then a definitely personalist and pluralist pattern of social life would come into effect in which new societal types of private ownership and enterprise would develop. And the State would leave to the multifarious organs of the social body the autonomous initiative and management of all the activities which by nature pertain to them. Its only prerogative in this respect would be its genuine prerogative as topmost umpire and supervisor, regulating these spontaneous and autonomous activities from the superior political point of view of the common good.

So perhaps it will be possible, in a pluralistically organized body politic, to make the State into a topmost agency concerned only with the final supervision of the achievements of institutions born out of freedom, whose free interplay expressed the vitality of a society integrally just in its basic structures.

* * *

To sum up, the common good of the body politic demands a network of authority and power in political society, and therefore a special agency endowed with uppermost power, for the sake of justice and law. The State is that uppermost political

---

my own purposes, I had not read Harold Laski's books; it was only later on that I became aware of the fundamental part played by the concept of pluralism in his political philosophy. Such phenomena of intellectual convergence between quite different, even conflicting, lines of thought (as was also the case, in another connection, with "personalism") are a sign of the inner necessity for the appearance of certain basic ideas at a given moment in history.

agency. But the State is neither a whole nor a subject of right, or a person. It is a part of the body politic, and, as such, inferior to the body politic as a whole, subordinate to it, and at the service of its common good. The common good of the political society is the final aim of the State, and comes before the immediate aim of the State, which is the maintenance of the public order. The State has a primary duty concerning justice, which should be exercised only in the manner of an ultimate supervision in a body politic basically just in its inner structures. Finally the body politic must control the State, which however contains the functions of government within its own fabric. At the point of the pyramid of all the particular structures of authority which in a democratic society should take form in the body politic from the bottom up, the State enjoys topmost supervising authority. But this supreme authority is received by the State *from the body politic*, that is, from the people; it is not a natural right to supreme power which the State possesses of itself. As follows from a critical elucidation of the concept of sovereignty—with which the second chapter of this book is concerned—the supreme authority of the State should in no way be called sovereignty.

In the eyes of a sound political philosophy there is no sovereignty, that is, no natural and inalienable right to *transcendent* or *separate* supreme power in political society. Neither the Prince nor the King nor the Emperor were really sovereign, though they bore the sword and the attributes of sovereignty. Nor is the State sovereign; nor are even the people sovereign. God alone is sovereign.

VII

THE PEOPLE

We have discussed the Nation, the Body Politic, the State. Now what about the People?

I just said that the people are not sovereign in the genuine sense of this word. For in its genuine sense the notion of sovereignty relates to a power and independence which are supreme *separately from* and *above* the whole ruled by the sovereign. And obviously the power and independence of the people are not supreme *separately from* and *above the people themselves*. Of the people as well as of the body politic we have to say, not that they are sovereign, but that they have a natural right to *full autonomy*, or to self-government.

The people exercise this right when they establish the Constitution, written or unwritten, of the body politic; or when, in a small political group, they meet together to make a law or a decision; or when they elect their representatives. And this right remains always in them. It is by virtue of it that they control the State and their own administrative officials. It is by virtue of it that they cause to pass into those who are designated to take care of the common good, the right to make laws and to govern, so that, by investing those particular men with authority, within certain fixed limits of duration and power, the very exercise of the right of the people to self-government restricts to the same extent its further *exercise*, but does not make the *possession* of this right itself cease or lessen in any way. The administrative officials, or the Administration, that is, the human persons who are invested with executive power, are (in the strictest sense of the word "governing") the governing organ *in the State*, because the people have made them, *in the body politic*, the deputies for the very whole. All this is fully consistent with our conclusion that the most accurate expression concerning the democratic régime is not "sovereignty of the people." It is Lincoln's saying: "government of the people, by the people, for the people." This means that the people are governed by men whom they themselves have chosen and entrusted with a right to command, for functions of a determined nature and duration, and over whose management they maintain a regular control—first of all by

means of their representatives and the assemblies thus constituted.[15]

* * *

As concerns furthermore the very notion of the people, I
would say that the modern concept of the people has a long
history and stems from a singular diversity of meanings which
have fused together.[16] But considering only the political significance of the word, suffice it to say that the people are the
multitude of human persons who, united under just laws, by
mutual friendship, and for the common good of their human
existence, constitute a political society or a body politic. The
notion of body politic means the whole unit composed of the
people. The notion of the people means the members organi-
cally united who compose the body politic. Thus what I have
said concerning either Body Politic and Nation or Body Politic
and State holds good for either People and Nation or People
and State. Nay more, since the people are human persons who
not only form a body politic, but who have each one a spiritual soul and a supratemporal destiny, the concept of the
people is the highest and noblest concept among the basic
concepts that we are analyzing. The people are the very substance, the living and free substance, of the body politic. The
people are above the State, the people are not for the State, the
State is for the people.

I should finally like to point out that the people have a special need of the State, precisely because the State is a particular
agency specializing in the care of the whole, and thus has
normally to defend and protect the people, their rights and the
improvement of their lives against the selfishness and par-
ticularism of privileged groups or classes. In ancient France the
people and the King relied upon each other, somewhat am-

15. See infra, pp. 65–66 and 127–39; and, on Lincoln's saying, *Scholasticism and
Politics* (New York: Macmillan Co., 1940), pp. 107–8.

16. Cf. our book *Raison et raisons* (Paris: Luf, 1947), chap. xi.

biguously, in their struggle against the supremacy of the great feudal lords or the nobility. In modern times it has been the same with the people and the State in regard to the struggle for social justice. Yet, as we have seen, this normal process, if it becomes corrupted by the absolutism of the totalitarian State, which raises itself to the supreme rule of good and evil, leads to the misfortune and enslavement of the people; and it is impaired and jeopardized if the people surrender themselves to a State, which, as good as it may be, has not been freed from the notion of its so-called sovereignty, as well as from the factual deficiencies of the body politic itself. In order both to maintain and make fruitful the movement for social improvement supported by the State, and to bring the State back to its true nature, it is necessary that many functions now exercised by the State should be distributed among the various autonomous organs of a pluralistically structured body politic—either after a period of State capitalism or of State socialism, or, as is to be hoped, in the very process of the present evolution. It is also necessary that the people have the will, and the means, to assert their own control over the State.

CHAPTER II
THE CONCEPT OF SOVEREIGNTY

✧

I
THE POINT AT ISSUE

NO CONCEPT has raised so many conflicting issues and involved XIXth Century jurists and political theorists in so desperate a maze as the concept of Sovereignty. The reason for this is perhaps the fact that the original, genuine philosophical meaning of the concept had not been, from the very start, sufficiently examined, tested, and taken seriously by them.

In the same measure as crucial practical problems dealing with international law developed, the controversies about State Sovereignty, considered in its external aspect (relations between States), grew deeper and more extended. The question was posed whether the international community as a whole is not the true holder of Sovereignty, rather than the individual States.[1] In some quarters, even the very notion of Sovereignty was challenged.[2] Such was the stand taken first by Triepel, then by several other international lawyers like Edmunds[3] and Foulke.[4] Yet that challenge to the concept of Sovereignty

1. Cf. Robert Lansing, *Notes on Sovereignty* (Washington: Carnegie Endowment for International Peace, 1921), chap. ii, "Notes on World Sovereignty." Reprinted from the *American Journal of International Law*, January, 1921.

2. Cf. Hymen Ezra Cohen, *Recent Theories of Sovereignty* (Chicago: University of Chicago Press, 1937), pp. 82 ff.

3. Sterling E. Edmunds, *The Lawless Law of Nations* (Washington, D.C.: Byrne & Co., 1925).

4. Roland R. Foulke, *A Treatise on International Law* (Philadelphia: John C. Winston Co., 1920): "The word sovereignty is ambiguous. . . . We propose to waste no time in

remained only juridical in nature, and did not come down to the philosophical roots of the matter.

My aim in this chapter is to discuss Sovereignty not in terms of juridical theory, but in terms of political philosophy. I think that the grounds for doing so are all the better as Sovereignty, in its historical origins, as Jellinek once observed, is "a political concept which later became transformed"[5] with a view to securing a juristic asset to the political power of the State.

It is my contention that political philosophy must get rid of the word, as well as the concept, of Sovereignty:—not because it is an antiquated concept,[6] or by virtue of a sociological-juridical theory of "objective law";[7] and not only because the concept of Sovereignty creates insuperable difficulties and theoretical entanglements in the field of international law; but because, considered in its genuine meaning, and in the perspective of the proper scientific realm to which it belongs—political philosophy—this concept is intrinsically wrong[8] and bound to mislead us if we keep on using it—assuming that it

---

chasing shadows, and will therefore discard the word entirely. The word 'independence' sufficiently indicates every idea embraced in the use of sovereignty necessary to be known in the study of international law" (p. 69).

5. Georg Jellinek, *Recht des modernen Staates: Allgemeine Staatslehre* (Berlin, 1900), p. 394.

6. Cf. Hugo Preuss, *Gemeinde, Staat, und Reich als Gebietskörperschaften* (Berlin, 1889); Charles E. Merriam, *History of the Theory of Sovereignty since Rousseau* (New York: Columbia University Press, 1900).

7. Cf. Léon Duguit, *Law in the Modern State* (New York: Viking Press, 1919). I am in agreement with Duguit as regards the necessity of discarding both the concept of the non-accountability of the State and the concept of State Sovereignty, not as regards the reasons upon which his conclusions are founded.

8. From another philosophic outlook, this is also the position of Harold J. Laski. Cf. his *Studies in the Problem of Sovereignty* (New Haven: Yale University Press, 1917) and *A Grammar of Politics* (New Haven: Yale University Press, 1925).

Professor MacIver, in his book *The Web of Government*, has made out the case against Sovereignty in a remarkably forceful manner (cf. R. M. MacIver, *The Web of Government* [New York: Macmillan Co., 1947], pp. 48–51, 69–73).

has been too long and too largely accepted to be permissibly rejected, and unaware of the false connotations that are inherent in it.

Is a somewhat pedantic remark, but dealing with accuracy in the use of words, permissible at this point?

Just as the words πόλις or *civitas* are often translated by "state" (though the most appropriate name is "commonwealth" or "body politic," not "state"), so the words *principatus* and *suprema potestas* are often translated by "sovereignty," the words κύριος or *princeps* ("ruler") by "sovereign."[9] This is a misleading translation, which muddles the issue from the start. *Principatus* ("principality") and *suprema potestas* ("supreme power") simply mean "highest ruling authority," not "sovereignty" as has been conceived since the moment when this word made its first appearance in the vocabulary of political theory. Conversely, "sovereignty" was rendered at that moment by *majestas* in Latin and ἄκρα ἐξουσία in Greek, as was well known at the time of Jean Bodin.[10]

II

JEAN BODIN'S SOVEREIGN PRINCE

Jean Bodin is rightly considered the father of the modern theory of Sovereignty. For Bodin, the king did not possess supra-mundane Sovereignty, which has absolutely nothing above itself. God was above the king, and the supreme power of the king over his subjects was itself submitted to "the law of God and nature,"[11] to the requirements of the moral

9. Cf. Aristotle *Politics* iii. 15. 1286b31; iv. 4. 1290a32, etc.; where Aristotle said κύριος, the Oxford translation, under the editorship of W. D. Ross, puts *sovereign*. Thomas Aquinas *Sum. theol.* i–ii. 90. 3, obj. 3; 96. 5, corp., obj. 3, and *ad* 3, etc.; where Aquinas said *princeps*, the translation edited by the English Dominicans puts *sovereign*.

10. Cf. Jean Bodin, *De la république* (Paris: Chez Jacques du Puys, 1583), Book I, chap. 8.

11. *Ibid.*, Book I, chap. 8.

order.[12] But the king was Sovereign, the king was possessed of human Sovereignty. Let us, then, listen to Bodin's words:

"Il est icy besoin de former la définition de souveraineté, par ce qu'il n'y a ny jurisconsulte, ny philosophe politique, qui l'ayt définie."[13]

"La souveraineté est *la puissance absolue et perpétuelle d'une République.*"[14]

12. Mr. Max Adam Shepard ("Sovereignty at the Crossroads: A Study of Bodin," *Political Science Quarterly*, XLV [1930], 580–603) has insisted that Bodin was at the crossroads between the medieval notion of the Prince—submitted to the law (the human law), not as to its *vis coactiva*, but as to its *vis directiva* (cf. *Sum. theol.* i–ii. 96. 5, *ad* 3)— and the modern ("monist") notion of the Prince, completely free from any law on earth. See also Professor Charles McIlwain's observations on Bodin and Hobbes in his article, "Sovereignty in the Present World," *Measure*, 3d issue, 1950. It is true that, inevitably, Bodin remained to some extent tributary to the Middle Ages and did not get the full distance on the road later traversed by Hobbes and Austin. But if he made the Sovereign bound to respect the *jus gentium* and the constitutional law of monarchy (*leges imperii*), this was because, in his view, when it came to such things as the inviolability of private property, or the precepts of *jus gentium*, or the "laws of the realm" like the Salic Law, expressing the basic agreement in which the power of the Prince originates, human laws and tribunals were *only the expressions or the organs of Natural Law itself*, so that, as a result, their pronouncements were valid even with regard to the Sovereign. This peculiar view of Bodin's (based, moreover, on a wrong idea of Natural Law) was to be discarded by the further theorists of Sovereignty, and in this sense he stopped halfway. Yet the fact remains that Bodin's sovereign was only subject to Natural Law, and to no human law whatsoever as distinct from Natural Law, and that is the core of political absolutism.

On Jean Bodin see Roger Chauviré, *Jean Bodin auteur de la République* (Paris, 1914); A. Ponthieux, "Quelques documents inédits sur Jean Bodin," *Revue du XVIe siècle*, Vol. XV (1928), fasc. 1–2; A. Garosci, *Jean Bodin* (Milan, 1935); Pierre Mesnard, *L'Essor de la philosophie politique au XVIe siècle* (Paris: Boivin, 1936), pp. 473–546, "La 'République' de Jean Bodin," and "Jean Bodin et la critique de la morale d'Aristote," *Revue Thomiste*, Vol. III (1949).

13. Bodin, *op. cit.*, Book I, chap. 8, p. 122. "For so here it behoveth first to define what majestie or Soveraigntie is, which neither lawyer nor politicall philosopher hath yet defined" (The Six Bookes of a Commonweale written by J. Bodin, a famous Lawyer, and a man of great Experience in matters of State; out of the French and Latine Copies, done into English, by Richard Knolles. London, Impensis G. Bishop, 1606, p. 84).

14. *Ibid.*, p. 122. "Majestie or Soveraigntie is the most high, absolute, and perpetuall power over the citisens and subjects in a Commonweale" (English trans., p. 84).

"Ceste puissance est *perpétuelle*,"[15] that is, "pour la vie de celuy qui a la puissance"[16] as opposed to those who "ne sont que dépositaires, et gardes de ceste puissance jusques à ce qu'il plaise au peuple ou au Prince la révoquer."[17]]

"Si le peuple octroye sa puissance à quelcun tant qu'il vivra, en qualité d'officier, ou lieutenant, ou bien pour se descharger seulement de l'exercice de sa puissance: en ce cas il n'est point souverain, ains simple officier, ou lieutenant, ou régent, ou gouverneur, ou gardien, et bail de la puissance d'autruy."[18]

But "*Si la puissance absolue luy est donnée purement et simplement*, sans qualité de magistrat, ny de commissaire, ny forme de précaire, *il est bien certain que cestuy-là est, et se peut dire monarque souverain: car le peuple s'est dessaisi et dépouillé de sa puissance souveraine, pour l'ensaisiner et investir: et à luy, et en luy transporté tout son pouvoir, auctorité, prérogatives, et souverainetés.*"[19]

Now what does "puissance *absolue*" mean?—"*Le peuple ou les seigneurs d'une République peuvent donner purement et simplement la puissance souveraine et perpétuelle à quelcun pour disposer des biens, des personnes, et de tout l'estat à son plaisir, et puis le laisser à qui il voudra, et tout ainsi que le propriétaire peut donner son bien purement et simplement*, sans autre cause que de sa libéralité, qui est

15. *Ibid.*, p. 122. "This power ought to be perpetuall" (p. 84).

16. *Ibid.*, p. 126. "For the tearme of the life of him that hath the power" (p. 87).

17. *Ibid.*, p. 122. "Seeing that they are but men put in trust, and keepers of this soveraigne power, untill it shall please the people or the prince that gave it them to recall it" (p. 84).

18. *Ibid.*, p. 127. "If the people shall give all their power unto any one so long as he liveth, by the name of a magistrat, lieutenant, or governour, or onely to discharge themselves of the exercise of their power: in this case he is not to be accounted any soveraigne, but a plaine officer, or lieutenant, regent, governour, or guerdon and keeper of another mans power" (p. 88).

19. *Ibid.*, p. 127. "If such absolute power bee given him purely and simply without the name of a magistrat, governour, or lieutenant, or other forme of deputation, it is certaine that such an one is, and may call himselfe a Soveraigne Monarch: for so the people hath voluntarily disseised and dispoyled it selfe of the soveraigne power, to sease and invest another therein; having on him, and uppon him transported all the power, authoritie, prerogatives, and soveraigneties thereof" (p. 88).

la vraye donation: et qui ne reçoit plus de conditions, estant une fois parfaicte et accomplie."[20]

Thus "*le Monarque est divisé du peuple.*"[21]

And "le poinct principal de la majesté souveraine et puissance absolue, gist principalement à donner loy aux subjects en général sans leur consentement."[22]

"*Le Prince souverain n'est tenu rendre conte qu'à Dieu.*"[23]

"*Le Prince souverain ne doit serment qu'à Dieu.*"[24]

"*La souveraineté n'est limitée, ny en puissance, ny en charge, ny à certain temps.*"[25]

"*Le Prince est l'image de Dieu.*"[26]

"*Or tout ainsi que ce grand Dieu souverain ne peut faire un Dieu pareil à luy,* attendu qu'il est infini, et qu'il ne se peut faire qu'il y ayt deux choses infinies, par démonstration nécessaire: aussi pouvons nous dire que le Prince que nous avons posé comme l'image de Dieu, ne peut faire un subject égal à luy, que sa puissance ne soit anéantie."[27]

20. *Ibid.*, p. 128. "For the people or the lords of a Commonweale, may purely and simply give the soveraigne and perpetuall power to any one, to dispose of the goods and lives, and of all the state at his pleasure: and so afterward to leave it to whom he list: like as the proprietarie or owner may purely and simply give his owne goods, without any other cause to be expressed, than of his owne meere bountie; which is indeed the true donation, which no more receiveth condition, being once accomplished and perfected" (pp. 88–89).

21. *Ibid.*, p. 143. "The monarch is divided from the people" (p. 99).

22. *Ibid.*, p. 142. "So wee see the principall point of soveraigne majestie, and absolute power, to consist principally in giving laws unto the subjects in generall, without their consent" (p. 98).

23. *Ibid.*, p. 125. "Whereas the prince or people themselves, in whome the Soveraigntie resteth, are to give account unto none, but to the immortall God alone" (p. 86).

24. *Ibid.*, p. 143. "A soveraign prince next under God, is not by oath bound unto any" (p. 99).

25. *Ibid.*, p. 124. "So that Soveraigntie is not limited either in power, charge, or time certaine" (p. 85).

26. *Ibid.*, pp. 156, 161. "The prince is the image of God."

27. *Ibid.*, Book I, chap. 10, p. 215. "For as the great soveraigne God, cannot make another God equall unto himself, considering that he is of infinit power and greatnes, and that there cannot bee two infinit things, as is by naturall demonstrations manifest:

III

The Original Error

Thus Bodin's position is perfectly clear. Since the people have absolutely deprived and divested themselves of their total power in order to transfer it to the Sovereign, and invest him with it, then the Sovereign is no longer a part of the people and the body politic: he is "divided from the people," he has been made into a whole, a *separate* and transcendent whole, which is his sovereign living Person, and by which the other whole, the immanent whole or the body politic, is ruled from above. When Jean Bodin says that the sovereign Prince is the image of God, this phrase must be understood in its full force, and means that the Sovereign—submitted to God, but accountable only to Him—transcends the political whole just as God transcends the cosmos. Either Sovereignty means nothing, or it means supreme power *separate* and *transcendent*—not at the peak but *above* the peak ("par dessus tous les subjects")[28] —and ruling the entire body politic *from above*. That is why this power is absolute (ab-solute, that is non-bound, separate), and consequently unlimited, in its extension as well as in its duration, and not accountable to anything on earth.

Let us observe at this point that there is no command without some kind of separation. *Segregatus ut imperet*, "separate, in order to command," Anaxagoras said of the νοῦς, the divine Intellect. After all, does not any man, once put in command, begin by separating himself from others in a certain measure, be it by means of a bigger chair or a less accessible office room? Yet it is the kind of separation which is the point at issue. As

---

so also may wee say, that the prince whom we have set down as the image of God, cannot make a subject equall unto himselfe, but that his owne soveraigntie must thereby be abased" (p. 155).

28. "Car souverain (c'est à dire, celuy qui est par dessus tous les subjects) ne pourra convenir à celuy qui a faict de son subject son compagnon" (*ibid.*, Book I, chap. 10; *ed. cit.*, p. 215).

regards political command, separation is truly and genuinely required only as an *existential* status or condition for the *exercise* of the right to govern. But with Sovereignty separation is required as an *essential* quality, one with the very *possession* of that right, which the people have supposedly given up entirely, so that all the essence of power—henceforth monadic, as indivisible as the very person of the Sovereign—resides in the Sovereign alone. No wonder that finally an essence other than common humanity was to be ascribed to the person itself of the Sovereign.

Here we are confronted with the basic wrong of the concept of Sovereignty, and the original error of the theorists of Sovereignty. They knew that the right to self-government is naturally possessed by the people. But for the consideration of this *right* they substituted that of the total *power* of the commonwealth. They knew that the "prince" receives from the people the authority with which he is invested. But they had overlooked and forgotten the concept of *vicariousness* stressed by the mediaeval authors. And they replaced it with the concept of physical transfer and donation.

In other words, they discussed the matter in terms of *goods* (or material *power*) held either in ownership or in trusteeship, instead of discussing it in terms of rights possessed by essence or by participation. If a material good is owned by the one, it cannot be owned by the other, and there can only be a question of transfer of ownership or a donation. But a right can be possessed by the one as belonging to his nature, and by the other as participated in by him. God is possessed by essence of the right to command; the people are possessed of this right both by participation in the divine right, and by essence insofar as it is a human right. The "vicars" of the people or deputies for the people are possessed (really possessed) of this right only by participation in the people's right.[29]

29. See infra, chap. v, pp. 133–38.

In reality, then, even in the case of monarchy—but not absolute—it should have been maintained that since the prince is the "vicar of the multitude" or the deputy for the people, his right in this capacity is the very right of the people, in which he has been made a participant by the trust of the people and which still exists in the people, far from having been uprooted from the people in order to be transferred to him. Thus the prince should have been considered at the peak (but not above the peak) of the political structure, as a part *representing* the whole (and not as a separate whole), or as a person commissioned to exercise the highest authority in the body politic, who has *vicariously* possession of this authority as a maximum *participation* in the right naturally possessed by the people. Such a prince (whose concept never materialized in human history, except perhaps, to some extent, in the case of St. Louis [Louis IX of France]) would have been separate from the people as to the existential status required by the exercise of the right to command. But he would not have been divided from the people as to the possession of this right—on the contrary! since he possessed it in a vicarious manner and by participation. He would have been accountable to the people. He would have been a king, but not an absolute king; a prince, but not a sovereign prince.

IV

What Does Sovereignty Mean. The Hobbesian Mortal God

The concept of Sovereignty took definite form at the moment when absolute monarchy was budding in Europe. No corresponding notion had been used in the Middle Ages with regard to political authority. St. Thomas treated of the Prince, not of the Sovereign. In the feudal times the king was but the Suzerain of Suzerains, each one of whom was pos-

sessed of his own rights and power. The jurists of the mediaeval kings only prepared in a more or less remote way the modern notion of Sovereignty. It is from the time of Jean Bodin on
that it forced itself upon the jurists of the baroque age.

Even leaving aside the theory of the *divine right* of kings,[30]
which was to flourish at the time of Louis XIV, the idea was
that the king as a person possessed a natural and inalienable
right to rule his subjects from above. Once the people had
agreed upon the fundamental law of the kingdom, and given
the king and his descendants power over them, they were deprived of any right to govern themselves, and the natural right
to govern the body politic resided henceforth in full only in
the person of the king. Thus the king had a right to supreme
power which was *natural and inalienable*, inalienable to such a
degree that dethroned kings and their descendants kept this
right forever, quite independently of any consideration of the
will of the subjects.

And since this natural and inalienable right to supreme
power resided only in the person of the king, with regard to
the body politic but independently of the body politic, the
power of the king was supreme not only as the topmost power
existing in the highest part of the body politic, but as a monadic and supernal power existing *above* the body politic and *separately* from it. So the king reigned over his subjects from above,
and took care of their common good from above; he was a
full-dress political image of God (a royal privilege which was
to become rather detrimental to God in the sequel). And any
restriction on the supernal independence and power of the king
could only come from a free and gracious concession granted
by the king (though most often, in actual fact, under pressure)
to such or such parts of the whole populace beneath.

Such was the idea, and the purpose for which the word Sov-

30. That is, absolute power directly conferred on the king by God, not indirectly
through the people's transferring the "absolute power of the Commonwealth" to him.

ereignty was coined.[31] We cannot use the concept of Sovereignty without evoking, even unawares, that original connotation.

∗ ∗ ∗

What is, therefore, the proper and genuine meaning of the notion of Sovereignty?

Sovereignty means two things:

First, a right to supreme independence and supreme power which is a *natural* and *inalienable* right.

Second, a right to an independence and a power which in their proper sphere are supreme *absolutely* or *transcendently*, not *comparatively* or as a *topmost part* in the whole. In other terms, it is *separately* from the whole which is ruled by the Sovereign that the independence of the Sovereign with regard to this whole and his power over it are supreme. His independence and power are not only supreme *in relation to* any other part of the political whole, as being at the top or highest part of this whole; they are supreme *absolutely* speaking as being above the whole in question.

Sovereignty is a property which is absolute and indivisible, which cannot be participated in and admits of no degrees, and which belongs to the Sovereign independently of the political whole, as a right of his own.

Such is genuine Sovereignty, that Sovereignty which the absolute kings believed they possessed, and the notion of which was inherited from them by the absolute States, and the full significance of which has been brought to light in the Hegelian State—and, long before Hegel, in the Hobbesian *Mortal God.*

31. I mean, in the vocabulary of political theory. The word "sovereign" (from Low Latin *superanus*, "Ex optimatum ordine, princeps") was employed long ago in the common language, meaning any official endowed with superior authority, for instance, "superior judge." Du Cange (see *Summus*) quotes an edict of the French King Charles V, made in 1367, which reads: "Voulons et ordonons que se ... le Bailli ou autre leur souverain. ..."

Let us re-read at this point Hobbes' unforgettable page: Whereas the agreement of irrational creatures is natural, he says, "that of men is by Covenant only, which is Artificiall: and therefore it is no wonder if there be somewhat else required (besides Covenant) to make their Agreement constant and lasting; which is a Common Power, to keep them in awe, and to direct their actions to the Common Benefit.

"The only way to erect such a Common Power, as may be able to defend them from the invasion of Forraigners and the injuries of one another and thereby to secure them in such sort, as that by their owne industrie, and by the fruites of the Earth, they may nourish themselves and live contentedly; is, *to conferre all their power and strength upon one Man, or upon one Assembly of men, that may reduce all their Wills, by plurality of voices, unto one Will: which is as much to say, to appoint one Man, or Assembly of men, to beare their Person;* and everyone to owne, and acknowledge himselfe to be Author of whatsoever he that so beareth their Person, shall Act, or cause to be Acted, in those things which concerne the Common Peace and Safetie; *and therein to submit their Wills, everyone to his Will, and their Judgments, to his Judgment.* This is more than Consent, or Concord; *it is a real Unitie of them all, in one and the same Person,* made by Covenant of every man with every man, in such manner, as if every man should say to every man, 'I Authorize and give up my Right of Governing my selfe, to this Man, or to this Assembly of men, on this condition, that thou give up thy Right to him, and Authorize all his Actions in like manner.' This done, the Multitude so united in one Person, is called a *Common-Wealth,* in Latin *Civitas.* This is the Generation of the great LEVIATHAN, *or rather (to speak more reverently) of that* MORTALL GOD, to which we owe under the *Immortall God,* our peace and defence. For by this Authoritie, given him by every particular man in the Common-Wealth, *he hath the use of so much Power and Strength conferred on him, that by terror thereof, he is inabled to forme the wills of them all,* to Peace at home, and mutuall ayd against their enemies abroad. *And in him consisteth the Essence of the Common-Wealth;* which (to define it) is One Person, of whose Acts a great Multitude, by naturall Covenants one with another, have made themselves every one the Author, to the end he may use the strength and means of them all, as he shall think expedient, for their Peace and Common Defence.

　"And he that carryeth this Person, is called SOVERAIGNE, *and said to have* SOVERAIGNE POWER; *and every one besides, his* SUBJECT.*"*[32]

V

NEITHER THE BODY POLITIC NOR THE STATE IS SOVEREIGN

Now what is the situation in reality, first, with regard to the body politic, and second, with regard to the State?

The *body politic* has a right to full autonomy. First, to full *internal* autonomy, or with respect to itself; and second, to full *external* autonomy, or with respect to the other bodies politic. The full *internal* autonomy of the body politic means that it governs itself with comparatively supreme independence (or greater than that of any part of it): so that no one of its parts can, by usurping government, substitute itself for the whole and infringe upon its freedom of action; the full internal autonomy of the body politic means also that it governs itself with comparatively supreme power (or greater than that of any part of it): so that no one of its parts can, by substituting itself for the whole, infringe upon the topmost power enjoyed by the agencies of government through which the whole governs itself.

The full *external* autonomy of the body politic means that it enjoys comparatively supreme independence with regard to the

---

32. *Leviathan,* ed. R. A. Waller (Cambridge: At the University Press, 1904), Part II, chap. xvii.

international community, that is, an independence which the international community—as long as it remains merely moral and does not exist as political society, therefore has no political independence of its own—has no right and no power forcibly to make lesser with respect to itself. As a result, each body politic, as long as it does not enter a superior, larger political society, has above itself no power on earth which it should be forced to obey. The full external autonomy of the body politic means also that it can exert externally topmost power in making war on another body politic.

The right of the body politic to such full autonomy derives from its nature as a perfect or self-sufficient society: a nature, be it observed in passing, which present bodies politic are losing, as a matter of fact, to a greater and greater extent, so that they keep their right to full autonomy only as a remnant, and because they are not yet integrated in a larger, really perfect and self-sufficient, political society. In any case, when a body politic decides to become part of a larger political society, say, a federal political society, it gives up, by the same token, its right to full autonomy, though it keeps, in fact and by right, a limited autonomy, much more limited, obviously, as external autonomy than as internal autonomy.

Now I say that the right of the body politic to full autonomy, which I have just analyzed, is a *natural* right, even an *inalienable* right: I mean *in the sense* that nobody may forcibly deprive it of this right; but *not at all in the sense* that the full independence in question is itself inalienable, and that the body politic cannot freely surrender its right to it, if it recognizes that it is no longer a perfect and self-sufficient society, and consents to enter a larger political society. As a result the full autonomy of the body politic implies the *first* element inherent in genuine Sovereignty, namely a *natural* and—in one sense—*inalienable* right to supreme independence and supreme power. But it does not imply the second element.

For it is clear that the body politic does not govern itself *separately from itself* and *from above itself*. In other words, its supreme independence and power are only comparatively or relatively supreme (as proper to this given whole with respect to its parts, and also with respect to the unorganized community of the other wholes). So the *second* element inherent in genuine Sovereignty, namely the *absolutely* or *transcendently* supreme character of independence and power, which in genuine Sovereignty are supreme *separately* from, and *above*, the whole ruled by the Sovereign (and which, in the external sphere, make even the possibility of any superior larger political society repugnant in itself to the very essence of the Sovereign)— the second element inherent in genuine Sovereignty is obviously irrelevant to the very concept of the full autonomy of the body politic.

* * *

Let us consider now the State. The State is a part and an instrumental agency of the body politic. Therefore it has neither supreme independence with regard to the whole or supreme power over the whole, nor a right of its own to such supreme independence and supreme power. It has supreme independence and power only with regard to the other parts of the body politic, subject to its laws and administration, and it has a right to such comparatively supreme independence and power only as come to it from the body politic, by virtue of the basic structure or constitution which the body politic has determined for itself. And the exercise of this right by the State remains subject to the control of the body politic.

As regards, furthermore, its *external* sphere of activity, it is only as representing the body politic, and under its control, that the State enjoys, with regard to the international community, a right to a supreme independence which (as we have seen apropos of the body politic) is only *comparatively* and *renounceably* supreme,—and can also exercise the topmost power in making war on another State.

As a result, neither the *first* element inherent in genuine Sovereignty, namely a *natural and inalienable* right to supreme independence and supreme power, nor the *second* element inherent in genuine Sovereignty, namely the *absolutely* and *transcendently* supreme character of that independence and power, which in genuine Sovereignty are supreme *separately* from, and *above*, the whole ruled by the Sovereign (and which, in the external sphere, make even the possibility of any superior, larger political society repugnant in itself to the very essence of the Sovereign)—neither the first nor the second element inherent in genuine Sovereignty can by any means be ascribed to the State. The State is not and has never been genuinely sovereign.

VI

Nor Are the People. Rousseau's Sovereign State

To sum up, let us then say that the concept of Sovereignty, taken in its proper and genuine meaning, does not apply to the body politic, except as regards the first of the two elements it implies; and that it does not apply at all to the State.

No doubt it is permissible to use the term sovereignty in an improper sense, meaning simply either the natural right of the body politic to full autonomy, or the right which the State receives from the body politic to topmost independence and topmost power with regard to the other parts and power agencies of the political society or with regard to the external relations between States. Yet in doing so one runs the risk of becoming involved in the worst confusion since the word Sovereignty always connotes obscurely its genuine, original meaning. And so one is in danger of forgetting that no human agency has by virtue of its own nature right to govern men. Any right to power, in political societies possessed by a man or a human agency in so far as he or it in the body politic a *part* at the service of the common good, a part which has received this right, within certain fixed bounds, from the people exercising their fundamental right to govern themselves.

As concerns finally the people, the second element inherent in genuine Sovereignty—namely the absolutely and transcendently supreme character of the independence and power, which in genuine Sovereignty are supreme separately from, and above, the whole ruled by the Sovereign—that second element inherent in genuine Sovereignty is obviously not present in the people any more than it is in the body politic. It is therefore better to say of them, as of the body politic, that they have a natural and inalienable right to *full autonomy*, that is, to comparatively supreme independence and power with regard to any part of the whole itself which is composed of them, and in order to have this very whole brought into existence and into activity. As we observed in the preceding chapter,[33] it would be simply nonsensical to conceive of the people as governing themselves *separately from themselves and from above themslves.*

* * *

Yet it is such a nonsensical notion which is at the core of Jean-Jacques Rousseau's *Contrat Social*. The myth of the *Volonté Générale*—which is in no way a simple majority will, but a monadic superio and indivisible Will emanating from the people as one single unit, and which is "always right"[34]—was only a means of having the separate and transcendent power of the absolute king transferred to the people while remaining separate and transcndent, in such a way that by the mystical operation of the General Will the people, becoming one single

33. Cf. above, p. 25.

34. Jean-Jacques Rousse *The Social Contract*, trans. Henry J. Tozer (London: Allen & Unwin, 1920), Book II, s. iii and iv, p. 123: "It follows from what precedes that the general will is always right . . ." and p. 126: "Why is the general will always right, and why do all invaily desire the prosperity of each. . . ."

Sovereign, would possess a separate, absolute, and transcendent power, a power from above over themselves as a multitude of individuals. As Rousseau put it, *"le pacte social donne au corps politique un* POUVOIR ABSOLU *sur tous ses membres; et c'est ce même pouvoir qui, dirigé par une volonté générale, porte le nom de* SOUVERAINETÉ."[35] *"La souveraineté, n'étant que l'exercice de la volonté générale, ne peut jamais s'aliéner, et le souverain, qui n'est qu'un être collectif,* NE PEUT ÊTRE REPRÉSENTÉ QUE PAR LUI-MÊME."[36] *"L'autorité suprême ne peut pas plus se modifier que s'aliéner;* LA LIMITER C'EST LA DÉTRUIRE."[37] *"La puissance souveraine n'a nul besoin de garant envers ses sujets. ... Le souverain,* PAR CELA SEUL QU'IL EST, EST TOUJOURS TOUT CE QU'IL DOIT ÊTRE."[38]

Thus Rousseau, who was not a democrat,[39] injected in nascent modern democracies a notion of Sovereignty which was destructive of democracy, and pointed toward the totalitarian State; because, instead of getting clear of the separate and transcendent power of the absolute kings, he carried, on the contrary, that spurious power of the absolute kings to the point of an unheard-of absolutism, in order to make a present of it to the people. So it is necessary that "each citizen should be in perfect independence of the others, *and excessively dependent on the State. . . . For it is only the power of the State* which

35. *Ibid.*, Book II, chap. iv, p. 125: ". . . the social pact gives the body politic an absolute power over all its members; and it is this same power which, when directed by the general will, bears, as I said, the name of sovereignty."

36. *Ibid.*, chap. i, p. 119: "I say, then, that sovereignty, being nothing but the exercise of the general will, can never be alienated, and that the sovereign power, which is only a collective being, can be represented by itself alone."

37. *Ibid.*, Book III, chap. xvi, p. 190: ". . . the supreme authority can no more be modified than alienated; to limit it is to destroy it."

38. *Ibid.*, Book I, chap. vii, p. 113: ". . . the sovereign power needs no guarantee toward its subjects. . . . The sovereign, for the simple reason that it is so, is always everything that it ought to be."

39. *Ibid.*, Book III, chap. iv, p. 160: "If there were a nation of gods, it would be governed democratically. So perfect a government is unsuited to men."

makes the freedom of its members."[40] The Legislator, that superman described in the *Contrat Social*, offers us a preview of our modern totalitarian dictators, whose "great soul is the true miracle which should prove" their "mission,"[41] and who have to "alter man's constitution in order to strengthen it."[42] Did not Rousseau think moreover, that the State has a right of life and death over the citizen? "When the prince has said to him: it is expedient for the state that you should die, he must die, since it is only on this condition that he has safely lived up to that time, and since his life is no longer a nature's boon only, but a conditional gift of the state."[43] Finally, as concerns matters of religion, he insisted that "the philosopher Hobbes is the only one who has clearly seen the evil and its remedy, and who has dared to suggest to unite in one single authority the two heads of the eagle, or *to reduce everything to political unity, without which never state or government will be rightly constituted.*"[44] Rousseau's State was but the Hobbesian Leviathan, crowned with the General Will instead of the crown of those whom the Jacobin vocabulary called "les rois et les tyrans."

But let us come back to our subject-matter. As a result of the principles set forth by Rousseau, and because the long-ad-

40. *Ibid.*, Book II, chap. xii. The original reads: "En sorte que chaque citoyen soit dans une parfaite indépendance de tous les autres, et dans une excessive dépendance de la cité. ... Car il n'y a que la force de l'état qui fasse la liberté de ses membres."

41. *Ibid.*, Book II, chap. vii.—"La grande âme du législateur est le vrai miracle qui doit prouver sa mission."

42. *Ibid.*—"Celui qui ose entreprendre d'instituer un peuple doit se sentir en état ... d'altérer la constitution de l'homme pour la renforcer."

43. *Ibid.*, chap. v.—"Et quand le prince lui a dit: Il est expédient à l'Etat que tu meures, il doit mourir, puisque ce n'est qu'à cette condition qu'il a vécu en sûreté jusqu'alors, et que sa vie n'est plus seulement un bienfait de la nature, mais un don conditionnel de l'Etat."

44. *Ibid.*, Book IV, chap. viii.—"De tous les auteurs chrétiens, le philosophe Hobbes est le seul qui ait bien vu le mal et le remède, qui ait osé proposer de réunir les deux têtes de l'aigle, et de tout ramener à l'unité politique, sans laquelle jamais état ni gouvernement ne sera jamais bien constitué."

mitted notion of the *transcendently* supreme independence and power of the king had been simply transferred to the people, thus making all individual wills lose any independence of their own in the indivisible *General Will*, it was held as a self-evident principle, at the time of the French Revolution, that the Sovereignty of the people,—absolute, monadic, transcendent as every Sovereignty,—excluded the possibility of any particular bodies or organizations of citizens enjoying in the State any kind of autonomy. "It is of necessity that no partial society should exist in the state."[45]

Similarly, such a transferring, to the people, of the mythical idea of the inalienable right of the king to *transcendently* supreme power resulted, in the early and mythical, purely Rousseauist stage of democratic (spurious democratic) philosophy, in making the deputies of the people mere instruments deprived of any right to govern:[46] whereas, in truth, they are possessed—vicariously, and by participation, but really—of this right, with the responsibility involved; since, having been put in charge, within certain fixed limits, by the people exercising their right to full autonomy, they have been, to the same extent, vested with authority, by virtue of that very

45. *Ibid.*, Book II, chap. iii.—"Il importe donc ... qu'il n'y ait pas de société partielle dans l'Etat."

46. "La souveraineté ne peut être représentée, par la même raison qu'elle ne peut être aliénée. ... *Les députés du peuple ne sont donc ni ne peuvent être ses représentants; ils ne sont que ses commissaires;* ils ne peuvent rien conclure définitivement. Toute loi que le peuple en personne n'a pas ratifiée est nulle; ce n'est point une loi. Le peuple anglais pense être libre, il se trompe fort; il ne l'est que durant l'élection des membres du parlement: sitôt qu'ils sont élus, il est esclave, il n'est rien. Dans les courts moments de sa liberté, l'usage qu'il en fait mérite bien qu'il la perde" (*Contrat Social*, Book III, chap. xv). Trans. Tozer, p. 187: "Sovereignty cannot be represented for the same reason that it cannot be alienated. ... *The deputies of the people, then, are not and cannot be its representatives; they are only its commissioners* and can conclude nothing definitely. Every law which the people in person have not ratified is invalid; it is not a law. The English nation thinks that it is free, but is greatly mistaken, for it is only during the election of members of Parliament; as soon as they are elected, it is enslaved and counts for nothing. The use which it makes of the brief moment of freedom renders the loss of liberty well-deserved."

choice of the people, and, first and foremost, by virtue of the order through which God maintains nature and societies, and through which alone men can be made bound in conscience to obey other men.

* * *

There is no need to add that the will of the people is not sovereign in the vicious sense that whatever would please the people would have the force of law. The right of the people to govern themselves proceeds from Natural Law: consequently, the very exercise of their right is subject to Natural Law. If Natural Law is sufficiently valid to give this basic right to the people, it is valid also to impose its unwritten precepts on the exercise of this same right. A law is not made *just* by the sole fact that it expresses the will of the people. An unjust law, even if it expresses the will of the people, is not law.

Here again the vicious dialectic of Sovereignty was at work. For Jean Bodin had indeed submitted the Sovereign to the law of God, but the inner logic of the concept was to make Sovereignty free from every—even heavenly—limitation. From the fact alone that he existed, was not the Sovereign always, as Rousseau put it, all that he ought to be? In actual fact Sovereignty required that no decision made by the Mortal God, or law established by the General Will, could possibly be resisted by the individual conscience in the name of justice. Law did not need to be *just* to have force of law. Sovereignty had a right to be obeyed, whatever it might command. Sovereignty was above moral law. The story came to its end once the Sovereignty of the abstract entity of the State had been substituted for the Sovereignty of the king, and the Sovereignty of the State had been confused with the Sovereignty of the Nation and the Sovereignty of the People. The Sovereignty of the totalitarian State is the master of good and evil as well as of life and death. That is *just* which serves the interest of the

Sovereign, that is, of the People, that is, of the State, that is, of the Party.

VII

Conclusions

It seems to me that the conclusion to be drawn from all the preceding considerations on the concept of Sovereignty is clear. The major texts that I have quoted from such unimpeachable witnesses as Jean Bodin, Thomas Hobbes, and Jean-Jacques Rousseau, should suffice to enlighten us as to the genuine meaning of this concept. In order to think in a consistent manner in political philosophy, we have to discard the concept of Sovereignty, which is but one with the concept of Absolutism.

The question is not a question of words only. Of course we are free to say "Sovereignty" while we are thinking full autonomy or right to decide without appeal—as we are free to say "omnipotence" while we are thinking limited power, or "drum" while we are thinking flute. Yet the result for our own way of thinking and for intelligible intercommunication would appear questionable. Professor Quincy Wright observes with good reason that "the state still seems to exist different from subordinate government agencies and other associations and a term is needed to define it."[47] The point is that the term needed is not Sovereignty.

Sovereignty is a curious example of those concepts which are right in one order of things and wrong in another. It loses its poison when it is transplanted from politics to metaphysics. In the spiritual sphere there is a valid concept of Sovereignty. God, the separate Whole, is Sovereign over the created world. According to the Catholic faith, the Pope, in his capacity of vicar of Christ, is sovereign over the Church. Even, in a merely moral sense, it may be said that the wise man, and first

47. Quincy Wright, *Mandates under the League of Nations* (Chicago: University of Chicago Press, 1930), pp. 281–82.

and foremost the spiritual man, have a kind of sovereignty. For they are possessed of an independence which is supreme *from above* (from the Spirit), with regard to the world of passions and the world of the law, to whose coercive force they are not subjected, since their will is of itself and spontaneously in tune with the law.[48] They are further "separate in order to command," that is, to tell the truth. And the spiritual man "judges all things, yet himself is judged of no man."[49]

But in the political sphere, and with respect to the men or agencies in charge of guiding peoples toward their earthly destinies, there is no valid use of the concept of Sovereignty. Because, in the last analysis, no earthly power is the image of God and deputy for God. God is the very source of the authority with which the people invest those men or agencies, but they are not the vicars of God. They are the vicars of the people; then they cannot be divided from the people by any superior essential property.

Sovereignty means independence and power which are *separately* or *transcendently* supreme and are exercised upon the body politic *from above:* because they are a natural and inalienable right belonging to a whole (originally the person of the sovereign Prince), which is superior to the whole constituted by the body politic or the people, and which, consequently, either is superimposed on them or absorbs them in itself. The quality thus defined does not belong to the State. Ascribed to it, it vitiates the State. Three implications of Sovereignty are especially to be considered in this connection.

First, as regards external Sovereignty: the sovereign State— each individual sovereign State—is by right *above* the community of nations and possessed of absolute independence with regard to this community. As a result, no international law binding the States can be consistently conceived. Furthermore,

48. Cf. Thomas Aquinas *Sum. theol.* i–ii. 96. 5.
49. Paul, I Cor. 2:15.

this absolute independence is inalienable (*unrenounceable*), because by virtue of its notion the sovereign State is a monadic entity which cannot cease to be sovereign without ceasing to be a State. As a result, no day can dawn—as long as the States behave consistently with their so-called Sovereignty—on which they could possibly give up their supreme independence in order to enter a larger political body, or a world society.

Secondly, as regards internal Sovereignty: the sovereign State is possessed of a power which—instead of being *relatively highest*, because in actual fact something must be at the top to decide without appeal—is a power *absolutely supreme*, as is necessary with a monadic whole superimposed on the body politic or absorbing it in itself. And this *absolute* power of the sovereign State over the body politic, or the people, is all the more unquestionable as the State is mistaken for the body politic itself or for the personification of the people themselves; do they not obey only themselves, by obeying the State? As a result, the pluralist idea is not only disregarded, but rejected by necessity of principle. Centralism, not pluralism, is required. It is at the price of a patent self-contradiction that the sovereign States will reluctantly accept the smallest amount of autonomy for particular agencies and associations born out of freedom. Through the inner logic of the notion of Sovereignty, they will tend to totalitarianism.

Thirdly, the sovereign State is possessed of a supreme power which is exercised *without accountability*. How could this notion of the non-accountability of the Sovereign be conceivable if it did not refer to something *separately* and *transcendently* supreme? As Mr. Robert Lansing observed, "the power to do all things without accountability" is coincident with the Sovereignty of God. As to human Sovereignty, it "may be defined as the power to the extent of human capacity to do all things on the earth without accountability."[50] Well, the attribute

50. Robert Lansing, *Notes on Sovereignty*, p. 3.

thus defined is all that could be wished for by the deified Potentates, Despots, and Emperors of ancient times in their most celestial ambitions. In modern times it has been ascribed to the State on the fictitious ground that the State is the people personified, and that the people can do anything without accountability. Yet the real process has been a transfer of the power without accountability of the personal Sovereign to the so-called juristic personality of the State. Thus was instilled in the latter a principle directly contrary to the principle which makes the people the final judge of the stewardship of their governmental officials; accordingly, the democratic States were involved in serious inconsistency. At all events the State was sovereign; as a result it was to endeavor perseveringly, in accordance with the principle of non-accountability, to escape the people's supervision and control.

To the extent to which the sovereign State succeeds in this effort, the non-accountability of the supreme decisions by which the body politic is committed has a clear meaning: it means in actual fact that *the people* will pay for the decisions made by the State in the name of their Sovereignty. As a French common saying puts it, "ce sont toujours les mêmes qui se font tuer," always the same ones are getting killed. The woes of the people settle the accounts of the not-accountable supreme persons or agencies, State, ministries, committees, boards, staffs, rulers, lawgivers, experts, advisers,—not to speak of the *intelligentsia*, writers, theorists, scientific utopians, connoisseurs, professors, and newspapermen.

The *intelligentsia* has not been commissioned by the people: it is not accountable to the people, except morally. (For to teach or write on the assumption that what one puts forth "is of no consequence" is permissible only to insane persons.) But the State is accountable indeed; the State, as well as all governmental agencies and officials, is accountable to the people. Do not the people have a right to supervise and control the

State? How could the State be subject to supervision if the power it exercises were a power without accountability?

But if the State is accountable and subject to supervision, how can it be sovereign? What can possibly be the concept of a *Sovereignty liable to supervision, and accountable?* Clearly, the State is not sovereign.

Nor, as we have seen, are the people. Nor do they exercise a power without accountability. Their right to self-government and full autonomy makes them not accountable to any tribunal or particular agency in the body politic. But the power they exercise, either by mass reflexes and extra-legal means, or through the regular channels of a truly democratic society, is in no way a power without accountability. For they are the very ones who always foot the bill. They are sure to account to their own sweat and blood for their mistakes.

The two concepts of Sovereignty and Absolutism have been forged together on the same anvil. They must be scrapped together.

CHAPTER III

THE PROBLEM OF MEANS

✻

THE Problem of Means is, as I see it, a twofold problem: first, the problem of *End and Means;* second, the problem of *the People and the State*, that is, of the means by which the people can supervise or control the State.

I

END AND MEANS

The problem of End and Means is a basic, *the* basic problem in political philosophy. Despite the difficulties involved, its solution is clear and inescapable in the philosophical field; yet, to be applied in the practical field, that solution demanded by truth demands in return from man a kind of heroism and hurls him into anguish and hardship.

What is the final aim and most essential task of the body politic or political society? It is not to ensure the material convenience of scattered individuals, each absorbed in his own well-being and in enriching himself. Nor is it to bring about either industrial mastery over nature, or political mastery over other men.

It is rather to better the conditions of human life itself, or to procure the common good of the multitude, in such a manner that each concrete person, not only in a privileged class but throughout the whole mass, may truly reach that measure of independence which is proper to civilized life and which is ensured alike by the economic guarantees of work and property, political rights, civil virtues, and the cultivation of the mind.

54

This means that the political task is essentially a task of civilization and culture, of helping man to conquer his genuine freedom of expansion or autonomy,[1] or, as Professor Nef put it, of "making faith, righteousness, wisdom and beauty ends of civilization";[2] a task of progress in an order which is essentially human or moral, for morality is concerned with nothing else than the true human good.

I should like to add that such a task requires historic achievements on so large a scale and is confronted with such obstacles in human nature that it cannot conceivably succeed —once the good tidings of the Gospel have been announced— without the impact of Christianity on the political life of mankind and the penetration of the Gospel inspiration in the substance of the body politic. As a result we are entitled to state that the end of the Body Politic is by nature something substantially good and ethical, implying, at least among peoples in whom Christianity has taken root, an actual—though doubtless always imperfect—materialization of the Gospel principles in terrestrial existence and social behavior.

And now, what about the means? Do we not know, as a universal and inviolable axiom, an obvious primary principle, that means must be proportioned and appropriate to the end, since they are *ways to the end* and, so to speak, the end itself in its very process of coming to existence? So that applying intrinsically evil means to attain an intrinsically good end is simply nonsense and a blunder. Yes, we know that, even without the help of Aldous Huxley's remarkable writings. And we know also that men in their practical behavior do not fail, as a rule, to make fun of that obvious and venerable axiom, especially in all that concerns politics. At this point we are

1. Cf. our essay on "The Conquest of Freedom," in *Freedom: Its Meaning*, ed. Ruth Nanda Anshen (New York: Harcourt, Brace & Co., 1940).

2. John U. Nef, *The United States and Civilization* (Chicago: University of Chicago Press, 1942), p. 252.

faced with the question of the *rationalization of political life*.
It is quite difficult for the rational animal to submit his own
life to the yard-stick of reason. It is quite difficult in our
individual lives. It is terribly, almost insuperably difficult
in the life of the body politic. As regards the rational management of collective and political life, we are still in a prehistoric age indeed.

There are two opposite ways of understanding the rationalization of political life. The easiest one—it comes to a bad
end—is the *technical* or *"artistic"*[3] one. The most exacting one
—but a constructive and progressive one—is the *moral* one.
Technical rationalization, through means external to man, ver-
sus *moral rationalization*, through means which are man himself, his freedom and virtue—such is the drama which human
history is facing.

II

The Technical Rationalization of Political Life

At the dawn of modern science and history, Machiavelli, in
his *Prince*, offered us a philosophy of the merely technical rationalization of politics: in other words, he made a rational
system out of the manner in which men most often behave in
fact, by submitting that behavior to a merely artistic form and
merely artistic rules. Thus good politics became by definition
non-moral and successful politics: the art of conquering and
keeping power by any means whatsoever—even good, should
an opportunity offer, a rare opportunity—on the sole condition that they be fit to ensure success.

I have tried to discuss Machiavellianism elsewhere.[4] Here I
should like only to point out that the great strength of
Machiavellianism comes from the incessant victories gained
by evil means in the political achievements of mankind, and

3. I mean, in the Aristotelian sense, pertaining to the realm and intellectual virtue
of Art, in contradistinction to Morality.
4. Cf. "The End of Machiavellianism," *Review of Politics*, January, 1942.

from the idea that if a prince or a nation respects justice, he or it is doomed to enslavement by other princes or nations trusting only in power, violence, perfidy, and lawless greed.

The answer is, first, that one can respect justice and have brains at the same time, and manage to be strong (I shall return to this point in a moment); second, that in reality Machiavellianism does not succeed. For the power of evil is only, in reality, the power of corruption—the squandering and dissipation of the substance and energy of Being and of Good. Such a power destroys itself in destroying that good which is its subject. So that the inner dialectic of the successes of evil condemn them not to be lasting. Let us take into account the dimension of time, the duration proper to the historical turns of nations and states, which considerably exceeds the duration of a man's life. According to the duration thus required by political reality to mature and fructify, I do not say that a just politics will, even in a distant future, always actually succeed, nor that Machiavellianism will, even in a distant future, always actually fail. For, with nations and states and civilizations we are in the order of nature, where mortality is natural and where life and death depend on physical as well as moral causes. I say that justice works through its own causality toward welfare and success in the future, as a healthy sap works toward the perfect fruit, and that Machiavellianism works through its own causality for ruin and bankruptcy, as poison in the sap works for the illness and death of the tree.

The illusion proper to Machiavellianism is the illusion of *immediate success*. The duration of the life of a man, or rather the duration of the activity of the prince, of the political man, circumscribes the maximum length of time required by what I call *immediate success*. Now immediate success is success for a man, it is not success for a state or a nation, according to the duration proper to state-vicissitudes and nation-vicissitudes. The more dreadful in intensity the power of evil appears, the weaker in historic duration are the internal improvements and the vigor of life which have been gained by a state using this power.

The more perfect and ruthless become the techniques of oppression, universal mutual spying, forced labor, mass deportation and mass destruction peculiar to the totalitarian States, the more difficult also becomes any attempt to change or overcome from the outside those gigantic Machiavellian robots. But they do not possess lasting inner force; their huge machinery of violence is a token of their inner human weakness. The breaking down of human freedom and conscience, because it engenders everywhere fear and insecurity, is in itself a process of self-destruction for the body politic. How long, then, can the power of a State endure which becomes more and more of a giant as regards the external or technical forces, and more and more of a dwarf as regards the internal, human, actually vital forces? It will do during some generations the job it has been assigned or permitted. I doubt that it can take root in the historical duration of nations.

Thus it is true that, politics being something intrinsically moral, the first political condition of good politics is that it be just. And it is true at the same time that justice and virtue do not, as a rule, lead men to success in this world, within that short time which separates the cradle from the grave, and in which success makes sense for them. But the antinomy is solved, as regards human societies, because the achievement of the common good, with the conditions of material prosperity which it involves, cannot be put in jeopardy or destroyed by the use of justice, if historical duration is taken into account and if the specific effect of the use of justice is considered in itself, apart from the effects of the other factors at play.

III

The Moral Rationalization of Political Life

There is another kind of rationalization of political life: not an artistic or technical, but a moral rationalization. This means the recognition of the essentially human ends of political life, and of its deepest springs: justice, law, and mutual friendship; it also means a ceaseless effort to make the living, moving structures and organs of the body politic serve the common good, the dignity of the human person, and the sense of fraternal love—to submit the huge material conditioning, both natural and technical, and the heavy setting up of conflicting interests, power and coercion inherent in social life, to the form and regulations of human reason spurring human freedom—and to base political activity not on childish greed, jealousy, selfishness, pride and guile, claims to prestige and domination transformed into sacred rules of the most serious game, but instead on a grown-up awareness of the innermost needs of mankind's life, of the real requirements of peace and love, and of the moral and spiritual energies of man.

That way of rationalizing politics was shown us by Aristotle and the great philosophers of antiquity, then by the great mediaeval thinkers. After a rationalistic stage, in which some basic errors preyed upon it, and vast illusions fostered genuine human hopes, it resulted in the democratic conception put into force during the last century.

Something particularly significant must be stressed at this point: democracy is the only way of bringing about a *moral rationalization* of politics.[5] Because democracy is a rational organization of freedoms founded upon law.

We may appreciate from this point of view the crucial importance of the survival and improvement of democracy for the evolution and earthly destiny of mankind. With democracy mankind has entered the road to the only genuine, that is *moral* rationalization, of political life: in other terms, to the highest terrestrial achievement of which the rational animal is capable here below. Democracy carries in a fragile vessel the

5. "L'Homme, tel est le but de la démocratie; sa voie historique, c'est la *rationalisation de l'État et du pouvoir*" (B. Mirkine-Guetzevitch, *Les nouvelles tendances du droit constitutionnel* [Paris: Giard, 1931], p. 46).

terrestrial hope, I would say the biological hope, of humanity. Of course the vessel is fragile. Of course we still are at the very first steps in the process. Of course we have paid and we are paying heavily for grave errors and moral failures. Democracy can be awkward, clumsy, defective, open to the risk of betraying itself by yielding to instincts of cowardice, or of oppressive violence. It can deserve the severe judgment passed upon its capacities in foreign policy by the French jurist Emile Giraud, former juridical counsellor of the League of Nations.[6] Yet democracy is the only way through which the progressive energies in human history do pass.

By the same token we may also appreciate the responsibility with which democracy is burdened. We may appreciate the unique, dramatic importance of the problem of End and Means for Democracy. In the process of moral rationalization of political life, the means must necessarily be moral. The end, for democracy, is both Justice and Freedom. The use, by democracy, of means basically incompatible with justice and freedom would be to that very extent an operation of self-destruction.

Let us not be deceived, moreover, by the Machiavellian sophistry: they say that justice and respect for moral values spell weakness and doom, and that strength is strong only if raised to the supreme standard of political existence. That is a lie. Not only, as we have seen, is evil incapable of succeeding in the long run, and not only does strength without justice weaken in the long run; but here and now strength *can exist* together with justice, and the power of nations struggling for freedom can be even greater than that of nations struggling for enslavement. The second world war was a proof of that. Yet the strength itself of a democratic body politic supposes justice, because it uses human energies as energies of free men, not

6. Émile Giraud, *La Nullité de la politique internationale des grandes démocraties (1919–1939)* (Paris: Recueil Sirey, 1948).

of slaves. Nay more: a supreme effort of all the energies of freedom, in their own spiritual realm, is needed to compensate for the momentary increase in physical strength that is given Machiavellian powers by their determination to use any means whatsoever. And such a supreme effort cannot arise if the body politic ignores moral values and standards. In reality strength is supremely strong only if not strength, but justice, is the supreme standard.

We know that the flesh is weak. It would be nonsense to require perfection and impeccability from anyone who seeks justice. We must forgive democracies for their accidental weaknesses and deficiencies. If, however, their exertions toward uprooting injustice from their own lives and toward making their means worthy of their ends were decidedly insufficient, then might history perhaps be less lenient with them than we would wish.

It is possible that the present and future course of human history will confront democracies with fearful trials and fateful alternatives. They might then be tempted to lose their reasons for living for their very lives' sake. As Henri Bergson put it, the democratic feeling and philosophy has its deepest root in the Gospel.[7] To try to reduce democracy to technocracy, and to expel from it the Gospel inspiration together with all faith in the supra-material, supra-mathematical, and supra-sensory realities, would be to try to deprive it of its very blood. Democracy can only live on Gospel inspiration. It is by virtue of the Gospel inspiration that democracy can overcome its direst trials and temptations. It is by virtue of the Gospel inspiration that democracy can progressively carry out its momentous task of the moral rationalization of political life.

Now my analysis would be incomplete if I did not observe that political hypermoralism is not better than political

7. Cf. Henri Bergson, *Les deux sources de la morale et de la religion* (Paris: Alcan, 1932), p. 304.

amoralism and, in the last analysis, answers the very purpose of political cynicism. Politics is a branch of Ethics, but a branch specifically distinct from the other branches of the same stem. For human life has two ultimate ends, the one subordinate to the other: an ultimate end *in a given order*, which is the terrestrial common good, or the *bonum vitae civilis;* and an *absolute* ultimate end, which is the transcendent, eternal common good. And individual ethics takes into account the subordinate ultimate end, but *directly aims* at the absolute ultimate one; whereas political ethics takes into account the absolute ultimate end, but its *direct aim* is the subordinate ultimate end, the good of the rational nature in its temporal achievement. Hence a specific difference of perspective between those two branches of Ethics.

Thus it is that many patterns of conduct of the body politic, which the pessimists of Machiavellianism turn to the advantage of political amorality—such as the use by the State of coercive force (even of means of war in case of absolute necessity against an unjust aggressor), the use of intelligence services and methods which should never corrupt people but cannot help utilizing corrupted people, the use of police methods which should never violate the human rights of people but cannot help being rough with them,[8] a lot of selfishness and self-assertion which would be blamed in individuals, a permanent distrust and suspicion, a cleverness not necessarily mischievous but yet not candid with regard to the other States, or the toleration of certain evil deeds by the law,[9] the recognition of the principle of the lesser evil and the recognition of the *fait accompli* (the so-called "statute of limitations") which permits the retention of gains ill-gotten long ago, because new human ties and vital relationships have infused

8. Cf. François Clerc, "Les mœurs de la police et la morale," *Nova et Vetera* (Fribourg, Switzerland), October–December, 1949.
9. Cf. Thomas Aquinas *Sum. theol.* i–ii. 96. 2.

them with new-born rights—all of these things are in reality ethically grounded.

The fear of soiling ourselves by entering the context of history is not virtue, but a way of escaping virtue. Some seem to think that to put our hands to the real, to this concrete universe of human things and human relations where sin exists and circulates, is in itself to contract sin, as if sin were contracted from without, not from within. This is pharisaical purism: it is not the doctrine of the purification of the means.

This doctrine primarily relates to the question of the *hierarchy of means*. It rests on the axiom that *the order of the means corresponds to that of ends*. It asks that an end worthy of man be pursued with means worthy of man. It insists first and foremost on the positive will to raise up means not only good in general, but truly proportionate to their end, truly bearing on them the stamp and imprint of their end: means in which that very justice which pertains to the essence of the common good and that very sanctification of secular life which pertains to its perfection shall be embodied.[10]

A final remark must be made, which deals with a particularly sad aspect of human collective life. When the social group is in a process of regression or perversion, and its moral level is sinking, then the precepts of morality do not change in themselves, of course, but the manner in which they must apply sinks also to a lower level: for our moral acts are concrete acts, the moral nature or specification of which can be changed by the nature of the situation which one has to face. I am quarrelling with a man: suppose I kill him, this will be a murder. Now suppose that this same man attacks me to kill me: it is a case of self-defense; I kill him and this will not be murder. Suppose we live in a completely barbarous social

10. See our books, *Freedom in the Modern World* (New York: Charles Scribner's Sons, 1936), chap. iii, and *True Humanism* (New York: Charles Scribner's Sons, 1938), pp. 240-48.

group, a tribe of bandits, in which no law, no tribunals, no public order exists. Then we should have to take the law into our own hands; which means that we might be placed in the position of justly killing some offender, and that in such a case the physical act of putting that man to death would not morally constitute a murder. For the moral essence of murder is to kill a man on one's own merely human authority, whereas in such a case we should not act on our own authority, but in the performance of a judicial function to which mankind in general is virtually yet really entitled, and which derives in mankind from the Creator of being. And though in civilized life this judicial authority must be held and exercised only by those who have been invested with judicial powers in the state, nevertheless, even in civilized life, a quite exceptional case of emergency, like the case of self-defense to which I just alluded, can call any man whatever to participate in it by defending his own right to live against an unjust aggressor.

IV

THE PEOPLE'S MEANS OF CONTROL AND THE DEMOCRATIC STATE

The second problem to be discussed is the problem of the people and the State, or of the means through which the people can supervise or control the State. That problem is not without connection with the first, because the people are naturally interested in justice, at least when passion does not blind them, whereas the State, when it becomes absolutist or despotic, sets itself above justice.

I should like to make only a few observations concerning two typically different cases: the case of a democratic State, in which freedom, law, and the dignity of the human person are basic tenets, and the rationalization of political life is sought in the perspective of moral values and norms; and the case of a totalitarian State, in which power and a certain work to be accomplished by the whole are the only things to be taken into consideration, and the rationalization of political life is sought in the perspective of merely artistic or technical values and norms.

Let us consider the case of a democratic State. Then the very control of the people over the State, even if in fact the State endeavors to escape it, is inscribed in the principles and constitutional fabric of the body politic. The people have regular, statutory means of exercising their control. They periodically choose their representatives, and either directly or indirectly their administrative officials. Not only will they remove the latter on the next polling day if they disapprove of them, but, through the assemblies of their representatives, they control, supervise, or put pressure on their Administration during the time when it exercises power.

I do not mean that the assemblies should govern in the place of the executive power or the Administration. But in order to supervise, check or modify the manner in which the Administration governs, they use the various devices put at their disposal by the Constitution—the most appropriate of which, in European democracies, is to throw the present administration out of office when they are dissatisfied with its policies. Does not a patient, while not being an expert in medicine, discharge a doctor when he is dissatisfied with his treatment? With greater reason the people—in whose basic right to govern themselves those who wield authority participate—the people are governed by their government, and the people control their government; they are the final judge of its stewardship.

In the second place the people have the means—though not directly used by themselves—of the press, the radio, and the other means of expressing public opinion, when they are free. By right, freedom of the press is not of itself a limitless freedom, the State may restrict it for the sake of the common good, but as a matter of fact, and in the face of the inevitably growing power of the State, as well as of the achievements of which the totalitarian States have been capable in the world, the people obey a sound political reflex when they stick to the freedom of the press as to a sacred good and protection.

In the third place, there are the pressure groups and the other non-institutional ways through which some particular fragments in the body politic act upon governmental agencies. A procedure which after all is normal, but which, as a means of control by the people, is rather questionable. There are also the means of political agitation, pressure, or propaganda which, in certain critical moments, a group of citizens regarding themselves as the standard-bearers of the people may use, and which I should like to call flesh-and-bone means of political warfare.

Now I would state, regarding all that first order of means, even to the basic, essential means provided by the one-man-one-vote suffrage and the representative system, that with them the real and active participation of the people in political life still remains insufficient. In his *Reveille for Radicals*, Saul Alinsky[11] quotes a page written by de Tocqueville in 1835, which I shall take the liberty of putting down here. "It must not be forgotten," de Tocqueville said, "that it is especially dangerous to enslave men in the minor details of life. For my own part, I should be inclined to think freedom less necessary in great things than in little ones, if it were possible to be secure of the one without possessing the other.

"Subjection in minor affairs breaks out every day, and is felt by the whole community indiscriminately. It does not drive men to resistance, but it crosses them at every turn, till they

11. Saul Alinsky, *Reveille for Radicals* (Chicago: University of Chicago Press, 1946), pp. 68–69.

are led to surrender the exercise of their will. . . . It is vain to summon a people, which has been rendered so dependent on the central power, to choose from time to time the representatives of that power; this rare and brief exercise of their free choice, however important it may be, will not prevent them from gradually losing the faculty of thinking, feeling, and acting for themselves. . . .

"I add that they will soon become incapable of exercising the great and only privilege which remains to them. The democratic nations which have introduced freedom into their political constitution, at the very time when they were augmenting the despotism of their administrative constitution, have been led into strange paradoxes. To manage those minor affairs in which good sense is all that is wanted—the people are held to be unequal to their task; but when the government of the country is at stake, the people are invested with immense powers; they are alternately made the playthings of their ruler, and his master—more than kings, and less than men.

"It is, indeed, difficult to conceive how men who have entirely given up the habit of self-government should succeed in making a proper choice of those by whom they are to be governed; and no one will ever believe that a liberal, wise, and energetic government can spring from the suffrages of a subservient people."[12]

Let us conclude, first, that according to the pluralist principle everything in the body politic which can be brought about by particular organs or societies inferior in degree to the State and born out of the free initiative of the people *should* be brought about by those particular organs or societies;[13] sec-

12. Alexis de Tocqueville, *Democracy in America* (New York: Barnes & Co., 1862), pp. 341–42.

13. "The set purpose to restrict the attributions of the State,—disquieting and dangerous as long as it is accompanied by any sort of hostility regarding the temporal supremacy of the State—becomes purely and simply salutary, as soon as the just notion

ond, that vital energy should unendingly rise from the people within the body politic. In other words the program of the people should not be offered from above to the people, and then accepted by them; it should be the work of the people.[14] This means that at the very bottom, at a level far deeper than that of the political parties, the interest and initiative of the people in civic matters should begin with an awakening of common consciousness in the smallest local communities, and remain constantly at work there. Here we enter the field of what may be called the means of organic edification. Those activities of spontaneous growth are for the people indirect but efficacious means of supervising or controlling the democratic State, not only because they have a normal repercussion on the behavior of the political parties, but also because they create and maintain in the body politic currents of high power and mighty propensities which the State cannot ignore.

Finally there is quite another order of means, of which our Western civilization is hardly aware, and which offers the human mind an infinite field of discovery—the spiritual means systematically applied to the temporal realm, a striking example of which has been Gandhi's *Satyagraha*.[15] I should like to call them "means of spiritual warfare."

As is known, Satyagraha means "the power of Truth."

---

of the State and its supremacy is duly re-established. This restrictive tendency then only expresses the fundamental idea of all philosophy of autonomy, to wit, that in a hierarchic whole, every function which *can* be assured by the inferior *must* be exercised by the latter, under pain of damage to the entire whole. For there is more perfection in a whole, all of whose parts are full of life and of initiative, than in a whole whose parts are but instruments conveying the initiative of the superior organs of the community" (Yves Simon, "Notes sur le fédéralisme proudhonien," *Esprit*, April 1, 1937).

14. Cf. Alinsky, *op. cit.*, chap. iv.

15. Cf. R. R. Diwakar, *Satyagraha: The Power of Truth*, Introduction by Clifford Manshardt (Hinsdale, Ill.: Henry Regnery Co., 1948).

Gandhi has constantly affirmed the value of the "Power of Love," or the "Power of the Soul," or the "Power of Truth" as an instrument or means of political and social action. "Patience," he said, "patience and voluntary suffering, the vindication of truth not by inflicting suffering on our opponent but on our own self" being "the arms of the strongest of the strong."

In my opinion Gandhi's theory and technique should be related to and clarified by the Thomistic notion that the principal act of the virtue of fortitude is not the act of attacking, but that of enduring, bearing, suffering with constancy. As a result it is to be recognized that there are two different orders of means of warfare (taken in the widest sense of the word), as there are two kinds of fortitude and courage, the courage that attacks and the courage that endures, the force of coercion or aggression and the force of patience, the force that inflicts suffering on others and the force that endures suffering inflicted on oneself. There you have two different keyboards that stretch along the two sides of our human nature, though the sounds they give are constantly intermingled: opposing evil through attack and coercion—a way which, at the last extremity, leads to the shedding, if need be, of the blood of others; and opposing evil through suffering and enduring—a way which, at the last extremity, leads to the sacrifice of one's own life. To the second keyboard the means of spiritual warfare belong.

Such are the means of spiritual warfare. Those means, the means peculiar to *courage in enduring*, correspond to the principal act of the virtue of fortitude, and thus are the privilege of "the strongest of the strong," as Gandhi put it. In a book written many years ago I tried to explain how, while being the most difficult, they are also by nature the most powerful means.[16]

16. *Du régime temporel et de la liberté* (Paris, 1933) (*Freedom in the Modern World*).

Gandhi himself was convinced that they can be applied in the West as they have been in the East. His own work of genius has been the systematic organization of patience and voluntary suffering as a special method or technique of political activity. Whether they follow the method of Gandhi or some method yet to be invented, men who attach importance to spiritual values are likely to be led willy-nilly to a solution along these lines. I think that such means of spiritual warfare would be especially appropriate in three kinds of struggle: first, in the struggle of a nation dominated by another to gain its own freedom (that was the case with Gandhi himself); second, in the struggle of the people to maintain or gain control over the State (this concerns the issue we are here examining); third, in the struggle of Christians to transform civilization by making it actually Christian, actually inspired by the Gospel. (At this point I should like to observe that if the Christian-minded parties which appeared on the political scene after the second World War had had a deeper sense of what men expected of them, that aspect of the problem of means, the discovery of a new technique akin to Gandhi's, would from the very first have occupied their thoughts.)

Coming back to our present issue, we have good reason to believe, it seems to me, that given on the one hand the normal growth—that I have so often mentioned—of the powers of the State, and the part that it necessarily plays in the achievement of social justice, on the other hand the illusory absolutist idea of itself and its so-called sovereignty with which even in democracies the State is still imbued, and which tends to make its big machinery oppressive and inhuman, the spiritual means of political warfare can provide the people with a supreme weapon to get or keep control not only of their government officials, but also of that big anonymous machinery itself. Even if they cannot know and supervise its complicated legal and administrative gears, they can confront the whole machine with the naked human strength of their patience in sustaining suffering on behalf of unyielding, just claims.

V

THE PROBLEM OF MEANS IN A REGRESSIVE OR BARBAROUS SOCIETY

I have examined the question of the people's weapons with regard to the State in a democratic society. The same question must now be discussed in the case of a totalitarian State. Which will be done in no time at all! By nature the totalitarian State suppresses any means whatever for the people to control or supervise it. Not only are the people deprived of any legal or institutional means of really controlling the State—the totalitarian State is a paternalistic State, in its view the people are infants, they do not know what's good for them, it is up to the State to make them happy—but the means which I have called means of organic edification are then entirely within the grasp of the State, as well as the temporal, flesh-and-blood means of political warfare. And as for the spiritual means of political warfare, they can be reduced to nothing by the pure and simple annihilation of those who look as though they might use them. As a matter of fact, Gandhi's successes were possible only against the background of the relative freedom granted to colonials by the British administration, both by virtue of an old liberal aristocratic tradition and a mistaken cynical belief—as has been rightly remarked[17]—in a possible utilization of Gandhi. The fate to which the inner logics of a totalitarian State tends is not a revolution which finally gives control to the people, but an ultimate disintegration by a slow rotting of human conscience within it.

All this is true, yet it does not do away with the problem of means; it makes it more serious and tragic. In order to pose it in the most extreme and striking terms, I should like to con-

17. Cf. George Orwell, "Reflections on Gandhi," *Partisan Review*, January, 1949.

template for a moment the most perfect case of political regression, namely the case of the inside life of a concentration camp—what has been called *l'univers concentrationnaire*. For Buchenwald, for instance, was not only a butchery, it was a society, a nightmare of a society, in which the conquest of power was a life-and-death issue, as the merciless struggle between the *greens* and the *reds*—that is, between the common law prisoners and the political prisoners—has shown.

Two opposite stands—the first questionable, the second simply bad—can be taken by a man forced to live in a concentrational universe. Either he can refuse to commit himself to any "political" activity, because the means to be used— spying, deceit, betrayal, co-operation with oppressors and torturers, not to speak of cruelties performed on fellow-prisoners, and indirect or direct homicide—are incompatible with the moral law; or, on the contrary, he can leave aside the moral law and accept using any kind of rotten means in order to wipe out the worst kind of torturers, to save at least a certain number of chosen people or to make preparations for some final insurrection. The first position assumes that one is confronted with a "catastrophe of the political," and that the only remaining means of activity are evangelical activities of self-purification, self-sacrifice, and fraternal love. I do not deny that such a position is justifiable, at least with regard to the possibilities or the highest calling of certain individuals. I think nevertheless that even in a concentrational universe it is not possible for man, in general, to give up any kind of political activity.

The second position assumes that the end justifies the means and that no God exists. For, as the French writer David Rousset put it in a significant book on his experiences in German concentration camps, "you cannot have moral principles playing the part of an umpire dividing bad and good means from each other unless you keep those moral principles out of historical, social relativity, and therefore find foundations for them outside the human species, that is to say, be it pleasant or not, in God.''[18] Let it be added that the one who takes the stand under discussion cannot help being himself corrupted in the long run by his total adaptation to a corrupted environment.

Thus the first position is not advisable as a rule, the second is wrong in itself? What, then, is the answer? The answer obliges us to face a most difficult problem in moral life and that sad law, which I previously pointed out, according to which the application of moral rules immutable in themselves takes lower and lower forms as the social environment declines. The moral law must never be given up, we must fasten on to it all the more as the social or political environment becomes more perverted or criminal. But the moral nature or specification, the moral *object* of the same physical acts, changes when the situation to which they pertain becomes so different that the inner relation of the will to the thing done becomes itself typically different. In our civilized societies it is not a murder, it is a meritorious deed for a fighting man to kill an enemy soldier in a just war. In utterly barbarized societies like a concentration camp, or even in quite particular conditions like those of clandestine resistance in an occupied country, many things which were, as to their moral nature, objectively fraud or murder or perfidy in ordinary civilized life cease, now, to come under the same definition and become, as to their moral nature, objectively permissible or ethical things. There are still, there are always good and evil actions; not every means whatever is permissible; it is still and it is always true that the end does not justify the means; moral principles keep on still and will always keep on dividing bad and good means from each other: but the line of demarcation has shifted. Conscience indeed, conscience apply-

18. Cf. David Rousset, *Les Jours de notre mort* (Paris: Pavois, 1947), p. 636.

ing principles is the actual umpire—not abstract principles seated in a Platonic heaven or in a dictionary of points of law. No written code is present, then, to help man; in a dark night full of snares it is up to one's personal conscience, reason and moral virtue to bear in each particular case the right moral judgment. In European resistance during the Second World War, the many convents which had become factories of false papers clearly knew that this manufacturing was physically but not morally a fraud. In Buchenwald not only those who professed that the end justifies the means, but Christians also, like Eugene Kogon and his friends, undertook with a certain amount of success an underground action to dodge the ferocious discipline of their jailers.[19] And in such an underground activity a right conscience, aware of the moral law, had to divide permissible from not-permissible acts in situations unheard of in civilized life.

Let us conclude that the same considerations apply to the political means to be used in an utterly regressive, barbarized political society. Even if they were questionable with respect to situations proper to civilized life, they would remain always subject to the principles of the moral law and to the judgment of conscience enlightened by moral virtues.

Moralists are unhappy people. When they insist on the immutability of moral principles, they are reproached for imposing unlivable requirements on us. When they explain the way in which those immutable principles are to be put into force, taking into account the diversity of concrete situations, they are reproached for making morality relative. In both cases, however, they are only upholding the claims of reason to direct life.

The worst temptation for mankind, in the epochs of dark night and universal perturbation, is to give up Moral Reason.

19. Cf. Eugène Kogon, *L'Enfer organisé*, translated from the German (Paris: La Jeune Parque, 1947).

Reason must never abdicate. The task of ethics is humble but it is also magnanimous in carrying the mutable application of immutable moral principles even in the midst of the agonies of an unhappy world, as far as there is in it a gleam of humanity.

CHAPTER IV

THE RIGHTS OF MAN

☼

I

Men Mutually Opposed in Their Theoretical Conceptions Can Come to a Merely Practical Agreement Regarding a List of Human Rights

OWING to the historical development of mankind, to ever widening crises in the modern world, and to the advance, however precarious, of moral conscience and reflection, men have today become aware, more fully than before, though still imperfectly, of a number of practical truths regarding their life in common upon which they can agree, but which are derived in the thought of each of them—depending upon their ideological allegiances, their philosophical and religious traditions, their cultural backgrounds and their historical experiences—from extremely different, or even basically opposed, theoretical conceptions. As the International Declaration of Rights published by the United Nations in 1948 showed very clearly, it is doubtless not easy but it is possible to establish a common formulation of such *practical conclusions*, or in other words, of the various rights possessed by man in his personal and social existence. Yet it would be quite futile to look for a common *rational justification* of these practical conclusions and these rights. If we did so, we would run the risk of imposing arbitrary dogmatism or of being stopped short by irreconcilable differences. The question raised at this point is that of the practical agreement among men who are theoretically opposed to one another.

Here we are confronted by the paradox that rational justifications are *indispensable* and at the same time *powerless* to create agreement among men. They are indispensable, because each of us believes instinctively in truth and only wishes to give his consent to what he has recognized as true and rationally valid. Yet rational justifications are powerless to create agreement among men, because they are basically different, even opposed to each other; and is this surprising? The problems raised by rational justifications are difficult, and the philosophical traditions in which those justifications originate have been in opposition for a long time.

During one of the meetings of the French National Commission of UNESCO at which the Rights of Man were being discussed, someone was astonished that certain proponents of violently opposed ideologies had agreed on the draft of a list of rights. Yes, they replied, we agree on these rights, *providing we are not asked why*. With the "why," the dispute begins.

The subject of the Rights of Man provides us with an eminent example of the situation that I tried to describe in an address to the second International Conference of UNESCO, from which I take the liberty of quoting a few passages. "How," I asked, "is an agreement conceivable among men assembled for the purpose of jointly accomplishing a task dealing with the future of the mind, who come from the four corners of the earth and who belong not only to different cultures and civilizations, but to different spiritual families and antagonistic schools of thought? Since the aim of UNESCO is a practical aim, agreement among its members can be spontaneously achieved, not on common speculative notions, but on common practical notions, not on the affirmation of the same conception of the world, man, and knowledge, but on the affirmation of the same set of convictions concerning action. This is doubtless very little, it is the last refuge of intellectual agreement among men. It is, however, enough to undertake a great work; and it would mean a great deal to become aware of this body of common practical convictions.

"I should like to note here that the word *ideology* and the word *principle* can be understood in two very different ways. I have just said that the present state of intellectual division among men does not permit agreement on a common *speculative* ideology, nor on common *explanatory* principles. However, when it concerns, on the contrary, the basic *practical* ideology and the basic principles of *action* implicitly recognized today, in a vital if not a formulated manner, by the consciousness of free peoples, this happens to constitute *grosso modo* a sort of common residue, a sort of unwritten common law, at the point of practical convergence of extremely different theoretical ideologies and spiritual traditions. To understand that, it is sufficient to distinguish properly between the rational justifications, inseparable from the spiritual dynamism of a philosophical doctrine or religious faith, and the practical conclusions which, separately justified for each, are, for all, analogically common principles of action. I am fully convinced that my way of justifying the belief in the rights of man and the ideal of freedom, equality, and fraternity is the only one which is solidly based on truth. That does not prevent me from agreeing on these practical tenets with those who are convinced that their way of justifying them, entirely different from mine or even opposed to mine in its theoretical dynamism, is likewise the only one that is based on truth. Assuming they both believe in the democratic charter, a Christian and a rationalist will, nevertheless, give justifications that are incompatible with each other, to which their souls, their minds, and their blood are committed, and about these justifications they will fight. And God keep me from saying that it is not important to know which of the two is right! That is essentially important. They remain, however, in agreement on the practical affirmation of that charter, and they can formulate together common principles of action."*

On the level of rational interpretations and justifications, on the speculative or theoretical level, the question of the rights of man brings into play the whole system of moral and metaphysical (or anti-metaphysical) certainties to which each individual subscribes. As long as there is no unity of faith or unity of philosophy in the minds of men, the interpretations and justifications will be in mutual conflict.

In the domain of practical assertion, on the contrary, an agreement on a common declaration is possible by means of an approach that is more pragmatic than theoretical, and by a collective effort of comparing, recasting, and perfecting the drafts in order to make them acceptable to all as points of practical convergence, regardless of the divergence in theoretical perspectives. Thus nothing prevents the attainment of formulations which would indicate notable progress in the process of world unification. It is not reasonably possible to hope for more than this practical convergence on a set of articles drafted in common. If a theoretical reconciliation, a truly philosophical synthesis, is desired, this could only come about as a result of a vast amount of probing and purification, which would require higher intuitions, a new systematization, and the radical criticism of a certain number of errors and confused ideas—which for these very reasons, even if it succeeded in exerting an important influence on culture, would remain one doctrine among many, accepted by a number and rejected by the rest, and could not claim to establish in actual fact universal ascendancy over men's minds.

Is there any reason to be surprised at seeing conflicting theoretical systems converge in their practical conclusions? The history of moral philosophy generally presents this very pic-

* Mexico City, November 6, 1947.

ture. This fact merely proves that systems of moral philosophy are the product of intellectual reflection on ethical data that precede and control them and reveal a very complicated type of geology of the conscience, in which the natural work of spontaneous, pre-scientific, and pre-philosophical reason is at every moment conditioned by the acquisitions, the servitudes, the structure and evolution of the social group. Thus there is a sort of vegetative development and growth, so to speak, of moral knowledge and moral feeling, which is in itself independent of the philosophical systems, although in a secondary way the latter in turn enter into reciprocal action with this spontaneous process. As a result these various systems, while disputing about the "why," prescribe in their practical conclusions rules of behavior which appear on the whole as almost the same for any given period and culture. Thus, from a sociological point of view, the most important factor in the moral progress of humanity is the experiential development of awareness which takes place outside of systems and on another logical basis—at times facilitated by systems when they awaken consciousness to itself, at other times thwarted by them when they obscure the apperceptions of spontaneous reason or when they jeopardize an authentic acquisition of moral experience by linking it to some theoretical error or some false philosophy.

II
The Philosophical Issue Deals with the Rational Foundation of Human Rights

Yet, from the point of view of intelligence, what is essential is to have a true justification of moral values and moral norms. With regard to Human Rights, what matters most to a philosopher is the question of their rational foundations.

The philosophical foundation of the Rights of man is Natural Law. Sorry that we cannot find another word! During the rationalist era jurists and philosophers have misused the notion of natural law to such a degree, either for conservative or for revolutionary purposes, they have put it forward in so oversimplified and so arbitrary a manner, that it is difficult to use it now without awakening distrust and suspicion in many of our contemporaries. They should realize, however, that the history of the rights of man is bound to the history of Natural Law,[1] and that the discredit into which for some time positivism brought the idea of Natural Law inevitably entailed a similar discrediting of the idea of the Rights of man.

As Mr. Laserson rightly said, "The doctrines of natural law must not be confused with natural law itself. The doctrines of natural law, like any other political and legal doctrines, may propound various arguments or theories in order to substantiate or justify natural law, but the overthrow of these theories cannot signify the overthrow of natural law itself, just as the overthrow of some theory or philosophy of law does not lead to the overthrow of law itself. The victory of judicial positivism in the XIXth Century over the doctrine of natural law did not signify the death of natural law itself, but only the victory of the conservative historical school over the revolutionary rationalistic school, called for by the general historical conditions in the first half of the XIXth Century. The best proof of this is the fact that at the end of that century, the so-called 'renaissance of natural law' was proclaimed."[2]

From the XVIIth Century on, people had begun to think of Nature with a capital N and Reason with a capital R, as

1. Cf. Heinrich A. Rommen, *Die ewige Wiederkehr des Naturrechts* (Leipzig: Hegner, 1936); English trans., *The Natural Law* (St. Louis: Herder, 1947). See also Charles G. Haines, *The Revival of Natural Law Concepts* (Cambridge: Harvard University Press, 1930).

2. Max M. Laserson, "Positive and Natural Law and Their Correlation," in *Interpretations of Modern Legal Philosophies: Essays in Honor of Roscoe Pound* (New York: Oxford University Press, 1947).

abstract divinities sitting in a Platonic heaven. As a result the consonance of a human act with reason was to mean that that act was traced from a ready-made, pre-existing pattern which infallible Reason had been instructed to lay down by infallible Nature, and which, consequently, should be immutably and universally recognized in all places of the earth and at all moments of time. Thus Pascal himself believed that justice among men should of itself have the same universal application as Euclid's propositions. If the human race knew justice, "the brilliance of true equity," he says, "would have subdued all nations, and legislators would not have taken as models, in place of this unchanging justice, the fantasies and caprices of Persians and Germans. One would see it established in all the states of the world and through all the ages. . . ."[3] Which is, I need not say, a wholly abstract and unreal conception of justice. Wait a little more than a century and you will hear Condorcet promulgate this dogma, which at first glance seems self-evident, yet which means nothing: "A good law should be good for everyone"—say, for man of the age of cave-dwellers as well as for man of the age of the steam-engine, for nomadic tribes as well as for agricultural peoples,—"a good law should be good for everyone, just as a true proposition is true for everyone."

So the XVIIIth Century conception of the Rights of man presupposed, no doubt, the long history of the idea of natural law evolved in ancient and mediaeval times; but it had its immediate origins in the artificial systematization and rationalist recasting to which this idea had been subjected since Grotius and more generally since the advent of a geometrising reason. Through a fatal mistake, natural law—which is *within* the being of things as their very essence is, and which precedes all formulation, and is even known to human reason *not* in terms

3. *Pensées*, II, *Œuvres* ("Grands écrivains de France" [Paris: Hachette, 1921], Vol. XIII, No. 294), 215.

of conceptual and rational knowledge—natural law was thus conceived after the pattern of a *written* code, applicable to all, of which any just law should be a transcription, and which would determine *a priori* and in all its aspects the norms of human behaviour through ordinances supposedly prescribed by Nature and Reason, but in reality arbitrarily and artificially formulated. "As Warnkoenig has shown, eight or more new systems of natural law made their appearance at every Leipzig booksellers' fair since 1780. Thus Jean-Paul Richter's ironical remark contained no exaggeration: Every fair and every war brings forth a new natural law."[4] Moreover, this philosophy of rights ended up, after Rousseau and Kant, by treating the individual as a god and making all the rights ascribed to him the absolute and unlimited rights of a god.

As to God himself, He had only been, from the XVIIth Century on, a superadded guarantor for that trine, self-subsistent absolute: Nature, Reason, Natural Law, which even if God did not exist would still hold sway over men. So that finally the human Will or human Freedom, also raised to Platonic self-subsistence in that intelligible, though unreachable, empyreal world which Kant inherited from Leibniz, was to replace God in actual fact as supreme source and origin of Natural Law. Natural Law was to be deduced from the so-called autonomy of the Will (there is a genuine notion of autonomy, that of St. Paul—unfortunately the XVIIIth Century had forgotten it). The rights of the human person were to be based on the claim that man is subject to no law other than that of his own will and freedom. "A person," Kant wrote, "is subject to no other laws than those which he (either alone or jointly with others) gives to himself."[5] In other words, man must "obey only himself," as Jean-Jacques Rousseau put it, because every measure or regulation springing from the

4. Rommen, *op. cit.*, p. 106.
5. *Introduction to the Metaphysics of Morals*, IV, 24.

world of nature (and finally from creative wisdom) would destroy at one and the same time his autonomy and his supreme dignity.

This philosophy built no solid foundations for the rights of the human person, because nothing can be founded on illusion: it compromised and squandered these rights, because it led men to conceive them as rights in themselves divine, hence infinite, escaping every objective measure, denying every limitation imposed upon the claims of the ego, and ultimately expressing the absolute independence of the human subject and a so-called absolute right—which supposedly pertains to everything in the human subject by the mere fact that it is in him—to unfold one's cherished possibilities at the expense of all other beings. When men thus instructed clashed on all sides with the impossible, they came to believe in the bankruptcy of the rights of the human person. Some have turned against these rights with an enslaver's fury; some have continued to invoke them, while in their inmost conscience they are weighed down by a temptation to scepticism which is one of the most alarming symptoms of the crisis of our civilization.

III

NATURAL LAW

Shall we try to reestablish our faith in human rights on the basis of a true philosophy? This true philosophy of the rights of the human person is based upon the true idea of natural law, as looked upon in an ontological perspective and as conveying through the essential structures and requirements of created nature the wisdom of the Author of Being.

The genuine idea of natural law is a heritage of Greek and Christian thought. It goes back not only to Grotius, who indeed began deforming it, but, before him to Suarez and Francisco de Vitoria; and further back to St. Thomas Aquinas (he alone grasped the matter in a wholly consistent doctrine, which unfortunately was expressed in an insufficiently clarified vocabulary,[6] so that its deepest features were soon overlooked and disregarded); and still further back to St. Augustine and the Church Fathers and St. Paul (we remember St. Paul's saying: "When the Gentiles who have not the Law, *do by nature* the things contained in the Law, these, having not the Law, are a law unto themselves . . .");[7] and even further back to Cicero, to the Stoics, to the great moralists of antiquity and its great poets, particularly Sophocles. Antigone, who was aware that in transgressing the human law and being crushed by it she was obeying a better commandment, the *unwritten and unchangeable laws*, is the eternal heroine of natural law: for, as she puts it, they were not, those unwritten laws, born out of today's or yesterday's sweet will, "but they live always and forever, and no man knows from where they have arisen."[8]

The First Element (Ontological) in Natural Law

Since I have not time here to discuss nonsense (we can always find very intelligent philosophers, not to quote Mr. Bertrand Russell, to defend it most brilliantly) I am taking it for granted that we admit that there is a human nature, and that this human nature is the same in all men. I am taking it

6. Especially because the vocabulary of the *Commentary on the Sentences*, as concerns the "primary" and "secondary" precepts of Natural Law, is at variance with the vocabulary of the *Summa theologica* (i–ii. 94). Thomas' respect for the stock phrases of the jurists also causes some trouble, particularly when it comes to Ulpian.

7. Paul, Rom. 2:14.

8.   "Nor did I deem
       Your ordinance of so much binding force,
       As that a mortal man could overbear
       The unchangeable unwritten code of Heaven;
       This is not of today and yesterday,
       But lives forever, having origin
       Whence no man knows: whose sanctions I were loath
       In Heaven's sight to provoke, fearing the will
       Of any man."
              (Sophocles *Antigone* ii. 452–60, George Young's translation)

for granted that we also admit that man is a being gifted with intelligence, and who, as such, acts with an understanding of what he is doing, and therefore with the power to determine for himself the ends which he pursues. On the other hand, possessed of a nature, or an ontologic structure which is a locus of intelligible necessities, man possesses ends which necessarily correspond to his essential constitution and which are the same for all—as all pianos, for instance, whatever their particular type and in whatever spot they may be, have as their end the production of certain attuned sounds. If they do not produce these sounds they must be tuned, or discarded as worthless. But since man is endowed with intelligence and determines nis own ends, it is up to him to put himself in tune with the ends necessarily demanded by his nature. This means that there is, by the very virtue of human nature, an order or a disposition which human reason can discover and according to which the human will must act in order to attune itself to the essential and necessary ends of the human being. The unwritten law, or natural law, is nothing more than that.

The example that I just used—taken from the world of human workmanship—was purposely crude and provocative: yet did not Plato himself have recourse to the idea of any work of human art whatever, the idea of the Bed, the idea of the Table, in order to make clear his theory (which I do not share) of eternal Ideas? What I mean is that every being has its own natural law, as well as it has its own essence. Any kind of thing produced by human industry has, like the stringed instrument that I brought up a moment ago, its own natural law, that is, the *normality of its functioning*, the proper way in which, by reason of its specific construction, it demands to be put into action, it *"should"* be used. Confronted with any supposedly unknown gadget, be it a corkscrew or a peg-top or a calculating machine or an atom bomb, children or scientists, in their eagerness to discover how to use it, will not question the existence of that inner typical law.

Any kind of thing existing in nature, a plant, a dog, a horse, has its own natural law, that is, the *normality of its functioning*, the proper way in which, by reason of its specific structure and specific ends, it *"should"* achieve fulness of being either in its growth or in its behaviour. Washington Carver, when he was a child and healed sick flowers in his garden, had an obscure knowledge, both by intelligence and congeniality, of that vegetative law of theirs. Horse-breeders have an experiential knowledge, both by intelligence and congeniality, of the natural law of horses, a natural law with respect to which a horse's behaviour makes him a *good horse* or a *vicious horse* in the herd. Well, horses do not enjoy free will, their natural law is but a part of the immense network of essential tendencies and regulations involved in the movement of the cosmos, and the individual horse who fails in that equine law only obeys the universal order of nature on which the deficiencies of his individual nature depend. If horses were free, there would be an ethical way of conforming to the specific natural law of horses, but that horsy morality is a dream because horses are not free.

When I said a moment ago that the natural law of all beings existing in nature is the proper way in which, by reason of their specific nature and specific ends, they *should* achieve fulness of being in their behaviour, this very word *should* had only a metaphysical meaning (as we say that a good or a normal eye "should" be able to read letters on a blackboard from a given distance.) The same word *should* starts to have a *moral* meaning, that is, to imply moral obligation, when we pass the threshold of the world of free agents. Natural law for man is *moral* law, because man obeys or disobeys it freely, not necessarily, and because human behaviour pertains to a particular, privileged order which is irreducible to the general order of the cosmos and tends to a final end superior to the immanent common good of the cosmos.

What I am emphasizing is the first basic element to be recognized in natural law, namely the *ontological* element; I mean the *normality of functioning* which is grounded on the essence of that being: man. Natural law in general, as we have just seen, is the ideal formula of development of a given being; it might be compared with an algebraical equation according to which a curve develops in space, yet with man the curve has freely to conform to the equation. Let us say, then, that in its ontological aspect, natural law is an *ideal order* relating to human actions, a *divide* between the suitable and the unsuitable, the proper and the improper, which depends on human nature or essence and the unchangeable necessities rooted in it. I do not mean that the proper regulation for each possible human situation is contained in the human essence, as Leibniz believed that every event in the life of Caesar was contained beforehand in the idea of Caesar. Human situations are something existential. Neither they nor their appropriate regulations are contained in the essence of man. I would say that they ask questions of that essence. Any given situation, for instance the situation of Cain with regard to Abel, implies a relation to the essence of man, and the possible murder of the one by the other is incompatible with the general ends and innermost dynamic structure of that rational essence. It is rejected by it. Hence the prohibition of murder is grounded on or required by the essence of man. The precept: thou shalt do no murder, is a precept of natural law. Because a primordial and most general end of human nature is to preserve being—the being of that existent who is a person, and a universe unto himself; and because man insofar as he is man has a right to live.

Suppose a completely new case or situation, unheard of in human history: suppose, for instance, that what we now call *genocide* were as new as that very name. In the fashion that I just explained, that possible behaviour will face the human essence as incompatible with its general ends and innermost dynamic structure: that is to say, as prohibited by natural law. The condemnation of genocide by the General Assembly of United Nations[9] has sanctioned the prohibition of the crime in question by natural law—which does not mean that that prohibition was part of the essence of man as I know not what metaphysical feature eternally inscribed in it—nor that it was a notion recognized from the start by the conscience of humanity.

To sum up, let us say that natural law is something both *ontological* and *ideal*. It is something *ideal*, because it is grounded on the human essence and its unchangeable structure and the intelligible necessities it involves. Natural law is something *ontological*, because the human essence is an ontological reality, which moreover does not exist separately, but in every human being, so that by the same token natural law dwells as an ideal order in the very being of all existing men.

In that first consideration, or with regard to the basic *ontological* element it implies, natural law is coextensive with the whole field of natural moral regulations, the whole field of natural morality. Not only the primary and fundamental regulations but the slightest regulations of natural ethics mean conformity to natural law—say, natural obligations or rights of which we perhaps have now no idea, and of which men will become aware in a distant future.

An angel who knew the human essence in his angelic manner and all the possible existential situations of man would know natural law in the infinity of its extension. But we do not. Though the Eighteenth Century theoreticians believed they did.

The Second Element (Gnoseological) in Natural Law

Thus we arrive at the *second* basic element to be recognized in natural law, namely natural law *as known*, and thus as measuring in actual fact human practical reason, which is the measure of human acts.

Natural law is not a written law. Men know it with greater

9. December 11, 1948.

or less difficulty, and in different degrees, running the risk of error here as elsewhere. The only practical knowledge all men have naturally and infallibly in common as a self-evident principle, intellectually perceived by virtue of the concepts involved, is that we must do good and avoid evil. This is the preamble and the principle of natural law; it is not the law itself. Natural law is the ensemble of things to do and not to do which follow therefrom in *necessary* fashion. That every sort of error and deviation is possible in the determination of these things merely proves that our sight is weak, our nature coarse, and that innumerable accidents can corrupt our judgment. Montaigne maliciously remarked that, among certain peoples, incest and thievery were considered virtuous acts. Pascal was scandalized by this. All this proves nothing against natural law, any more than a mistake in addition proves anything against arithmetic, or the mistakes of certain primitive peoples, for whom the stars were holes in the tent which covered the world, prove anything against astronomy.

Natural law is an unwritten law. Man's knowledge of it has increased little by little as man's moral conscience has developed. The latter was at first in a twilight state.[10] Anthropologists have taught us within what structures of tribal life and in the midst of what half-awakened magic it was primitively formed. This proves merely that the knowledge men have had of the unwritten law has passed through more diverse forms and stages than certain philosophers or theologians have believed. The knowledge which our own moral conscience has of this law is doubtless still imperfect, and very likely it will continue to develop and to become more refined as long as humanity exists. Only when the Gospel has penetrated to the very depth of human substance will natural law appear in its flower and its perfection.

10. Cf. Raïssa Maritain, *Histoire d'Abraham ou les premiers âges de la conscience morale* (Paris: Desclée De Brouwer, 1947).

So the law and the knowledge of the law are two different things. Yet the law has force of law only when it is promulgated. It is only insofar as it is known and expressed in assertions of practical reason that natural law has force of law. At this point let us stress that human reason does not discover the regulations of natural law in an abstract and theoretical manner, as a series of geometrical theorems. Nay more, it does not discover them through the conceptual exercise of the intellect, or by way of rational knowledge. I think that Thomas Aquinas' teaching, here, should be understood in a much deeper and more precise fashion than is usual. When he says that human reason discovers the regulations of natural law through the guidance of the *inclinations* of human nature, he means that the very mode or manner in which human reason knows natural law is not rational knowledge, but knowledge *through inclination.*[11] That kind of knowledge is not clear knowledge through concepts and conceptual judgments; it is obscure, unsystematic, vital knowledge by connaturality or

11. This is, in my opinion, the real meaning implied by St. Thomas, even though he did not use the very expression when treating of Natural Law. Knowledge through inclination is generally understood in all his doctrine on Natural Law. It alone makes this doctrine perfectly consistent. It alone squares with such statements as the following ones: "Omnia illa ad quae homo *habet naturalem inclinationem, ratio naturaliter apprehendit ut bona*, et per consequens ut opere prosequenda; et contraria eorum, ut mala et vitanda" (i–ii. 94. 2); "Ad legem naturae pertinet omne illud ad quod homo inclinatur secundum naturam. . . . Sed, si loquamur de actibus virtuosis secundum seipsos, prout scilicet in propriis speciebus considerantur, sic *non* omnes actus virtuosi sunt de lege naturae. Multa enim secundum virtutem fiunt *ad quae natura non primo inclinat; sed per rationis inquisitionem ea homines adinvenerunt*, quasi utilia ad bene vivendum" (i–ii. 94. 3). The matter has been somewhat obscured because of the perpetual comparison that St. Thomas uses in these articles between the speculative and the practical intellect, and by reason of which he speaks of the *propria principia* of Natural Law as "*quasi conclusiones principiorum communium*" (i–ii. 94. 4). As a matter of fact, those *propria principia* or specific precepts of Natural Law are in no way conclusions rationally deduced; they play in the practical realm a part *similar* to that of conclusions in the speculative realm. (And they appear as inferred conclusions to the "after-knowledge" of the philosophers who have to reflect upon and explain the precepts of Natural Law.)

congeniality, in which the intellect, in order to bear judgment, consults and listens to the inner melody that the vibrat-
ing strings of abiding tendencies make present in the subject.

When one has clearly seen this basic fact, and when, moreover, one has realized that St. Thomas' views on the matter
call for an historical approach and a philosophical enforcement of the idea of development that the Middles Ages were
not equipped to carry into effect, then at last one is enabled to
get a completely comprehensive concept of Natural Law. And
one understands that the human knowledge of natural law has
been progressively shaped and molded by the inclinations of
human nature, starting from the most basic ones. Do not expect me to offer an a priori picture of those genuine inclinations which are rooted in man's being as vitally permeated
with the preconscious life of the mind, and which either developed or were released as the movement of mankind went
on. They are evinced by the very history of human conscience.
Those inclinations *were really genuine* which in the immensity of
the human past have guided reason in becoming aware, little
by little, of the regulations that have been most definitely and
most generally recognized by the human race, starting from
the most ancient social communities. For the knowledge of the
primordial aspects of natural law was first expressed in social
patterns rather than in personal judgments: so that we might
say that that knowledge has developed within the double protecting tissue of human inclinations and human society.

With regard to the second basic element, the element of
knowledge which natural law implies in order to have force
of law, it thus can be said that natural law—that is, natural
law *naturally known*, or, more exactly, natural law *the knowledge of which is embodied in the most general and most ancient
heritage* of mankind—covers only the field of the ethical regulations of which men have become aware by virtue of knowledge *through inclination*, and which are *basic principles* in moral

life—progressively recognized from the most common principles to the more and more specific ones.

All the previous remarks may help us to understand why, on the one hand, a careful examination of the data of anthropology would show that the fundamental *dynamic schemes* of natural law, if they are understood in their authentic, that is, still undetermined meaning (for instance: to take a man's life is not like taking another animal's life; or, the family group has to comply with some fixed pattern; or, sexual intercourse has to be contained within given limitations; or, we are bound to look at the Invisible; or, we are bound to live together under certain rules and prohibitions), are subject to a much more universal awareness—everywhere and in every time—than would appear to a superficial glance; and why, on the other hand, an immense amount of relativity and variability is to be found in the particular rules, customs, and standards in which, among all peoples of the earth, human reason has expressed its knowledge even of the most basic aspects of natural law: for, as I pointed out above, that spontaneous knowledge does not bear on moral regulations conceptually discovered and rationally deduced, but on moral regulations known through inclination, and, at the start, on general tendential forms or frameworks, I just said on *dynamic schemes* of moral regulations, such as can be obtained by the first, "primitive" achievements of knowledge through inclination. And in such tendential frameworks or dynamic schemes many various, still defective contents can occur,—not to speak of the warped, deviated, or perverted inclinations which can mingle with the basic ones.

We may understand at the same time why natural law essentially involves a dynamic development, and why moral conscience, or the knowledge of natural law, has progressed from the age of the cave-man in a double manner: first, as regards the way in which human reason has become aware in a less and less crepuscular, rough, and confused manner, of the primordial regulations of natural law; second, as regards the way in which it has become aware—always by means of knowledge through inclination—of its further, higher regulations. And such knowledge is still progressing, it will progress as long as human history endures. That progress of moral conscience is indeed the most unquestionable instance of progress in humanity.

I have said that natural law is unwritten law: it is unwritten law in the deepest sense of that expression, because our knowledge of it is no work of free conceptualization, but results from a conceptualization *bound* to the essential inclinations of being, of living nature, and of reason, which are at work in man, and because it develops in proportion to the degree of moral experience and self-reflection, and of social experience also, of which man is capable in the various ages of his history. Thus it is that in ancient and mediaeval times attention was paid, in natural law, to the *obligations* of man more than to his *rights*. The proper achievement—a great achievement indeed—of the XVIIIth Century has been to bring out in full light the *rights* of man as also required by natural law. That discovery was essentially due to a progress in moral and social experience, through which the root *inclinations* of human nature as regards the rights of the human person were set free, and consequently, *knowledge through inclination* with regard to them developed. But, according to a sad law of human knowledge, that great achievement was paid for by the ideological errors, in the theoretical field, that I have stressed at the beginning. Attention even shifted from the obligations of man to his rights only. A genuine and comprehensive view would pay attention *both* to the obligations and the rights involved in the requirements of natural law.

IV

HUMAN RIGHTS AND NATURAL LAW

I need not apologize for having dwelt so long on the subject of natural law. How could we understand human rights if we had not a sufficiently adequate notion of natural law? The same natural law which lays down our most fundamental duties, and by virtue of which every law is binding, is the very law which assigns to us our fundamental rights.[12] It is because we are enmeshed in the universal order, in the laws and regulations of the cosmos and of the immense family of created natures (and finally in the order of creative wisdom), and it is because we have at the same time the privilege of sharing in spiritual nature, that we possess rights vis-à-vis

12. Cf. Edward S. Dore, associate justice of New York Supreme Court, "Human Rights and Natural Law," *New York Law Journal*, 1946; McKinnon, "The Higher Law," *American Bar Association Journal*, 1947; Laserson, *op. cit.*; Lord Wright, chairman of the United Nations War Crimes Commission, "Natural Law and International Law," *Essays in Honor of Roscoe Pound;* Godfrey P. Schmidt, *An Approach to Natural Law* (in preparation).

The concept of Natural Law played, as is well known, a basic part in the thought of the Founding Fathers. In insisting (cf. Cornelia Geer Le Boutillier, *American Democracy and Natural Law* [New York: Columbia University Press, 1950], chap. iii) that they were men of government rather than metaphysicians and that they used the concept for practical rather than philosophical purpose, in a more or less vague, even in a "utilitarianist," sense (as if any concern for the common good and the implementing of the ends of human life were to be labeled utilitarianism!), one makes only more manifest the impossibility of tearing Natural Law away from the moral tenets upon which this country was founded.

In his vigorous and stimulating book, *Courts on Trial* (Princeton, N.J.: Princeton University Press, 1949), Judge Jerome Frank also views Natural Law more in a practical than in a metaphysical perspective. This very fact gives a particularly significant experiential value to his judgment, when he writes: "No decent non-Catholic can fail to accept the few basic Natural Law principles or precepts as representing, at the present time and for any reasonably foreseeable future, essential parts of the foundation of civilization" (pp. 364–65).

Be it finally noted that when it comes to the application of basic requirements of justice in cases where positive law's provisions are lacking to a certain extent, a recourse to the principles of Natural Law is unavoidable, thus creating a precedent and new judicial rules. That is what happened, in a remarkable manner, with the epoch-making Nazi war crimes trial in Nuremberg.

other men and all the assemblage of creatures. In the last analysis, as every creature acts by virtue of its Principle, which is the Pure Act; as every authority worthy of the name (that is to say, just) is binding in conscience by virtue of the Principle of beings, which is pure Wisdom: so too every right possessed by man is possessed by virtue of the right possessed by God, Who is pure Justice, to see the order of His wisdom in beings respected, obeyed, and loved by every intelligence. It is essential to law to be an order of *reason;* and natural law, or the normality of functioning of human nature known by knowledge through inclination, is *law*, binding in conscience, only because nature and the inclinations of nature manifest an order of reason,—that is of *Divine Reason*. Natural law is law only because it is a participation in Eternal Law.

At this point we see that a positivistic philosophy recognizing Fact alone—as well as either an idealistic or a materialistic philosophy of absolute Immanence—is powerless to establish the existence of rights which are naturally possessed by the human being, prior and superior to written legislation and to agreements between governments, rights which the civil society does not have to *grant* but to *recognize* and sanction as universally valid, and which no social necessity can authorize us even momentarily to abolish or disregard. Logically, the concept of such rights can seem only a superstition to these philosophies. It is only valid and rationally tenable if each existing individual has a nature or essence which is the locus of intelligible necessities and necessary truths, that is to say, if the realm of Nature taken as a constellation of facts and events envelops and reveals a realm of Nature taken as a universe of Essences transcending the fact and the event. In other words there is no right unless a certain order—which can be violated in fact—is inviolably required by *what things are* in their intelligible type or their essence, or by what the nature of man is, and is cut out for: an order by virtue of which certain things like life, work, freedom are due to the human person, an existent who is endowed with a spiritual soul and free will. Such an order, which is not a factual datum in things, but demands to be realized by them, and which imposes itself upon our minds to the point of binding us in conscience, exists in things in a certain way, I mean as a requirement of their essence. But that very fact, the fact that things participate in an ideal order which transcends their existence and requires to govern it, would not be possible if the foundation of this ideal order, like the foundation of essences themselves and eternal truths, did not exist in a separate Spirit, in an Absolute which is superior to the world, in what perennial philosophy calls the Eternal Law.

For a philosophy which recognizes Fact alone, the notion of Value,—I mean Value objectively true in itself—is not conceivable. How, then, can one claim rights if one does not believe in values? If the affirmation of the intrinsic value and dignity of man is nonsense, the affirmation of the natural rights of man is nonsense also.

V

About Human Rights in General

Let us now discuss further some problems which deal with human rights in general. My first point will relate to the distinction between Natural Law and Positive Law. One of the main errors of the rationalist philosophy of human rights has been to regard positive law as a mere transcript traced off from natural law, which would supposedly prescribe in the name of Nature all that which positive law prescribes in the name of society. They forgot the immense field of human things which depend on the variable conditions of social life and on the free initiative of human reason, and which natural law leaves undetermined.

As I have pointed out, *natural law* deals with the rights and the duties which are connected in a *necessary* manner with the first principle: "Do good and avoid evil." This is why the precepts of the unwritten law are in themselves or in the nature of things (I am not saying in man's knowledge of them) universal and invariable.

Jus gentium, or the *Law of Nations*, is difficult to define exactly, because it is intermediary between natural law and positive law. Let us say that in its deepest and most genuine meaning, such as put forward by Thomas Aquinas, the law of nations, or better to say, the common law of civilization, differs from natural law because it is *known*, not through inclination, but through the *conceptual exercise of reason*, or through rational knowledge;[13] in this sense it pertains to positive law, and formally constitutes a juridical order (though not necessarily written in a code). But as concerns its content, *jus gentium* comprises both things which belong also to natural

---

13. According to St. Thomas (*Sum. theol.* i-ii. 95. 4), *jus gentium*—which he sharply distinguishes from natural law and connects rather with positive law—is concerned with all things that derive from natural law as *conclusions* from principles.

Yet he also teaches that the *propria principia* of Natural Law are like conclusions derived from *principia communia* (i-ii. 94. 4, 5, and 6). And assuredly the *propria principia* of natural law belong to Natural Law, not to *jus gentium!* Well, in 95. 2, St. Thomas gives the prohibition of murder as an example of a conclusion derived from a principle of natural law ("do nobody evil"), and pertaining to what is defined as *jus gentium* in art. 4. It is obvious, however, that the prohibition of murder, which is inscribed in the Decalogue, is a precept of natural law. What then?

The only way to realize the inner consistency of all that, and correctly to grasp the Thomistic distinction between Natural Law and *jus gentium*, is to understand that a precept which is *like* a conclusion derived from a principle of natural law but which in actual fact is *known through inclination, not through rational deduction*, is part of *natural law;* but that a precept which is *known through rational deduction, and as a conclusion conceptually inferred* from a principle of natural law, is part of *jus gentium*. The latter pertains to positive law more than to natural law precisely by virtue of the manner in which it is known and because of the intervention of human reason in the establishment of the precepts conceptually concluded (whereas the *only* reason on which natural law depends is divine Reason). The prohibition of murder, in so far as this precept is *known by inclination*, belongs to natural law. The same prohibition of murder, if this precept is known as a conclusion *rationally* inferred from a principle of natural law, pertains to *jus gentium*.

law (insofar as they are not only known as rationally inferred, but also known through inclination) and things which—though obligatory in a universal manner, since concluded from a principle of natural law—are beyond the content of natural law (because they are *only* rationally inferred, and not known through inclination). In both cases *jus gentium* or the common law of civilization deals, like natural law, with rights and duties which are connected with the first principle in a *necessary* manner. And precisely because it is known through rational knowledge, and is itself a work of reason, it is more especially concerned with such rights and duties as exist in the realm of the basic natural work achieved by human reason, that is, the state of civil life.

Positive Law, or the body of laws (either customary law or statute law) in force in a given social group, deals with the rights and the duties which are connected with the first principle, but in a *contingent* manner, by virtue of the determinate ways of conduct set down by the reason and the will of man when they institute the laws or give birth to the customs of a particular society, thus stating of themselves that in the particular group in question certain things will be good and permissible, certain other things bad and not permissible.

But it is by virtue of natural law that the law of Nations and positive law take on the force of law, and impose themselves upon the conscience. They are a prolongation or an extension of natural law, passing into objective zones which can less and less be sufficiently determined by the essential inclinations of human nature. For it is *natural law itself which requires that whatever it leaves undetermined shall subsequently be determined*, either as a right or a duty existing for all men, and of which they are made aware, not by knowledge through inclination, but by conceptual reason—that's for *jus gentium*—or—this is for positive law—as a right or a duty existing for certain men by reason of the human and contingent regulations proper to the social group of which they are a part. Thus there are imperceptible transitions (at least from the point of view of historical experience) between Natural Law, the Law of Nations, and Positive Law. There is a dynamism which impels the unwritten law to flower forth in human law, and to render the latter ever more perfect and just in the very field of its contingent determinations. It is in accordance with this dynamism that the rights of the human person take political and social form in the community.

Man's right to existence, to personal freedom, and to the pursuit of the perfection of moral life, belongs, strictly speaking, to natural law.

The right to the private ownership of material goods[14] pertains to natural law, insofar as mankind is naturally entitled to possess for its own common use the material goods of nature; it pertains to the law of Nations, or *jus gentium*, in so far as reason necessarily concludes that for the sake of the common good those material goods must be privately owned, as a result of the conditions naturally required for their management and for human work (I mean human work performed in a genuinely human manner, ensuring the freedom of the human person in the face of the community). And the particular modalities of the right to private ownership, which vary according to the form of a society and the state of the development of its economy, are determined by positive law.

The freedom of nations to live unburdened by the yoke of want or distress ("freedom from want") and the freedom for them to live unburdened by the yoke of fear or terror ("freedom from fear"), as President Roosevelt defined them in his Four Points, correspond to requirements of the law of Nations which are to be fulfilled by positive law and by a possible economic and political organization of the civilized world.

14. Cf. our book, *Freedom in the Modern World* (New York: Charles Scribner's Sons, 1936), Appendix I.

The right of suffrage granted to each one of us for the election of the officials of the State arises from positive law, determining the way in which the natural right of the people to self-government has to apply in a democratic society.

* * *

My second point will deal with the inalienable character of natural human rights. They are inalienable since they are grounded on the very nature of man, which of course no man can lose. This does not mean that they reject by nature any limitation, or that they are the infinite rights of God. Just as every law,—notably the natural law, on which they are grounded,—aims at the common good, so human rights have an intrinsic relation to the common good. Some of them, like the right to existence or to the pursuit of happiness, are of such a nature that the common good would be jeopardized if the body politic could restrict in any measure the possession that men naturally have of them. Let us say that they are absolutely inalienable. Others, like the right of association or of free speech, are of such a nature that the common good would be jeopardized if the body politic could not restrict in some measure (all the less as societies are more capable of and based upon common freedom) the possession that men naturally have of them. Let us say that they are inalienable only substantially.

* * *

Yet, even absolutely inalienable rights are liable to limitation, if not as to their possession, at least as to their exercise. So my third point will deal with the distinction between the *possession* and the *exercise* of a right. Even for the absolutely inalienable rights, we must distinguish between possession and exercise—the latter being subject to conditions and limitations dictated in each case by justice. If a criminal can be justly condemned to die, it is because by his crime he has deprived himself, let us not say of the right to live, but of the possibility of justly asserting this right: he has morally cut himself off from the human community, precisely as regards the use of this fundamental and "inalienable" right which the punishment inflicted upon him prevents him from exercising.

The right to receive the heritage of human culture through education is also a fundamental, absolutely inalienable right: the exercise of it is subject to a given society's concrete possibilities; and it can be contrary to justice to claim the use of this right for each and all *hic et nunc* if that can only be realized by ruining the social body, as in the case of the slave society of ancient Rome or the feudal society of the Middle Ages— though of course this claim to education for all remained legitimate, as something to be fulfilled in time. In such cases what remains is to endeavor to change the social state involved. We see from this example—and I note this parenthetically—that the basis for the secret stimulus which incessantly fosters the transformation of societies lies in the fact that man *possesses* inalienable rights but is deprived of the possibility of justly claiming the *exercise* of certain of these rights because of the inhuman element that remains in the social structure of each period.

This distinction between the possession and the exercise of a right is, in my opinion, of serious importance. I have just indicated how it enables us to explain the limitations that can be justly imposed upon the assertion of certain rights under certain circumstances, either by the guilt of some delinquent or criminal individual, or by social structures whose vice or primitiveness prevents the claim, legitimate in itself, from being immediately fulfilled without encroaching upon major rights.

I should like to add that this distinction also enables us to understand that it is fitting at times, as history advances, to forego the exercise of certain rights which we nevertheless

continue to possess. These considerations apply to many problems concerning either the modalities of private property in a
society that is in the process of economic transformation, or
the limitations on the so-called "sovereignty" of States in
an international community that is in the process of being
organized.

VI

HUMAN RIGHTS IN PARTICULAR

Coming finally to the problems dealing with the enumeration of human rights taken in particular, I shall first recall to
our minds what I have previously stated: namely the fact that
in natural law there is immutability as regards things, or the
law itself ontologically considered, but progress and relativity
as regards human awareness of it. We have especially a tendency to inflate and make absolute, limitless, unrestricted in
every respect, the rights of which we are aware, thus blind-
ing ourselves to any other right which would counterbalance
them. Thus in human history no "new" right, I mean no
right of which common consciousness was becoming newly
aware, has been recognized in actual fact without having had
to struggle against and overcome the bitter opposition of
some "old rights." That was the story of the right to a just
wage and similar rights in the face of the right to free mutual
agreement and the right to private ownership. The fight of the
latter to claim for itself a privilege of divine, limitless absolutism was the unhappy epic of the XIXth Century. (Another unhappy epic was to follow, in which on the contrary
the very principle of private ownership was under fire, and
every other personal freedom with it.) Well! In 1850, when the
law against fugitive slaves was enforced, was not any help
given to a fugitive slave held by the conscience of many people
to be a criminal attempt against the right to ownership?

Conversely "new" rights often wage war against the "old"
ones, and cause them to be unfairly disregarded. At the time

of the French Revolution, for instance, a law promulgated in 1791 prohibited as "an attack on freedom and on the Declaration of the Rights of Man" any attempt by workers to associate in trade unions and join forces in refusing to work except for a given wage. This was considered an indirect return to the old system of corporations.

As concerns the problems of the present time, it is obvious that human reason has now become aware not only of the rights of man as a human and a civic person, but also of his rights as a social person engaged in the process of production and consumption, especially of his rights as a working person.

Generally speaking, a new age of civilization will be called upon to recognize and define the rights of the human being in his social, economic, and cultural functions—producers' and consumers' rights, technicians' rights, rights of those who devote themselves to labor of the mind, rights of everyone to share in the educational and cultural heritage of civilized life. But the most urgent problems are concerned on the one hand with the rights of that primordial society which is family society, and which is prior to the political state; on the other hand with the rights of the human being as he is engaged in the function of labor.[15]

I am alluding to rights such as the right to work and freely to choose one's work.—The right freely to form vocational groups or unions.—The right of the worker to be considered socially as an adult, and to have, some way or other, a share and active participation in the responsibilities of economic life.—The right of economic groups (unions and working communities) and other social groups to freedom and autonomy.—The right to a just wage, that is, sufficient to secure the family's living.—The right to relief, unemployment insurance, sick benefits, and social security.—The right to have

15. Cf. our book, *The Rights of Man and Natural Law* (New York: Charles Scribner's Sons, 1943); Georges Gurvitch, *La Déclaration des droits sociaux* (New York: Maison Française, 1944).

a part, free of charge, depending on the possibilities of the social body, in the elementary goods, both material and spiritual, of civilization.

What is involved in all this is first of all the dignity of work, the feeling for the rights of the human person in the worker, the rights in the name of which the worker stands before his employer in a relationship of justice and as an adult person, not as a child or as a servant. There is here an essential datum which far surpasses every problem of merely economic and social technique, for it is a *moral* datum, affecting man in his spiritual depths.

I am convinced that the antagonism between the "old" and the "new" rights of man—I mean the social rights to which I just alluded, especially those which relate to social justice and aim both at the efficacy of the social group and at the freedom from want and economic bondage of the working person—I am convinced that that antagonism, which many contemporary writers take pleasure in magnifying, is by no means insuperable. These two categories of rights seem irreconcilable only because of the clash between the two opposed ideologies and political systems which appeal to them, and of which they are independent in actual reality. Too much stress cannot be placed on the fact that the recognition of a particular category of rights is not the privilege of one school of thought at the expense of the others; it is no more necessary to be a follower of Rousseau to recognize the rights of the individual than it is to be a Marxist to recognize the economic and social rights. As a matter of fact, the universal Declaration of the Rights of Man adopted and proclaimed by the United Nations on December 10, 1948, makes room for the "old" and the "new" rights together.[16]

16. Even after the first World War, the Declarations of Rights attached to the new constitutions which then appeared on the European scene recognized the importance of social rights. Cf. Boris Mirkine-Guetzevitch, *Les nouvelles tendances du droit constitutionnel* (Paris: Giard, 1931), chap. iii.

If each of the human rights were by its nature absolutely unconditional and exclusive of any limitation, like a divine attribute, obviously any conflict between them would be irreconcilable. But who does not know in reality that these rights, being human, are, like everything human, subject to conditioning and limitation, at least, as we have seen, as far as their exercise is concerned? That the various rights ascribed to the human being limit each other, particularly that the economic and social rights, the rights of man as a person involved in the life of the community, cannot be given room in human history without restricting, to some extent, the freedoms and rights of man as an individual person, is only normal. What creates irreducible differences and antagonisms among men is the determination of the degree of such restriction, and more generally the determination of the scale of values that governs the exercise and the concrete organization of these various rights. Here we are confronted with the clash between incompatible political philosophies. Because here we are no longer dealing with the simple recognition of the diverse categories of human rights, but with the principle of dynamic unification in accordance with which they are carried into effect; we are dealing with the tonality, the specific key, by virtue of which different music is played on this same keyboard, either in harmony or in discord with human dignity.

We can imagine—in accordance with the views set forward in the first part of this chapter—that the advocates of a liberal-individualistic, a communistic, or a personalist[17] type of society will lay down on paper similar, perhaps identical, lists of the rights of man. They will not, however, play that instrument in the same way. Everything depends upon the supreme value in accordance with which all these rights will be ordered and will mutually limit each other. It is by virtue of

17. Cf. our books, *Freedom in the Modern World*, pp. 46 ff., and *True Humanism* (New York: Charles Scribner's Sons, 1938), pp. 127 ff.

the hierarchy of values to which we thus subscribe that we determine the way in which the rights of man, economic and social as well as individual, should, in our eyes, pass into the
realm of existence. Those whom, for want of a better name, I
just called the advocates of a liberal-individualistic type of society, see the mark of human dignity first and foremost in the
power of each person to appropriate individually the goods of
nature in order to do freely whatever he wants; the advocates
of a communistic type of society see the mark of human dignity first and foremost in the power to submit these same
goods to the collective command of the social body in order to
"free" human labor (by subduing it to the economic community) and to gain the control of history; the advocates of a
personalistic type of society see the mark of human dignity
first and foremost in the power to make these same goods of
nature serve the common conquest of intrinsically human,
moral, and spiritual goods and of man's freedom of autonomy.
Those three groups inevitably will accuse each other of ignor-
ing certain essential rights of the human being. It remains to
be seen who makes a faithful image and who a distorted image
of man. As far as I am concerned, I know where I stand: with
the third of the three schools of thought I just mentioned.

CHAPTER V

THE DEMOCRATIC CHARTER

✲

I

The Democratic Secular Faith

IN THE "sacral" era of the Middle Ages a great attempt was made to build the life of the earthly community and civilization on the foundation of the unity of theological faith and religious creed. This attempt succeeded for a certain number of centuries but failed in the course of time, after the Reformation and the Renaissance; and a return to the mediaeval sacral pattern is in no way conceivable. In proportion as the civil society, or the body politic, has become more perfectly distinguished from the spiritual realm of the Church—a process which was in itself but a development of the Gospel distinction between the things that are Caesar's and the things that are God's—the civil society has become grounded on a common good and a common task which are of an earthly, "temporal," or "secular" order, and in which citizens belonging to diverse spiritual groups or lineages share equally. Religious division among men is in itself a misfortune. But it is a fact that we must willy-nilly recognize.

In modern times an attempt was made to base the life of civilization and the earthly community on the foundation of mere reason—reason separated from religion and from the Gospel. This attempt fostered immense hopes in the last two centuries,— and rapidly failed. Pure reason showed itself more incapable than faith of ensuring the spiritual unity of mankind, and the dream of a "scientific" creed, uniting men in peace and in common convictions about the aims and basic principles of human life and society, vanished in our contemporary catastrophes. In proportion as the tragic events of the last decades have given the lie to the bourgeois rationalism of the XVIIIth and XIXth Centuries, we have been confronted with the fact that religion and metaphysics are an essential part of human culture, primary and indispensable incentives in the very life of society.

As a result, it seems likely that, if democracy enters its next historical stage with sufficient intelligence and vitality, a renewed democracy will not ignore religion, as the bourgeois XIXth Century society, both individualist and "neutral," did; and that this renewed, "personalist" democracy will be of a *pluralistic* type.

Thus we would have—supposing that the people have regained their Christian faith, or at least recognized the value and sensibleness of the Christian conception of freedom, social progress, and the political establishment—we would have, on the one hand, a body politic Christianly inspired in its own political life. On the other hand, this personalist body politic would recognize that men belonging to most different philosophical or religious creeds and lineages could and should cooperate in the common task and for the common welfare, provided they similarly assent to the basic tenets of a society of free men. These common tenets, that is the subject matter which requests our attention and which I should like to discuss.

For a society of free men implies basic tenets which are at the core of its very existence. A genuine democracy implies a fundamental agreement between minds and wills on the bases of life in common; it is aware of itself and of its principles, and it must be capable of defending and promoting its own conception of social and political life; *it must bear within itself a common human creed, the creed of freedom*. The mistake of bourgeois liberalism has been to conceive democratic society to be a kind of lists or arena in which all the conceptions of the bases of common life, even those most destructive to freedom and law, meet with no more than the pure and simple indifference of the body politic, while they compete before public opinion in a kind of free market of the mother-ideas, healthy or poisoned, of political life. Nineteenth Century bourgeois democracy was *neutral* even with regard to freedom. Just as it had no real *common good*, it had no real *common thought*—no brains of its own, but a neutral, empty skull clad with mirrors: no wonder that before the second world war, in countries that fascist, racist, or communist propaganda was to disturb or to corrupt, it had become a society without any idea of itself and without faith in itself, without any *common faith* which could enable it to resist disintegration.

But the all-important point to be noted here is that this faith and inspiration, and the concept of itself which democracy needs—all these do not belong to the order of religious creed and eternal life, but to the temporal or secular order of earthly life, of culture or civilization. The *faith* in question is a *civic or secular* faith, not a religious one. Nor is it that philosophic substitute for religious faith, that adherence forced upon all by reason's demonstrations, which the XVIIIth and XIXth Century philosophers sought in vain. A genuine democracy cannot impose on its citizens or demand from them, as a condition for their belonging to the city, any philosophic or any religious creed. This conception of the city was possible during the "sacral" period of our civilization, when communion in the Christian faith was a prerequisite for the constitution of the body politic. In our own day it has been able to produce only the inhuman counterfeit, whether hypocritical or violent, offered by the totalitarian States which lay claim to the faith, the obedience, and the love of the religious man for his God; it has produced only their effort to impose their creed on the mind of the masses by the power of propaganda, lies, and the police.

What is, then, the object of the *secular faith* that we are discussing? This object is a merely practical one, not a theoretical or dogmatic one. The secular faith in question deals with *practical* tenets which the human mind can try to justify—more or less successfully, that's another affair—from quite different philosophical outlooks, probably because they depend basically on simple, "natural" apperceptions, of which the human heart becomes capable with the progress of moral conscience, and which, as a matter of fact, have been awakened by the Gospel leaven fermenting in the obscure depths of human history. Thus it is that men possessing quite different, even opposite metaphysical or religious outlooks, can converge, not by virtue of any identity of doctrine, but by virtue of an analogical similitude in practical principles, toward the same practical conclusions, and can share in the same practical secular faith, provided that they similarly revere, perhaps for quite diverse reasons, truth and intelligence, human dignity, freedom, brotherly love, and the absolute value of moral good.

We must therefore maintain a sharp and clear distinction between the human and temporal creed which lies at the root of common life and which is but a set of *practical conclusions* or of *practical points of convergence*—on the one hand; and on the other, the *theoretical justifications*, the conceptions of the world and of life, the philosophical or religious creeds which found, or claim to found, these practical conclusions in reason.

The body politic has the right and the duty to promote among its citizens, mainly through education, the human and temporal—and essentially practical—creed on which depend national communion and civil peace. It has no right, as a merely temporal or secular body, enclosed in the sphere where the modern State enjoys its autonomous authority, to impose on the citizens or to demand from them a rule of faith or a conformism of reason, a philosophical or religious creed which would present itself as the only possible justification of the practical charter through which the people's common secular faith expresses itself. The important thing for the body politic is that the democratic sense be in fact kept alive by the adherence of minds, however diverse, to this moral charter. The ways and the justifications by means of which this common adherence is brought about pertain to the freedom of minds and consciences.

Certainly, it is supremely important to the common good that the practical assertions which make up the charter in question be true in themselves. But the democratic State does not judge of that truth; it is born out of that truth, as recognized and asserted by the people—by each one of us, to the extent of his abilities.

What would be the content of the moral charter, the code of social and political morality which I am speaking about and the validity of which is implied by the fundamental compact of a society of free men? Such a charter would deal, for instance, with the following points: rights and liberties of the human person, political rights and liberties, social rights and social liberties, corresponding responsibilities; rights and duties of persons who are part of a family society, and liberties and obligations of the latter toward the body politic; mutual rights and duties of groups and the State; government of the people, by the people, and for the people; functions of authority in a political and social democracy, moral obligation, binding in conscience, regarding just laws as well as the Constitution which guarantees the people's liberties; exclusion of the resort to political coups (coups d'état) in a society that is truly free and ruled by laws whose change and evolution depend on the popular majority; human equality, justice between persons and the body politic, justice between the body politic and persons, civil friendship and an ideal of fraternity,

religious freedom, mutual tolerance and mutual respect between various spiritual communities and schools of thought,
civic self-devotion and love of the motherland, reverence for
its history and heritage, and understanding of the various traditions that combine to create its unity; obligations of each
person toward the common good of the body politic and obligations of each nation toward the common good of civilized
society, and the necessity of becoming aware of the unity of
the world and of the existence of a community of peoples.

It is a fact that in democratic nations, which, like the
United States and France, have a hard historic experience of
the struggles for freedom, practically everybody would be
ready to endorse all the tenets of such a charter. Given that
virtue of universality with which the civilization inherited
from Christianity is endowed, and which Arnold Toynbee has
insisted upon in a persuasive manner, we have good reason to
hope that in all nations of the world the people—I say the
people, whatever the case of their governments may be—
would be likely to offer the same endorsement.

I should like to add two remarks which do not deal directly
with the issue that I just discussed, but rather with the problems that we shall consider in the next chapter.

First: as a matter of fact, the more the body politic—that
is, the people—were imbued with Christian convictions and
aware of the *religious* faith which inspires it, the more deeply
it would adhere to the *secular* faith in the democratic charter;
for, as a matter of fact, the latter has taken shape in human
history as a result of the Gospel inspiration awakening the
"naturally Christian" potentialities of common secular consciousness, even among the diversity of spiritual lineages and
schools of thought opposed to each other, and sometimes
warped by a vitiated ideology.

Second: to the extent that the body politic—that is, the

people—were imbued with Christian convictions, to the same extent, as a matter of fact, the justification of the democratic charter offered by Christian philosophy would be recognized as the truest one—not at all as a result of any interference of the State, but only as a result of the free adherence which larger parts of the people would have given to Christian faith and Christian philosophy in actual fact.

And of course no religious pressure would be exercised by the majority. Non-Christian citizens' freedom to found their democratic beliefs on grounds different from those more generally accepted would by no means be jeopardized. What the civil authority and the State would be concerned with is only the common secular faith in the common secular charter.

II

The Political Heretics

The fact must be recognized that the body politic has its own heretics, as the Church has hers. Nay more, St. Paul tells us that there must be heretics[1]—and they are probably still less inevitable in the State than in the Church. Did we not insist that there is a democratic charter, nay, a democratic creed? That there is a democratic secular faith? Well, everywhere where faith is, divine or human, religious or secular, there are also heretics who threaten the unity of the community, either religious or civil. In the sacral society of the Middle Ages the heretic was the breaker of religious unity. In a lay society of free men the heretic is the breaker of the "common democratic beliefs and practices," the one who takes a stand against freedom, or against the basic equality of men, or the dignity and rights of the human person, or the moral power of law.

People who remember the lessons of history know that a democratic society should not be an unarmed society, which

1. I Cor. 11:19.

the enemies of liberty may calmly lead to the slaughterhouse in the name of liberty. Precisely because it is a commonwealth of free men, it must defend itself with particular energy against those who, out of principle, refuse to accept, and who even work to destroy, the foundations of common life in such a régime, the foundations which are freedom and the practical secular faith expressed in the democratic charter.

When the political heretic embarks on *political activity*, he will be met with, and checked by, opposite political activity freely developed by citizens in a body politic sufficiently lively and alive. When he embarks on *illegal activity*, trying to use violence, he will be met with, and checked by, the authority of the State, which in a society of free men, is exercised against him only in granting him, in a real, not a fake manner, the institutional guarantees of justice and law. There is no problem here. The difficulty begins when it comes to the *speaking and writing activity* of the political heretic.

The question of the freedom of expression[2] is not a simple

2. See the important report, *A Free and Responsible Press*, published by the Commission on the Freedom of the Press under the chairmanship of Robert M. Hutchins (Chicago: University of Chicago Press, 1947).

I would like to recall in this note the various recommendations made by the commission.

I. As concerns government: (1) That the constitutional guaranties of the freedom of the press be recognized as including the radio and motion pictures. (2) That government facilitate new ventures in the communications industry, that it foster the introduction of new techniques, that it maintain competition among large units through the antitrust laws, but that those laws be sparingly used to break up such units, and that, where concentration is necessary in communications, the government endeavor to see to it that the public gets the benefit of such concentration. (3) As an alternative to the present remedy for libel, legislation by which the injured party might obtain a retraction or a restatement of the facts by the offender or an opportunity to reply. (4) The repeal of legislation prohibiting expressions in favor of revolutionary changes in our institutions where there is no clear and present danger that violence will result from the expressions. (5) That the government, through the media of mass communication, inform the public of the facts with respect to its policies and of the purposes underlying those policies and that, to the extent that private agencies of mass communication are unable or unwilling to supply such media to the government, the government itself

one. So great is the confusion today that we see commonsense principles, which have been ignored in the past by the worshippers of a false and deceiving liberty, being now used in a false and deceiving manner in order to destroy true liberty. Those maxims—dealing with our obligations toward objective truth and with the rights of the common good—which were branded as an outrage against human autonomy when the Catholic Church set them forth to condemn theological liberalism, and which, by opposing unbridled, divinely unlimited freedom of expression, were of a nature to save freedom of expression—the Communist State is now trumpeting them and perverting them in order simply to annihilate freedom of expression. A sad Time's revenge. And, for everybody, an opportunity for melancholy reflections.

In discussing freedom of expression we have to take into account a variety of aspects. On the one hand, it is not true that every thought as such, because of the mere fact that

---

may employ media of its own. Also that, where the private agencies of mass communication are unable or unwilling to supply information about this country to a particular foreign country or countries, the government employ mass-communication media of its own to supplement this deficiency.

II. As concerns the press and mass communication media: (1) That the agencies of mass communication accept the responsibilities of common carriers of information and discussion. (2) That they assume the responsibility of financing new, experimental activities in their fields. (3) That the members of the press engage in vigorous mutual criticism. (4) That the press use every means that can be devised to increase the competence, independence, and effectiveness of its staff. (5) That the radio industry take control of its programs and that it treat advertising as it is treated by the best newspapers.

III. As concerns the public: (1) That nonprofit organizations help supply the variety, quantity, and quality of press service required by the American people. (2) That academic-professional centers of advanced study, research, and publication in the field of communications be created; and, further, that existing schools of journalism exploit the total resources of their universities to the end that their students may obtain the broadest and most liberal training. (3) That a new and independent agency be established to appraise and report annually upon the performance of the press.

it was born in a human intellect, has the right to be spread about in the body politic.[3]

On the other hand, not only censorship and police methods, but any direct restriction of freedom of expression, though unavoidable in certain cases of necessity, are the worst way to ensure the rights of the body politic to defend freedom and the common charter and common morality. Because any such restriction runs against the very spirit of a democratic society: a democratic society knows that human subjectivity's inner energies, reason, and conscience are the most valuable springs of political life. It also knows that it is no use fighting ideas with *cordons sanitaires* and repressive measures (even totalitarian States know that; consequently they simply kill their heretics, while using psychotechnical means to tame or corrupt ideas themselves).

Moreover we have seen that the common agreement expressed in democratic faith is not of a doctrinal, but merely practical nature. As a result the criterion for any interference of the State in the field of the expression of thought is also to be practical, not ideological: the more extraneous this cri-

---

3. In order to sum up the considerations presented in this section, I would say:

A. Freedom of expression is a human right, but this right is only a "substantially," not an "absolutely," inalienable right (see above, p. 101). There are limits to freedom of expression, which are inevitably demanded both by the common good and by this very freedom, that would become self-destructive if it were made limitless.

B. The State is entitled to impose limitations on freedom of expression, in view of particularly serious circumstances. But in actual fact it can do so in a manner beneficial to a democratic society only in most obvious and externally palpable matters and with regard to those basic ingredients in the common good which are the simplest and the most elementary.

C. When it comes to higher matters, in which freedom of inquiry and the inner values of intelligence and conscience are involved, and with regard to the most vital and spiritual ingredients (which *in themselves* are the most important) in the common good, the factual limitations to be brought to bear on freedom of expression depend on the constructive and regulative institutions, organs, and agencies and the free activities spontaneously developed in the body politic.

terion is to the very content of thought, the better it will be. It is too much for the State, for instance, to judge whether a work of art is possessed of an intrinsic quality of immorality (then it would condemn Baudelaire or Joyce); it is enough for it to judge whether an author or a publisher plans to make money in selling obscenities. It is too much for the State to judge whether a political theory is heretical with regard to the democratic faith; it is enough for it to judge—always with the institutional guarantees of justice and law—whether a political heretic threatens the democratic charter by the tangible acts he undertakes or by receiving money from a foreign State to subsidize antidemocratic propaganda.

You will answer quite rightly: is not the intellectual corruption of human minds, is not the ruining of primary verities, exceedingly more detrimental to the common good of the body politic than any other work of corruption?—Yes, it is.—But the fact is that the State is not equipped to deal with matters of intelligence.

Each time the State disregards that basic truth, which depends on its own nature, intelligence is victimized. And since intelligence has always its revenge, it is the body politic which, in one way or another, is finally victimized. Only one society can deal with matters of intelligence—that is the Church, because she is a spiritual society. Yet she, who knows what's what, had in the past some sad experiences in giving an eye to such ideas as the movement of the earth, and she does not use without thoughtful misgivings her spiritual weapons against her own heretics.[4]

Do I mean to imply that even with regard to superior matters the democratic body politic is disarmed? I mean just the

4. The Church, of course, is entitled to bring limitations to bear on freedom of expression in her own spiritual realm, as regards matters of faith and morals and with respect to the common good of the Kingdom of God. The claim to limitless freedom of expression laid by theological liberalism was a direct challenge to that right of the Church.

contrary. I mean that positive, constructive means are exceedingly more efficacious than mere restriction of freedom of expression. And there are in a living democracy innumerable means of such a nature. Let us consider especially the matter of political heretics: Groups and leagues of citizens could devote themselves to the progress of democratic philosophy, the enlightenment of people with regard to the common charter, and the intellectual struggle against warped political trends. The State itself could have the people informed of the judgments passed upon anti-democratic ideologies by some special body made up of men whose intellectual wisdom and moral integrity would be universally recognized.[5] Still more important, the various organizations, freely starting from the bottom, which in a pluralist society would unite readers and listeners on the one hand, writers and speakers on the other, could develop, as regards the use of the media of mass communication, a ceaseless process of self-regulation, as well as a growing sense of responsibility. Still more important, the body politic, with the sense of community which it normally entails, has at its disposal the spontaneous pressure of the common consciousness and public opinion, which spring from the national ethos when it is firmly established, and which are strong enough to keep political heretics out of leadership. First and foremost it has at its disposal the work of democratic education.

III

EDUCATION AND THE DEMOCRATIC CHARTER

Education is obviously the primary means to foster common secular faith in the democratic charter.

Education depends first and foremost on the family. For the end of the family is not only to beget offspring—promiscuity would be enough for that—but to beget them as children of

5. See also Recommendation I, 5, of the Commission on the Freedom of the Press above, p. 115, n. 2).

man or to bring them up spiritually as well as physically. Under various particular forms and patterns, everywhere and in every time, men have been aware of this requirement of natural law. So the function of the educational system and the educational function of the State are only auxiliary functions with regard to the family group—normal auxiliary functions, moreover, since the family group is unable to supply the youth with the full stock of knowledge needed for the formation of a man in civilized life. My point is that in exercising this normal auxiliary function, the educational system and the State have to provide the future citizens not only with a treasure of skills, knowledge, and wisdom—liberal education for all[6]—but also with a genuine and reasoned-out belief in the common democratic charter, such as is required for the very unity of the body politic.

The educational system and the State have a duty to see to the teaching of that charter of common life, and thus to defend and promote the common good and the fundamental statute of the body politic even up to the common secular faith involved.

Yet the educational system and the State can do this only in the name of the common assent through which the charter in question is held true by the people, and in so far as it proceeds from that agreement between minds and wills which lies at the root of the political society. And thus—since in actual fact the body politic is divided in its fundamental theoretical conceptions, and since the democratic State, as we have seen, cannot impose a philosophical or a religious creed—the State and the educational system, in seeing to the teaching of the common charter, can and must cling only to the common practical recognition of the merely practical tenets upon which the people have agreed to live together, despite the diversity or the op-

6. Cf. Robert M. Hutchins, *Education for Freedom* (Baton Rouge: Louisiana State University Press, 1943).

position between their spiritual traditions and schools of thought.

Nay more, there is no belief except in what is held to be intrinsically established in truth, nor any assent of the intellect without a theoretical foundation and justification: thus if the State and the educational system are to perform their duty and inculcate the democratic charter in a really efficacious way, they cannot help resorting—so that minds be put in possession of such a foundation and justification, and perceive as true what is taught them—to the philosophical or religious traditions and schools of thought which are spontaneously at work in the consciousness of the nation and which have contributed historically to its formation.

Adherence to one of these schools of thought or another rests with the freedom of each person. But it would be sheer illusion to think that the democratic charter could be efficiently taught if it were separated from the roots that give it consistence and vigor in the mind of each one, and if it were reduced to a mere series of abstract formulas—bookish, bloodless, and cut off from life. Those who teach the democratic charter must believe in it with their whole hearts, and stake on it their personal convictions, their consciences, and the depths of their moral life. They must therefore explain and justify its articles in the light of the philosophical or religious faith to which they cling and which quickens their belief in the common charter.

Now, if every teacher does thus put all his philosophical or religious convictions, his personal faith, and his soul into the effort to confirm and vivify the moral charter of democracy, then it is clear that such a teaching demands a certain spontaneous adaptation between the one who gives and the one who receives, between the inspiration animating the teacher and the basic conceptions that the student holds from his home circle and his social milieu and that his family feels the duty of fostering and developing in him. In other words, this teaching should awaken in those who receive it the deep interest which depends on the moral beliefs already formed or started in them, and without which it would lose the greater part of its vital efficacy.

The conclusion is obvious. The goal aimed at by the educational system and the State is unity—unity in the common adherence to the democratic charter. But for the very sake of attaining this practical unity a sound pluralism must obtain in the means; inner differentiations must come into force in the structure of the educational system so as to afford an efficacious teaching of the democratic charter. On the one hand the State—or the groups and agencies in the body politic which are concerned with education, or the authorities that govern the educational system—should see to it that the democratic charter be taught—and taught in a comprehensive, far-reaching, and vitally convincing manner—in all the schools and educational institutions. On the other hand, and for the very sake of fostering the democratic faith in people's minds, the educational system should admit within itself *pluralistic* patterns enabling teachers to put their entire convictions and most personal inspiration in their teaching of the democratic charter.

* * *

These are quite general principles. When it comes to application, I am aware of the great diversity in educational systems between countries where schools are mainly supported by the State or mainly privately endowed.

As concerns the educational system mainly grounded, as in France, on State support and control, I have offered some suggestions of my own in an annex to the French edition of *Educa-*

tion at the Crossroads.[7] The pluralism which I am advocating for public schools should relate, in my opinion, not to the curriculum, but to the various inspirations with which the common curriculum would be taught if the members of the teaching body were distributed and grouped in the various areas of a city, or of the whole country, according to their own wishes as well as to the moral geography of local communities and the requests of associations of parents—so that their own personal religious or philosophical convictions would roughly correspond to those which prevail in the social environment.

In educational systems grounded to a degree, as in this country, on privately endowed schools, colleges, and universities, pluralistic teaching of the democratic charter would still more easily come into force, if the denominational institutions were more aware of the impact of religious inspiration on the whole realm of intelligence, and if the secular institutions freed themselves of the secularist prejudices they have progressively developed despite their not infrequent religious origins.

I am not treating here of the problem of religious instruction with regard to the youth educated in secular schools and colleges and State institutions, and of the facilities for a serious religious education which should be offered to those children whose parents desired it. What I am discussing is the teaching of the democratic charter in these institutions.

The most rational solution, in tune with the pluralistic principle, would consist, to my mind, in having the teaching of the democratic charter given not by one, but by several teachers belonging to the main religious or philosophical traditions represented in the student population of a given school or college, each one of those teachers addressing the students of his own spiritual tradition. Yet as logical as it may be, such

7. *L'Éducation à la croisée des chemins* (Paris: Luf, 1947), Annexe: "Le Problème de l'école publique en France."

a solution has little chance, I am afraid, to appear feasible to our contemporaries. Something else should be carried into effect, in every country, to insure a real and efficient teaching of the democratic charter in public schools.

The idea is that a *new discipline* should be introduced in the curriculum: this new discipline would bring together such diverse branches of knowledge as National history and History of Civilization as basic framework, and then Humanities, Social Science, Social Philosophy, and Philosophy of Law, all these to be centered on the development and significance of the great ideas comprised in the common charter: so this charter would be taught in a concrete and comprehensive manner, in the light of the great poets and thinkers and heroes of mankind, and in connection with the historical life of the nation, seen as woven of deeds and truths always full of meaning and deservedly treasured. As to the teachers, those only would be put in charge of this new part of the curriculum who felt able to swear that they sincerely believe in all the tenets of the democratic charter; they would also swear that if some day they ceased to believe in it, then they would request to be shifted to the teaching of another part of the curriculum—full assurance being given them, moreover, that they would not incur for that any professional drawback.

As concerns the role of the State, I do not believe that it is difficult to determine, if only one keeps in mind the golden rule of the common good. The State (precisely because it is not a substitute for the body politic, but a special agency concerned with keeping *that which exists* in the body politic in line with the common good)—the State should not stand aloof from, it should help and encourage (I do not mean as concerns any financial subsidization of the schools themselves,[8] I

8. As regards the very controversial issue dealing with the financial subsidizing of denominational *schools* by the State, the general principle to be considered could, in my opinion, be expressed as follows: Either the various religious inspirations traditional in

mean as concerns *welfare services* to all children and all students) the educational effort accomplished by the various privately-endowed institutions, either denominational or secular, which emanate from and correspond to the diverse spiritual lineages at work in the nation. And as to its own State-supported schools and colleges, not only should every extra-curricular facility be offered by them for religious instruction, but in their very teaching full recognition should be given to the essential role played by the Judeo-Christian tenets and inspiration in the birth and maintenance of the democratic charter. To ignore, on the plea of a "separation" between State and

---

the nation are integrated in the public school system, or they give rise to merely private schools.

In the first case the public school system admits of an inner pluralistic organization, according to the diversity of spiritual lineages in the nation (cf. the Dutch school system); and the denominational schools—or those sections of the public school system which correspond to them—are State-supported. But the denominational schools are no longer autonomous, they are subject to the general regulations of the public school system.

In the second case, the denominational schools are completely autonomous. But they are not State-supported.

Given the conditions and difficulties of our times, it seems that, at least in Europe, the most appropriate situation would obtain if the first solution were applied as a rule and the second in particular instances as a complement.

Now if the public school system refuses any kind of inner pluralism and sticks to a merely "neutral" or areligious common teaching, then a basically unsound situation occurs. For such a public school system claims to be a *public* service and is *not* in reality, since it does not meet the basic needs and requirements—which, in justice, should be equally satisfied—of the various categories of citizens which compose the nation. As a result of that fundamental, intrinsic self-contradiction, the unsound situation in question cannot be remedied: some lack of justice will block either one way out or the other. If the denominational schools are subsidized by the State, public funds will be used for private aims. If the denominational schools are not subsidized by the State, some categories of citizens will be obliged to pay the same bill twice (first, taxes for the public school system; second, financial support of their own private schools). The drawback implied in the first part of the alternative might be regarded, it is true, as making up for the more serious drawback involved in a public service which is not public. But, as a matter of fact, if the State is unwilling to adapt the school system to the legitimate requirements of all categories of citizens, it will probably be still more unwilling to use public funds to compensate for this defect.

Church wrongly and anti-politically understood, the religious traditions and schools of thought which are part of the heritage of the body politic, would simply mean for democracy to separate itself, and democratic faith, from the deepest of its living sources.

IV

Problems concerning Authority

I have treated of authority in democracy in another book.[9] Yet it is necessary to sum up a few considerations of the subject in order to have our concept of the democratic charter sufficiently complete. I am not dissatisfied, moreover, to have an opportunity to make certain positions clearer and more definite—and truer, I hope—than in my previous essays.

Authority and Power are two different things: *Power* is the force by means of which you can oblige others to obey you. *Authority* is the *right* to direct and command, to be listened to or obeyed by others. Authority requests Power. Power without authority is tyranny.

Thus authority means right. If, in the cosmos, a nature, such as human nature, can be preserved and developed only in a state of culture, and if the state of culture necessarily entails the existence in the social group of a function of commandment and government directed to the common good, then this function is demanded by Natural Law, and implies a *right* to command and govern.

Furthermore, if said function, which in direct democracy is exercised by the "multitude" or the people themselves, can be properly exercised, in larger and more differentiated societies, only on the condition that the people entrust it to certain men who will be henceforth especially concerned with the affairs of the whole, then those men, once put in charge of the direc-

9. *Scholasticism and Politics* (New York: Macmillan Co., 1940), chap. iv (French corresponding text in *Principes d'une politique humaniste* [New York: Maison Française, 1944], chap. ii).

tion òf the community, have a *right* (received from and through the people) to be obeyed for the sake of the common good: in other words, the relation of authority among men proceeds from Natural Law. I mean here the relation of authority taken as yet indeterminately, and not in the sense that *some* in particular must command and *some* in particular must obey; but rather in the general sense that there must be people who command and people who obey, the mode of designation of those who shall command being a different matter to be determined later and according to reason.[10]

Finally, since authority means *right*, it has to be obeyed by reason of conscience, that is, in the manner in which free men obey, and for the sake of the common good.[11]

But by the same token there is no authority where there is no justice. Unjust authority is not authority, as an unjust law is not law. At the origin of the democratic sense, there is not the desire to "obey only oneself," as Rousseau put it, but rather the desire to obey only *because it is just*.

* * *

Whatever the régime of political life may be, authority, that is, the right to direct and to command, derives from the people, but has its primary source in the Author of nature. Authority derives from the will or *consensus* of the people, and from their basic right to govern themselves, as from a channel through which nature causes a body politic to be and to act.

These two statements, expressed as they are in the most general and still undetermined way, have been a matter of com-

10. Cf. Suarez, *De legibus*, Lib. III, c. 4, n. 5: "Unde potestas regia formaliter ut talis est de jure humano."

11. For a thorough discussion of the matter see Yves Simon, *Nature and Functions of Authority* (Milwaukee: Marquette University Press, 1940); and *Democracy* (in preparation; to be published by the University of Chicago Press). Professor Yves Simon has rightly stressed the fact that the basic problem of authority (as a right of the people as a whole) comes prior to the problem of the necessity for having authority entrusted to a distinct governing personnel.

mon agreement for a century-old tradition in political philosophy. But they have been understood in quite different and
sharply opposed manners.

A first issue, dealing with the relationship between the
people and God, has been: do the people receive from God the
right to self-government and authority to rule themselves in a
merely *transient and transitory* way? So that when they designate their rulers they act only as an *instrumental cause*[12] through
which God alone (as principal agent) invests with authority
the one or ones designated?

Or do the people receive from God the right to self-government and authority to rule themselves in an *inherent* manner? So
that they are possessed of this right and this authority as a
"principal agent" (though "secondary" or subordinate with
respect to the Primary Cause) which through its own causal
power—acting, as everything acts, in the virtue of God's universal activation—invests with authority the one or ones
designated?[13] It is this second part of the alternative which has
proved to be the true one.

And a second issue, dealing with the relationship between
the people and their rulers, has been: do the people, when they
invest certain men with authority, *divest themselves* of their
right to self-government and their authority to rule themselves (whatever the way may be—transient or inherent—in
which they have received these rights from God)? So that
once the ruler or rulers have been put in charge, the people
lose their right to self-government and their authority to rule

12. Instrumental, not with respect to the choice or designation made, but with respect to the transmission of authority.

13. Thus this authority comes from God as Primary Source and Primary Cause, even
comes from Him "immediately," in the sense that human nature, naturally demanding what is necessarily implied in social life, immediately proceeds from God. Cf.
Josephus Gredt, O.S.B., *Elementa philosophiae Aristotelico-Thomisticae* (St. Louis: Herder,
1946), t. II, n. 1029, 4: "Auctoritas politica immediate est a Deo seu a lege aeterna,
quatenus immediate a Deo est humana natura naturaliter ad societatem ordinata."

themselves, which have been transferred to the ruler or rulers and are henceforth possessed by them alone?

Or do the people, when they invest certain men with authority, *keep* their right to self-government and their authority to rule themselves? So that they possess these rights, not only *inherently* with respect to the manner in which they receive them from God, but also *permanently* with respect to the manner in which they convey them to their rulers?

In modern history the age of the absolute kings, as we have seen in discussing Sovereignty,[14] has answered affirmatively the first part of this alternative, negatively the second. Yet the right answer is *no* to the first part of the alternative, and *yes* to the second. The realization of this basic verity (long ago pointed out by some great Schoolmen) has been a conquest of democratic philosophy. In this connection, whatever the political *régime* may be, monarchical, aristocratic, or democratic, democratic *philosophy* appears as the only true political philosophy.

The trouble has been that from the very moment when it took the upper hand, this philosophy was imperiled by a counterfeit ideology, the ideology of Sovereignty. Instead of getting clear of the concept of Sovereignty (which implies *transcendent* or *separate* supreme power, supreme power *from above*), Rousseau transferred to the people, as we have pointed out in Chapter II, the Sovereignty of the absolute monarch conceived in the most absolute manner; in other terms he made a mythical people—the people as the monadic subject of the indivisible General Will—into a sovereign Person separated from the real people (the multitude) and ruling them from above. As a result, since a figment of the imagination cannot really rule, it is to the State—to the State which, in genuine democratic philosophy, should be supervised and controlled

14. See chap. ii.

by the people,—that, as a matter of fact, Sovereignty, indivisible and not-accountable Sovereignty, was to be transferred. On the other hand, Sovereignty cannot be shared in; consequently, the people, or the Sovereign Person, could not invest any official with authority over them; only the people as a whole could make laws, and the men elected by them did not hold any real authority, or right to command. The elected of the people were only passive instruments, not representatives. As a matter of principle, the very concept of representative of the people was to be wiped away.

This concept, however, is absolutely essential to genuine democratic philosophy. It is on the notion of representation or vicariousness, by virtue of which the very right of the people to rule themselves is exercised by the officials whom the people have chosen, that all the theory of power in democratic society rests. As I shall emphasize further, the representatives of the people are "sent," missioned or commissioned, by the people to exercise authority because they are made by the people participants, to some given extent, in the very authority of the people, in other words because they are made by the people *images* of and *deputies* for the people.

Those who represent the people are not the image of God. The Pope in the Church, being the vicar of Christ, is the image of Christ. The Prince in political society, being the vicar of the people, is the image of the people. A great deal of confusion occurred in this regard in the age of absolutism, because the authority of the king was often conceived of on the pattern of the authority of the Pope, that is to say, as coming down from above, whereas in reality it came up from below. For another reason a great deal of confusion had previously occurred in the Middle Ages: because the solemn anointing or coronation of the king, by sanctioning from the sacred heights of the supernatural order his right to command in the natural order, conveyed to him, as servant or secular arm of the Church, a reflection of the supernatural royal virtues, bounty, justice, and the paternal love of Christ, Head of the Church. From this point of view the Middle Ages might regard the king as the image of Christ.[15] But in the natural order, which is the order of political life, he was not the image of Christ, he was the image of the people. Theologians, especially in the Thomist lineage, were able clearly to make that distinction. But mediaeval common consciousness remained enmeshed in an ambivalent idea of the Prince.

The civil power bears the impress of majesty: this is not because it represents God. It is because it represents the people, the whole multitude and its common will to live together. And by the same token, since it represents the people, the civil power holds its authority, through the people, from the Primary Cause of Nature and of human society.[16] St. Paul teaches that "there is no authority that is not from God" and that those who bear the sword are "God's ministers" or "functionaries of God," "appointed by God" (let us understand, through the people) "to inflict his wrathful vengeance upon him that doth wrong."[17] Never did he teach that they were the image of God. What essentially constituted, in its own temporal or political order, the majesty of the king is the same as what the majesty of the President of a democratic nation consists of, especially when he is invested with such constitutional powers as those in this country. For the President, just as the king, can be a quite ordinary man deprived of any personal prestige; yet look at him when he acts in his capacity of

15. Cf. this passage from Bracton's *De rerum divisione*, quoted by Richard O'Sullivan in his Introduction to *Under God and the Law: Papers Read to the Thomas More Society of London, Second Series* (Oxford: Blackwell, 1949): The king "ought to be under the law since he is God's vicar, as evidently appears after the likeness of Jesus Christ whose representative he is on earth" (*cujus vices gerit in terris*).

16. And in a sense—a theologian would add—from Christ's universal kingship. But this no more makes him a representative of Christ than an image of God.

17. Rom. 13:1–7.

supreme chief of the body politic: millions of citizens, with their collective power, their hopes, their trust, their century-old heritage of suffering and glory, their prospective collective destiny, their collective calling in mankind's history, are there, in his person, as in a sign which makes them present to our eyes. Here is majesty, here is the essence of his political majesty. Not because he is a Sovereign! since in the political domain there is no such thing as sovereignty. But because he is the image of the people, and the topmost deputy of the people. And behind this majesty, as its supreme foundation, there is the eternal Law of the primary cause of being, source of the authority which is in the people and in which the vicar of the people participates. And if the man is righteous and faithful to his mission, there is reason to believe that, when the common good of the people is at stake, and when he acts in communion with the people, he may somehow receive, in whatever obscure or even tortuous way, some particular inspiration ("grâce d'état," aid called for by one's vocational duty) from the One who is the supreme governor of human history.

The majesty of which I am speaking exists also (in the European parliamentary régimes it exists mainly) in the assemblies composed of the representatives of the people, insofar as they are a collective image of the people and a collective deputy for the people. (They should be conscious of that; when they themselves lose the sense of their inherent majesty, and behave like a throng of irresponsible school-boys or clan fighters at feud, this is a bad sign for democracy.) And in each one of these representatives separately taken, as deputy for a fragment of the people, part of that very majesty, broken so to speak into pieces, still really exists.

* * *

Thus, in a democratic regime, the fundamental truth, recognized by democratic philosophy, that authority in the rulers derives from the right to rule themselves inherent in the people and permanent in them, is given a particular and particularly appropriate expression in the typical structural law of the body politic. Then authority deriving from the people rises from the base to the summit of the structure of the body politic. Power is exercised by men in whom authority, within certain fixed limits, is brought periodically to reside through the designation of the people, and whose management is controlled by the people: and this very fact is a sign of the continued possession, by the people, of that right to govern themselves, the exercise of which has entitled the men in question to be in command—in political command—of other men, in the virtue of the primary Source of all authority. I mean that the supremely just establishment of Uncreated Reason, which gives force of law, or of a just ordinance, to what is necessary for the very existence and common good of nature and society, causes the governing function of those men chosen by the people to be held *by right*, and, by the same token, obedience to them within the limits of their powers to be *required in justice*.

To understand these things correctly, we need, it seems to me, to sharpen the philosophical concepts traditionally used in this matter. In other words, I think that in order to bring to its full significance the political theory of Thomas Aquinas, which has been developed in so valuable a manner by Cajetan,[18] Bellarmine[19] and Suarez[20] in the XVIth and early XVIIth

18. Cf. Cajetan, *Com. on Sum. theol.*, i–ii. 90. 3; *De comparatione auctoritatis papae et concilii* (Romae: Apud Institutum Angelicum, 1936), c. 1, 12; c. 11, 190; c. 24, 359; c. 27, 415; *Apologia ejusdem tractatus* (in the same volume), c. 1, 449–50; c. 8, 533; c. 9, 550, 557–64, 572, 590; c. 16, 801.

19. Cf. Bellarmine, *Controversiarum de membris Ecclesiae liber tertius, De laicis sive secularibus*, c. 6; *Opera omnia* (Paris: Vives, 1870), III, 10–12. English translation by Kathleen E. Murphy, *De Laicis or the Treatise on Civil Government* (New York: Fordham University Press, 1928).

20. Cf. Suarez, *Defensio fidei catholicae et apostolicae adversus anglicanae sectae errores*, Lib. III: *De summi pontificis supra temporales reges excellentia, et potestate*, c. 2; *Opera* (Venetiis, 1749), fols. 114 ff.; *De legibus*, Lib. III, c. 4.

Centuries, we have still to add certain further clarifications, the principle of which is to be found in the very notion of *vicariousness*, as used by St. Thomas himself with respect to the Prince "vicar of the multitude,"[21] and elaborated by him in quite another field, namely the theory of the sign as "vicar" of the thing signified.[22]

Then two main points of doctrine, to which our preceding remarks have already alluded, would be clearly brought out. The first relates to the fact that in investing rulers with authority the people lose in no way possession of their basic right to self-government. The second relates to the fact that the representatives of the people are not mere instruments, but rulers invested with real authority, or right to command.

When I possess a material good, I cannot give it to another without losing by the very fact my possession of it. Conceiving things in that way has been the trouble with the classical theories of political power, especially, as we have seen, with the misleading theory of Sovereignty.[23] But when it is a question of a moral or spiritual quality, such as a right is, I can invest another man with a right of mine without myself losing possession of it, if this man receives this right in a vicarious manner—as a vicar of myself. Then he is made into an image of myself, and it is in this capacity that he participates in the very same right which is mine by essence. (Similarly, the disciple *as such* participates in the very same science which is in his teacher, and if he teaches in his turn—I mean in his mere capacity as a disciple, conveying the science of another—he

21. "Vicem gerens multitudinis" (*Sum. theol.* i–ii. 90. 3).

22. Cf. our chapter "Sign and Symbol," in *Ransoming the Time* (New York: Charles Scribner's Sons, 1941).

23. See above, chap. ii. I am afraid such a concept remains in the background of some current Scholasticist views, which would finally reduce the democratic process to a moment of free choice, by the people, of their masters (just as Rousseau fancied that the representative system acted, when he condemned it). Cf. Gredt, *op. cit.*, t. II, nn. 1032, 1033.

will teach as a vicar, or an image of his teacher, and as a deputy for him;—and for all that, his teacher will not have divested himself of any bit of his own science). The people are possessed of their right to govern themselves in an inherent and permanent manner. And the rulers, because they have been made into the vicars of the people, or into an image of them, are invested *per participationem*—to the extent of their powers—with the *very same* right and authority to govern which exists in the people *per essentiam*, as given them by the Author of nature and grounded upon His transcendent, uncreated authority. The people, by designating their representatives, do not lose or give up possession of their own authority to govern themselves and of their right to supreme autonomy.

Now there is a distinction between the *possession* of a right and the *exercise* of it.[24] It is the very exercise of the people's right to self-government which causes the rulers chosen by the people to be invested with authority, according to the duration of the office, and to the measure and the degree of their attributions: the very exercise of the right of the people to self-government restricts therefore to that extent, not this right itself, but the further *exercise* of it (in other words, the "power" of the people)—since the right of the people to self-government cannot be exercised in actual fact (except in the smallest groups or in the particular case of popular *referendum*) without placing certain men in public service, and, by the same token, having them invested with genuine authority. There is no lack of similar examples, where the very exercise of a right (for instance the right to choose one's vocation or state of life) restricts further exercise without causing to end, or lessening in any way, the possession of that right itself.

Thus we come to the second point. The representatives of the people are possessed of authority in a vicarious manner, in their capacity as vicars or image of the people, and deputies for

24. See chap.; iv, pp. 101–3.

them. But they are a living and active, not a dead image of the people, an image which is a human person, endowed with reason, free will, and responsibility. And they cannot *exercise* the vicarious authority of which they are possessed if not as human persons and free agents, whose personal conscience is committed in the performance of their mission. So the authority they exercise, which is the very same authority of the people participated in to some given extent and within certain given limits, is a vicarious but a genuine authority, held, like the people's authority, in the virtue of the primary Source of all authority; they really hold a right to command and to be obeyed. They are not mere instruments of a mythical general will; they are actual rulers of the people; they have to make their decisions conformably to the dictates of their conscience, to the laws of that specific branch of Ethics which is political Ethics, to the judgment of their virtue (if they have any) of political prudence, and to what they see required by the common good—even if by so doing they incur the displeasure of the people.

The fact remains that they are accountable to the people, and that their management has to be supervised and controlled by the people. The fact also remains that, since their authority is but the authority of the people vicariously participated in, they have to rule, not as *separated* from the people (except as regards the existential conditions for exercising authority),[25] but as *united* with the people in their very essence of deputies for them. Here is a difficult question, which I should like to try to make clear. I just said that the representatives of the people must be ready to incur the displeasure of the people, if their conscience demands it. Now I am saying that they must carry out their obligations in communion with the people. Are these two statements contradictory? They are not, on the

25. See chap. ii, pp. 34–35.

condition that this expression "in communion with the people" be correctly understood.

In what can be called the common psyche of the people there is a huge variety of levels and degrees. At the most superficial level there are the momentary trends of opinion, as transient as the waves on the sea, and subjected to all winds of anxiety, fear, particular passions, or particular interests. At deeper levels, there are the real needs of the multitude. At the deepest level, there is the will to live together, and the obscure consciousness of a common destiny and vocation, and finally the natural trend of the human will, considered in its essence, toward the good. Furthermore—this is a point we shall meet in the next section—people are ordinarily distracted from their most capital aspirations and interests, as a people, by each one's everyday business and suffering. Under such circumstances, to rule in communion with the people means on the one hand educating and awakening the people in the very process of governing them, so as to demand of them, at each progressive step, what they themselves have been made aware of and eager for (I am thinking of a real work of education, grounded on respect for them and trust in them, and in which they are the "principal agent"[26]—just the contrary to selling them ideas through sheer propaganda and advertising techniques). It means on the other hand, being intent on what is deep and lasting, and most really worthy of man, in the aspirations and psyche of the people. Thus it is that in incurring the disfavor of the people a ruler can still act in communion with the people, in the truest sense of this expression. And if he is a great ruler, he will perhaps make that disfavor into a renewed and more profound trust. In any case there is nothing in common between despotically imposing

26. Cf. our book, *Education at the Crossroads* (New Haven: Yale University Press, 1943), pp. 29–31.

one's own will on the people—as a ruler from above separated from them—and resisting the people, or becoming hated and rejected by them, while being united with them in one's inmost intentions, and heedful of keeping communion with their deepest human will, which they ignore.

If this question is intricate, it is because no relation is more complex and mysterious than the relation between a man and the multitude for whose common good he is responsible, precisely because the authority he possesses is a vicarious authority, ultimately grounded in God, which he exercises as a free and responsible agent, image of the multitude and deputy for it. If we are looking for the most significant—though too transcendent for our purpose—type of a Legislator, let us think of Moses and his relation with the Jewish people. But the rulers of our political societies are not prophets directly commissioned by God, and this makes their case a little more simple.

At this point it would perhaps be appropriate to use the distinction, which I have emphasized in another essay, between a *law* and a *decree*. "Law and decree belong to two specifically distinct spheres: law, to the sphere of the *structural forms* of authority; decree, to the sphere of the *existential exercise* of authority. . . . A *law* is a general and lasting rule (general, that is to say, which determines in the social body a certain *functional relation;* lasting, that is to say, which is directed to something beyond the present moment or circumstance, and *calculated not to change*). A decree is a particular ordinance, determining a *point of fact* in the framework of the law, and confronted with a given circumstance for a given time."[27] Then I would say that a decree can without too much drawback be promulgated contrary to the trends prevalent at the moment in the people, and forced upon a reluctant public

27. *Principes d'une politique humaniste*, Annexe to chap. ii, "Pouvoir législatif et pouvoir exécutif."

opinion. But a law should normally be laid down (always supposing that it be just) in accordance with the common consciousness of the people as expressed in the mores or in collective needs and requests of organic groups of the population, or in spontaneous social and public service regulations in the making. Here could be saved the element of truth in Duguit's theory, unacceptable in itself, of "objective law." Contrary to this theory, the law is and will always remain a work of the reason of those who are in charge of the common good: but this same reason of the Legislator has to give shape to, or to express in a formed "word," an achieved *verbum*, what exists in the common mind in an inchoate, unformulated manner.

V

THE PROPHETIC SHOCK-MINORITIES

The last issue to be discussed no longer deals with *the people*, but with—how shall I designate them?—well, with the *inspired servants or prophets of the people*.

What I mean is that it is not enough to define a democratic society by its legal structure. Another element plays also a basic part, namely the dynamic leaven or energy which fosters political *movement*, and which cannot be inscribed in any constitution or embodied in any institution, since it is both personal and contingent in nature, and rooted in free initiative. I should like to call that existential factor a prophetic factor. Democracy cannot do without it. The people need prophets.

And those servants or prophets of the people are not—not necessarily—elected representatives of the people. Their mission starts in their own hearts and consciousness. In this sense they are self-appointed prophets. They are needed in the normal functioning of a democratic society. They are needed especially in the periods of crisis, birth, or basic renewal of a democratic society.

Truly speaking, something similar is to be found in every political régime. The kings of past ages were surrounded with *grands commis*, great stewards, favorite counsellors or ministers, in ruthless competition with one another; each one of them believed or alleged that his own views and endeavors expressed the hidden *real* will of the king. They took a risk. When they were mistaken, they were broken by the king, sometimes they were sent into exile or they were hanged. The same story takes place in totalitarian States with rival high officials and political cliques in the bosom of the party.

In democratic societies the people play the part of the king, and the inspired servants of the people that of the great counsellors. As a rule they are prophets of emancipation—national, political, or social emancipation.

In the normal functioning of a democratic society the political animation thus proceeds from men who, feeling themselves designated for a vocation of leadership, follow the usual channels of political activity—they will become chiefs of political parties, they will come to power through the legal machinery of elections. The happiest circumstance for the body politic obtains when the top men in the state are at the same time genuine prophets of the people. I think that in a renewed democracy the vocation of leadership which I just mentioned, —a sinister image of which is offered us by the *unique Party* of the totalitarian States,—should normally be exercised by small dynamic groups freely organized and multiple in nature, which would not be concerned with electoral success but with devoting themselves entirely to a great social and political idea, and which would act as a ferment either inside or outside the political parties.[28]

But it is in periods of crisis, birth, or basic transformation that the role of the inspired servants, the prophets of the people, takes on full importance. Let us think, for example, of

` 28. Cf. *True Humanism* (New York: Charles Scribner's Sons, 1938), pp. 162 ff.

the fathers of the French Revolution or of the American Constitution, of men like Tom Paine or Thomas Jefferson; or of that John Brown—still a criminal for Southerners, a hero for Northerners—who was convinced he had a divine commission to destroy slavery by the force of arms, and who captured the arsenal of Harper's Ferry, to be hanged some months later, in December 1859:

> John Brown's body lies a-mouldering in the grave,
> But his soul goes marching on.

Or of the originators of the Italian Risorgimento,[29] or of the liberation of Ireland; let us think of Gandhi once again, or of the pioneers of unionism and the labor movement. The primary work of the inspired servant of the people is to *awaken* the people, to awaken them to something better than everyone's daily business, to the sense of a supra-individual task to be performed.

That is a quite vital and necessary social phenomenon. And it is a quite dangerous phenomenon. For where there is inspiration and prophecy, there are false prophets and true prophets; thieves aiming to dominate men and servants aiming to set them free; inspiration from dark instincts and inspiration from genuine love. And nothing is more difficult than what is called "discrimination between spirits." It is easy to mistake impure inspiration for unsullied inspiration; nay more, it is easy to slip from genuine inspiration to a corrupt one. And we know that *optimi corruptio pessima*, corruption of what is best is what is worst.

The political problem we are confronted with at this point is the problem of the prophetic pioneering minorities or shock-minorities,—I say shock-minorities as one says shock-troops—a problem which any theory of democracy should frankly face.

29. Cf. Carlo Rosselli, *Socialisme libéral* (Paris, 1930), pp. 47 ff.

The people are to be awakened—that means that the people are asleep. People as a rule prefer to sleep. Awakenings are always bitter. Insofar as their daily interests are involved, what people would like is business as usual: everyday misery and humiliation as usual. People would like not to know that they are *the* people. It is a fact that, for good or evil, the great historical changes in political societies have been brought about by a few, who were convinced that they embodied the real will—to be awakened—of the people, as contrasting with the people's wish to sleep. At the time of the Risorgimento, the great majority of Italians surely preferred not to be set free from the Austrian yoke. If a popular poll had been taken at the time of Samuel Adams, we may wonder whether the majority would have voted for the war of Independence. If a popular poll had been taken in France in 1940, it is highly probable that the majority would have voted for Marshal Pétain,—they believed he hated collaboration with the Germans as they did. In all these cases, the majority went wrong, and the shock-minorities were right.—Well, but we have also been able to contemplate how the makers of totalitarian States have used the power of vanguard insurgent minorities.

The question is: are the people to be *awakened* or to be *used?* to be awakened like men or to be whipped and driven like cattle? The prophetic minorities say *we the people* when in actual fact they alone, not the people, are speaking. Only the final decision of the people can prove whether that figure of speech was right or wrong. But each time a part speaks in the name of the whole, that part is tempted to believe that *it is* the whole. As a result the part will endeavor to substitute itself for the whole, or rather to oblige the whole to be "really" the whole, that is, what the part wills the whole to be. Thus the entire process will become rotten, and instead of awakening the people to freedom, as they believed or pretended they were doing, that prophetic shock-minority will dominate the people and make them more enslaved than they had been.

During the course of the XIXth Century a dreadful ambiguity existed in this regard in democratic ideology; concepts and trends inspired from genuine devotion to the people and genuine democratic philosophy were mixed up with concepts and trends inspired from spurious democratic philosophy and would-be dictatorial, mistaken devotion to the people. There were men who believed that, as Jean-Jacques Rousseau put it, they should *force* the people *to be free*.[30] I say they were betrayers of the people. For they treated the people like sick children while they were clamoring for the rights and freedom of the people. Those who distrust the people while appealing to the highest feelings and to the blood of the people cheat and betray the people. The first axiom and precept in democracy is to trust the people. Trust the people, respect the people, trust them even and first of all while awakening them, that is, while putting yourself at the service of their human dignity.

The actual contempt for and distrust of the people involved in the principle "to force the people to be free" was to impair in some places the democratic mind and to develop a spurious philosophy of the mission of the self-styled enlightened minorities.

Let us summarize that spurious philosophy in the three following points. First, since the action of what I just called a prophetic shock-minority results in a showdown, and since only the fact, the event, can decide whether they were right or wrong in offering themselves as the personification of the people, then there is only one way to make good the risk that such a minority is taking, namely, *the out and out use of violence*, in order to succeed at any cost and by any means.

Second, once they have succeeded, they have to use *terror* to wipe out any possible opponent.

30. Cf. *Contrat social*, Book I, chap. vii: "Quiconque refusera d'obéir à la volonté générale y sera contraint par tout le corps: ce qui ne signifie autre chose sinon qu'on le forcera d'être libre."

Third, given on the one hand the congenital dullness and infirmity of the people, on the other hand the indispensable role of prophetic shock-minorities in human history, the deep trend toward emancipation which is at work in that history requires *breaking of the law* as a perpetual and necessary condition of progress, and blossoms forth into the messianic myth of *the Revolution*. Thus the basic tenets of democratic faith were denied in the very name of democracy; and the myth of the Revolution, with a capital R, was to bring to naught the real changes of structure, let us say the particular revolutions, (without a capital R) which could be possibly needed at certain given moments in human history, and which will be needed in actual fact as long as human history lasts.

How could we be surprised at seeing such spurious philosophy end up in totalitarianism, and the principle: *to force the people to be free*, reach its logical conclusion in the totalitarian dream: to force the people to be obedient in order that the State be free and all-powerful, or in order to make the people happy despite themselves, as Dostoievsky expressed it in his Legend of the Great Inquisitor?

The above-mentioned remarks, as well as the consideration of the present plight of the world, oblige us to take a serious view of the issue involved, and to ask from democratic philosophy a clear restatement of the theory of the role of prophetic shock-minorities. Such a restatement, as I see it, would emphasize the three following points, in accordance with the democratic charter.

First, the recourse to illegal activity is in itself *an exception*, not a rule, and should always remain exceptional; and it is only justified—as a lesser evil—when a prophetic shock-minority is confronted with a situation in which law has been already broken or suspended, that is, when it is confronted with some form of *tyrannical power*.

Second, just as exceptional as illegal activity, the use of

force, or of hard measures of coercion, may be needed in such circumstances; but *justice* must always hold sway. The use of terror striking the innocent and the guilty indiscriminately is always a crime. Innocent persons can indirectly suffer from just public measures directed to the social group in which they belong; but no innocent person should ever be punished, put into captivity, put to death.

Third, it is true that only the fact, the event, can decide whether a prophetic shock-minority was right or wrong in offering itself as the personification of the people, but the only thing which can make that test a success is the *free approval by the people*, as soon as the people can express their will. This means on the one hand that the use of force should always be provisional as well as exceptional, and the free consultation of the people always intended as an urgent, unpostponable aim; on the other hand, that the risk that a prophetic shock-minority is taking must be fairly taken, that this minority would betray itself as well as the people if it clung to power by any means whatever, and that it must be ready to lose the game if the people say so.

Finally what can be the weapons of the people to protect themselves and the body politic either against false servants of the people and spurious prophetic shock-minorities or against the corruption of true servants of the people and genuine prophetic shock-minorities shifting from the struggle for freedom to the struggle for domination? Nothing can replace in this connection the strength of the common ethos, the inner energy of democratic faith and civil morality in the people themselves, the enjoyment by them of real freedom in their everyday life and of a truly human standard of living, and the active participation of them in political life from the bottom up. If these conditions are lacking, the door is open to deception.

Yet there is in any case a weapon which they should particularly treasure as a bulwark of their political liberties. Namely the freedom of expression and criticism. That's a new reason to confirm what has been said in this chapter about the vital necessity in democracy for the freedom of the press and of the means of expression of thought, even at the price of great risks,—still less great than the loss of liberty. A free people needs a free press, I mean free from the State, and free also from economic bondage and the power of money.

* * *

I have said that democracy cannot do without the prophetic element; that the people need prophets. I should like to conclude that it is a sad necessity; or, rather, that in a democracy which has come of age, in a society of free men, expert in the virtues of freedom and just in its fundamental structures, the prophetic function would be integrated in the normal and regular life of the body politic, and issue from the people themselves. In such a society inspiration would rise from the free common activity of the people in their most elementary, most humble local communities. By choosing their leaders, at this most elementary level, through a natural and experiential process, as fellow-men personally known to them and deserving their trust in the minor affairs of the community, the people would grow more and more conscious of political realities and more ready to choose their leaders, at the level of the common good of the body politic, with true political awareness, as genuine deputies for them.

CHAPTER VI
CHURCH AND STATE

✢

PRELIMINARY REMARKS

BEFORE embarking on the problems of Church and State, I should like to make two preliminary remarks: First, my own faith is the Roman Catholic one; hence the concept of the Church which I shall rely upon in my discussion is the Catholic concept of the Church. As far as the relation of other Churches or religious institutions with the State is concerned, my line of argumentation therefore will apply only in an indirect and qualified manner. Second, I shall try to discuss my subject in the perspective of adequate practical philosophy: that is to say, as a philosopher, not as a theologian, but as a Christian philosopher, who takes into account the theological data fit to provide a genuine grasp of the concrete realities he is talking about.

I shall divide my discussion into three main parts: First, the general immutable principles; second, the analogical way in which, by virtue of their very transcendence, they are to be applied; third, some practical conclusions relating to our time. The issue is a highly controversial one. At the beginning of the XVIIth Century Cardinal Bellarmine's positions were strongly attacked, before he became one of the greatest authorities on the question. Today a conflict of opinion exists on the matter among men who belong to the same faith, but whose historical outlooks can be traced back either to St. Louis or to Philip the Second. I shall express my own opinion with the candor and humility of a layman firmly attached to his faith and seeking a right solution—which, after all, should

147

not be so difficult of attainment if one is attentive both to eternal truths and to human history.

I have meditated and written on these problems for twenty-five years or so. I have a bit of a hope, nevertheless, that I shall not get entangled too much in the labyrinthine ways of the issue, and that I shall be able to discuss it in less than twenty-five "disputations."

I

The General Immutable Principles

1. *The Human Person and the Body Politic*

From a philosophical point of view, the first thing, it seems to me, that we have to stress is the relationship between the human person and the body politic, namely the fact that the human person is both part of the body politic and superior to it through what is supra-temporal, or eternal, in him, in his spiritual interests and his final destination.

That very superiority of what is eternal in man over the political society can already be seen in the merely natural realm. We know that the whole man is engaged in the common good of civil society. But we also know that in respect to things *which are not Caesar's*, both society itself and its common good are indirectly subordinated to the perfect accomplishment of the person and his supra-temporal aspirations as to an end of another order—an end which transcends the body politic.

I say that this subordination exists already in the natural order, with regard to supra-temporal natural goods, which of themselves are related to the common good of what might be called civilization as a whole or the spiritual community of minds; for instance the sense of justice for all men and love for all men; the life of the spirit and all that which, in us, is a natural beginning of contemplation; the intangible dignity of truth, in all domains and all degrees, however humble they may be, of knowledge, and the intangible dignity of beauty: both of which—truth and beauty—are nobler than the social ingredients of life and, if curbed by the latter, never fail to avenge themselves. In the measure that human society attempts to free itself from this subordination and to proclaim itself the supreme good, in the very same measure it perverts its own nature and that of the political common good. The common good of civil life is an ultimate end, but an ultimate end in a relative sense and in a certain order, not the absolute ultimate end. This common good is lost if it is closed within itself, for, of its very nature, it is intended to foster the higher ends of the human person. The human person's vocation to goods which transcend the political common good is embodied in the essence of the political common good. To ignore these truths is to sin simultaneously against both the human person and the political common good. Thus, even in the natural order, the common good of the body politic implies an intrinsic though indirect ordination to something which transcends it.[1]

Now the Christian knows that there is a supernatural order, and that the ultimate end—the absolute ultimate end—of the human person is God causing His own personal life and eternal bliss to be participated in by man. The direct ordination of the human person to God transcends every created common good —both the common good of the political society and the intrinsic common good of the universe. Here is the rock of the dignity of the human person as well as of the unshakeable requirements of the Christian message. Thus the indirect subordination of the body politic,—not as a mere means, but as an end worthy in itself yet of lesser dignity—to the supratemporal values to which human life is appendent, refers first and foremost, as matter of fact, to the supernatural end to

1. Cf. our book, *The Person and the Common Good* (New York: Charles Scribner's Sons, 1947), chap. iv.

which the human person is directly ordained. To sum up all
this in one single expression, let us say that the law we are
faced with here is the law of the *primacy of the spiritual*.[2]

2. The Freedom of the Church

Let us now go one step further, and consider the Church in
her own realm or order. What is the Church? To begin with,
what is the Church *for the unbeliever?* In the eyes of the unbeliever, the Church is, or the Churches are, organized bodies
or associations especially concerned with the religious needs
and creeds of a number of his fellow-men, that is, with spiritual values to which they have committed themselves, and to
which their moral standards are appendent. These spiritual
values are part—in actual fact the most important part, as
history shows it—of those supra-temporal goods with respect
to which, even in the natural order, the human person transcends, as we have seen, political society, and which constitute the moral heritage of mankind, the spiritual common
good of civilization or of the community of minds. Even
though the unbeliever does not believe in these particular
spiritual values, he has to respect them. In his eyes the
Church, or the Churches, are in the social community particular bodies which must enjoy that *right to freedom* which is but
one, not only with the right to free association naturally belonging to the human person, but with the right freely to believe the truth recognized by one's conscience, that is, with
the most basic and inalienable of all human rights. Thus, the
unbeliever, from his own point of view—I mean, of course, the
unbeliever who, at least, is not an unbeliever in reason, and,
furthermore, who is a democratically-minded unbeliever—
acknowledges as a normal and necessary thing the freedom of
the Church, or of the Churches.

2. Cf. our book, *Primauté du spirituel* (English translation, *The Things That Are Not
Caesar's* [New York: Charles Scribner's Sons, 1930]).

But what is the Church *for the believer?*[3] For the believer the Church is a supernatural society, both divine and human—the very type of perfect or achieved-in-itself, self-sufficient, and independent society—which unites in itself men as co-citizens of the Kingdom of God and leads them to eternal life, already begun here below; which teaches them the revealed truth received in trust from the Incarnate Word Himself; and which is the very body of which the head is Christ, a body *visible*, by reason of its essence, in its professed creed, its worship, its discipline and sacraments, and in the refraction of its supernatural personality through its human structure and activity,[4] *invisible* in the mystery of the divine grace and charity vivifying human souls, even those which belong to that body without knowing it and only through the inner movement of their hearts, because they live outside the sphere of explicit faith but seek for God in truth. For the believer the Church is the body of Christ supernaturally made up of the human race, or, as Bossuct put it, *le Christ répandu et communiqué*, Christ Himself diffused and communicated.

In such a perspective, not only is the freedom of the Church to be recognized as required by freedom of association and freedom of religious belief without interference from the State, but that freedom of the Church appears as grounded on the very rights of God and as identical with His own freedom in the face of any human institution. The freedom of the Church does express the very independence of the Incarnate Word. As a result, the first general principle to be stated, with respect to the problems we are examining, is *the freedom of the Church to*

3. Cf. Humbert Clérissac, O.P., *Le Mystère de l'Église* (Paris: Crès, 1918; ed. du Cerf, 1934) (English translation, *The Mystery of the Church* [New York: Sheed & Ward, 1937]); and, first and foremost, the admirable treatise by Msgr. Charles Journet, *L'Église du Verbe Incarné* (Paris: Desclée De Brouwer, 1941); with the additional essays published by him in the review *Nova et Vetera* (Fribourg, Switzerland), and in *Revue Thomiste* (particularly Nos. 1–2 [1949], "Nature du corps de l'Église").

4. Cf. Charles Journet, "L'Église mystérieuse et visible," *Nova et Vetera*, July–September, 1940.

teach and preach and worship, the freedom of the Gospel, the freedom of the word of God.

3. *The Church and the Body Politic*

We come now to a further point, namely the relation between the Church and the body politic. It is clear, on the one hand, that the freedom and independence of which I just spoke, since they belong to a true and genuine society, imply for the Church the freedom of developing her own institutions and governing herself without interference by the body politic. Here we are confronted with the basic distinction, stated by Christ himself, between the things which are God's and the things which are Caesar's. From the advent of Christianity on, religion has been taken out of the hands of the State; the terrestrial and national frameworks in which the spiritual was confined have been shattered; its universality together with its freedom have been manifested in full bloom. Nay more, how could that universality of the Church be manifested except as a token of her superiority?

From the point of view of the political common good, the activities of the citizens as members of the Church have an impact on that common good; they and the institutions supported by them are part of the political society and the national community; under this aspect and in this manner it can be said that the Church is *in* the body politic. But this very point of view remains partial and inadequate. While being *in* the body politic—in every body politic—through a given number of her members and her institutions, the Church as such, the Church in her essence, is not a part but a whole; she is an absolutely universal realm stretching all over the world —*above* the body politic and every body politic.

There is no distinction without an order of values. If the things that are God's are distinct from the things that are Caesar's, that means that they are better. The said distinction, developing its virtualities in the course of human history, has resulted in the notion of the intrinsically *lay* or *secular* nature of the body politic. I do not say that the body politic is by nature irreligious or indifferent to religion ("lay" and "laicized," "secular" and "secularized" are two quite different things); I say that by nature the body politic, which belongs strictly to the natural order, is only concerned with the temporal life of men and their temporal common good. In that temporal realm the body politic, as Pope Leo XIII has insisted, is fully autonomous;[5] the State, the modern State, is under the command of no superior authority in its own order. But the order of eternal life is superior in itself to the order of temporal life.[6]

The Kingdom of God is essentially spiritual, and by the very fact that its own order is not of this world, it in no way threatens the kingdoms and republics of the earth. *Non eripit mortalia, qui regna dat caelestia.*[7] But precisely because it is spiritual, the Kingdom of God is of a better and higher nature than the kingdoms and republics of the earth. Let us remove from the word "superiority" any accidental connotation of domination and hegemony; let us understand this word in its pure sense; it means a higher place in the scale of values, a higher dignity. The second general principle to be stated, with respect to the problems we are examining, is *the superiority of the Church—that is, of the spiritual—over the body politic or the State.*

On the other hand it is clear that, as sharply distinct as they may be, the Church and the body politic cannot live and develop in sheer isolation from and ignorance of one another. This would be simply anti-natural. From the very fact that the same human person is simultaneously a member of that so-

5. Cf. encyclicals *Immortale Dei* ("utraque potestas est, in suo genere, maxima") and *Sapientiae Christianae.*

6. Cf. Charles Journet, *Exigences chrétiennes en politique* (Paris: Egloff, 1944), chap. ii.

7. Cf. Pope Pius XI, encyclical *Quas primas.*

ciety which is the Church and a member of that society which is the body politic, an absolute division between those two societies would mean that the human person must be cut in two. The third general principle to be stated with respect to the problems we are examining is *the necessary cooperation between the Church and the body politic or the State.*

II
THE APPLICATION OF THE IMMUTABLE PRINCIPLES IN ACTUAL HISTORICAL EXISTENCE
1. *Thesis and Hypothesis. Historical Climates and Concrete Historical Ideals*

And now what is the form, or what are the forms, that the principle of the spiritual superiority of the Church will take in practical application? What is the form, or what are the forms, which the principle of the necessary cooperation between Church and State will take in practical application? With those questions we are tackling our second issue—the way in which the general immutable principles that sway the issue are to be applied amidst the adventures and the vicissitudes of the terrestrial powers.

At this point we meet with a distinction often used by theologians, the distinction between what they call (in their own vocabulary, quite different from the vernacular) the *thesis* and the *hypothesis:*[8] the "thesis" expressing the way in which the general principles at stake should be applied; the "hypothesis" meaning the field of practical possibilities and impediments offered by actual circumstances.

That distinction between the thesis and the hypothesis is quite respectable and can of course be used in a valid manner. Yet I do not believe that it has very deep traditional roots. And, what matters more, it is often incorrectly construed,

8. Cf. our book, *Du régime temporel et de la liberté* (English translation, *Freedom in the Modern World* [New York: Charles Scribner's Sons, 1936]), chap. ii.

namely understood in a *univocal* sense. Then the thesis is regarded as *the ideal*—the absolute ideal, the ideal in itself—as
to the way of applying principles; and it is only because we are
prevented by circumstances stronger than our wills that we
renounce enforcing—or enforce only indifferently—that unique
ideal way of applying principles.

Such a univocal conception does not take into account the
intrinsic reality as well as the intelligible meaning of time.
On the one hand the very notion of an absolute ideal, an ideal
in itself, a supra-temporal ideal as to the way of *applying* or
realizing principles, is self-contradictory, since any application
or realization is existential and takes place in time, therefore is
relative to some given set of historical conditions. On the
other hand the corresponding conception of the hypothesis
deals with conditions and circumstances considered in a merely
empirical manner and from the point of view of mere expediency, as if time were but a refuse-bin in which we would
have to pick up more or less profitable opportunities; whereas
in actual fact time has a meaning and a direction, human history is made up of periods each one of which is possessed of a
particular intelligible structure and therefore of basic particular requirements, a fact that no political brain should ignore.

Furthermore the univocal conception of the thesis and the
hypothesis entails for us a risk of mistaking either for the so-
called absolute ideal as to the way of applying principles, or
even for the immutable principles themselves, the particular
way in which the general principles at stake were applied in a
more or less idealized past; then we shall disregard the relativity of the existential forms of the past, and a contingent
example offered to our imagination will be raised to an absolute. Finally the *hypothesis*, which is incompatible with that
image of the past—owing of course to the wickedness of our
contemporaries!—will mean a forced abandonment of the principles, and we shall yield to such abandonment with a con-

science all the more untroubled as we fiercely claim a *thesis* which we have no means of realizing—except when we get a chance to enforce our image of the past by violence, which is another way of betraying the immutable principles, by putting a ghost in their place.

We shall have an intellectual equipment more fit to deal with the problem if we understand the genuine value of the philosophical notion of *analogy*, which plays so great a part in Thomas Aquinas' metaphysics, and if we place ourselves in the perspective of analogy, in contradistinction to the perspective of univocity. I do not mean, assuredly, that the *meaning* of the general principles which hold sway over the issue is analogical, in such a manner that they would acquire in the course of time I know not what new meanings, having driven out the former ones; the meaning of statements like: "the full freedom of the Church is both a God-given right belonging to her and a requirement of the common good of political society," or "the spiritual order is superior to the temporal one," or "Church and State must cooperate"—the meaning of such statements is immutable. What I mean is that the *application* of the principles is analogical—the more transcendent the principles are, the more analogical is the application—and that this application takes various typical forms in reference to the *historical climates* or *historical constellations* through which the development of mankind is passing; in such a manner that the same immutable principles are to be applied or realized in the course of time according to typically different patterns.

For there are in human history typical climates or constellations of existential conditions, which express given intelligible structures, both as concerns the social, political, and juridical dominant characteristics and the moral and ideological dominant characteristics in the temporal life of the human community, and which constitute frames of reference for the ways of applying in human existence the immutable principles that hold sway over the latter. And it is according to these historical climates, as are recognized by a sound philosophy of history, which is here indispensable, that we have to conceive the *concrete historical ideals* or prospective images of what is to be hoped for in our age: ideals which are neither absolute nor bound to an unrealizable past, but which are *relative*—relative to a given time—and which moreover can be claimed and asserted as *realizable*.[9]

Thus the *principles* are absolute and immutable and supratemporal. And the particular, concrete applications through which they are to be analogically realized, and which are called for by the various typical climates that replace each other in human history, change, according to the specific patterns of civilization, the intelligible features of which it is imperative to recognize as peculiar to every given historical age.

2. *The Historical Climate of Modern Civilization*

I would therefore say, summing up quite briefly what would require a long historical analysis:[10] there was a *sacral* age, the age of mediaeval Christendom, mainly characterized on the one hand by the fact that the unity of faith was a prerequisite for political unity, and that the basic frame of reference was the unity of that social body, religio-political in nature, which was the *respublica Christiana*,[11] on the other hand by the dominant dynamic idea of strength or fortitude at the service of justice. In that sacral era, the principles that we are considering were therefore applied principally in terms of the social power of the Church;—the superior dignity of the Church (that is, the principle) found its ways of realization in her

9. Cf. *ibid.* and *Humanisme intégral* (English translation, *True Humanism* [New York: Charles Scribner's Sons, 1938]), chap. iv.

10. Cf. *Humanisme intégral* (*True Humanism*), chaps. iv and v.

11. Cf. John Courtney Murray, *Governmental Repression of Heresy*, reprinted from the *Proceedings of the Catholic Theological Society of America*, 1949, pp. 56–57.

superior power over the prince (that is, the application);—and as a result the political power of the Holy Empire and the kings was an instrument for the spiritual aims of the Church. In this way the Church was to assert the freedom of the spirit in the face of the ruthlessness of the temporal power, and to impose on it such restraints as the truce of God. Let us not forget, moreover, that in the Middle Ages not only the differentiation of the body politic as such was not completely achieved, but the Church had, as a matter of fact, to make up for a number of deficiencies in the civil order, and to take upon herself, because she was shaping civilization in her own womb, many functions and responsibilities pertaining of themselves to political society.[12] In post-mediaeval centuries—a period which can be called the baroque age—sacral civilization disintegrated, while in the political order the notion and reality of the State was gradually arising, yet the tenets of

12. On the distinction between the "sacral" and the "secular" age of civilization see Charles Journet, *L'Église du Verbe Incarné*, p. 243. The régime of "sacral Christendom," peculiar to the Middle Ages, is thoroughly analyzed in this book (pp. 253–96). Let us quote p. 254: "Il serait inexact [the author says] de définir l'époque médiévale comme une époque de confusion du spirituel et du temporel. Depuis la parole décisive du Christ sur les choses de Dieu et les choses de César, les deux pouvoirs, même quand ils seront réunis dans un même sujet, resteront pour les chrétiens formellement distincts. Mais leurs rapports seront caractérisés par le fait que, dans la cité médiévale, le spirituel ne se bornait pas à agir sur le temporel comme un élément régulateur des valeurs politiques, sociales, culturelles. Il tendait en outre, en vertu d'un processus qui s'explique historiquement, à associer une portion de lui-même au temporel, à devenir, uni au temporel, un élément *composant* de la cité. La notion de chrétien tendait à entrer dans la notion de citoyen, et la notion de christianisme dans la définition de la cité, non pas seulement comme une cause extrinsèque et une *puissance inspiratrice*, mais encore comme une cause intrinsèque et une *partie intégrante*. Il fallait être, en effet, chrétien, membre visible de l'Église, pour être citoyen; la cité, en vertu de son principe constitutionnel, n'était faite que de chrétiens. Ceux qui n'appartenaient pas visiblement à l'Église étaient d'emblée rejetés hors de la cité: les Gentils aux frontières, les Juifs dans les ghettos; pour ceux qui, d'abord chrétiens, brisaient ensuite avec l'Église, comme les hérétiques et les schismatiques, ils étaient un danger bien pire: ils ébranlaient les assises de la nouvelle cité et apparaissaient comme des ennemis du salut public."

Further (pp. 298–300), the author explains in what sense this "sacral" régime was not a "theocratic" régime, as some historians put it in an oversimplified manner.

sacral civilization were more or less preserved—in forms which were hardening, since they became more legal than vital—so that the notion of State-religion,[13] for instance, then came to the fore.

The modern age is not a sacral, but a secular age. The order of terrestrial civilization and of temporal society has gained complete differentiation and full autonomy,[14] which is something normal in itself, required by the Gospel's very distinction between God's and Caesar's domains. But that normal process was accompanied—and spoiled—by a most aggressive and stupid process of insulation from, and finally rejection of, God and the Gospel in the sphere of social and political life. The fruit of this we can contemplate today in the theocratic atheism of the Communist State.

Well, those Christians who are turned toward the future and who hope—be it a long range hope—for a new Christendom, a new Christianly inspired civilization, know that "the world has done with neutrality. Willingly or unwillingly, States will be obliged to make a choice for or against the Gospel. They will be shaped either by the totalitarian spirit or by the Christian spirit."[15] They know that a new Christianly inspired civilization, if and when it evolves in history, will by no means be a return to the Middle Ages, but a typically different attempt to make the leaven of the Gospel quicken the depths of temporal existence. They feel that such a new age

13. Without embarking on a discussion on the *Syllabus* and the degree of authority of its various articles, as excerpts taken from other papal documents, I would like only to observe that, at the time (1855) when proposition 77 (about State-religion) was set forth, Concordats previously agreed upon were being brutally violated in the name of Liberalism, whose struggle against the Church was in full swing, so that, by virtue of this factual context, the vicious manner in which a false ideology often spoils a historical process in the making was then especially conspicuous. At such moments no one is prepared to discard weapons that are at his command in actual fact.

14. I mean, in its own sphere and domain. See supra, pp. 152–53.

15. Cf. our book, *The Rights of Man and Natural Law* (New York: Charles Scribner's Sons, 1943), p. 23.

will aim at rehabilitating man in God and through God, not apart from God, and will be an age of sanctification of secular life. But along what lines can this be imagined? This means that the Christians of whom I am speaking have to establish and develop a sound philosophy of modern history, as well as to separate from the genuine growth of time, from the genuine progress of human consciousness and civilization, the deadly errors which have preyed upon them, and the tares which are also growing among the wheat and which foster the wickedness of the time. In order to conceive our own concrete historical image of what is to be hoped for in our age, we have to determine and take into account, as an existential frame of reference, the basic typical features which characterize the structure of our age, in other words the *historical climate* or the *historical constellation* by which the existence and activity of the human community is conditioned today.

As I just put it, the historical climate of modern civilization, in contradistinction to mediaeval civilization, is characterized by the fact that it is a "lay" or "secular," not a "sacral" civilization. On the one hand the dominant dynamic idea is not the idea of strength or fortitude at the service of justice, but rather that of the conquest of freedom and the realization of human dignity. On the other hand the root requirement for a sound mutual cooperation between the Church and the body politic is not the unity of a religio-political body, as the *respublica Christiana* of the Middle Ages was, but the very unity of the human person, simultaneously a member of the body politic and of the Church, if he freely adheres to her. The unity of religion is not a prerequisite for political unity, and men subscribing to diverse religious or non-religious creeds have to share in and work for the same political or temporal common good. Whereas "medieval man," as Father Courtney Murray puts it,[16] "entered the State (what

16. Murray, *op. cit.*, p. 57.

State there was) to become a 'citizen,' through the Church and his membership in the Church, modern man is a citizen with full civic rights whether he is a member of the Church or not."

Hence many consequences derive. First, the political power is not the secular arm[17] of the spiritual power, the body politic is autonomous and independent within its own sphere. Second, the equality of all members of the body politic has been recognized as a basic tenet. Third, the importance of the inner forces at work in the human person, in contradistinction to the external forces of coercion; the freedom of individual conscience with regard to the State; the axiom—always taught by the Catholic Church, but disregarded as a rule by the princes and kings of old—that faith cannot be imposed by constraint[18]—all these assertions have become, more explicitly than before, crucial assets to civilization, and are to be especially emphasized if we are to escape the worst dangers of perversion of the social body and of state totalitarianism. Fourth, a reasoned-out awareness has developed, at least in those parts of the civilized world where love for freedom is still treasured —and is growing all the keener as freedom is more threatened—with regard to the fact that nothing more imperils both the common good of the earthly city and the supra-temporal interests of truth in human minds than a weakening and breaking down of the internal springs of conscience. Common consciousness has also become aware of the fact that freedom of

17. On the question of the "secular arm" see *ibid.*, pp. 62 ff.; Journet, *L'Église du Verbe Incarné*, pp. 249, 317–26. Be it noted in passing that the stock phrase "recourse to the secular arm," that is, to civil law, to enforce, in certain circumstances dealing with the public order and the temporal domain, a canonic regulation concerning the members of the Church, means something quite different from the concept of the political power as being the secular arm or instrument of the Church. In a pluralistic society it is but normal that the particular regulations of an autonomous body may be sanctioned by civil law, from the civil society's own viewpoint, when the interests of the common good are concerned.

18. See Journet, *L'Église du Verbe Incarné*, pp. 261–64.

inquiry, even at the risk of error, is the normal condition for men to get access to truth, so that freedom to search for God in their own way, for those who have been brought up in ignorance or semi-ignorance of Him, is the normal condition in which to listen to the message of the Gospel and the teachings of the Church, when grace will illumine their hearts.[19]

Given such an existential frame of reference, what can be the ways of applying and realizing, in our historical age, the supreme principles that hold sway over the relationship between Church and State? Let us say that in a new Christianly inspired civilization, as far as we are able to see it,[20] those principles would in general be applied less in terms of the social power than in terms of the vivifying inspiration of the Church. The very modality of her action upon the body politic has been spiritualized, the emphasis having shifted from power and legal constraints (which the Church exercises, now as ever, in her own spiritual sphere over her own subjects, but not over the State) to moral influence and authority; in other words, to a fashion or "style," in the external relations of the Church, more appropriate to the Church herself, and more detached from the modalities that had inevitably been introduced by the Christian Empire of Constantine. Thus the superior dignity of the Church is to find its ways of realization in the full exercise of her *superior strength of all-pervading inspiration.*

3. *The Principle of the Superiority of the Church*

The supreme, immutable principle of the superiority of the Kingdom of God over the earthly kingdoms can apply in other ways than in making the civil government the secular arm of the Church, in asking kings to expel heretics, or in using the

19. Cf. infra, pp. 181–82 (and nn. 33 and 34).

20. On the notion, and possible advent, of a "Chrétienté profane" (lay or secular Christendom, in contradistinction to the sacral Christendom of the Middle Ages) see Journet, *L'Église du verbe incarné*, pp. 243–52.

rights of the spiritual sword to seize upon temporal affairs for the sake of some spiritual necessity (for instance in releasing the subjects of an apostate prince from their oath of allegiance). These things we can admire in the Middle Ages; they are a dead letter in our age. The supreme, immutable principle of the primacy of the spiritual and the superiority of the Church can apply otherwise—but not less truly, and even more purely[21]—when, from the very fact that the State has become secular, the supreme functions of moral enlightenment and moral guidance of men, even as concerns the standards and principles which deal with the social and political order, are

21. Commenting upon the Concordat concluded in 1940 between the Holy See and the Portuguese State (according to which the Portuguese State, while ensuring full freedom to the Catholic Church, does not support any official Church, and the clergy, except for the assistance given some overseas mission works, do not receive any subsistence from the State), Cardinal Cerejeira, patriarch of Lisbon, said in a remarkable address delivered on November 18, 1941:

"Another aspect of the agreement instituted by the Concordat is the reciprocal autonomy of the Church and the State. Each one is independent and free in its respective sphere of competence. Neither does the State keep the Church under its tutelage, nor does the Church interfere with matters pertaining to the State.

"The advocates of the supremacy of the State would like to add: enslavement of the Church, and, by the same token, of Catholic conscience. But we say: according to the very doctrine of the Church, the State has full authority, but only in its own field.

"It was Christianity which introduced into the world that separation between the temporal and the spiritual, upon which rests the foundation of all Christian civilization. Here is the fountainhead of liberty of conscience. . . .

"The Portuguese State recognizes the Church as she is, and ensures her freedom; but it does not support or protect her as a State established religion. . . .

"What the Church loses in official protection, she regains in virginal freedom of action. Free from any liability toward the political power, her voice gains greater authority upon consciences. She leaves Caesar a completely clear field, in order for herself better to attend to the things that are God's. She is the pure crystal from which the treasure of the Christian revelation is streaming forth."

Cardinal Cerejeira gave another important address on the same subject, November 18, 1946.

On the Portuguese Concordat see our book *Raison et raisons* (Paris: Luf, 1947), chap. xiii; *Commonweal*, February 5, 1943 (in that issue excerpts from the 1941 address are unfortunately often translated in a defective manner); the London *Tablet*, October 2, 1948; Yves de la Brière, "Le Concordat du Portugal," *Construire*, 1941 (*Construire* was the wartime substitute for the Jesuit periodical, *Études*); Murray, *op. cit.*, pp. 71–72 n.

exercised by the Church in a completely free and autonomous manner, and when the moral authority of the Church freely moves human consciences in every particular case in which some major spiritual interest is at stake.[22] Then the superior dignity and authority of the Church asserts itself, not by virtue of a coercion exercized on the civil power, but by virtue of the spiritual enlightenment conveyed to the souls of the citizens, who must freely bear judgment, according to their own personal conscience, on every matter pertaining to the political common good. This way of carrying into effect the primacy of the spiritual can be thwarted or checked by the opposite course of action chosen by other citizens (no infallible way has ever existed). But, other things being equal, it seems to be surer in the long run than the ways conceived of in terms of State power, and it manifests in a clearer manner the freedom and purity of the spiritual, because the latter is under no obligation to a secular arm always eager to take the upper hand, and has not to extricate itself more or less painfully from the too mighty embrace of the State, which never serves unless with a view to be served.

Let us not forget what constitutes the essential sign and property of superiority. A superior agent is not confined or shut up within itself. It radiates. It stimulates the inner forces and energies of other agents—even autonomous in their own peculiar spheres—whose place is less high in the scale of being. Superiority implies a penetrating and vivifying influence. The very token of the superiority of the Church is the moral power with which she vitally influences, penetrates, and quickens, as a spiritual leaven, temporal existence and the inner energies of nature, so as to carry them to a higher and more

22. "Through the free citizen, who freely consents to her doctrine and law, and who likewise by his free consent directs the processes of the City, the Church indirectly touches the life of the City. Through him too the processes of the City are so directed that they indirectly aid the supernatural mission of the Church" (Murray, *op. cit.*, p. 43).

perfect level in their own order[23]—in that very order of the world and of the life of civilization, within which the body politic is supremely autonomous, and yet inferior with regard to the spiritual order and the things that are of the eternal life. This is exactly what the absolutist or the totalitarian States (as well as, in the intellectual realm, rationalist philosophy) most stubbornly refuse to admit, even when they claim to respect freedom of religion (by shutting up religion in its own heavenly sphere, and forbidding it any influence on earthly life, as if it were possible to forbid heaven to send rain on the earth or shine upon it). But this—the vivifying influence of the Church and the Gospel on the things of the world —is, on the contrary, what is actually and genuinely ensured in a type of Christian civilization and a "style" of Church-State relations such as those we are now discussing.

* * *

At this point I should like to observe that the stock phrase, "the problem of Church and State," is to some extent ambiguous, for what is the meaning of this word *State?* There was an age in which the Church had to do with the kings of Christendom and the Germanic Emperors. There was an age in which she had to do with absolute kings, then with modern absolute States claiming to be personal or supra-personal entities ruling the body politic from above. Today she has to do either with totalitarian States bound by nature to persecute her, or with democratic States still entangled in the remnants of the past, which do not know exactly how to deal with her because they have not yet realized that not they, but the body politic in the whole range of its institutional organization, is henceforth the *dramatis persona* with whom the Church is confronted. If the democratic principle is to develop fully in the world, there will be an age in which the Church will have to

23. See Journet, *L'Église du Verbe Incarné,* pp. 229–42.

do with the peoples; I mean with political societies in which the State will cease pretending to be a person and will only play its true part as central agency of the body politic. The problem of Church and State has not the same significance in these various instances.

Let us consider especially the obligations that the human being, not only in his individual life but also in his social life, bears toward truth. Everyone is obliged to truth to the extent that he knows it. The kings of old—or the absolutist States, heirs of the kings, and conceived in a kind of Hegelian manner—had an obligation to the truth to which *they themselves*, as distinct from the people and ruling over the body politic, adhered in conscience. But the body politic as such has an obligation to the truth to which *the people themselves*, the citizens—who constitute the body politic—adhere in conscience. The body politic does not know another truth than that which the people know.

As a result, the supreme principle that the political society bears obligations toward truth, and that its common good implies the recognition, not in words only, but in actual fact, of the existence of God, was implemented in the past by the duty incumbent on the kings—or on the absolutist States, heirs of the kings—of leading the body politic or the people to what those kings, or (supposing they had a soul of their own) those absolutist States held to be the true religion. But in our historical climate (once the genuine notion of the State and its merely instrumental function in a democratic society has been recognized) the same supreme principle is to be implemented by the duty incumbent on the people, and enforced by their own consciences, of giving expression to, and adopting as the enlightening and inspiring moral standard in their own social and political life, what the people themselves, or the citizens, hold to be the true religion. Thus everything will depend, in practice, on what the people freely believe in conscience;—and on the full freedom of teaching and preaching the word of God, which is the fundamental right of the Church and which is also needed by the people in their search for the truth;—and on the degree of efficacy with which the members of the Church, laity as well as clergy, give testimony, in actual existence, to their living faith and to the Spirit of God.

If a new civilization is to be Christianly inspired, if the body politic is to be quickened by the leaven of the Gospel in temporal existence itself, it will be because Christians will have been able, as free men speaking to free men, to revive in the people the often unconscious Christian feelings and moral structures embodied in the history of the nations born out of old Christendom, and to persuade the people, or the majority of the people, of the truth of Christian faith, or at least of the validity of Christian social and political philosophy.

Such a body politic Christianly inspired, such a political society really and vitally Christian, by virtue of the very spirit that would animate it and give shape to its structure—let us say, a political society evangelically Christian—would have its own social and political morality, its own conception of justice and civic friendship, temporal common good and common task, human progress and civilization, vitally rooted in Christian awareness. Considering now a new and particularly difficult issue, which deals with the temporal society itself in its proper order and life, and with its legislation, we may ask ourselves what kind of notions this legislation would call into play when it comes to matters of conscience or questions directly concerned with personal creeds and standards as well as with civil law. At this point we have to maintain that the legislation of the Christian society in question could and should never *endorse* or *approve* any way of conduct contrary to Natural Law. But we have also to realize that this legislation could and should *permit* or *give allowance to* certain ways of conduct which depart in some measure from Natural Law, if the prohibition by civil law of these ways of conduct were to impair the common good, either because such prohibition would be at variance with the ethical code of communities of citizens whose loyalty to the nation and faithfulness to their own moral creed, however imperfect it may be, essentially matter to the common good, or even because it would result in a worse conduct, disturbing or disintegrating the social body, for a great many people whose moral strength is not on a level with the enforcement of this prohibition.[24]

24. Thomas Aquinas states the principles of the matter in a basically significant article: "Law," he says, "is established as a certain rule and measure of human acts. Now every measure must be homogeneous with the thing measured. . . . Hence it is necessary that even laws be imposed on men according to the condition of them: for, as Isidore puts it (*Etym.*, Bk. V, c. 21) law must be *possible, both with regard to nature and to fatherland's custom.*

"Now the power or ability to act proceeds fom the inner disposition or *habitus* of the subject: for the same thing is not possible to the one who does not possess virtue, and to the virtuous man; just as to the child and to the perfect man (the grownup). As a result, we do not have the same law laid down for children and for adults; and many things are permitted to children which for adults are punished by the law or held to be shameful. Similarly, many things must be permitted to men who are not perfected by virtue, which could not be tolerated in virtuous men.

"Now human law is laid down for the multitude, the major part of which is composed of men not perfected by virtue. Consequently, all and every vice, from which virtuous men abstain, is not prohibited by human law, but only the gravest vicious actions, from which it is possible for the major part of the multitude to abstain, and mainly those—like homicide, theft, etc.—which are harmful to others, and without the prohibition of which human society could not be preserved" (*Sum. theol.* i–ii. 96. 2).

And he goes on to say: "Human law aims at leading men to virtue, not at one sweep, but gradually. As a result, it does not immediately impose on the multitude of the imperfect those things which are required from already virtuous men, so that they would be obliged by the law to abstain from every kind of evil. Otherwise imperfect people, being unable to bear such obligations, would plunge into worse evils, as is said in Prov. 30:33: *the wringing of the nose bringeth forth blood,* and in Matt. 9:17: *if they put new wine*—that is, the

I would say, therefore, that in the matters we are considering, civil legislation should adapt itself to the variety of moral creeds of the diverse spiritual lineages which essentially bear on the common good of the social body—not by endorsing them or approving of them, but rather by giving allowance to them. In other words, civil law would only lay down the regulations concerned with the allowance of the actions sanctioned by those various moral codes, or grant such actions the juridical effects requested by their nature; and consequently the State would not take upon itself the responsibility for them, or make them valid by its own pronouncement, but only register (when the matter is of a nature to require a decision of civil authorities) the validity acknowledged to them by the moral codes in question.

Thus, in the sense which I just defined, a sound application of the pluralist principle[25] and of the principle of the lesser evil

---

precepts of perfect life—*into old wine-skins*—that is, into imperfect men—*the skins burst, and the wine is spilled*—that is, the precepts are contemned, and from such contempt men plunge into worse evils" (*Ibid., ad* 2).

25. Let us not understand "that because all human opinions of whatsoever kind have a right to be taught and propagated the commonweal should be obliged to recognize as juridically valid for each spiritual group the law worked out by this group according to its own principles. This is not my meaning. To me this principle signifies that, in order to avoid greater evils (that is, the ruin of the society's peace and either the petrification or the disintegration of consciences), the commonweal could and should tolerate (to tolerate is not to approve) ways of worship more or less distant from the true one: *the rites of the unfaithful must be tolerated*, St. Thomas Aquinas taught (*Sum. theol.* ii-ii. 10. 11); ways of worship, and then also ways of conceiving the meaning of life and modes of behavior; and that in consequence the various spiritual groups which live within the body politic should be granted a particular juridical status which the legislative power *of the commonweal itself in its political wisdom* would adapt on the one hand to their condition and, on the other, to the general line of legislation leading toward virtuous life, and to the prescriptions of the moral law, to the full realization of which it should endeavor to direct as far as possible this diversity of forms" (*Humanisme intégral*, pp. 172–73; *True Humanism*, pp. 160–61; I made some amendments to the English translation). Cf. also *Du régime temporel et de la liberté* (*Freedom in the Modern World*), chap. i, n. 12. In such a pluralist conception, as I noted (p. 80, French ed.; p. 66,

would require from the State a juridical recognition of the moral codes peculiar to those minorities comprised in the body politic whose rules of morality, though defective in some regard with respect to perfect Christian morality, would prove to be a real asset in the heritage of the nation and its common trend toward good human life. Such recognition would not be grounded on a right, I know not what, of which any moral way of life whatsoever would be possessed with regard to civil law, but on the requirements of the political common good, which in a democratic society demands on the one hand a particular respect for the inner forces and conscience of the human subject, and, on the other hand, a particular care not to impose by force of law rules of morality too heavy for the moral capacity of large groups of the population. It would be up to the political wisdom of the lawmaker, furthermore, to determine what communities of citizens could enjoy the pluralistic legal status which I have described.

As a result, I would see, in some conceivable future society, the laws of the body politic recognizing in such matters—not by virtue of a right belonging to any moral way of life whatever, but by virtue of the free decisions of political wisdom— the moral codes to which the consciences of the main spiritual stocks or lineages that make up the national community and its complex moral heritage are attached; of course on the condition that the body politic, while granting such freedoms to its own parts, were heedful of the moral interests of the whole, and made as restricted as possible, in actual existence, the derogations to the highest requirements of Natural Law which

English ed.), "civil legislation might coincide or concur with Canon Law for the Catholics," while for other spiritual lineages it might be different, yet always *orientated* in the direction of the true moral principles. It can be observed in this connection that art. 24 of the Portuguese Concordat forbids divorce only to those who have contracted a Catholic marriage. "This provision," Father John Courtney Murray comments, "illustrates what I meant by saying that the State organizes what is 'there' in society" (*op. cit.*, p. 72 n.).

the legislators would allow as a lesser evil for the sake of the common good. The final objective of law is to make men morally good. Civil law would adapt itself, with a view to the maximum good of which the multitude is capable, to various ways of life sanctioned by various moral creeds, but it should resist changes which were requested through sheer relaxation of morality and decaying mores. And it should always maintain a general orientation toward virtuous life, and make the common behavior *tend*, at each level, to the full accomplishment of moral law.

4. *The Principle of Cooperation*

But let us now turn back to the relationship between Church and State, and consider our second immutable principle, the principle of cooperation. The things that are Caesar's are not only distinct from the things that are God's; but they must cooperate with them. What, then, in the particular type of Christian political society which I am discussing, would be the appropriate means through which the principle of the *necessary cooperation* between the Church and the body politic would apply?

The question, it seems to me, has three implications: the first, which concerns both the body politic and the State, deals with the most general and indirect form of mutual assistance between them and the Church; the second, which concerns especially the State or the civil authority, deals with the public acknowledgement of God; the third, which concerns in one case especially the State, in another case especially the body politic, deals with the specific forms of mutual help between the Church and the political society.

The Most General and Indirect Form of Cooperation

As regards the first point (the most general and indirect form of mutual assistance), I would say with Father John Courtney Murray, in his paper to the American Society of

Theology, that "the major assistance, aid and favor" that the body politic and the State "owe to the Church (one might better say, to the human person with respect to his eternal destiny)" consists in the entire fulfillment of their own duties with respect to their own ends, in their own attention to Natural Law, and in the full accomplishment of their political duty of creating "those conditions in society—political, social, economic, cultural—which will favor the ends of human personality, the peaceful enjoyment of all its rights, the unobstructed performance of all its duties, the full development of all its powers. There is here a material task, the promotion of prosperity, the equitable distribution of the material things that are the support of human dignity. There is also a moral task, the effective guarantee of the juridical order. This organization of society according to the demands of justice" is "the first, most proper and necessary contribution" of the body politic and the State to the spiritual interests of the Church,—"an indirect contribution, but one apart from which the end of the Church is impossible, or too difficult, of attainment."[26]

The Public Acknowledgment of the Existence of God

As concerns the second point (the public acknowledgment of the existence of God), I have already observed that a political society really and vitally Christian would be conscious of the doctrine and morality which enlighten for it—that is, for the majority of the people—the tenets of the democratic charter, and which guide it in putting those tenets into force. It would be conscious of the faith that inspired it, and it would express this faith publicly. Obviously, indeed, for any given

26. Murray, *op. cit.*, p. 48. "Nothing is clearer than the Pope's insistence that the conscientious exercise by the State of its direct power over temporal life is the essential exercise of its indirect power and duty to favor and assist the ends of the Church. . . . The spiritual problem of our times is in fact centered in the temporal order. And the modern 'welfare-state,' simply by serving human welfare, would serve the Church better than Justinian or Charlemagne ever did" (*ibid.*, p. 49).

people such public expression of common faith would by preference assume the forms of that Christian confession to which
the history and traditions of this people were most vitally
linked. But the other religious confessions institutionally
recognized would also take part in this public expression—just
as it happens now in this country—and they would also be
represented in the councils of the nation, in order that they
might defend their own rights and liberties and help in the
common task. As for the citizens who were unbelievers, they
would have only to realize that the body politic as a whole
was just as free with regard to the public expression of its
own faith as they, as individuals, were free with regard to the
private expression of their own non-religious convictions.

The Specific Forms of Mutual Cooperation

With respect to the third point—the specific forms of mutual help between the body politic and the Church—I should
like first to make clear some preliminary remarks. It is obvious
that it is the spiritual mission of the Church which is to be
helped, not the political power or the temporal advantages to
which certain of her members might lay claim in her name.
In the stage of development and self-awareness which modern
societies have reached, a social or political discrimination in
favor of the Church, or the granting of juridical privileges to
her ministers[27] or to her faithful, would be precisely of a nature to jeopardize, rather than to help, this spiritual mission.

I just spoke of the ministers of the Church. Regarding their
particular position, it is appropriate to enter into some more
detailed elucidations.

The exemption from military obligations granted to the
clergy in many countries is not a *social privilege*. To be exempt-
ed from having to shed blood is for a man a high moral privilege, but it is, at the same time, from the temporal and terrestrial point of view—because in the modern régime of "a nation

in arms" it involves an exception to a common rule and to common dangers—a socially humiliating condition (not to speak of the resentment it may sometimes engender) imposed on men consecrated to God by the recognition of their essentially peaceful mission in the human community.

On the other hand, a distinction must be made between *simple adjustment of law and custom* to various functions or states of life which matter to the common good of the social body, and *juridical privilege* favoring a particular category with certain temporal advantages by virtue of an infraction of the principle of the equality of all before the law. The rights enumerated in the Code of Canon Law, in the chapter *de privilegiis clericorum*, through which the Church sanctions from her own point of view certain requirements of the priestly condition, should be recognized by a civil society of a pluralistic type as pertaining to the first case: adjustment of law and custom to various functions or states of life.

Instances of the same case are obviously to be found in certain advantages sometimes granted to the clergy, which it would never occur to the Church, for her own part, and at her own level as an autonomous society, to inscribe in her Code, and which she does not regard as rights required by the priestly condition. Thus it is that in certain countries, the United States for instance, the railroad companies offer clergymen reduced fares. Similar advantages might conceivably be granted to persons exercising other functions, the medical function, for instance. The fact remains that in any case the use of such advantages supposes in those who profit by them a general behavior that is modest enough to prevent these minor inequalities from seeming offensive, or even scandalous, as the equestrian array of Benedictine Abbots did in the XIIIth Century (St. Thomas Aquinas rode a donkey, as was suitable for a member of a mendicant Order).[27]

27. Let us note, finally, in order to avoid any misinterpretation, that, from the point of view of what is usually called the "thesis," and on the condition that one be aware

But let us leave this digression and return to our purpose, namely, to the discussion of the specific forms of mutual cooperation between the body politic and the Church in our historical age. The care that the State must take not to encroach upon matters of religion does not imply that as soon as it comes to the moral and religious realm the State should stand aloof and be reduced to sheer impotency. The State has no authority to impose any faith whatsoever upon, or expel any faith whatsoever from, the inner domain of conscience. But the State, as we have seen in a preceding chapter, has to foster in its own way general morality, by the exercise of justice and the enforcement of law, and by supervising the development of sound conditions and means in the body politic for good human life, both material and rational. And as to religious matters, the State has to deal with them on a certain level, which is the level of civil peace and welfare, and from its own point

---

of the real bearing of words, there is no opposition between all that is said in this chapter and the fact of considering a privileged juridical situation for the Catholic Church the ideal situation to be sought, by virtue of the rights she possesses as a messenger of divine truth. For, given the factual circumstances created by the advent of modern societies and democratic régimes, the conditions of realization (what is called the "hypothesis") for such an ideal situation suppose a people in whom division in religious matters has disappeared, and in whom the Catholic faith is accepted by all. (And let us not forget that, by reason of the intercommunications between all nations of the world, no religious unanimity is possible in a given people if such unanimity does not actually extend to mankind as a whole.)

Then the Catholic Church would obviously be alone in enjoying in actual fact the rights and liberties granted *de jure* to the various religious bodies institutionally recognized in a Christian society of the type we are describing: consequently the ideal envisaged in the thesis would be fulfilled in a situation which was actually privileged, but which implied neither temporal advantages granted to a category of citizens as opposed to the others, nor any departure from the principle of the equality of all before the law, nor, with greater reason, any pressure exercised by the State in matters of conscience, nor any instrumental rôle played by the State as secular arm of the Church.

And, to tell the truth, the ideal situation in question would correspond to the rights of the Church—the first of which is to convey divine truth—as well as to the dearest aspirations of the Christian heart, first and foremost through that which it pre-supposes, namely the general disappearance of religious division in the world, and the general adherence to the true faith.

of view, which is the point of view of the temporal common good; for instance, as we just said, the civil power has, as representing the people, to request the prayers of the religious communities historically rooted in the life of the people. And it is but normal that in applying the laws concerned with the exercise of the right of association, it should grant institutional recognition to those religious communities—as well as to all associations, religious or secular, educational, scientific, or devoted to social service, whose activity is of major importance for the common welfare—in contradistinction to other religious groups or secular associations which enjoy freedom but not institutional recognition. Moreover, assuming the formation of some religious sect aimed at the destruction of the bases of common life, say, prescribing collective suicide or racial annihilation, it would be up to the State to dissolve such a religious sect, as well as any other association either criminal or destructive of national security. All this deals with the administration of justice, and implies the equality of rights of all citizens, whatever their race, their social standing, or their religious denomination may be.

It should be pointed out in this connection, first, that the subjects of rights are not abstract entities like "truth" or "error," but human persons, individually or collectively taken; second, that the equality of rights of all citizens is the basic tenet of modern democratic societies. Therefore the very fact (on which I have so often laid stress in this chapter) that the temporal society, become secular or strictly temporal, unites in its common task and common good men belonging to different religious lineages, has as its consequence that the principle of equality of rights is to be applied—not to "doctrines" or "creeds," this would have no meaning—but to the *citizens* who belong in these different religious lineages, which the body politic, from its own point of view, regards as parts of its own common moral heritage. Is it not, as I have previously remarked, through the citizens who are members of the Church that the Church, who is above the body politic, enters the sphere of the body politic and of its temporal common good? As a result it is from the point of view of the rights of the citizens who compose the body politic that the State will define its own positions with regard to the juridical status of the Church within the temporal sphere and in relation to the temporal common good.

Thus the Christian political society which I am discussing— supposing that the faith to which the majority of the people belonged were the Catholic faith—would know perfectly well that the Church herself was no part of it, but above it. And in this connection it would recognize the juridical personality of the Church as well as her spiritual authority in ruling her members in her spiritual realm, and it would deal with her as a perfect and perfectly independent society, with which it would conclude agreements and with the supreme authority of which it would maintain diplomatic relations. Yet, for all that, this Christian political society would have to hold that, in its own temporal sphere, and with regard to the rights they possess, Christian citizens (with the collective activities they and their multifarious institutions freely display in the national community) are no more legally privileged than any other citizens.

In other terms, this Christian political society would realize that there is only one temporal common good, that of the body politic, as there is only one supernatural common good, that of the Kingdom of God, which is supra-political. Once the political society had been fully differentiated in its secular type, the fact of inserting into the body politic a particular or partial common good, the temporal common good of the faithful of one religion (even though it were the true religion), and

of claiming for them, accordingly, a privileged juridical position in the body politic, would be inserting into the latter a
divisive principle and, to that extent, interfering with the
temporal common good.[28]

* * *

After these preliminary remarks, I come to the point under
discussion, namely the specific forms of mutual help between
the Church and the political society.

As I have observed in the first part of this chapter, man is a
member both of the body politic and, if he adheres to the
Church, of that supra-temporal society which is the Church.
He would be cut in two if his temporal membership were cut
off from his spiritual membership. They must be in actual contact and connection. And an actual contact and connection, if
it is not a contact and connection of mutual antagonism, is a
contact and connection of mutual help. Moreover the common
good itself of the temporal society implies that human persons are indirectly assisted by the latter in their movement
toward supra-temporal achievement, which is an essential
part of the pursuit of happiness. Finally (not to speak even
of the fact, defined by theology, that human nature in its
existential condition needs divine grace in order to achieve its
highest human ends, social as well as individual), the Christian political society which we are discussing would be aware
of the fact that Christian truths and incentives and the inspiration of the Gospel, awakening common consciousness and
passing into the sphere of temporal existence, are the very
soul, inner strength, and spiritual stronghold of democracy.
Just as democracy must, under penalty of disintegration, foster
and defend the democratic charter; so a Christian democracy,

28. Cf. our book, *The Rights of Man and Natural Law*, pp. 26–27.—See also Heinrich
Rommen, "Church and State," *Review of Politics*, July, 1950.

that is, a democracy fully aware of its own sources, must, under penalty of disintegration, keep alive in itself the Christian sense of human dignity and human equality, of justice and freedom. For the political society really and vitally Christian which we are contemplating, the suppression of any actual contact and connection, that is, of any mutual help, between the Church and the body politic would simply spell suicide.

What are then, the specific forms of mutual assistance to which I am alluding?

The most basic of them is the recognition and guarantee by the State of the full freedom of the Church. For the fact of insuring the freedom of somebody is surely an actual, and most actual, though negative, form of cooperation with him and assistance to him. It has been an illusion of modern times to believe that mutual freedom means mutual ignorance. Can I be ignorant of the one whose freedom I insure? The theory of mutual ignorance between State and Church is self-deluding: either it veers in actual fact (as was the case in France in the XIXth Century) to having the State encroach upon spiritual matters and oppose the Church in order to define and enforce in its own way a so-called freedom of the Church; or it veers in actual fact to having the State know the Church (without confessing it) in order really to insure, somehow or other, the freedom of the Church.

Insuring to the Church her full liberty and the free exercise of her spiritual mission is fundamentally required by the God-given rights of the Church as well as by the basic rights of the human person. But it is also required by the common good of the body politic. For it is the condition for that spreading of the leaven of the Gospel throughout the whole social body which the temporal common good needs in its own sphere.

The State acts simply in its own way, as providing the common good of the body politic, in guaranteeing the full freedom of the Church in her spiritual mission. And, as we have seen, it can insure that guarantee—in our historical age it ensures it in the best way—without granting any juridical privilege to the citizens who are members of the Church.

Finally there is a second specific form of mutual assistance which is also required. I mean not only a negative assistance, as is the insurance of freedom, but a positive one. This time I am not speaking of the State, but of the body politic with its free agencies and institutions. In the Christian political society which we are discussing this positive form of assistance would in no way infringe upon the basic rule of equal laws and equal rights for all citizens. The State would not assist the Church by granting her favored juridical treatment, and by seeking to gain her adherence through temporal advantages paid for at the price of her liberty. It is rather by *asking the assistance* of the Church for its own temporal common good that the body politic would assist her in her spiritual mission. For the concept of help is not a one-way concept; help is a two-way traffic. And after all, is it not more normal to have what is superior, or of greater worth in itself, aiding what is of lesser dignity, than to have what is terrestrial aiding what is spiritual? For the latter, moreover, giving more help amounts to being better assisted in its proper task.

Thus the body politic, its free agencies and institutions, using their own freedom of existential activity within the framework of laws, would ask more of the Church. They would ask, on the basis of freedom and equality of rights for all citizens, her cooperation in the field of all the activities which aim at enlightening human minds and life. They would positively facilitate the religious, social, and educational work by means of which she—as well as the other spiritual or cultural groups whose helpfulness for the common good would be recognized by them—freely cooperates in the common welfare. By removing obstacles and opening the doors, the body politic, its free agencies and institutions, would positively facilitate the effort of the apostles of the Gospel to go to the masses and share their life, to assist the social and moral work of the nation, to provide people with leisure worthy of human dignity, and to develop within them the sense of liberty and fraternity.[29]

Such would be, as I see it, the positive cooperation between the body politic and the Church. And because of the fecundity of truth, we may have confidence that among all the religious or cultural institutions thus freely cooperating with the body politic, the Church which holds in trust the true faith—in contradistinction to religious creeds whose message is more or less faltering, and with greater reason to more or less erroneous human philosophies,—would, as a matter of fact, turn to better account the opportunities offered to all by freedom.

III

SOME PRACTICAL CONCLUSIONS

The present is but a limit, a line of demarcation between the past and the future. So we can understand the present only in terms of the past or in terms of the future. That is why I think it would be advisable for Christians to dedicate in their own way a bit of meditation to the future.

As concerns my attempt to outline a future type of Christian political society, whatever one may think of its particular features, what matters essentially to me is the fact that the supreme general principles are immutable; and that the ways

29. Cf. our books, *Humanisme intégral*, pp. 184–85 (*True Humanism*, pp. 172–73), and *The Rights of Man and Natural Law*, pp. 28–29.

of applying or realizing them are analogical, and change according to the variety of historical climates. So the principles which were applied in a given way by the sacral civilization of the Middle Ages always hold true, but they are to be applied in another way in modern secular civilization.[30]

These things being understood, we see that many problems which embarrass contemporary consciousness are solved by the same token.

On the one hand we see that the condemnation of theological liberalism by the Catholic Church will never be amended. This is because theological liberalism implied the false philosophy of the absolute metaphysical autonomy of human reason and will. It made the so-called "modern liberties" absolute and limitless to such an extent that man's obligations either toward truth or toward the common good simply vanished away. And it insisted that the very principles which had been applied in the Middle Ages or in the baroque age in a way inapplicable today were perishable principles, which have been dismissed by the evolution of ideas and societies. Such positions are intrinsically erroneous. Yet that does not mean that the "modern liberties" soundly understood are to be denied. And that does not prevent the Church from putting for-

---

30. To express the same point otherwise, we might make use of the distinction, which I stressed in a previous chapter, between the possession of a right and its exercise. I can possess a right, for instance, to personal freedom, and be prevented in justice from claiming its actual exercise if my country is waging a just war and assigns me to be drafted.

The Church does not lose any of the essential rights she has claimed or exercised in the past. Nevertheless, she can renounce the exercise of certain of them, not because she is forced to do so, but voluntarily and by virtue of the consideration of the common good, the historical context having changed. She exercised in the past the right of making null and void a civil law which severely impaired the spiritual welfare of the people. She always possesses this right in its roots. If she made it emerge in actual exercise in the historical climate of today, this very exercise would harm the common good both of the Church and of civil society. So by reason of justice (justice toward the common good both of civilization and of the Kingdom of God) does the Church give up the exercise of such a right.

ward today such freedoms as freedom of conscience, freedom of teaching, etc.[31]

On the other hand we see that statements like Cardinal Manning's famous reply to Gladstone are unquestionably true. "If Catholics were in power tomorrow in England," Cardinal Manning wrote, "not a penal law would be proposed, not the shadow of a constraint put upon the faith of any man. We would that all men fully believed the truth; but a forced faith is a hypocrisy hateful to God and man. . . . If the Catholics were tomorrow the 'Imperial race' in these kingdoms they would not use political power to molest the divided and hereditary religious state of the people. We would not shut one of their Churches, or Colleges, or Schools. They would have the same liberties we enjoy as a minority."[32] Such a statement is valid, not only for England, but for every freedom-loving country. It does not refer to the requirements of an hypothesis reluctantly accepted, but to the requirements of the very principles soundly applied in the existential framework of the modern historical climate. Even if one single citizen dissented from the religious faith of all the people, his right to dissent could by no means be infringed upon by the State in a Christianly inspired modern democratic society. Even if, by the grace of God, religious unity were to return, no return to the sacral régime in which the civil power was the instrument or secular arm of the spiritual power could be conceivable in a Christianly inspired modern democratic society. The Catholics who are ready to give their lives for freedom do not cling to these assertions as a matter of expediency, but as a matter of moral obligation or of justice. Yet that does not mean that they disregard in any respect, it means that they assert and maintain more than ever, the principle of the su-

31. Cf. our book, *Raison et raisons*, pp. 280–83.

32. Henry Edward Manning, *The Vatican Decrees in Their Bearing on Civil Allegiance* (London, 1875), pp. 93–96.

periority of the spiritual order over the temporal order and the principle of the necessary cooperation between the Church and the body politic.

I know that there are people who would like, for the sake of religious truth, to set forth the concept of civil intolerance.[33] Well, they should frankly propose their own solution to the world, require that the State make all non-Christians and non-orthodox second-rate citizens, and they should be ready to contemplate the consequences that such a claim would entail, not only for themselves but for the very work of the Church in the world, as well as for the peace and common good of the civil society.[34]

I also know that, from the opposite side, there are people who would like, for the sake of civic tolerance, to make the Church and the body politic live in total and absolute isolation. Well, let me say, as the testimony of one who loves this country, that a European who comes to America is struck by the fact that the expression "separation between Church and State," which is in itself a misleading expression, does not have the same meaning here and in Europe. In Europe it means, or it meant, that complete isolation which derives from century-old misunderstandings and struggles, and which has produced most unfortunate results. Here it means, as a matter of fact, together with a refusal to grant any privilege to one religious denomination in preference to others and to have a State established religion, a distinction between the State and the Churches which is compatible with good feeling

33. Cf. the remarks made by Father Max Pribilla, "Dogmatische Intoleranz und bürgerliche Toleranz," *Stimmen der Zeit*, April, 1949, and by Father Robert Rouquette, S.J., in his "Chronique de la vie religieuse," *Études*, September, 1949.

34. In the theological vocabulary the notion of "civil tolerance" (imposing on the State respect for consciences) has been coined in contradistinction to that, obviously erroneous, of "dogmatic tolerance," which means that in the very sphere of the conscience and with regard to divine revelation man has a right to freedom *from* truth, or that the human mind has no obligation toward truth.

and mutual cooperation. Sharp distinction *and* actual cooperation, that's an historical treasure, the value of which a European is perhaps more prepared to appreciate, because of his
own bitter experiences. Please to God that you keep it carefully, and do not let your concept of separation veer round to
the European one.

Far beyond the influences received either from Locke or the
XVIIIth Century Enlightenment, the Constitution of this
country is deep-rooted in the age-old heritage of Christian
thought and civilization.[35] Paradoxically enough, and by virtue of the serious religious feelings of the Founding Fathers, it
appeared, at a moment of unstable equilibrium (as all moments
in time are) in the history of ideas, as a lay—even, to some extent, rationalist—fruit of the perennial Christian life-force,
which despite three centuries of tragic vicissitudes and spiritual division was able to produce this momentous temporal
achievement at the dawn of the American nation: as if the
losses suffered by human history in the supreme domain of the
integrity and unity of faith, and in the interest in theological
truth, had been the price paid, with respect to human weakness and entanglements, for the release at that given moment
of humbler, temporal Christian energies that must at any
cost penetrate the historical existence of mankind. Peerless is
the significance, for political philosophy, of the establishment
of the American Constitution at the end of the XVIIIth Century. This Constitution can be described as an outstanding lay
Christian document tinged with the philosophy of the day.
The spirit and inspiration of this great political Christian

35. As I put it in *Scholasticism and Politics* (New York: Macmillan Co., 1940), p. 91,
"its structure owes little to Rousseau, if I am to believe some Dominican friends of
mine that this Constitution has rather some relation to ideas which presided in the
Middle Ages at the constitution of St. Dominic's Order."—On the history and meaning of
the American attitude toward the problem of Church and State, see Anson Phelps Stokes,
Church and State in the United States (New York: Harper & Bros., 1950); Wilfrid Parsons,
S.J., *The First Freedom* (New York: The Declan X. McMullen Co., Inc., 1948).

document is basically repugnant to the idea of making human society stand aloof from God and from any religious faith. Thanksgiving and public prayer, the invocation of the name of God at the occasion of any major official gathering, are, in the practical behavior of the nation, a token of this very same spirit and inspiration.

＊ ＊ ＊

The Catholic Church is sometimes reproached with being an "authoritarian Church," as if the authority—that is, the right to be listened to—that she exercises on her faithful in seeing to the preservation of revealed truth and Christian morality were to result in fostering authoritarian trends in the sphere of civil life and activities.[36] May I be allowed to say that those who make such reproaches lack both in theological and historical insight.

They lack in historical insight, because they do not grasp the significance of the diversity of historical climates which in past times made the authority of the Church over the State—and now make the mutual freedom of the State and the Church—requisites of the common good of civilization.

They lack in theological insight, for they do not see that the authority of the Church in her own spiritual sphere is nothing else than her bondage to God and to her mission. This authority concerns her own organization precisely as contrasted in essence with the organization of civil society. As Pope Pius XII has put it in an address delivered on October 2, 1945, the foundation of the Church as a society was accomplished from above downwards, but political society origi-

36. I am alluding to serious-minded authors, not to Mr. Paul Blanshard. His handling of the question (*American Freedom and Catholic Power* [Boston: Beacon Press, 1949], chap. iii) is not worth discussion because it is simply unfair, like the rest of his book, whose criticisms, instead of clarifying matters, are constantly vitiated by biased and devious interpretation, and which confuses all issues in a slandering manner, up to ascribing to the Catholic Church "a full-blown system of fetishism and sorcery" (p. 215).

nates from below upwards.[37] In other words, authority in the Church comes down from above, but authority in political society rises from below; and whereas the Pope in the Church is the Vicar of Christ, the rulers in political society are the vicars of the people. As a result, it is a particular emphasis on political freedom which corresponds, in the sphere of civil society, to the particular emphasis on teaching authority in the sphere of the Church.

Be it noted, furthermore, that, as a matter of fact, no government is less authoritarian than the government of the Catholic Church. It governs without police force and physical coercion the immense people for whose spiritual common good it is responsible. Here we have a society the order of which primarily depends on the non-material influence on human souls of teaching, preaching, worshipping, and the sacramental life, and only secondarily on the external power of the law. The Pope speaks to the conscience of men, he counts upon the inner vitality of faith to make his word listened to; to enforce his doctrinal and moral directions in the Catholic people he has recourse to the spiritual sanctions of Canon Law but on comparatively infrequent occasions.

He has over the Church an authority that is supreme and sovereign.[38] But this supreme authority is exercised on a vast and infinitely variegated structure made up of all local Churches, which have their own particular life in the whole, and whose heads enjoy in their own sphere genuine and autonomous, though subordinate, authority. The bishops are not to the Pope as generals to a chief of supreme headquarters,

37. "La Fondazione della chiesa come società si e effettuata, contrariamente all' origine dello stato, non dal basso all' alto, ma dall' alto al basso" (address for the inauguration of the new juridical year of the Tribunal of the Rota, October 2, 1945, reported in *Osservatore romano*, October 3, 1945).

Cajetan, in 1511, had already made clear that difference between the origin of power in the Church and in civil society, in his opuscule *De comparatione auctoritatis papae et concilii*.

38. Cf. supra, p. 49.

or as civil servants to the central administration. According to the basic tenets on which the constitution of the Catholic Church is grounded, they are invested with the fulness of priesthood; they are the successors to the Apostles; each one of them is the spouse of his local Church. The central government of the Church respects their rights and legitimate freedom of action. It takes into account, to a degree much more considerable than is ordinarily fancied, the various trends and initiatives, rooted in particular circumstances, of the episcopate and the faithful of each nation, and the *feeling of the Church*, who is not the ecclesiastical hierarchy only, but the whole body of Christ, laity and clergy together.

The Church in her very essence is an object of theological faith—belongs to the order of those realities hidden in divine life and made known by divine revelation which are called supernatural mysteries. As a result, between the believer, who thinks of the Church in terms of faith, and the unbeliever, who thinks of her in terms merely human, there is a kind of unavoidable mutual misapprehension. The first one knows that the life which animates her is the life of the God-given grace of Christ, which is received in deficient human beings, and from which these human beings slip away each time they do evil. He knows, therefore, that she is sinless while composed of sinful members. The unbeliever, on the contrary, ascribes to her all the faults of her members. He does not realize that even in the natural order a nation for instance is possessed of a life of its own which is, fortunately for those who cherish it, superior (though not come down from God) to the disheartening pettiness of a great many of its nationals. Those men of faith who have the truest and highest idea of the transcendent essence of the Church and her substantial holiness— tangibly manifested in her saints and all the fruits of sanctity that proceed from her—are best able to see without flinching the lapses of her members, and the way in which, to a greater or lesser extent, the behavior of Christians cannot help proving false to Christianity.

In the course of twenty centuries, by preaching the Gospel to the nations and by standing up to the flesh and blood powers in order to defend against them the liberties of the spirit, the Church has taught men freedom. Today the blind forces which for two hundred years attacked her in the name of freedom and of the human person deified, are at last dropping the mask. They appear as they are. They yearn to enslave man. Present times, however miserable they may be, have the wherewithal to elate those who love the Church and love freedom. The historical situation they are facing is definitely clear. The great drama of the present day is the confrontation of man with the totalitarian State, which is but the old spurious God of the lawless Empire bending everything to his adoration. The cause of freedom and the cause of the Church are one in the defense of man.

CHAPTER VII

THE PROBLEM OF WORLD GOVERNMENT*

✻

I

The Alternative

IN 1944, Mr. Mortimer Adler published a book entitled
How to Think About War and Peace, in which he advocated
in a conclusive manner World Government as the only means
of insuring peace. This book was written just on the eve of the
advent of what they now call the atomic age;—that's a proof
that philosophers do not need to be stimulated by the atomic
bomb in order to think. Yet the advent of the atomic bomb is

* In this chapter I consider the problem of world government from the point of view
of political philosophy and not from that of immediate practical activity. Furthermore,
I aim in my discussion to clarify the positions of the particular group whose approach
to the problem is most closely concerned, in my opinion, with the philosophical issues
involved; I refer to the group at the University of Chicago.

As a result, (1) the development of my own views on the philosophical theory of
world government being my main purpose, no attempt has been made to analyze the
huge diversity of conflicting views with which a complete practical discussion of the
matter would have had to deal; (2) as regards the material quoted, I have restricted
myself to a few books from the Chicago group which happen to be more closely linked
with the topic of my discussion. In order to ward off the reproach of provincialism
which such an approach might seem to deserve (if the reader were mistaken about the
author's actual aim), I should like to lay stress here on the importance and interest of
the various contributions that have come from other quarters, and more especially
from such authorities in the matter as Messrs. MacIver, Carr, Clarence Streit, Cord Meyer,
Kelsen, Herbert Hoover, Culbertson, Goodrich, Hambro, Woodward, and the Shotwell
Commission—without forgetting the strong objections made by Messrs. Walter Lippmann
and Reinhold Niebuhr. I should like also to mention Julia E. Johnsen's books: *United Nations or World Government* ("The Reference Shelf," Vol. XIX, No. 5 [April, 1947]) and
Federal World Government ("The Reference Shelf," Vol. XX, No. 5 [September, 1948]), as
well as the general survey undertaken by Duke University, under the direction of Professor
Hornell Hart. See also J. Warburg, *Faith, Purpose and Power* (New York, 1950), chap. v.

a strong invitation to think, directed both to the States, which, having no soul of their own, find it a harder matter to think than mechanical brains do, and to the peoples, which, as long as they are not atomized, still have human brains.

The problem of World Government—I would prefer to say, of a genuinely political organization of the world—is the problem of lasting peace. And in a sense we might say that the problem of lasting peace is simply the problem of peace, meaning that mankind is confronted today with the alternative: either lasting peace or a serious risk of total destruction.

I need not emphasize the reality and significance of this alternative, which results from the fact that modern wars are world wars, and total wars, involving the whole of human existence, with regard to the deepest structures of social life as well as to the extent of the population mobilized by war, and threatened by it, in every nation.

What I should like is rather to seek for the reasons for this alternative.

The basic fact is the henceforth unquestionable interdependence of nations, a fact which is not a token of peace, as people for a moment believed in their wishful thinking, but rather a token of war: why? because that interdependence of nations is essentially an economic interdependence, not a politically agreed-upon, willed, and built up interdependence, in other words, because it has come to exist by virtue of a merely technical or material process, not by virtue of a simultaneous genuinely political or rational process.

Quoting a statement of Mr. Emery Reves, Mortimer Adler, in his chapter on *The Economic Community*, points out that "the technical developments which render the world smaller, and its parts more interdependent, can have two consequences: '1) a political and economic rapprochement, or 2) fights and quarrels more devastating than ever, precisely because of the proximity of men to each other. Which one of these two possibilities will occur depends on matters essentially nontechnical.' " And he rightly adds: "Both will occur within the next great historic epoch, but the second before the first."[1]

An essentially *economic* interdependence, without any corresponding fundamental recasting of the *moral* and *political* structures of human existence, can but impose by material necessity a partial and fragmentary, growing bit by bit, political interdependence which is reluctantly and hatefully accepted, because it runs against the grain of nature as long as nations live on the assumption of their full political autonomy. In the framework and against the background of that assumed full political autonomy of nations, an essentially economic interdependence can but exasperate the rival needs and prides of nations; and the industrial progress only accelerates the process, as Professor John Nef has shown in his book *La Route de la guerre totale.*[2] Thus it is that we have the privilege of contemplating today a world more and more economically one, and more and more divided by the pathological claims of opposed nationalisms.

At this point we may make two remarks. In the first place, both economic life and political life depend on *nature* and *reason*, I mean *nature* as dominated by material forces and laws and by deterministic evolution, even when the human mind interferes in the process with its technical discoveries—and on *reason* as concerned with the ends of human existence and the realm of freedom and morality, and as freely establishing, in consonance with Natural Law, an order of human relations. In the second place, it is nature and matter that have the upper hand in the economic process; and it is reason and freedom that have the upper hand in the political, the genuinely political process.

1. Mortimer J. Adler, *How To Think about War and Peace* (New York: Simon & Schuster, 1944), pp. 228–29. Mr. Emery Reves's quotation is taken from his *Democratic Manifesto.*

2. John U. Nef, *La Route de la guerre totale* (Paris: Armand Colin, 1949).

As a result, it is permissible to say that the spectacle we are contemplating today is but an instance of that unfortunate law that in human history matter goes faster than the spirit. The human intellect is always getting winded in catching up with the advance of matter. It is probable that with the discovery of fire the cave-man had to face predicaments not unlike those which our civilization is facing now. The question is whether human conscience and moral intelligence, teamed with the effort of creative energies, will be able to make the Machine a positive force in the service of mankind—in other words, to impose on man's instinctive greed, with its unsurpassable technical equipment, a collective reason grown stronger than instinct—without a period of trial and error more terrible to our kind than the prehistoric eras.[3]

* * *

Now the preceding considerations are not enough. Another factor must be considered, which plays a far-reaching part in the development of that alternative: *either lasting peace or a serious risk of total destruction*, the reasons for which we are seeking.

This factor is the modern State, with its false pretense to be a person, a superhuman person, and to enjoy, as a result, a right of absolute sovereignty.

In a remarkable essay, entitled "The Modern State a Danger for Peace,"[4] the Belgian jurist Fernand de Visscher offers this primary fact for our consideration: the fundamental amorality of the foreign policy of modern States; a fundamental amorality whose unique rule and principle is the *raison d'État*, which raises the particular interest of a State to a supreme law of its activity, especially as to its relations with the other States.

3. Cf. *France, My Country* (New York: Longmans, Green & Co., 1941), p. 108.

4. Fernand de Visscher, *L'État moderne: Un Danger pour la paix: Extrait de la revue Le Flambeau* (1940–47).

And the same author goes on to explain that the root of this evil is the false assumption that the State is a person, a supreme person, which consequently has its supreme justification, supreme reason for being and supreme end in itself, and possesses a supreme right to its own preservation and growth in power by any means whatever.

This false assumption has been previously discussed.[5] Mr. de Visscher calls it a political "heresy," and thinks that it derives from a fatal misunderstanding, by virtue of which a mere metaphor, technically useful in the language of jurists—the notion of "juridical personality"—has been mistaken for a reality, and has given birth in this way to "one of the most baneful myths of our times." As we have seen, such a myth has much deeper roots, I would say Hegelian roots. Hegel did not invent, he gave full metaphysical expression to the idea of the State as a superhuman person. The modern States were Hegelian in practice long before Hegel and his theory. The modern State, heir of the kings of old, has conceived of itself as a person superior to the body politic, and either dominating the body politic from above or absorbing the body politic in itself. Now, since the State in actual fact is not a person, but a mere impersonal mechanism of abstract laws and concrete power, it is this impersonal mechanism which will become suprahuman, when that vicious idea comes to develop its whole potentialities; and as a result the natural order of things will be turned upside down: the State will be no longer in the service of men, men will be in the service of the peculiar ends of the State.

Let us not forget, moreover, that this trend toward supreme domination and supreme amorality, which has fully developed and is in full swing in the totalitarian States, is by no means inherent in the State in its real nature and its true and necessary functions, but depends on a perverted notion which preys

5. See supra, chaps. i and ii.

upon the modern State, and of which democracy, if it is to survive, will get clear.

Let us also observe with de Visscher that this trend of modern States toward supreme domination and supreme amorality, which runs against the nature of the genuinely democratic State and can but impair its most beneficial initiatives, is constantly thwarted, in democratic nations, as concerns especially the *internal or domestic* activity of the State. Because in democratic nations the basic idea of justice, law, and common welfare, on which the State itself is grounded, the rights and freedom of the citizens, the constitution and the free institutions of the body politic, the control exercised by the assemblies of the representatives of the people, the pressure of public opinion, the freedom of expression, freedom of teaching and freedom of the press, tend of themselves to check the vicious trend in question and keep, somehow or other, the State within its proper and natural limits.

But as concerns the *external or foreign* activity of the State, that is, its relations with the other States, there is nothing to check the trend of modern States—to the extent to which they are infected with the Hegelian virus—toward supreme domination and supreme amorality, nothing except the opposite force of the other States. For there is no more powerful control, no organized international public opinion, to which these States can be submitted. And as to the superior law of justice, they deem it to be embodied in their own supreme interests. I by no means disregard the work which international institutions like the late League of Nations or the present United Nations Organization were or are performing in order to remedy that situation. Yet this work cannot touch the root of the evil, and remains inevitably precarious and subsidiary, from the very fact that such institutions are organs created and put into action by the sovereign States, whose decisions they can only register. As a matter of fact, modern States, with respect to international relations, are acting in a kind of vacuum, as supreme and adamantine, transcendent, absolute entities. While the modern State grows inevitably stronger as regards its supervision over national life, and the powers with which it is armed more and more dangerous for the peace of nations, at the same time the external relations of foreign policy between nations are strictly reduced to relations between those supreme entities in their harsh mutual competition, with an only remote participation of the people—their human aspirations and their human wills—in the course of fateful events developing above them in an unattainable Jovian heaven.

II

Discarding the So-called Sovereignty of the State

From all that I have said it appears that the two main obstacles to the establishment of a lasting peace are, first, the so-called absolute sovereignty of modern States; second, the impact of the economic interdependence of all nations upon our present irrational stage of political evolution, in which no world political organization corresponds to world material unification.

As concerns the so-called absolute sovereignty of modern States, I am not unaware of the fact that we may use, and we often use, the expression "sovereignty of the State" to mean a genuine political concept, namely the full independence or autonomy of the body politic. Unfortunately, "sovereignty of the State" is exactly the wrong expression for that concept, because the subject involved is not the State but the body politic, and because, as we have seen in Chapter II, the body politic itself is not genuinely sovereign. The right name is autonomy. No less unfortunately, this very autonomy of the body politic no longer exists in full: as a matter of fact, the nations are no longer autonomous in their economic life; they are even only half autonomous in their political life, because their political life is impaired by the lasting threat of war and interfered with, in domestic affairs, by the ideology and pressure of other nations. Now I say that it is not enough to remark that modern bodies politic have ceased in actual fact to be "sovereign" in that improper sense which means full autonomy. It is also not enough to request from sovereign States limitations and partial surrenders of their sovereignty, as if it were only a matter of making more or less restricted in its extension a privilege genuinely and really inherent in the State, and as if, moreover, sovereignty could be limited in its own sphere.

That is not enough. We must come down to the roots, that is, we must get rid of the Hegelian or pseudo-Hegelian concept of the State as a person, a supra-human person, and understand that the State is only a *part* (a topmost part, but a part) and an *instrumental agency* in the body politic,—thus bringing the State back to its true, normal, and necessary functions as well as to its genuine dignity. And we must realize that the State is not and has never been sovereign, because sovereignty means a *natural* right (which does not belong to the State but to the body politic as perfect society) to a supreme power and independence which are supreme *separately from* and *above* the whole that the sovereign rules (and of which neither the State nor the body politic is possessed). If the State were sovereign, in the genuine sense of this word, it could never surrender its sovereignty, nor even have it restricted. Whereas the body politic, which is not sovereign, but has a right to full autonomy, can freely surrender this right if it recognizes that it is no longer a perfect society, and decides to enter a larger, truly perfect political society.[6]

6. See chaps. i and ii.

III

NECESSITY FOR A WORLD POLITICAL SOCIETY

As concerns the second main obstacle to the establishment of a lasting peace, namely the present state of political *in-organization* of the world, well, here we are getting to the core of the problem we have to discuss.

If we place ourselves in the perspective of rational necessities, neglecting for a moment the factual entanglements of history, and if we transfer ourselves to the final conclusions made clear by the logical requirements of the issue, then we shall see how cogently the advocates of World Government, or of a *one world* politically organized, make out their case.

Suffice it briefly to recall the arguments they have developed to substantiate their contention.

Distinguishing from the various causes which are incitations to war (and which are epitomized in human nature and its need for material goods) the basic structural condition presupposed by war, Mr. Mortimer Adler states that "the only cause of war is anarchy," that is, "the condition of those who try to live together without government." "Anarchy occurs wherever men or nations try to live together without each surrendering their sovereignty."[7] As a result, if a time arrives in which war is made impossible, this will be a time in which anarchy between nations has been suppressed, in other words, a time in which world government has been established.

In a similar line of reasoning, Mr. Stringfellow Barr, having described *The Pilgrimage of Western Man*, writes: "The problem which confronted the generation of Armistice Two, the first generation of the Atomic Age, was clearly the oldest political problem of all: how to find government for a community that lacked it, even if each fraction of the community already lived under a government of its own. It had been solved by tribes

7. Adler, *op. cit.*, p. 69.

that had merged to form a village, by villages that had merged to form city-states like those of Renaissance Italy, by city-states that had merged to form empires or to form sovereign nation-states. Now it was nation-states, not villages, that were the governed fractions of an ungoverned community. What was terribly new about the problem was that this time the community was world-wide, bound together for weal or woe by modern science, modern technology, and the clamorous needs of modern industry." Thus man today, broadening his imagination, has to grasp with respect to a whole planet the force of the argument of Alexander Hamilton in the first of the *Federalist Papers*, that is to say, as Stringfellow Barr puts it, "that the price of peace is justice, the price of justice is law, that the price of law is government, and that government must apply law to men and women, not merely to subordinate governments."[8]

Finally Chancellor Hutchins has admirably shown, in his lecture on *St. Thomas and the World State*,[9] that the concept of a pluralist world-wide political society perfectly squares with the basic principles of Thomas Aquinas' political philosophy. For Thomas Aquinas as well as for Aristotle, self-sufficiency (I do not say total self-sufficiency, I say real, if relative, self-sufficiency), self-sufficiency is the essential property of *perfect society*, which is the goal to which the evolution of political forms in mankind tends; and the primary good ensured by a perfect society—a good which is one indeed with its very unity and life—is its own internal and external peace. As a result, when neither peace nor self-sufficiency can be achieved by a particular form of society, like the city, it is no longer that particular form, but a broader one, for instance the kingdom, which is perfect society. Hence we are entitled to conclude,

8. *The Pilgrimage of Western Man* (New York: Harcourt, Brace & Co., 1949), p. 341.

9. Robert M. Hutchins, *St. Thomas and the World State* (Aquinas Lecture, 1949 [Milwaukee: Marquette University Press, 1949]). "Perfect society" does not mean a society without defect, but a society which has reached full formation.

following the same line of argumentation: when neither peace nor self-sufficiency can be achieved by particular kingdoms, nations, or states, they are no longer perfect societies, and it is a broader society, defined by its capacity to achieve self-sufficiency and peace—therefore, in actual fact, with reference to our historical age, the international community politically organized—which is to become perfect society.

According to the same principles, it was on a merely moral ground, reinforced as far as possible by legal and customary bonds born of mutual agreement, in other words, it was by virtue of *natural law* and *jus gentium* or the common law of civilization, that kingdoms and States, as long as they answered in an approximate yet sufficient manner the concept of perfect society, had to fulfil their obligations toward that "community of the whole world," that international society whose existence and dignity have always been affirmed by Christian doctors and jurists, as well as by the common consciousness of mankind. And God knows how the obligations in question were fulfilled in the absence of the sword of the law. But when the particular bodies politic, our so-called national States, grown incapable of achieving self-sufficiency and assuring peace, definitely recede from the concept of perfect society, then the picture necessarily changes: since it is the international society which must become henceforth the perfect society, it is not only on a *moral*, but on a fully *juridical* ground that the obligations of the particular bodies politic, once they have become parts of a politically organized whole, will have to fulfil their obligations toward this whole: not only by virtue of *natural law* and *jus gentium*, but also by virtue of the *positive laws* which the politically organized world society will establish and which its government will enforce.

In the transitional period, or as long as a world government has not yet been founded by the only normal and genuine process of generation of political societies, that is, through the ex-

ercise of freedom, reason, and human virtues, it is obvious, as
Mr. Hutchins points out, that the foundation of a World
State by force, as well as any attempt by one State forcibly to
impose its will upon another, should be opposed as contrary to
Natural Law. As long as a pluralist world political society has
not yet been founded, the particular bodies politic shaped by
history remain the only political units in which the concept of
perfect society, though they are now falling short of it, has
been carried into effect: be they great or small, powerful or
weak, they keep their right to full independence, as well as
that right to make war and peace which is inherent in perfect
society, and in the exercise of which moral law demands of
them today more self-restraint than ever.

Yet the final aim is clearly determined. Once the perfect society required by our historical age, that is the world political society, has been brought into being, it will be bound in
justice to respect to the greatest possible extent the freedoms—
essential to the common good of the world—of those invalu-
able vessels of political, moral, and cultural life which will be
its parts; but the particular States will have surrendered their
full independence,— much more indeed in their external than
in their internal sphere of activity, and the World State will
have to enjoy, within the strict limits and the well-balanced
modalities proper to such a completely new creation of human
reason, the powers naturally required by a perfect society: legislative power, executive power, judicial power, with the
coercive power necessary to enforce the law.

I should like to add that the Constitution in which the
rights and duties and the governmental structures of such a
World State will perhaps be defined some day can only be the
fruit of the common efforts, experiences, and hard trials met
with by present and future history; but that the *Preliminary
Draft for a World Constitution* which is known as the Chicago
Plan, or Hutchins Plan, appears as a particularly valuable in-

ception. If this *Preliminary Draft* is understood, according to the purpose of its authors, as a merely tentative "proposal to history, to promote further study and discussion," it seems to me to be both the best among the many plans of international organization which are being elaborated today, and the most comprehensive and well-balanced ideal pattern that prominent political scientists[10] could work out in order to exasperate frowning realists, and to prod the thought and meditation of men of good will and far-sighted ingenuousness.

* * *

A good many objections have been raised, of course, to the idea of a World Government. I should like only to allude to the most conspicuous one, which insists that the idea is fine and beautiful, but utterly impossible of realization, and therefore most dangerous, for it runs the risk of diverting toward a brilliant utopia efforts which should be directed toward more humble but possible achievements. The reply is that if the idea is grounded, as we believe, on true and sound political philosophy, it cannot be impossible *in itself*. Therefore it is up to human intelligence and energy to make it, in the long run, not impossible *with respect to* the enormous yet contingent obstacles and impediments that the sociological and historical conditions which lie heavy on mankind have piled up against it.

At this point I must confess that in my capacity as an Aristotelian I am not much of an idealist. If the idea of a world political society were only a beautiful idea, I would not

10. The Committee To Frame a World Constitution was composed of Messrs. Robert M. Hutchins, G. A. Borgese, Mortimer J. Adler, Stringfellow Barr, Albert Guérard, Harold A. Innis, Erich Kahler, Wilber G. Katz, Charles H. McIlwain, Robert Redfield, and Rexford G. Tugwell.

The "Preliminary Draft" was printed in the March, 1948, issue of the monthly *Common Cause* (University of Chicago), a "journal of one world" dedicated to the defense and diffusion of this plan, under the direction of Mr. G. A. Borgese, whose untiring intentness was particularly instrumental in the drafting of the plan.

care much for it. I hold it to be a great idea, but also a sound and right idea. Yet the greater an idea is with respect to the weakness and entanglements of the human condition, the more cautious one must be in handling it. And the more attentive one must be in *not* demanding its immediate realization (a warning which, if I may be allowed to say, sounds especially distasteful in a generous country where good ideas are looked upon as something to be immediately applied and seem worthy of interest only to that extent). It would not be good, either for the cause of the idea or for the cause of peace, to use the idea of World Government as a weapon against the limited and precarious international agencies which for the time being are the only existing political means at the disposal of men to protract the truce among nations. Moreover the supporters of the concept of World Government perfectly know—Mr. Mortimer Adler has especially stressed that aspect of the question —that this concept can be brought into being only after many years of struggle and effort. They know, therefore, that their solution for a future perpetual peace has surely no more efficacy for the precarious peace to be ensured today than the work of the agencies to which I just alluded. The pros and cons, in the issue of World Government, do not concern our day, but the generations to come.

IV

FULLY POLITICAL VS. MERELY GOVERNMENTAL THEORY

So far I have dealt with the most general aspects of the problem. Perhaps I could be tempted to end my essay here; so at least I would spare the patience of the reader. Yet further consideration seems to me to be needed. My discussion is not finished, and this chapter has to set forth a new series of considerations.

The reason for this is that the problem has been posed in terms of its ultimate solution, and in terms of world government,—therefore, first of all in terms of *State* and *government*. Now, if we remember the distinction, emphasized in the first chapter of this book, between *state* and *body politic*, we shall see that the very idea of world government can be conceived in two opposite ways. The question, therefore, is: in which way should a sound political philosophy conceive of world government? A first possible manner of conceiving world government would reduce the whole matter to the *sole and exclusive* consideration of the *state and government*. Let us call it the *merely governmental* theory of world organization. The second possible manner of conceiving world government envisages the matter under the universal or integral consideration of the *body politic* or *political society*. Let us call it the *fully political* theory of world organization.

I think that the *fully political* theory is the good one, and that a *merely governmental* theory would be wrong and disastrous. I do not know of anybody having ever taken a stand in its behalf. But sins of omission are to be avoided like the others. My point is that it is necessary to clarify the issue, in order to brush aside any possibility of mistaking one theory for the other, and to get rid of misunderstandings quite detrimental to the very idea of world political organization.

Let me emphasize once again that the basic political reality is not the State, but the body politic with its multifarious institutions, the multiple communities which it involves, and the moral community which grows out of it. The body politic is the people organized under just laws. The State is the particular agency which specializes in matters dealing with the common good of the body politic, it is therefore the topmost political agency, but the State is a part, not a whole, and its functions are merely instrumental: it is for the body politic and for the people that it sees to the public order, enforces laws, possesses power; and being a part in the service of the people, it must be controlled by the people.

What is called in French *le gouvernement*, and here the Administration or the administrative officials, that is, the men who are in charge of the common good, are part both of the body politic and of the State; but because they are the head of the people, and deputies for the people with respect to whom they exercise a vicarious function, and by whom, in a democratic régime, they are chosen, their governing function is rooted in the body politic, not in the State; it is not because their function is rooted in the State that they are part of the body politic; it is because their function is rooted in the body politic that they are part of the State.

Since that is how things are, we might better say, as I observed at the start, the *Problem of the World's Political Organization* than the *Problem of World Government*. The whole issue is not simply *World Government*. It is *World Political Society*.

What I just called a *merely governmental* theory would consider the whole thing, Existence and Nature of World Government, as well as Passage from the present state of affairs to the World Government, in the perspective of the State and government *separately* from that of the body politic. As a result, we would have to contemplate a process developed artificially, and against the grain of nature, resulting in a State without a body politic or a political society of its own, a world brain without a world body; and the World Government would be an absolute Super-state, or a superior State deprived of body politic and merely *superimposed* on and interfering with the life of the particular States—even though it were born of popular election and representation. For this procedure is of course the only authentic one—it is not through delegation from the various governments, it is through the free suffrage of men and women that the World State is to be founded and maintained—but this necessary procedure is a merely technical or juridical one and would be entirely insufficient to change in any way the fact that I am pointing out.

Just, then, as the ambition to become a sovereign person was transferred from the Holy Germanic Emperor to the kings— at the time when the French kings refused obedience to the Holy Empire—and from the kings to the States, so this same ambition would be transferred from the States to the World Superstate. So that by a tragic inconsistency, while putting an end to the modern myth of the State as regards all the particular States, men would again find this myth, the myth of the State as person and sovereign person and supra-human person, enthroned at the top of the universe. All the consequences involved in the Hegelian conception of the State could then spread over humanity with irresistible power.

The quest of such a Superstate capping the nations is nothing else, in fact, than the quest of the old utopia of a universal Empire. This utopia was pursued in past ages in the form of the Empire of one single nation over all others. The pursuit, in the modern age, of an absolute World Superstate would be the pursuit of a democratic multinational Empire, which would be no better than the others.

* * *

What I have just characterized as a merely governmental theory of world government is the exact opposite of what all of us who support the idea of world government are thinking, and, in particular, of the political philosophy of the Chicago plan's authors. But other people may come along, and be in a hurry, and be mistaken. And the more we insist on the right way, the more we must be aware of, and point out, the dangers of the wrong one. A *merely governmental* theory of world organization would go the wrong way, because from the very start it would pursue the analogy between *State with respect to individuals* and *World State with respect to particular States* in the mere perspective of the topmost power.

The *fully political* theory of world organization goes the right way, because it pursues the same analogy in the perspective of the basic requirements of political life and freedom. As Adler and Hutchins have repeatedly pointed out, the problem is to raise international community to the condition of a perfect society, or of a politically organized international society.

At this point I should like to make a few remarks on the comparison which suggests itself, and which, quoting Mr. Stringfellow Barr, I used in the first part of this chapter, between the passage from the tribe to the village, from the village to the city, from the city to the kingdom or to the modern political society, and the passage from our present political society to a world political society. The processes in question are only analogical, of course, and took place in multiple and exceedingly various fashions. Mr. Max Ascoli has sharply criticized that comparison,[11] and accused of utter naïveté the notion that our present political societies, ripened by history, could or should develop into a world political society by a so-to-speak mechanical process of broadening in extension. This criticism, in my opinion, applies to the manner in which things would be conceived in a merely governmental theory. It does not apply to the manner in which things are conceived in the fully political theory of world organization.

From another point of view, Henri Bergson, distinguishing *closed societies*, which are temporal and terrestrial, from *open society*, which is spiritual, insisted that that kind of friendship which unites members of the village or the city can broaden from a closed society to another, larger, closed society, but that when it comes to love for all men, then it is a question of passing from one order to another; from the realm of closed societies to the realm, infinitely different, of open and spiritual society, in which man is united with that very Love which has

11. Cf. Max Ascoli, *The Power of Freedom* (New York: Farrar, Straus, 1949), Part III, chap. iv.

created the world.[12] All that is true. But here also the mere consideration of extension is only accidental. If men are to pass from our present political societies to a world political society, they will pass to a larger *closed* society, as large as the whole company of nations, and civic friendship will have to broaden in the same manner. Civic friendship will still remain infinitely different from charity, just as the world society will remain infinitely different from the Kingdom of God.

Yet these remarks make us aware of a crucial point. The passage of which we are speaking implies a change not only in the dimension of extension, but first of all in the dimension of depth: a change in the inner structures of man's morality and sociality.

In the past epochs of history the will of men to live together, which is basic in the formation of political societies, was as a rule—with the splendid exception of this country— brought into being by any kind of means, save freedom. It has been enforced even by war; for, it is sad to say, wars have been the most general means—because they are the most primitive and brutal—of mixing and brewing peoples together and forcing them to know each other and to live with one another, conqueror and conquered, in the same place, and in the long run to develop between each other a kind of unhappy congeniality. Later on civic friendship could occur.

That time is past, at least as concerns democratic principles and the requirements of justice. Now, if a world political society is some day founded, it will be by means of freedom. *It is by means of freedom that the peoples of the earth will have been brought to a common will to live together.* This simple sentence makes us measure the magnitude of the moral revolution—the *real* revolution now proposed to the hopes and virtues of man-

12. Cf. Henri Bergson, *Les deux sources de la morale et de la religion* (Paris: Alcan, 1932), chap. iv. "De la société close à la société ouverte, de la cité à l'humanité, on ne passera jamais par voie d'élargissement. Elles ne sont pas de la même essence" (p. 288).

kind—on the necessity for which Mr. Mortimer Adler laid stress in his book.

Living together does not mean occupying the same place in space. It does not mean, either, being subjected to the same physical or external conditions or pressures or to the same pattern of life; it does not mean *Zusammenmarschieren*. Living together means sharing as men, not as beasts, that is, with basic free acceptance, in certain common sufferings and in a certain common task.

The reason for which men will to live together is a positive, creative reason. It is not because they fear some danger that men will to live together. Fear of war is not and never has been the reason for which men have wanted to form a political society. Men want to live together and form a political society for a given task to be undertaken in common. When men will have a will to live together in a world-wide society, it will be because they will have a will to achieve a world-wide common task. What task indeed? The conquest of freedom. The point is to have men become aware of that task, and of the fact that it is worthy of self-sacrifice.

Given the human condition, the most significant synonym of *living together* is *suffering together*. When men form a political society, they do not want to share in common suffering out of love for each other. They want to accept common suffering out of love for the common task and the common good. The will to achieve a world-wide common task must therefore be strong enough to entail a will to share in certain common sufferings made inevitable by that task, and by the common good of a world-wide society. What sufferings indeed? Sufferings due to solidarity. Suffice it to observe that the very existence of a world-wide society will inevitably imply deep changes in the social and economic structures of the national and international life of peoples, and a serious repercussion of these changes on the free business of a number of individuals, who are not the most numerous in the world, but the most attached to profit-making. The very existence of a world-wide society will also inevitably imply a certain—relative no doubt, yet quite serious and appreciable—equalization of the standards of life of all individuals. Let us put it in crude terms: perhaps, if the issue were made sufficiently clear to them, people in occidental nations would be ready to accept, for the sake of peace and of a world political organization ensuring lasting peace, a serious lowering of their standards of life in order to provide people on the other side of the iron curtain with an equivalent raising of their standards of life. Yet this would suppose a kind of moral heroism, for which, I deem, we are badly prepared.—People are unhappy, and it will be necessary for them to confront new obligations and sacrifices, connected with the life of other men at the other end of the world, in order to promote in the long run peace, happiness, and freedom for all.

We can meditate in this connection two far-reaching sentences of Mr. John Nef: "Science and machinery," he wrote, "have enabled humanity to command the material resources of the planet in ways which have made world government indispensable. At the same time science and machinery are depriving individuals and societies of the vision and of the control over themselves, which alone might make world government human and worth having."[13] And: "The price of peace is the renunciation, to a large extent, of success as the principal driving force in thought, work and politics."[14] The matter is nothing less than having science perfected by wis-

13. From a chapter, "Renewal (1950)," in a still unpublished book, "French Civilization and Universal Community."

14. Nef, *La Route de la guerre totale*, p. 161: "Le prix de la paix ... est l'abandon, dans une large mesure, du succès comme principe à la fois de la pensée, du travail et de la politique."

dom, and the criterion of success superseded by the criterion of good and devotion to the good.

One body politic is *one* organized people. Of course the unity of a world body politic would be quite different from the unity which characterizes kingdoms or nations, and to which our thought is accustomed. It would be not even a federal unity, but rather, let me say, a *pluralist unity*, taking place only through the lasting diversity of the particular bodies politic, and fostering that diversity. The fact remains that when we say that the community of nations must form *one* body politic, even taking into account the qualifications to which such a unity would be subject, we are saying that the community of peoples must form *one* people, even taking into account the qualifications to which such a pluralist unity would be subject. That means that among all peoples the sense of the common good of that *one people* should develop, and supersede the sense of the common good peculiar to each body politic. A sense of civic friendship as large as that one people should also and simultaneously develop, since civic love or friendship is the very soul or animating form of every political society. To insist that this sense of a world-wide civic friendship and a world-wide common good is a prerequisite condition for the foundation of a world political society would be putting the cart before the horse. Yet some beginnings should actually take shape in the peoples; moreover the sense of the common good of the community of peoples, with the mood of good will and fellow-feeling it implies, is implicitly and virtually involved in the freely developed will to live together, which *is* the basic condition prerequired for the foundation of a world political society coming into existence by means of freedom.

* * *

We see, therefore, that the birth of a world political society would result from a growing, vital process, in which the work of all official and private institutions interested in any form of international rapprochement and cooperation would participate, but in which the essential part would be played by the will of the people, in every nation, to live together, in the world, I mean a will growing so powerful as to sweep away the obstacles caused by the myth of the States as sovereign persons or by the bias of governments, and the obstacles, still greater, caused in the people themselves by misfortune and fatigue, slowness of reason, and natural self-interest.

We also see in this way how the World State would have a body politic of its own: this pluralist world body politic would be made up, not only of the international and supranational institutions required by the world government, but also, and first of all, of the particular bodies politic themselves, with their own political structures and lives, their own national and cultural heritages, their own multifarious institutions and communities—all this being enveloped, treasured and held sacred by the same will which would tend, beyond all this, to a world-wide living together, and which would have achieved this aim by the foundation of a world political society.

At this point it is advisable for us to elaborate a new concept, the concept of *imperfect* political society,—I mean, of course, as *part* of a kind of perfect society that the Ancients did not know, and in which, because of its very extension, the functions and properties inherent in self-sufficiency are divided between a multiplicity of particular bodies politic and a central common organism. In a world political society the nations would become *by right* and with the guarantees of a superior juridical order what they already are in fact, but anarchically, namely non-self-sufficient or imperfect bodies politic; and the World State, considered separately from them, and only in its supra-national institutions and life, would also be an imperfect political society. Only the world society taken as a whole both with the supra-national State and the multiplicity of nations, would be a perfect political society.

By the same token we may realize that the independence of nations would not be jeopardized—it would rather be better assured—by the creation of a world political society. The States would have to surrender their privilege of being sovereign persons, that is, a privilege which they have never possessed. They would have to give up their full independence, that is, something which they have lost. They would have to give up something which they have now, but the use of which has become more detrimental than profitable to them, to the nations, and to the world, namely the property of each one of enjoying *top* independence. Yet in their mutual interdependence the nations could achieve a degree of real, though imperfect, independence higher than that they possess now, from the very fact that their inner political life, being freed from the threat of war and from the interference of rival nations, could become more autonomous in actual fact than it is at present.

Some people are afraid that making the concern for justice, as the Chicago draft does, the chief duty of the World State, would result in extending over everything the celestial power of the world government.[15] They are thinking of a State without a body politic. Ensuring justice by law, which is the main function of the State, should obviously be the main function of the World State; but presupposing and needing all the other channels—legal, customary, social, moral, even merely vegetative—through which justice is ensured, somehow or other, in the infinitely diversified existence of nations. Limping as human justice is, justice is the primary need of the human community. And in this respect it is hard to say that our present world suffers from overnutrition.

15. Cf. McGeorge Bundy, "An Impossible World Republic," *Reporter*, November 22, 1949.

V

A Supra-National Advisory Council

As to practical application, a conclusion follows from all the preceding considerations: namely, that the passage to a world political society presupposes a will to live together developed in all the peoples, especially all great peoples in the world; any effort to found a World State in the absence of such a universal basis, thus creating a half-universality to be extended progressively to the whole, would, I am afraid, invite war rather than peace.

A second conclusion is that the passage to a one world politically organized can only occur after a long time. I know that time is relative, not only in the sense that a long time with respect to our experience is a short time with respect to history, but also in the sense that time runs faster in proportion as human history goes on. Nevertheless the period of maturation will seem very long to our unhappy race.

It is regrettable that perpetual peace cannot be established immediately after the discovery of the atomic bomb. This is no more regrettable than the fact that it *was necessary* to discover the atomic bomb; this is no more regrettable than the fact that, twenty centuries after the good tidings in Bethlehem, mankind is still in a prehistoric age with regard to the application of the Gospel in actual life. Now the business of human history is not in a stage of free creative development, rather it reckons up its losses; we are paying century-old historical debts. Ancient Israel, in such moments, turned to God in self-accusation and hope. We are more proud, and less hopeful. I have often expressed the opinion that our major problems cannot be decisively settled before the time of great crisis and great reconciliation announced by St. Paul.

Yet the creative process, visibly or invisibly, is always at work in history; and the saddest periods are often the most fecund ones. If nations have still to extricate themselves, in a most precarious and far from brilliant way, from the dangers of universal destruction, and if the foundation of a politically organized community of the world is only to be expected in a distant future, this is but reason to hope for that foundation more strongly, and to undertake, right now, with greater energy, the task of preparing it, and of awakening common consciousness to the imperative necessity of moving toward it.

This task, as we well know, has already been undertaken by the most courageous and far-seeing pioneers—in Chicago especially it was undertaken six days after the first atomic bomb dropped on Hiroshima. Such a task will obviously develop first of all as a deep and continuing task of education and enlightenment, discussion and study. It will also develop through the efforts, limited as they may be, of the diverse co-operative agencies of the United Nations, and through all the various efforts that have been started everywhere to promote the federal idea, and which are especially valuable, in my opinion, when they tend to well defined objectives actually achievable in one partial field or another, and are on their guard, at the same time, against the risk of only creating new and larger patterns for the world competition they are trying to eliminate.

But is there no means whatever of inserting in the present structure of the world a germ, however small it may be, or a first beginning, however weak it may be, which would have a chance of proving useful, if, some day, better times make possible the *political preparation* for the foundation of a world political society? Everyone's imagination can exert itself in this regard. Well, at this point may I also be permitted to make, in the most tentative way, a suggestion of my own?

My own suggestion is that a new superior agency, which would be deprived of any *power* whatsoever, but endowed with unquestionable *moral authority*, would perhaps have a chance of being accepted by the States, and would also have a chance of becoming the first beginning of which I just spoke.

Let us suppose a kind of world council whose function would be only a function of ethical and political wisdom, and which would be made up of the highest and most experienced authorities in moral and juridical sciences. Let us suppose that the members of this supreme advisory council would be picked from the nations of the world according to some equitable method of apportionment, and would be directly elected by the people of all nations, among men previously proposed by the highest institutions and the governments of every State. But let us suppose that, once elected, they would lose their national citizenship and would be given world citizenship, so as to become independent of any government and completely free in the exercise of their spiritual responsibility.

Let us suppose that they would be materially disarmed, without any other means of action than their own pronouncements, and only protected by the mutual commitments of the States. And let us suppose that they would be deprived of any powers, even, in contradistinction to the present International Court of Justice, of any judicial power. No government could appeal to them to make any decision, they would have no juridical connection with the United Nations, they would be simply free to tell the governments and the nations what they held to be just.

In proportion as such a supreme advisory council acted in a really wise, independent, and firm manner, and resisted the pressures exerted upon it, its moral authority would grow stronger, as well as its influence on public opinion. It would give a voice to the conscience of the peoples.

I think that being really a world institution, shielded by its constitution from the interference of any government; being, at the same time, deprived of powers; and exercising a merely moral function, it would have a chance of disarming the fears—fears of manoeuvres, of encirclement, of loss of prestige, etc.—which spoil the activities of international organizations; as a result, and taking into account the lip service which even the most cynical governments deem it necessary to pay to the moral factor, I think that some day, perhaps after new ordeals shall have made the situation more desperate, the idea of such a supreme advisory council could perhaps have a chance of being accepted by all States and governments.

What makes me fond of that idea is the fact that by this means a possibility could be offered for the coming into being of something indispensable and badly needed—namely an organized international opinion.

It is also the fact that, by this means, people could be enlightened and helped with regard to the most intricate temporal problems which concern the common good of the world, and on which, in democratic nations, they have to make a decision. Some of such problems are even of a nature to put their consciences on the rack—I am thinking especially of the problem of just war. People know that participating in an unjust war is sharing in homicide. They are told, on the other hand, that things have become so obscure and entangled that they lack competence to bear judgment on each particular case: am I bound, then, to share in what is *perhaps* a crime, because my government is a better judge than I on the matter, even if I were a German at the time of the Hitlerian war? On the opposite side, systematic conscientious objection is a tragic illusion, no less harmful to justice than blind obedience. The old standards with respect to which a war was to be considered just or unjust are outworn, and nevertheless the fact of giving up the distinction between the just and the unjust, in the case of war as in any other case, would boil down to a simple abdication of moral reason. It would be good if, in given and especially serious international conjunctures, a senate of wise men were to tell people where, in their opinion, the road to justice was.

But first and foremost, if such a senate of wise men existed, it would be the first token of the possibility of a really supra-national world organization, and it would foster in the consciousness of the peoples that great movement of intelligence and will on which depends the genuine and constructive revolution needed by our historical age, the foundation of a world community politically organized.

I am afraid that in expressing at the end of this chapter a practical suggestion of my own, I have perhaps yielded to the old temptation of philosophers, who would have reason, through the instrumentality of certain wise men, be accepted as an authority in human affairs. After all, this would be less serious an illusion, I suppose,—and in any case a less frequent one—than the conviction treasured by so many fatalists, that any reliance on reason has to be carefully avoided in the conduct of *Man, and the State.*

INDEX

✻

217

PHOENIX BOOKS
in Political Science and Law

Women in America

FROM COLONIAL TIMES TO THE 20TH CENTURY

Women in America

FROM COLONIAL TIMES TO THE 20TH CENTURY

Advisory Editors
LEON STEIN
ANNETTE K. BAXTER

A Note About This Volume

Elizabeth Parsons Ware Packard (1816-1897) became a teacher at the age of 19, but was committed to the state hospital at Jacksonville, Illinois, by her husband (whose six children she bore) because she openly differed with him on religious matters in the church in which he served as pastor. He was an orthodox Calvinist, she a mystic convinced that the Divine Spirit moved within her. Using her intelligence she won release and then vindication of her sanity by a court. She then undertook to expose the plight of married women, including those unjustly incarcerated by their husbands in asylums, by writing a series of books which she sold on an advance subscription basis. She also lobbied in state legislatures, buttonholed important people, and gained publicity in the newspapers interjecting herself into the movement to reform the care of th insane. Her efforts led to liberalizing changes in commitment laws Massachusetts, Illinois, Maine and Iowa. But, until the end, waged a battle with medical professionals whom she accus conspiring against her, while they publicly insinuated concerning her sanity. Her book is a powerful statement of h

GREAT DISCLOSURE

OF

Spiritual Wickedness!!

IN HIGH PLACES.

WITH

AN APPEAL TO THE GOVERNMENT

TO

Protect the Inalienable Rights

OF

Married Women

[ELIZABETH PARSONS WARE PACKARD]

ARNO PRESS
A New York Times Company
NEW YORK – 1974

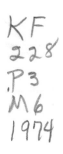
Reprint Edition 1974 by Arno Press Inc.

Reprinted from a copy in The Francis A. Countway
Library of Medicine

WOMEN IN AMERICA
From Colonial Times to the 20th Century
ISBN for complete set: 0-405-06070-X
See last pages of this volume for titles.

Publisher's Note: This volume was reprinted
from the best available copy.

Manufactured in the United States of America

Library of Congress Cataloging in Publication Data

Packard, Elizabeth Parsons Ware, 1816-1895.
    Great disclosure of spiritual wickedness!! in high
places.

    (Women in America: from colonial times to the 20th
century)
    Reprint of the ed. published by the author, Boston.
    1. Packard, Elizabeth Parsons Ware, 1816-1895.
2. Insanity--Jurisprudence--United States. 3. Women--
Legal status, laws, etc.--United States. I. Title.
II. Series.
KF228.P3M6 1974   346'.73'013   74-3965
ISBN 0-405-06114-5

GREAT DISCLOSURE

OF

Spiritual Wickedness!!

IN HIGH PLACES.

The House from which Mrs. Packard was Kidnapped.

GREAT DISCLOSURE

OF

Spiritual Wickedness!!

IN HIGH PLACES.

WITH

AN APPEAL TO THE GOVERNMENT

TO

Protect the Inalienable Rights

OF

Married Women.

WRITTEN UNDER THE INSPECTION OF DR. M'FARLAND, SUPERINTENDENT
OF INSANE ASYLUM JACKSONVILLE, ILLINOIS.

FOURTH EDITION.

BOSTON:
PUBLISHED BY THE AUTHORESS.
1865.

CONTENTS.

TO MY BELOVED CHILDREN

IS THIS BOOK

MOST AFFECTIONATELY DEDICATED.

———

To you, my first-born son, THEOPHILUS PACKARD, JR., born March 17, 1842; and you, my second child, ISAAC WARE PACKARD, born June 24, 1844; and you, my third child, SAMUEL PACKARD, born November 2, 1847; and you, my only daughter, ELIZABETH WARE PACKARD, born May 10, 1850; and you, my fifth child, GEORGE HASTINGS PACKARD, born July 18, 1853; and you, my sixth child, ARTHUR DWIGHT PACKARD, born December 18, 1858; — I dedicate this "book of nature," or a record of your Mother's life — of that life of which you are the sun, moon and stars. Yes, it is for you, my jewels, I have lived — it is for you I have suffered the agonies of Gethsemane's Garden — it is for you I have hung on this cross of crucifixion; and been entombed three years in this living cemetery; and oh! it is for your sakes I hope to rise again, to find my maternal joys immortalized.

Children dear, I have been deserted by my father, cast off by my husband, uncared for by my brothers; but you, my treasures, have, all, save one, stood by me during my persecutions. Yes, when all the world forsook me and fled, *you stood* firm for right, firm for truth, firm for duty. You, and you alone, were true to the mother who bore you, for you *knew* she was true to man, and true to God.

Yes, your tender, loving hearts have writhed in secret agony over your mother's sorrows — but you have been denied the boon of human sympathy for yourselves; and, what is harder still, you have not been allowed to bestow it upon your persecuted mother, even, while her lacerated heart was panting to receive it from you.

Yes, you, my first-born son, Theophilus, have been threatened with disinheritance from our family and home, because you loved your faithful, kind-hearted mother *so well*, that you sought to visit her in hei prison-home in defiance of your father's edict. Oh, my son! Thy Father, God, will not disinherit thee for loving thy mother, even, when the world forsook her. You have, on this account, become my "Ishmael," but you are not the "fugitive and vagabond" your father represents you to be. Four times has thy hard-earned wages, my filial Theophilus, been cheerfully expended to see your mother.

And you, my Isaac, I have consented to lay upon the altar of my country — a living sacrifice for its sins. God has accepted the sacrifice and *spared my Isaac!* You toiled early and late to accumulate a treasure, with which you could visit your mother. God succeeded you — you paid me one clandestine visit in my prison.

Your faces are the only ones of my kindred* whom I have seen within my cell. Your two clandestine letters are all the letters from my kindred I have been permitted to receive.

But oh! I needed no such proofs of your *true love*, to assure me it was not dead within you. No, death and a living tomb cannot separate us. We are one in Christ. Oh, my children! Every earthly love has died within me — but oh! the death agonies of the *maternal love* well nigh rent soul and body asunder. Yes, the mother has died! But she has risen again — the mother of her country — and her sons and daughters are — *The American Republic.*

Children, it is for the service of your country your mother has dedicated you, one and all. May you, my sons, be fitted to adorn the garden of American freedom, "as plants," grown up in your youth, from the rocky but luxuriant soil of family persecution. And may you, my daughter, be as a "corner-stone," in our new temple of American freedom — "polished after the similitude of a palace."

---

* Since writing the above; cousin Angeline S. Field, of Granville, Ill., visited me once, and has written me once.

PREFACE.

In presenting this volume before the public, *I—the first person sin-gular*—assume the entire responsibility of the statements and opinions it contains.

Before the reader has proceeded far, he will doubtless see the significance of my singular assumption. It contains many singular thoughts and expressions, and is, thereby, a transcript of my own individuality upon paper.

It has always been my fortune (since my spirit tenanted this body, for the last forty-six years of its existence) or rather *misfortune*, in the present phase of the world's history, to be a pioneer, just about twenty-five years in advance of my cotemporaries, — therefore, I am called crazy, or insane, by those so far in my rear, that they cannot see the reasonableness of the positions and opinions I assume to advocate and defend. And their lack of christian charity incapacitates them for holding me in the bonds of christian fellowship as a sister, while I dare, fearlessly, to use my inalienable right of *opinion*, especially if that opinion differs from their own.

I freely accord to the insane party — my enemies — their right of opinion, in *believing* me to be an insane person ; and so long as these opinions do not lead them to trespass *upon my inalienable rights*, I have no right or desire to interfere with them.

But, since I differ from my enemies in opinion on *this* point, just as much as they differ from me, and, since my opinion is as dear to me as are these of my enemies to them, and, since we have no right to do wrong, therefore, when these opinions of my enemies lead them to *kidnap* my accountability, by placing me on a level with the beasts, for opinion's sake merely, the law of self-defense compels me to resist this, their interference with my inalienable rights, as a trespass upon my identity. Neither will conscience allow me to compromise with my persecutors by yielding my own individuality to their dictation.

This inflexibility of purpose has resulted in a long and wearisome persecution and *false imprisonment* of three years for conscience sake.

At this point, through the manliness of Dr. McFarland, I am allowed to speak for myself, by presenting my own statement before the public, in my own way and manner. And in doing so, I am conscience-bound to be true to man, and true to God.

Truth is my argument — truth is my only weapon — truth is my only defense — truth is my only refuge. On this immovable rock I take my stand, fearless of the foaming billows which dash at its base. Daring to be true to God, with this foundation to stand upon, I shall give free utterance to the inspirations of the Divinity within me, fearlessly trusting the results of this act of loyalty to the overruling providence of that God whose cause I have dared to espouse and defend, in spite of the mighty power of my persecutors.

But, to my friends — the sane party — I must say, that you must expect to find some crazy things in it; for, unless you do, you see our game is lost; for should all chance to think me a sane person, we should then have none to defeat. There could be no victory, no triumph.

And, besides, my benevolent regard for the insane party tempts me to give them some occasion for believing me insane by giving utterance to what, *to them*, will be insane opinions. We must respect the feelings of that party, for they are all our brothers and sisters; and among them are some nobly developed intellects, (though under an eclipse,) such as Dr. McFarland, who, himself, for a time, was tempted to call my views of things — insanity. But thanks to God, the scales are being removed from his eyes, so that he can, even now, "see men as trees walking."

I have purposed in this volume, to pack my thoughts into the form of cannon balls to shoot Calvinism with, instead of beating them out into a shield of self-defense, by giving my reasons for my opinions. But, justice to the sane party, as well as to myself, demands that I add, that I have reasons — sound and good reasons — for all the new views of truth herein advanced; and I pledge myself ready and willing to defend them by giving my reasons whenever Christianity makes the demand.

The author of the good things in this book is God, himself. The author of the evil things, and God's writing medium of the whole, is

E. P. W. PACKARD.

INTRODUCTION.*

AT the suggestion of Dr. McFarland, I have concluded to present my book, before the public, in twelve distinct or separate parts, or volumes, since I find the whole would make a volume of such mammoth size, that I fear the sight of it would be enough to frighten away the *practical* reader — the very one 't was written for.

And besides, I am in such a hurry to get to my children. And since I find that as the square of the distance of time between us decreases, so does the attraction which draws me to them, increase; so I want to put the press on to a little "hand-car" to tell the public what's on the track, so they can clear the track for it, and also for me to go home, to Manteno, to my family.

I can assure you, I have engineered the government clear through to Chicago, the New York city of "Young America." And I have found, in auctioneering off our old useless plunder, at Washington, I have had a working time of it. For our government stock contained so much chaff, in the Calvinism of its institutions, that it took a strong wind to blow it all away. Although 't was light stuff, yet there was a *good deal* of it. I can tell you, I found it buried up so deep, in the very centre of the stack, that I was compelled to tear it *all to pieces*, to be sure I had got it *all out*. The little bundles themselves, had all to be unbound, and scattered to the four winds. The chaff, I mean — not the wheat; that's too heavy to fly up at a light breeze. It takes a whirlwind to do that. And then, I've had to bind all this cleaned wheat again into little and big bundles, and stack it all up again myself, *all alone* — not even Dr. McFarland has helped one bit!

---

* This Introduction has special reference to the allegorical style in which the succeeding volumes of this Drama are written.

And then I've had to metamorphose that great metallic image, stand·ing there in the old white house, at Washington, with his golden head and his clayey, useless, conservative feet, into a real, live, practical man, and set him at *work too.*

And I can tell you, it has been no small job, to convert that *splendid inertility,* or useless splendor, into a *protective* government.

Lincoln is such a long man, and I've had to tell him so many stories to keep him in good spirits, while I *soft-soaped* him, to clean him, for I found him pretty dirty, I can tell you — especially behind his ears. I guess that's the reason he's been so hard of hearing of late ! * But I've got most through using this liey soap — the hard soap will answer my present purpose, or where I've got him to, and I like it much better; he has a better scent now.

I tell you, I had all this to do for father Abraham, before I could get him to mind *me,* and do as I told him to do !

Another thing, he's so cautious I've had to run my emancipation and government car, too, *clean through* from Washington to Chicago, or he would n't believe me, I could put it through, until he had seen it done !

But I think he can see his way now, for he's *breaking up* there at Washington as fast as he can, with more than 1,000,000 of soldiers at work, helping him. And I guess when he undertakes to break up our government 't will be done — even quicker than we can move the valuables, and get *well settled* in our new home out West.

Then I've had to tell of so many sights I've seen on our way. How we stopped one year in the limey soil of Ohio, just long enough to see that a limey soil would n't do to build our new temple on. 'T would do well enough to build a brick one of, like our old one. But we want a better one than that — built of *free stone granite,* found only in the Mt. Pleasant regions of the West — where we must build our temple superior to Solomon's — in the centre square of our New Jerusalem of Old Columbia, which is bounded, north, by the will of

---

* This was written while the country was calling in vain upon him to eman·cipate.

God, south, by the purposes of God, east, by the decrees of God, and west, by our deserts. And I warn you, *New Columbia !* that you toe the mark of justice, lest your deserts shoot you dead, in this hollow square, as Young America's did ! !

I've had to build this temple, too, and put the ark of the testimony in the Shekinah, and draw it all the way from Washington on a cart, *my own self*—and I run, too, fast, by Uzzah field, lest his hands should follow his eyes and try to stop me from getting to my calves at home, *so quick.*

I've had to build the dome, and make a new flag for it, too; the old staff will do to hang it on. I had to put in the sun and moon in the place of the stripes, for we have no more fools, in our family, to whip. And besides, our children are of age, and they can govern and take care of themselves. God governs the whole family, wife, children, servants and all, and no one is wronged or trode upon, or abused, not even an infant son or daughter. The *rights of all* are respected by the united government of a *Christian pair.*

In short, I've had to engineer *two trains*, clear through to their terminus. The personified, Calvin, I've had to escort to his tomb in Shelburne, Mass., and the personified, Christ, I've escorted to his throne in the new temple, at the New Jerusalem of Old Columbia.

And this cosmoplastic work has cost me thirty-three and a half days of hard work, I can tell you—for my engineer, the *"lightning express,"* goes quick through what he undertakes to do.

I have already got one Uncle Tom's Cabin full of material ready for copying for the press, and I do n't know how many more cabins I shall fill, before I get through.

I've got many valuable receipts in it, infallible ones too, to cure the most inveterate cases, such as crying babies, insanity, sin, drunkenness, licentiousness, and all other demoniacal possessions. I do not mean to say, that insanity is a sin, but I do say, sin is insanity. And you'll see when you read my book, what a sight better government we'll have, when we, women, get back into our good old places, where *God* put us, in rank and file with our husbands, instead of being separated, as Calvinistic influences do, from what God hath joined together. If

't want for this plaguey old Calvinism, our seats would not have been
vacant in our legislative halls, and in our Congress sessions, and our
female power, *joined with* the male power, would have saved our government from corruption. For men are nothing but boors and tyrants
without woman to tame their lion natures into a *protective* instead of an
oppressive power. I assure you, no man will run on our ticket, who aint
woman's friend in our new republic. We shall pick out the wise
Solomons at our caucusses, who do n't confine their protection to one
woman. Mrs. Packard's vote goes in for the "*woman-lover*" president,
mind you! No office at all for the "*woman-hater*," except that of
fourth corporal of the woman's rights regiment, but women do n't fight,
mind you!

And I've had to settle *the harsh* between me and Dr. McFarland,
and put him in his "own place," too. And I've had to tell how he's
been sick, and how I doctored him. But I shant tell you the result,
for whether he's "dead to sin" or "alive to righteousness," he must
report himself, by his *own actions*. I shant venture to prophesy, lest
I share Seward's fate. But I have prophecies in the last volume; for
I've run the emancipation car beyond the settlements of the continent,
into the unexplored territory on the Pacific bank.

And I've had to praise his wife, too, because she's such a good
woman, and is so kind to the patients, especially the *sick* ones.

And I've had to whip the Trustees for *falsely imprisoning* me here
three years, and tell on them, too, to Uncle Sam.

And I've got a long speech to report from Gen. George Washington, from the upper regions, to his countrymen, telling them just what
to do to get out of their troubles.

And I've to tell you how I've trained my five sons to be the states-
men and orators of their country; and how I've trained my model
daughter — a second edition of "Eva," revised, improved and corrected
— to be a model wife and housekeeper, and a *model mother*.

And I've told you of our model farmer Jones, of this hospital — of
Haslet and Comstock, the Abraham and Lot of the Sodom of America
— of the theology of Parks — of the star of the Beech — of Spring on
the car, as our fourth corporal of the anti-slavery regiment — of the

Greeley and Cheever lions—of the engineer, McClellan—of the phrenologist, Fowler—of Elliot, the auctioneer who knocked off my bedstead and chairs to the two and three cent. bidders on Shelburne hills—of Dr. Duncan, who *can dun*, but dont, because Shelburne folks wont give him, nor their minister, a chance to—of Dr. Packard, who packed such a load of infamy to his grave with him, because he became a Universalist and a Spiritualist, in his old age—of our generous cousin Ophelia, and her brimming ladle of flowing sweet—of my husband's treacherous sister Sybil, who, after having helped her brother to make his children orphans, now wants me and my orphans to *thank her* for taking care of them, *for me !* Look out for *the* matron of Young America's orphan asylums ! ! Not New Columbia's charity institutions— of my kind sister Mary, wife of my brother Samuel, who has longed to express her sympathy for me, but *dares not*, for fear of her husband's and his father's mandates to the contrary—of my model step-mother, who, like the British Queen, longs to extend succor to her *persecuted* step-daughter, but is prevented by the parliament, her husband, from doing so—of Tiffany, the magnanimous landlord—of Jenet Warner, the magdalen—of Betsey, the model servant girl—of Mr. Packard's cousin, Sophia Porter Smith, Calvin sycophant or parasite —of cousin Bethiah Nichols, a jealous spy—of Hon. Gerritt Smith, the cedar of Lebanon— of Dr. Sylvester, the dentist—of Angeline, the adopted sister—of the modern king David, the woman-lover—of cousin Laura, the woman's rights wife—of the "pack of wolves," visitors—of John Clary, my teacher—of Gordon Hall, my pupil—of Brown, the Uzzahish trustee—of Club, the trustee who clubs the women to keep them under proper subjection to the "lords of creation" —of Mr. and Mrs. J. C. Coe, model partners and model cooks—of the Eagle Bell, the asylum belle—of Antonio, the model porter—of Mr. Carter, the model attendant—of Persis Hansen Joslyn, the importunate widow—of Baker, the love-letter writer—of Hasselton, the banker—of Dr. Pettigue, the renter—of Rev. Samuel Ware, my Calvinistic father, the defender of *total* depravity—of Dr. Sturtevant, our chaplain—of my sainted mother—of Austin Ware, my kind, but halting brother—of Mrs. Waldo, our man-fearing matron—of Fanny

Arms, my schoolmate — of my accomplished dancing master, farmer Jones, and my first promenade lesson — of Woodman, merchant of Jacksonville — of Gen. Fremont, the freedom-loving freeman — and of the "*natural woman*," the natural writer of natural scenes — of family scenes — of hospital scenes, boat scenes, car scenes, depot scenes, hotel scenes.

And I've got many more things, which I can't begin to mention in my introduction, without making the portico larger than the house! or rather without making the introduction longer than the first volume of my book. For I can't afford to give you much, if any, of the solid part of the book, in this volume; because I'm now a pauper, and the book itself, is so heavy with thoughts, that the drapery hardly conceals them; some are even in a state of shameless nudity; for I have n't got a cent to my name, and do n't expect to have, until the public pay for my first volume. I've had to borrow all the paper to write upon, from my kind and accommodating attendants, Miss Martha Mills, Miss Mattie Stephens, Miss Mary Bailey and Miss Adelaide Trion, and our doctors — Drs. Tenny and McFarland. And I've got to give it to the public in its *pauper dress*, for I can't afford to offer drapery instead of thoughts; for you know I'm imprisoned on the charge of *thinking*, and if I do n't prove the charge to be a true one, Uncle Sam may have to pay for my *false imprisonment!* And I should n't like to borrow money enough of Dr. McFarland, to pay for anything but naked thoughts, for fear my hand note could n't indorse a great sum. However, my right hand has done a *great deal*, for the interest of Uncle Sam, for the last thirty-three and a half days, and I have n't got quite through yet. I fear I shall have to give my country forty days work, save one, before I've whipped her enough to punish her, for being afraid to *do right*, even after God has promised to protect her, if she will. But if Judas continues to carry the *treasury bag*, I shall run a poor chance of getting money of him, to pay for my voluntary services, as a volunteer soldier. Its been no small undertaking, I can assure you, for *me*, to emancipate all the slaves alone! But I have given them all their freedom, without sending them through death and hell to get it, either — as my husband did me, and as Lincoln *proposes* to colonize, to

Central America. I've had to report the Central America depot, from personal observation made within the last three years I've spent there, myself.

And I, for one, speak for the whole class of slaves, and petition, that instead of depriving our Calvinistic husbands of the services of their married slaves, or the slaveholders South, of the services of their slaves, that we be *protected in the homes* Providence has placed us in, until God's providence emancipates us from the relation of slave to our fellows.

'T is *freedom*, or *natural liberty* that we want, and it is all we ask of our country to bestow upon us; but emancipation we ask of God, as his prerogative alone, to bestow. We ask our government for our *freedom to do right*, where God has placed us, and protection from the abuse of our inalienable rights. My husband will not consent to the government divorcing me, *against his consent* — neither will the Southerners consent to have their domestic institution trampled upon, without *their* consent.

God has a right to emancipate the slaves, with or without the slaveholders' consent. But God has not delegated this right to us.

One sinner has no right to punish another sinner. "Vengeance is my right" alone, says God.

The slaves most needing emancipation in America, are the slaves of lust and sin, from the only slaveholder in the universe, Satan, himself. Kill Satan, or Calvinism, and bury them together in one and the *same grave*, which they have dug for the republic, and then we will have one universal jubilee on the continent which Columbus — not Americus Vespucius — discovered.

In short, if you do n't believe my book is *The Book* of the present age, it is only because you do n't know what *smart things* it contains, as well as I do; and the only way you can see I do n't lie about it, is, to buy it, and read it for yourselves!

If we do n't think alike about it, then, it's only because we differ in opinion on the same subject! But I shan't vote to have you put into an Insane Asylum, if you do n't *think* as I do. For I fear I should be hung as a traitor to our constitution, by and by, if I should *imprison you for opinion's sake*.

Father Abraham, have n't I a *right*, under your free government, to think as I please?

Won't you take care of that conspiracy of forty, headed by my husband, and see that they do n't imprison another of your best subjects, as they have me, just for thinking as I pleased; and pleasing to be just as kind and charitable to every body else, as Christ was?

I do n't want another sister in America, to suffer as much as I have, for *conscience sake;* when *God* says we have a right to judge *for ourselves*, what is right for us to do.

And I think it is right for me, to train up *my own children*, instead of letting Calvin, my husband, do it all alone, in his batchelor-hall style.

I 'm afraid my sons won't learn of him, how to fold their napkins right, when they sit at your Congress festivals!!

I have so set my heart upon keeping the next Christmas festival at home with my children, that, unless my "hand-car" returns with orders enough for books, to pay the cost of its outfit, and enough more to fire up my big engine, to steam on my "emancipation-car," and have enough left to pay my fare home to Manteno, on the cars, I shan't offer my country my second volume. I 'll give it to sister Victoria first!

My county must bear in mind that this book is written for *its profits*, the "Prophets of Baal." And you see I cannot get my share of these profits, unless you help me slay them.

And perhaps Victoria has n't any Baals in her kingdom, to speculate upon — and if she has, her Parliament, or her Lancaster operatives will need all their profits, to prevent the bankruptcy of her kingdom.

I intend our American kingdom — "the kingdom of Heaven" — shall stand on the immovable foundation of eternal truth and justice. On this rock we shall take our stand, and from it, wield the sword of eternal justice, fearless of consequences to ourselves, or all others. For 't is with God we stand, and with God we fall. For God and our country's interests are eternally identified.

JACKSONVILLE, OCTOBER, 1862.

BIRTH OF MY BOOK.

HAVING concluded to publish a statement of facts as they exist, and, after looking at the mighty array of facts, which cluster around this complex "family rebellion," I felt almost startled at the size of the volume it would take to give a just and adequate delineation of them; and, as I commenced with the prospect of printing only a small tract, since I am a penniless pauper, is it not presumption to extend the statement much beyond its original dimensions? Yes, I fear it is. Still, it is against my principle to half do anything. "What is worth doing at all, is worth doing well," and thorough.

And, does not the magnitude of the results justify, yea, even demand the publication of a volume large enough to contain all the facts necessary to elucidate the momentous principles involved in the just settlement of this rebellion? My understanding, heart, and conscience, all combine in an affirmative answer to the question.

Therefore I feel again called upon to put into practical use, my long standing principle, that it is always both wise and politic to do right while under the superintending Providence of a just God. Yes, I will "cast my bread upon the waters," trusting, I may find it again after "many days" of waiting for it.

Possibly the sale of the volume may meet all the expenses attending its publication, and Dr. McFarland's purse and patience may be equal to the exigencies of the case.*

O, the relief my full heart feels in coming to this conclusion. I feel now that I have sea-room, where I can navigate my boat, fearless of the shoals and quicksands and harbors of a circumscribed coasting limit. Trusting to the inspirations of the Almighty to guide my pen in making it a truthful medium of *his truth* — the truth of providential events, — I go forward and assume the office of God's scribe, as recorder of his revealed will to men, as indicated *by facts* as they exist.

---

* Dr. McFarland did not keep his promise to lend me money to publish my book; but, on the contrary, tried to prevent its publication. May God forgive him for his treason against me.

2

MY PASSPORT.

THE following statement was presented to the Trustees of the Jacksonville Insane Asylum, September meeting, 1862, through the kindness of Dr. McFarland. It being a self-evident truth that my cause had met with favor on the part of the trustees, Dr. McFarland, with generous magnanimity of purpose, suggested of his own free will to go with me before the legislature, and let me there plead my own case if I chose.

Seeing his noble, manly heart had been moved to espouse the cause of the defenseless, I ventured to propose the publication of my statement, in a handbill form, or that of a small tract, to be circulated among my friends, as a means of procuring their aid and sympathy in my behalf. Dr. McFarland most promptly and heartily acceded to my proposal, and also generously offered to pay the printer himself, depending upon me to refund the money at my convenience.

At his suggestion I commenced to prepare it for the press immediately. But, to my surprise, the subject so opened before my mind, that I could not find a stopping place until my papers had accumulated to the size of a large volume. He then suggested that I send out the first volume under its present auspices.

The statement is verbatim as it was presented to the trustees. The result is contained in the succeeding correspondence with Mrs. Chapman, who is confined by her friends here on the charge of insanity, based on her embracing Swedenborgian views, while her friends remain Presbyterians. She occupies a separate ward from me, and Dr. Tenny is our mail-carrier.

STATEMENT BEFORE THE TRUSTEES.

CALVINISM AND CHRISTIANITY COMPARED.

Gentlemen : — I am accused of teaching my children doctrines ruinous in their tendency, and such as alienate them from their father.

I reply, that my teachings and practice both, are ruinous to Satan's cause, and do alienate my children from satanic influences. *I* teach Christianity; my *husband* teaches Calvinism. They are antagonistic systems, and uphold antagonistic authorities.

Christianity upholds God's authority. Calvinism, the devil's authority.

Calvinism befriends slavery. Christianity befriends liberty.

The kingdom of Christ and the kingdom of Satan can no longer exist in one and the same family or government. The time has come when the tares and the wheat must be separated; for the harvest of the world is fully ripe.

I am gathering the wheat, the fruits of Christianity, into God's granary. My husband is gathering the tares, the fruits of Calvinism, and binding them in bundles to be burned.

He is a consistent Calvinist. I am a consistent Christian.

Calvin was a bigot — an intolerant despot — a murderer. Christ was a kind, liberal, charitable and tolerant friend and protector to all, and the Saviour of all.

Calvin trespassed upon the inalienable rights of others. Christ protected the rights of all.

Calvin hated with a deadly hate his christian brother. Christ loved with saving power his enemies.

Calvinism is treason to God's government. Christianity is loyalty to God's government.

Calvinistic marriage requires the subjection of woman. Christian marriage requires the protection of woman.

Christ's teachings, and Calvin's, were antagonistic.

Christ taught there is but one God. Calvin taught there are three Gods.

Christ taught that he was the Son of God. Calvin taught that he was God, himself.

Christ taught that the Son could not be as old as his Father. Calvin taught that they could be of the same age.

Christ taught that he was a subordinate being, subject to God's authority, and that he acted with delegated power as the world's Saviour, and that when this end was fully achieved, he should deliver up his delegated authority to his Father, and he himself, be subject to him, and God would then be "all and in all." Calvin taught that he was God himself, and acted by his own self-derived authority.

Christ taught that God was the Father of all the human family, and, as such, purposes and designs the best good of all his children; and he taught that he had Omnipotent power to carry out and accomplish all the benevolent purposes of his fatherly nature. Calvin taught that the largest part of the human family were the children of the devil, and that he had Omnipotent power to *thwart* God's purposes concerning such, and could ensure to them eternal destruction in spite of God's inten tion and purpose to redeem the *whole* of the human family from destruction.

Christ taught that every sin would receive its just punishment — that the law of justice was inexorable — that the only way to escape punishment was to escape the *cause* of punishment. Calvin taught that the favorites in God's family would be exonerated from this law, simply because they believed that Christ died for sinners.

Christ taught that punishment would continue so long as transgression continued, that whenever repentance took place, pardon ensued; and that all would sometime repent, because he had purposed to *save all* in *this way alone;* and he taught that death and hell would finally be destroyed, and of course, if the effect ceased, the *cause* must have ceased. Calvin taught that the greater part of God's family would transcend God's ability to discipline into subjugation to his authority and obedience to his commands; and that failing in his ability so to do, he was determined to show his power over them by keeping them in endless, hopeless torment, and thus, fiend-like, manifest his despotic authority by torturing forever his helpless victims.

Calvin taught that the day of probation terminated with the death of our natural bodies. Christ taught that there were no limits to God's mercy, that he was unchangeable, "the same yesterday, to-day, and forever" — therefore, repentance will always remain a condition of pardon — that free-agency is an indispensable law of our moral nature, over which the death of our natural body has no influence — that this

natural law of our *physical* being has no more influence or control over the laws of our *moral* nature than the natural law of eating or sleeping has over them — or, that putting off our natural body has no more power to change the laws of our moral nature than a change of clothing has to change the character.

Christ taught that our natures are holy — that all their God-given instincts and laws, are but a type of his own nature which we cannot violate with impunity — that to disregard *nature's* claim, is to disregard *God's* claims. And he has shown us what these claims are, by living a natural life himself, on earth, for our example. He has shown us that sin consists in violating the laws of our God-given nature — thus depraving, or perverting it, from its original tendencies; that he came to restore human nature from its present, perverted condition, to its original, natural state of innocence. Calvin taught that our natures are sinful, that to live a natural life, is to live a sinful life. He taught that human nature is our worst foe, which we must conquer into subjection to his perverted standard of faith and practice, or be lost eternally.

Christ taught that to be baptized we must go down into the water and come up out of the water, as he did. Calvin taught that to be baptized we must stand up in a house and be sprinkled.

Christ taught that to feel right we must first *do* right. Calvin taught that to do right we must first *feel* right.

Christ taught us to "overcome evil with good." Calvin taught us to overcome evil with evil — that the first step towards becoming better, was to believe you were very bad, and if you are too honest to say you were bad when you felt that you were not, it was the darkest sign of guilt — so that the upright, sincere soul felt driven to become bad, so that he could make an *honest* confession of his guilt in order to secure the confidence of his christian brethren that he was converted.

Christ taught that to clothe ourselves with his righteousness, was to do like him, be like him, by doing right, in everything. Calvin taught that to clothe ourselves with Christ's righteousness, was to act contrary to the dictates of human nature and utterly repudiate obedience as a meritorious act, or as a reason why we should be acquitted and justified in God's sight, and depend wholly upon the merits of Christ, entirely independent of our own ; or, in other words, to continue in an unnatural state, depending upon a sovereign act of God to appropriate the vicarious sufferings of Christ for our benefit, independent of our accountability.

Calvin taught that the elect were all that would or could be saved, and that these were God's children, and all others the devil's children. Christ taught that all were God's dear children — that all had good and

evil in them, but that all the evil in them he came to destroy. And that ior this purpose, he had elected some of his children and capacitated them by peculiar sufferings and trials to be co-workers with him for the good of the many. As if a father should bestow peculiar advantages upon one child, that he might be fitted to be the educator of his other children. This is "the economy of grace."

I believe that with these, his educated company of sanctified ones, who have come out of great tribulation, such as he endured on earth, he will make such assaults upon Satan's kingdom as will ensure its entire overthrow and destruction.

I believe that this reign of Christ on the earth, with his elect co-workers, is about to be inaugurated; and that these troublous times are only the day of preparation for a better state than has ever been experienced on earth. The clouds which precede this bright, millenial day, will soon be dispersed by the Sun of Righteousness; and that a kingdom is about to be established, which shall never be destroyed.

Then will the great work of redeeming a lost world commence, with accelerated power and efficiency.

Christ, with his chosen band of purified ones, will then make *practical* the beneficent, self-sacrificing principles of his unselfish nature, so that no inveterate foe to his government and reign—not even the stoutest Calvinist—will be able then to resist, effectually, any one of his benevolent plans to save the whole class of Calvinists from endless torment, by leading them to bow to his sceptre, and become kind and tolerant toward others, as Christ and his followers are toward them.

I believe that all who have died unsanctified, will live again on the earth, where their surroundings will be so favorable, that they will be able to live natural lives, and, in this manner, take the *first step* to a higher spiritual life. For God says, with no exception, "first the natural, then the spiritual." And the poor deluded Calvinist, who has been led to despise nature, will not be found to have committed a sin too great for his benevolent Sovereign to pardon, on the ground of late repentance.

I believe that some incorrigible Calvinists may compel God to punish them one thousand years in what, *to them*, is endless torment, before they will be willing to renounce Calvin's creed, and adopt Christ's creed —"to do unto others as they would wish to be done by"—in its stead.

But since no man ever lived more than one thousand years in one body on earth, so, I think, one thousand years of punishment will be as long time as will be necessary to subdue the most *inveterate Calvinist*.

The sum of my practical theology is contained in the following stanza:

> " With cheerful feet thy path of duty run,
> God nothing does, nor *suffers* to be done,
> But what thou wouldst thyself, couldst thou but see
> Through all events of things as well as he."

REFLECTIONS.

1. This impious, Calvinistic attempt to *chain my thoughts*, by calling me " insane," for opinion's sake, and imprisoning me on this account, is a *crime* against the constitution of this free government, and also a crime against civilization and human progress. For who will dare to be true to the inspirations of the divinity within them, if the pioneers of truth are thus liable to lose their personal liberty for life, for so doing?

2. The law by which I am imprisoned, which entirely deprives a married wóman of the primeval law of heaven—the *right of self-defense*—is a Calvinistic law, since it conflicts with the gospel—the golden rule.

3. This notorious family rebellion, is the legitimate fruit of the Calvinistic law of marriage, which enslaves the wife. And the only cure for it is, legal, constitutional emancipation, based upon the principles of God's government, which demand *liberty to all.*

4. This kidnapping intelligent moral agents of their accountability, is the climax of all human wrongs, to which Calvinism gravitates; for this impious attempt to place the divinity within me, a spiritual woman—a "temple of the Holy Ghost"—upon a level with the brutes, is "blasphemy against the Holy Ghost." For, if calling Christ, the son of man, " mad" or insane, because he uttered opinions which his cotemporaries could not understand, was blaspheming him, as he said it was, it is "blasphemy against the Holy Ghost" so to treat a spiritual woman; inasmuch as she is a more spiritual being, and, therefore, more sensitive to abuses of her spiritual nature; and, since her position in society renders her a more weak, defenseless being than a man, therefore it is a much more aggravated offense to kidnap a woman's accountability than a man's.

Gentlemen, Trustees of this Institution, I, as your best friend, advise you to follow the dictates of your individual consciences, God's secretary within you, in performing the ₊part Providence has assigned you to perform in this great drama; *for, as is my fate, so will be that of my country.*

A REQUEST.

Gentlemen, I claim ability to defend every sentiment herein advanced by sound argument, and I pledge myself ready now to do so, either in an extemporaneous defense, or a written discussion. And I will engage to write a volume in their defense and elucidation, and have it ready for publication at your next meeting, if you will be so kind as to furnish me with paper to write it upon.

It would be the greatest luxury to me, to thus be able to improve this opportunity, afforded by my prison life, to advance the cause of truth and righteousness on earth, so that when called to give an account of my earthly stewardship, it may appear, that while *numbered* with the incapacitated, useless members of society, I did what I could for the cause most dear to my heart.

Another favor I ask of you is, to furnish me with a key or a pass, so that I can enjoy the privileges of the other patients. in riding out. I cannot do so without, since I should violate my conscience, by telling a lie, to return to the ward a voluntary prisoner. But with a key or a pass I could do so, since I should then be virtually my own keeper. I will engage to use the key for no purpose, except what Dr. McFarland specifies, and I will engage to deliver up my key to him whenever he thinks I abuse my liberty. I cannot, even now, return to my ward again, without the help of his porters to put me back.

Dr. McFarland, please to accept my most grateful thanks for permitting me this privilege of presenting some of my most radical views of religious truth, before the trustees.

I now ask you, if you have any objection to my exposing the sophistry of my husband's demand upon this institution to perpetuate my imprisonment, on the plea that the good of his children requires it? I think I can do it in no better way than by reading this manuscript, which I prepared with the intention of reading to you alone. But since no such opportunity has offered itself, I will read it now, with your permission. It is written upon the leaves of our ward Bible, which some patient tore out and left upon my table; and, as I have no paper, I appropriated them to this use.

SOPHISTRY EXPOSED.

You say, Dr. McFarland, that my abuses must be balanced by my children's abuses.

Now I wish to inquire, can one abuse be balanced or corrected by inflicting another abuse? Can my husband be justified in his abuse of me, by the plea that the good of the children demands it?

Suppose I had abused them, (which thing I never did, thank God!) is he therefore justified in abusing me? Has he a right to cure an evil by inflicting an evil? Again, who made him my overseer? Did God delegate my parental authority to his guardianship? Am I responsible to *him* for the use I make of my maternal rights? Did he bestow them? Has he authority bestowed upon him to take them away, or to interfere with their lawful exercise?

Has he a right to assume that my teachings are ruinous in their tendency? Have I not a right to teach them what I *think* is God's revealed will, or must I yield my own convictions of truth and duty to his dictation? Would he be willing that I should assume this authority over him, or, in other words, is he doing by me as he would wish to be done by?

How would you, Dr. McFarland, receive such a demand from me, as you seem bound to respect from him? Suppose I should say to you: Dr. McFarland, I conscientiously believe that the legitimate tendency of the Calvinistic creed is to make hard, unfeeling, bigoted, cruel, tyrannical characters, like himself; and now, out of regard to these helpless children's interests, I demand that you take Mr. Packard from his position in society, his family, and from all his constitutional rights as an American citizen, and imprison him in this Insane Asylum, for life, or until I can remove his children out of the reach of his influence. How would you receive such a demand from me, the mother of the children, whose interest in their welfare is as deep, at least, as their father's? Would you not regard it as an *insane* request, and would you not employ it as a *proof* that I was a fit subject for the Insane Asylum?

Now how can you listen to this same demand, involving precisely the same principle, and urge it as a reason to justify you in perpetuating *my* imprisonment, based on the same principle?

Again, for illustration, suppose a male and female teacher were employed by the trustees of an academy, and were intrusted by them with equal rights and privileges; with especial instructions that they should teach Astronomy to their pupils, according to their respective systems, viz.: the male teacher the Ptolemaic, and the female the Copernican; and suppose, in process of time, that the female teacher, by her fidelity and kindness, was found to be gaining in influence over the minds and hearts of the pupils; while the male teacher, by his neglect and hardness, was losing his influence correspondingly; and suppose the class of Copernicans was increasing over the Ptolemaic believers, so that at length the Ptolemaic had not one left to believe its system. And sup

pose the male teacher, chagrined and crest-fallen by his position, at being eclipsed and outshone by a *woman's* virtues and corresponding success, should attempt to remedy this state of things by ejecting his female partner *by force* from the school-room, upon his own responsibility, and placing her in a prison on the false charge of insanity, supported by no proofs but *lies* of his own malicious invention ; and suppose he should attempt to quiet his own conscience, and that of her keeper, by assuming that the good of the pupils demanded this course.

Well, suppose the pupils, mourning the loss of their beloved and faithful teacher, and knowing how she had been misrepresented, should desire to expose him, in order to defend their abused teacher, but could not, by his power over them to keep them from doing so. This his treatment of his female partner, so alienated them from him that he had no hold upon their affections ; and all this alienation of feeling he laid to the female influence, when due wholly to his own actions, not hers.

And suppose the appeals of the injured teacher to her keeper for help, on the ground of her innocence, were met by the response, that as an offset to her abuse she must remember that the good of the pupils required that the male teacher's wishes be carried out respecting her, for she was alienating the heart of the pupils from their male teacher, and from his system of astronomy ! ! !

Now, what think you the trustees will say, when they come to look into this business ? Will they not inquire by whose authority he has revolutionized their school ? Would they not say, " You have gone entirely out of your province and trespassed most egregiously upon our authority, and have proved yourself a traitor of the basest kind to our government and institution ? You justly merit, by your conduct, not only expulsion from your office, but also disgrace and imprisonment, for this malicious defamation of insanity which you have put upon our best teacher, to carry out your own base purpose, of supplanting her well-earned and well-deserved influence, which she employed only for their best good. Your purpose is exposed, and your doom is sealed. And your accomplice, the prison keeper, deserves to share your fate, for his heartless, unfeeling response to the appeals of injured, helpless innocence ! ! "

Here is a slip which I cut from a speech in a paper, containing a sentiment which, if true, proves my husband to have not only committed treason against God's government, in treating me as an insane person, but also proves him to be a traitor to our government and constitution :

" We are a free people, and every man living under this government, has the right to form his own opinions, and having formed them, he has the right to express his individual opinions wherever he may think proper ; and whoever seeks to imprison him because he does that, is a traitor to that flag and the cause which it represents."

And to show that he, and all my persecutors, are exposed to receive a traitor's doom, I will state two facts, viz. :

A gentleman in Jacksonville, after having become personally acquainted with me, remarked to another : "That man who will call Mrs. Packard an insane person, is not fit to live." Another fact : One of the most intelligent of the employees here, and who has had ample opportunity for knowing whereof she affirms, remarked to me a few days since, "Mrs. Packard, I can assure you, that there is not a single individual in this house who *believes* that you are an insane person, and as for Dr. McFarland, he *knows* you are not, whatever he may choose to *say* upon the subject."

In conclusion, I feel conscience-bound to add, as my own testimony, — the testimony of my feelings, viz. : — that when I consider my husband's real character, as developed in his abuse of me, who have invariably been one of the kindest, truest, and most faithful of Christian wives and mothers, my sanctified nature *instinctively* revolts from him, as from a most loathsome serpent or viper, and I feel like giving utterance to this heavenly inspiration, in the words of Christ to Peter, viz.: "Get thee behind me, Satan, thou art an offense unto me, for thou savorest not the things that be of God, but the things that be of man."

THE CHAPMAN CORRESPONDENCE.

A DAY or two after I had presented the foregoing statement to the Trustees, I sent it to Mrs. Chapman to read for her amusement. The next day, the bearer, Dr. Tenny, brought it back, with the following note, and a blank sheet of paper for me to write my reply upon :

Dear Mrs. Packard :

I have read your "Statement to the Trustees," and am anxious to know what success you had with them in pleading your cause, and if Mr. Packard was present with the trustees when you read your statement.

You have been so brave in fighting your own battles, I do hope it will not be in vain. What is your prospect of liberation since Mr. Packard left ?

Write me a note, and let me know all about it.

Truly your friend,   MARIA CHAPMAN.

MY REPLY.

JACKSONVILLE, SEPT. 8, 1862.

Yes, my dear Mrs. Chapman, Satan did present himself among the "Sons of God," and heard my statement read by me, and also heard many more hard things said by me. Such as, All those evil statements respecting me were lies, and I could prove it ! That he would not allow me the rights of conscience, and Dr. McFarland did, therefore I preferred him for my protector before my husband ! That so long as he did that for me, I should "trust him though he slay me." That my husband had forced me from him, and now no law but brute force could return me to him. That self-defense demanded this course. That I could spend my days here, if it was God's will. That my life might be cut short by my trials, as Mr. Wells' had been. That I intended to follow the dictates of my conscience come what would, for only by so doing could I insure God as my advocate. That justice would

be done me at God's bar, if I failed to secure it at the bar of my country. That Christ would reward them if they befriended me, etc. In short, instead of occupying ten minutes only, as the chairman specified was allotted to me when I entered, they passed two different full votes to have me go on. When I came to where I asked Dr. McFarland if I might be allowed to expose the sophistry of my husband's plea to perpetuate my imprisonment, by reading what I had written upon the Bible leaves, he referred the answer to Mr. Brown, the chairman, and he put it to vote, when several cried out, "Let her go on!" "Let us hear the whole!" I playfully remarked, in view of so generous and cheerful a response, that I "thought the indications betokened that I was in the element where freedom of opinion was tolerated." Mr. Club responded to this remark by saying, "We don't know about letting *women* think as they please, we must look after *them*." Here he was silenced by the noble "woman's rights" Miner, by his remarking, in a very decided tone, "Go on! Mrs. Packard! Go on!"

After thanking friend Miner for his generous advocacy, I proceeded to read on to very attentive eye and ear listeners. In all, I occupied our hour, lacking ten minutes, instead of the ten minutes only, in talking as fast as I could. And you know *I* can say a great many things in that time!

Well, the result which you want to know is this. After having been absent from the room, some ten minutes in the matron's room, adjoining the trustees' room, where I could hear roars and roars of laughter from the trustees, Dr. McFarland came, with a face radiant with smiles, and asked me to go to the trustees and tell them what I wanted to have done.

I went back with him and found them in high spirits. All their sanctimonious gravity had gone — I was now one of them, instead of a culprit under the grace of court! They seemed ready to do anything and everything I asked. Mr. Brown told me himself, he saw it was of no use for me to think of again returning to my husband, and advised me to consult with Dr. McFarland and try to devise some other disposal of myself, and if I was willing, he would advise me to stay here until it was done. I consented to that, and told him I was willing to follow his advice, since I saw he now understood my case and was disposed to befriend me.

I told them I had a place offered me up town where I could go, if they thought best to discharge me thus. They seemed perfectly willing to do so if I preferred that, or they would send me home alone, or, as Mr. Brown suggested, send for my father to come for me. I told him I

had no reason to hope for help from him, for he was a thorough Calvinistic clergyman, and I fully believed that he would rather have me regarded as hopelessly insane, than have it known that I had departed from the faith of my fathers!

He has stood entirely aloof from me in my persecutions, has not even so much as answered my two long, kind and affectionate letters, which I have sent him from this Asylum, nor even sent me one message of love or sympathy in the letter he sent to Dr. McFarland, in reply to my first; but, on the contrary, impiously solicited that the charities of this institution might be extended to his insane daughter, out of pecuniary regard to her afflicted husband and his now dependent children, whom he feared would never outgrow the deleterious influence their mother had exerted over them, since she still retained a most tenacious hold upon their loving hearts! He has volunteered his entire influence in favor of the course my husband has pursued toward me, boldly .declaring that he considered this asylum as the very best place for me in the world, provided no demands were made upon his own or her husband's purses in securing it for a life-long home for his only, but hopelessly insane daughter!

Knowing these facts to exist, I can assure you, Mrs. Chapman, I do not feel much like applying to him a third time for help in delivering me out of my present perplexities, any more than does America like to apply to England for help. I altogether prefer to stand self-reliant and alone, depending upon my own intrinsic character, capacities, qualifications and deserts, for my own support, entirely independent of help from friends, who have thus encouraged my husband in casting me off as an "insane pauper" for life! O, how I should rejoice to let them see I could support not only myself but also my six infant children, entirely independent of them, by my own abilities, in a style fully equal to what they feel that they have supported us hitherto.

And who knows but what Providence is now providing the way for me thus to demonstrate the self-supporting talent and capacities of one whom they are so desirous should be regarded by community as only a hopelessly insane pauper?

Possibly the publication of this statement may serve as a certificate of recommendation to some lucrative post of honor and usefulness, where I can do so. Let us do our duty, and wait, and trust an overruling Providence with the result. I told them also, if they sent me home I should do my duty until sent off and hid in some other prison ; and there I should try to wait patiently as I had here, hoping for deliverance from an overruling Providence.

But they saw the difficulties, which Dr. McFarland and I had ever seen, that I could have no protection secured to me outside of this institution, from falling into my husband's hands, since the law protected him in claiming me anywhere out of here, and no individual would like to assume the responsibility of standing between me and my husband, as protection against him, while in his present standing in society. Seeing the insuperable difficulties to be met in disposing of me, independently of my husband, they felt unprepared to decide upon any course with their present light. Therefore they postponed the matter until the next meeting in December, and I am satisfied and gratified, both. There could not have been a more complete victory. My case is now known to them to be one of persecution for opinion's sake. Not one of them believes me to be an insane person. *They know I am not.*

The heavy gun which Dr. McFarland allowed me to fire at the rotten carcass of Calvinism has done a great work, the result of which is yet to be made manifest.

I told Dr. McFarland that I had loaded my gun so heavily that I feared it might burst the cannon! still, I determined to risk it, and improve my chance lest I should not get another. But it did not burst. They believed me to be a *sane* person.

Yes, Mrs. Chapman, the tide has turned. "Our tacklings are loosed— they could not well strengthen the mast — the lame have taken the prey."

A very sensible woman remarked to me, as I came out of their presence, "I'm pretty sure they found you the smartest of their number." This is the same one who remarked to me, that when the Dr. and I held an argument, "*two hard heads meet.*" I guess, between you and I, they did secretly think that I should be a match for them! I could tell how they felt. We women instinctively see at a glance how the tide is moving.

Dr. McFarland took me down, the *gentleman,* and introduced me in, leaning on his arm. He took me back, the *superintendent,* carrying me in his arms!

I explained to the trustees how I came to need a key or a pass in order to return to the ward — that I felt it to be my duty to protest against my *false imprisonment,* as being both unjust and illegal, and I should feel conscience-bound to seek a legal redress of my wrongs at the bar of my country; and that in doing so, I was obliged to make use of the expression, "I shall never return again, a voluntary prisoner, to my ward." I was in the office, with Dr. Sturtevant as my witness,

when I entered this protest. A porter, with Dr. Tenny's help, carried me back to my ward *that time.*

It was about a year and a half since, and I have not been out of the wards since, except once, and that was when my son, Theophilus, came to see me, and Dr. McFarland invited me down into the parlor to visit with him.

I supposed, when I accepted the invitation, I was to be discharged and leave with him. Dr. McFarland then forced me back. So that, although I have sworn to my own hurt, in that I have cut myself off from many of the privileges of the house by so doing, still, I have not changed my purpose, nor broken my vow—neither shall I *perjure myself,* if I die as a consequence. "He that sweareth to his own hurt and changeth not," is bearing one mark of those who shall dwell in God's temple.

I believe that our confidence in God ought to be so genuine, deep, and unwavering, that we shall dare, fearlessly, to do our duty, and leave results entirely with God. I think, that, by the strict observance of the laws of my physical nature, so far as my present surroundings will admit, I shall be able to preserve my health, unimpaired, until Providence prepares the way for my deliverance.

However that may be, I shall continue to trust God, by *doing right,* and never presume upon any claim to God's protection, by doing what *I think* is wrong.

What others think is my duty, is not my present standard of action; but what *I think* is my duty to do, I shall do, in spite of all the opposition of men and devils combined, to break down my conscience —God's vicegerent in my soul—ever bearing in mind that our just God never requires of us *impossibilities.*

The trustees did not grant either of my requests. But the Dr. says he will let me have paper to write to my children. Many thanks are due him for allowing me this opportunity of *self-defense.* I think he will, now, send my letters, and not intercept the replies.

I tell him he is doing better and better—that I shall claim him among *my sheaves,* to be secured in God's granary!

Mrs. Chapman, "this is the Lord's doing, and it is marvellous in our eyes." He is executing his own plan in emancipating married women from servitude! Let us work as *His* instruments, and *fear nothing.*   Your sympathizing sister,

                                    E. P. W. PACKARD.

P. S.—Good! better!! best!!! Dr. McFarland has consented to let me publish my "Statement," and he has volunteered to stand re-

sponsible to the printer for the pay, trusting to my word to refund the money to him!!! Your paper is spent, as you see. Still I have many, many more things to tell you about our interview, and if we cannot meet and talk them over, I will get the Dr.'s consent to write you further particulars another time. Yours truly,   E. P. W. P.

Mrs. Chapman's reply to the above letter is misplaced, so that I cannot give it to the public. I regret it, for although very short, it was *very good*. The substance of it was, that she should withhold the expression of any opinion upon the subject, lest she, by so doing, interfere with my entire "spiritual freedom." She hoped my own *reason* would ever continue to be the guide of my own actions, unfettered by human dictation. A part of my reply, the answer to the above sentiment, is also among the missing documents. It was, of course, a grateful response to the spiritual freedom she so unquestionably allowed me, as a God-given right. O, that the Mrs. Chapmans were multiplied, in the same ratio as human beings are personified, for the millennium would then have fully dawned upon us!

ANOTHER LETTER TO MRS. CHAPMAN.

JACKSONVILLE, SEPTEMBER 12, 1862.

My Dear Sister Chapman:

You will perhaps like to hear of the compliment which my husband bestowed upon my intelligence, while here. I will tell you. He accompanied Dr. McFarland to the door of my room, and the Dr. very politely asked admittance for his company. I positively declined — utterly refusing his admittance into my room or presence. I told him my *principles* compelled me so to treat him. He stood in my door-way, listening to my talk with the Dr. Seeing my persistent determination to have nothing to do with him, not even so much as to cast a look at him, (although I could see, by reflection, his *white* vest, an even *groom* attraction!) he then extended me a pair of shoes, saying, "Will you, my dear, accept a present from your friend, Mrs. Rugg?"

Not understanding who Mrs. Rugg was, I asked the Dr. who it was to whom I was indebted for the shoes?

Mr. Packard replied, "Mrs. Rugg was Miss Philena Kellogg when you knew her."

Addressing the Dr., I replied, "O! yes, I remember Philena Kellogg, of Shelburne, Mass. She was the little girl who used to help me wait upon the association, in taking care of my little children," etc.

3

My husband then remarked, in a soliloquizing, drawling tone of voice, "Yes — she remembers — !" closing the sentence with the rising inflection of *sadness*.

I instantly caught the arch look of the Dr.'s eye, and seeing that he noticed what a striking compliment my intelligence had received from my husband, I gave utterance to my indignant feelings, in the expression, "Aint I *bright?* I can remember so well, Dr.!"

I told the Dr., afterwards, he might have extended his soliloquy in words like these:—"Yes, there is *one* ray of intelligence left,—possibly my poor insane wife may yet recover her reason, so as to be fit to resume her former position in society, as a moral, accountable agent! May God grant that my great, self-sacrificing efforts for her good may be rewarded in her voluntary surrender of her conscience to her husband, and his bigoted, creed-bound church's dictation! O, God! grant that she may see that it is her own willful spirit that dictates her actions, rather than the Spirit of God within her, as she claims it to be. O, that she might be converted into an automaton, or a parasite, so that *my* will concerning her might be personified within her, and secure as undisputed possession of her inner life as the will of God now seems to have obtained of the temple of her loving and confiding heart."

"No, husband, 't is too late! My case is a hopeless one! My Christianity is incurable; and, in your vain attempts to dethrone God within me, you have forever severed the last link or tie by which you were held in respect by me, as a human being. I now fully believe you to be *not a man*, entitled to my respect on *that* ground, but only a *personified demon*—and as for me, I must treat you only as such. I cannot act the hypocrite, by pretending to respect a being whom my whole nature *abhors*. Yes, husband, you now find that I have hating faculties as well as loving faculties, although you have so often doubted it. Yes, I can hate *evil*, as well as love *good*. But since you never before knew me to hate a human being, it was because I never before found one whom I considered as *totally depraved*, until your own actions developed *you* to be so. Yes, you have illustrated the truth of your favorite doctrine of total depravity, by presenting one living example of its truth to the world, in your own entirely perverted nature. God grant that you find no company! Alone—alone—may you stand as the world's beacon and warning of the infinite hazard one ventures, by daring to despise their God-given natures by trampling its laws and instincts into the dust, through the continuous force of educational influences based on doctrines of devils."

Mrs. Chapman, it is no satisfaction for me to know that there are

others beside myself who *believe* him to be as bad as I *know* him to be. But the fact exists. A little incident took place one morning while he was here, proving this point.

Mrs. Grapes, our sewing room superintendent, came to my room, and, closing the door, said she, "I must tell you something in confidence." Said she, "Mrs. Packard, your husband is not a man — he is an evil spirit. I can see it in his eye. When I meet him in the halls, I feel like going to him, and saying :— You are a bad man, and unless you repent, you will have to go to the bad place, if you do preach to others." Another fact: Miss Mary Salgal, the Dr.'s chambermaid, remarked to another, at the time he officiated at chapel evening prayers, when he first brought me here, after leaving chapel, "I wonder who that was who officiated to-night — he is not a man — he is an evil spirit!"

Several of our spiritual women in the wards remarked to each other, on their return to the wards — "We had an evil spirit to officiate to-night! he is not a human being." This fact Mary Salgal told me of about a year since. Mrs. McFarland told me herself, that she felt an instinctive shrinking from his presence, which she could not account for.

A gentleman in Manteno, Mr. Haslet, a man of most noble, manly developments, once remarked to me, "Mrs. Packard, unless I am very much mistaken, I can see the devil in your husband's eye." I replied, "It is there, and if you knew what I do of him, you could not question it."

One devilish development which he showed while here, was, in his showing me four different letters from four of my children, written to him, but which contained not one word or allusion to mother, any more than as if no such being had ever existed! Of course, this is what I might expect; for had there been any such allusion, I should not have been allowed to see them at all. This is one of his devilish devices to instill into my mind the falsehood, that my children are wholly and entirely lost to me, except as I will make him my medium of communication with them. He will take upon himself to dole out this love to me, just according to his own sovereign pleasure, since a wife has no right to her children's love only so far as he sees fit to bestow it upon her, as a special favor, meriting her thanks to him — the generous almoner or giver of maternal rights, duties and privileges! How often has this generous soul been heard to say to his children, "Yes, you may obey your mother"! About as often as he has tried to get me to express my thanks to him, for letting me have a home in his house for so many long years!!

Mr Devil! I can assure you, you are greatly mistaken in relation to holding my children's love at *your* discretion, for it is an immutable law of God's government, that parents shall receive just the homage and love from their children, which their own characters deserve, as developed in their own individual actions.

So, sir, it is a moral impossibility which you have undertaken to accomplish — that of alienating my children from a mother, whose own conduct claims and demands their entire love and confidence. They, being natural children, cannot be made to hate good and love evil. You have, for three years, had everything your own way in making this experiment, to see if you could not change one of heaven's established, immutable laws; and we will see how you will come out!

Time will test all doubtful questions. And then we shall see who holds these natural children by the strongest cords — whether kindness and faithful love form the strongest cord, or whether abuse, hate and neglect are the strongest.

I am no prophet, if the issue does not establish the fact, that God is stronger than Satan, and, moreover, show how God has omnipotent power to bring good out of evil, by using the very means designed to *overthrow* God's authority, as a most efficient instrumentality in *establishing* that authority on earth. Yes, I risk my character as a prophet on the result of this drama, as showing that the very means Satan has employed, through my husband's agency, to *destroy* my maternal influence, and extinguish the practical influence of my example, will be overruled to *enhance* that influence, and extend the notoriety of my example a hundred fold! Satan doubtless foresaw that his purpose to defeat the influence of *my system of family training*, was one very important *necessity* to the maintenance of his power on earth: for if *this practice* was followed extensively, his subjects must necessarily be greatly diminished. And fearing this result, he devised, by means of his satanic sagacity, this nefarious plot, to make the impression that these indefatigable efforts which Mrs. Packard had put forth to educate her own children in the paths of virtue and piety, resulted in her complete ruin, by causing her to become hopelessly insane for life — fit only for the tenant of a mad house!

Those who were favorably inclined to adopt my system of family training might reflect thus: "Well, if this *is* the inevitable result of training our children in the way they should go, it is better to let them go as they are born, untrained, like the wild ass colts, rather than to make a sacrifice of ourselves to the demon of insanity, in thus attempting to train them."

He, being the father of liars, had become such an adept in his profession, that he trusted to his sagacity in sustaining the defamation with lies, so adroitly fabricated, as to delude many an unwary soul into the belief of this monster lie — that of calling a highly cultivated, intelligent, Christian woman a maniac, without her ever having given one proof of being lost to reason, by doing or saying one unreasonable thing ! !

Well, Mr. Devil ! your sagacity has been defeated by the superior wisdom of God, who will surely cause these lies to return upon your own head, and thereby secure your destruction. And God's own work of grace on me will, by these very means, be made to shine out with increasing splendor and notoriety.

Thus does God let Satan work out his own destruction, while he not only protects and defends his own cause and interests from contamination thereby, but also enhances the splendor of the same by the very means employed for its destruction.

That man who has made such a sinner of his own conscience, as to believe his own lies, is the only one who is fully competent to be employed as the devil's uncompromising agent, in conceiving and acting out a drama based on the malign principles of this.

Well, Mrs. Chapman, have I not spun a long yarn out of my husband's compliment? Can't I do a good business upon a small capital? Fowler says I can, and he of course knows, even better than we do ourselves ! You may expect one more letter by the next mail. So, good bye, for to-day. Your loving sister,

ELIZABETH.

ANOTHER LETTER TO MRS. CHAPMAN.

My Dear Mrs. Chapman :

One thing more I told the trustees, which I tell you in confidence, hoping you will not make use of the illustration before *undeveloped*, minds to my injury, since such might be disposed to regard the simile as a vulgarism or an impropriety. This seemingly indelicate illustration came in, in this manner.

I told them that my father and husband claimed that I must be insane now, *because I was not as I used to be* — that I used to credit their interpretation of the Bible as correct, and as demanding my *entire confidence ;* but that now I discredited them, seeming to have lost confidence in them as my *spiritual guides.*

I acknowledge 't is even so. Still, I claim that this increasing intel-

ligence on my part, which capacitates me to assume the position of a self-reliant, independent thinker, instead of being insanity, an unnatural development of mind, is only a *natural* growth of intellect, and is a natural result of practical godliness. For, as I have uniformly striven to do the will of God, by living a consistent, holy life, (not a sinless life,) the Lord has thus made me "to know of the doctrine"—for he says, "they that *do* his commandments, *shall* know of the doctrine."

I said, that my husband placing me in an Insane Asylum to be cured of this natural development, was like his placing me under the treatment of a cancer doctor to have my breasts removed, insisting upon it that my breasts were cancers, since they were not there when I was a girl ! !

I asked pardon of the trustees for making use of such an illustration, claiming the peculiar aptness of the illustration as my only apology for its seeming indelicacy.

A roar of laughter, accompanied by the expressions, "That's good!"· "'Tis apt !" "To the point !" etc., was the only response !

In confirmation of the above position, I will tell you one thing which I did not tell the trustees. It is a compliment, in a remark by Rev. Mr. Nichols, of Chicago, to Mr. Smith, our Deacon in Manteno, when he exchanged with my husband, a few Sabbaths before he put me here. He said he had known me from a child, and these three things were true of me : "first, he had never seen so amiable a disposed person in his life ; second, he never saw so devoted a Christian ; third, he never saw so useful a person as I had always been."

Another thing I told the trustees was, that I had been most wantonly and unjustly called upon to bear the "reproach of my youth," in that, my husband made a wanton use of the fact of my having been once in an asylum as a reason why I ought to be in one now. And as he had used the fact, he led many to believe that, since I was insane once, it is very probable I am so now.

This fact only serves as an illustration, to show how he maliciously warps facts, so as to make them serve his own base purpose, to destroy my moral influence.

My father very needlessly and unkindly placed me in the Worcester Asylum, Mass., when I was eighteen years old, to cure me of a derangement which followed a severe brain fever, the result of malign medical treatment—that of bleeding me and reducing me with allopathic drugs, when tonics alone were required to sustain the excessive action of the brain, occasioned by an excess of mental and physical effort combined. I remained there five weeks, until the blood had had

time to form again so that I could control my mind. Therefore, I am insane now! although I have never taken a particle of drug-poison since, nor even been sick so as to necessitate him to pay five dollars, doctor's bill, in all my married life, for twenty-one years; but have been uniformly healthy, cheerful, well and happy. And have done all my housework and sewing, for my family of eight, with no hired girl, except one for nine months, in all that time. And I hardly think a more healthy, perfectly sound, robust, elastic constitution than I still have, at forty-six years of age, can be found among American women. And I claim also, that my mind is as comparatively sound as my body is.

Thanks to the reverence I have long felt for *nature* and her laws, my health of body and mind is still unimpaired : although they have both been severely tested by the strongly counteracting influence of a long, cruel and very severe persecution and imprisonment.

I think I might have replied to Mr. Brown's inquiry — "Mrs. Packard, aint you afraid you'll grow *too fast?*"— that he ought to look for a strong and vigorous growth, where he gave me such a rich, luxuriant soil to grow in, as *imprisonment* afforded. I told him, "that I claimed my individuality;" and I think I have a right to grow *as fast* as a life of practical godliness, in doing .or suffering the will of God, *develops me.*

The trustees all manifested a kindly interest in my welfare. I regard them all, now, as my friends; and shall of course try to shield all their past neglect of me under my capacious mantle of charity, which my forgiving spirit instinctively prompts me to extend to the erring, especially when the least indication of gospel repentance is apparent.

I do think they now see the injustice they have done me, to keep me so long unjustly imprisoned. I expect they will discharge me at their next meeting, as a proof of their acknowledgement of the truth. But if they should not, and conclude to violate the dictates of their reason and conscience by treating me as an insane person, judicial blindness will come upon them and they will be left to become consistent Calvinists, and, like my husband, will conscientiously believe this lie, which will ensure to them a place in the bundle which my husband is gathering together to be burned.

But Dr. McFarland I shall claim among my sheaves, since his act of practical repentance, in becoming my protector at last, secures his title to God's forgiveness. Let us pray for them, and may God be their guide as well as ours unto death.

Yours in the best of bonds,

E. P. W. PACKARD.

P. S.   When I asked permission of Dr. McFarland to fire one gun at Calvinism before the trustees, I do n't know but he meant to scare me by telling me that Mr. Brown, the chairman, was a member of the "General Assembly," intimating that he might be a Calvinist! and if so, what might be the effect of this movement on my interests? But, if he thought I could be scared by a Calvinist, he does n't know me as well as I do myself!

But I did n't tell him so, of course.   I simply remarked, Well, if he and the others are consistent Calvinists, of course they will call me an insane person, and then you may be agreed in consigning me to perpetual imprisonment!

So he consented to let me shoot one gun.   I did n't load it near as heavily as I might, had I had more time to shoot in ; but however, I think I hit the mark, and shall risk a heavier charge another time I go hunting!

The fact is, Mrs. Chapman, there is not a consistent Calvinist among them, except "Satan, who presented himself among the sons of God;" for in heart, they all secretly rejoiced to see the rotten carcass of Calvinism thus blown to pieces with the charge of my heavy gun.

O, if I only had a chance, would n't I like to give my mind in full upon the subject!

There is one thing we get, Mrs. Chapman, by being called insane, that but few have, and that is — our "spiritual liberty."   Do n't we? For we cannot be called anything worse than to be called insane, and it is a pity to have the name without the game.

I intend my Presbyterian friends shall see, that I am not so afraid of his bugbear as they thought they could make me.   I am not so afraid of apparitions as some folks, I guess they will find, before this game is played out!   I have not been sent to school three years for nothing, they will soon find out, I guess!   Do n't you?   E. P. W. P.

"SEEING EYE TO EYE."

On the distant hill-top stands the Observatory — the observed of all observing — Christ — "the Model Man.

Each human heart pulsates in sympathy more or less strong, to gain that eminence. At various stand-points on the hillside, are seen the individual, the sects, the tribes, the nations of the earth, all, all moving onward, upward.

At the base stands the conservative, the Presbyterian, the Calvinist, whom no entreaties, no prospective views. can induce to try the ascending slope. Friends urge — enemies deride — but all in vain. Immovable he stands, confident he sees, from his low stand-point, all there is to be seen of the vast landscape of eternal truth spread out before him.

A "Spring" leaps from their ranks and rises one step above his cotemporaries. He reports his views from his new stand-point to his mundanes below him. But no. The spring was unpropitious. "Our confidence in your firmness and inflexibility of purpose is shaken." Spring has lost the confidence of his former friends: but in losing old friends he has found new and untried ones, who gladly extend to him the welcome hand. Upward they all move in company: and as they rise, new and more extended views of the surrounding country break upon their pleased and excited vision.

Again they report to the conservatives at the base — "Nay, verily, we will not heed thy tales of new truths. Our Bibles confidently say, there is nothing new under the sun." "But come and see for yourselves." "No, no. We are satisfied — trouble us not."

Onward and upward the ascending party go, until they behold on the right side, the Methodist creed — on the left, the Baptist creed in view. On they go in a winding course, and they see the Unitarian view. Onward they move to the Universalist stand-point, and they see the Universalist view. Onward they see the Christian view. Again, the Swedenborgian view, the Episcopalian, the Puseyite, and at length, the Catholic position. All and each presenting a distinctly different view of the same landscape below.

The further they ascend the more friends they find in the great human family, all equally intent to get to the Observatory above them all. At length one man from the summit shouts out, " *You are all right !*" The Presbyterian, the Methodist, the Baptist, the Unitarian, the Universalist, the Christian, the Swedenborgian, the Episcopal, the Puseyite, the Catholic, each, and all, from your own stand-point have reported correctly. He ascends to the top of the Observatory and takes the footprints of his Master — he and Christ "see eye to eye," for they see from the same stand-point.

One by one the travelers after holiness or likeness to Christ, arrive at the stand-point upon the pinnacle of the Observatory. All see now, as Christ sees: and all "see eye to eye." Their charity is now Godlike. It embraces all races, all sects, all men : and as they ascended through distinct paths, yet each being true to himself, has safely arrived at his destined goal. But no one can see just as he did; for his angle of vision, his organization, differs from each and all others, and yet he is true to himself—and true to God.

So, can we but start the conservative, we shall at length all see eye to eye. But I fear some will compel us to pull them with a lasso up to a higher stand-point before we can convince them there is one. But let us try chafing them before hanging them; rub their feet — give a start to the circulation, by tempting a retaliatory passion, even, rather than let them become pillars of salt, or die of dyspepsia, for we cannot have an universal jubilee until the last tardy conservative has attained the pinnacle of the Observatory. Oh, Conservative ! For the sake of the world above you, if not for your own sake, be persuaded to try one advance movement. And let not the consummate age of righteousness be longer retarded by your obstinate, inflexible determination never to know any more than you do at present !

Again — from the sunny side of this vast hill, enlightened by the sun of civilization, can be seen the cultivated farm, the verdant stream whose banks are studded with the mill, the factory — and from the peaceful, quiet village stands out in bold relief, the school-house, the academy, the college, the university — and above all, is seen the church-spire, pointing heavenward to the fount and source of all the blessings of cultivated life.

And from the shady side, which the sun of civilization has not yet reached, is seen the unbroken forest, where the wild man roams, hunting his forest prey. And from India's vast plains may be seen the heathen temple, the car of Juggernaut, the Mahommedan paradise, bounded by the Ganges, upon whose banks may be seen the devoted Christian

mother sacrificing the object dearer than her own life, to the crocodile and the floods, to propitiate the favor of her deity.

But as the sun of civilization moves onward in its westward course, leaving the sunny plains of civilization eclipsed by the principles of Calvinism, it is only to chase away the darkness of ignorance by which its Christianity has been hitherto eclipsed. And the civilized mother finds, to her shame and sorrow, that her selfishness has been eclipsed by refinement—while the kind mother's self-sacrificing benevolence has been only eclipsed by her ignorance. Day of judgment! Day of wonders!

Again—on the side of this hill stand the different trees of God's great unbroken forest—each perfect—because true to the respective functions with which God has endowed it. And being true to itself, each perfects its own appropriate fruit—the walnut, the chestnut, the butternut, the hazelnut—all perfect—yet all different; all unlike, yet all right. All good, that have life enough in the nut to sprout another like it: all bad, that have not vitality enough to rise again. But, from whence comes the mouldy, rotten, shriveled nut? From the gnarly, old, decayed, rotten and crumbling trees of Calvinism!

Let the woodman's axe level it, and prepare it for the flames—but let the fair young twigs of *nature's* verdant soil remain, to fill the welcome vacuums, with the fragrant foliage, and spreading boughs, and teeming fruits of the perfected *Christianity of nature.*

So, in God's great family of human trees—the sects, tribes, races, nations of men—each and all, have a shell, and a nut, peculiar to itself. For God has made us to differ. How shall we perfect ourselves? Shall the butternut strive to be a walnut? Shall the chestnut strive to be a hazelnut? No. Be what God has made you to be— a good butternut, a good chestnut. Some like chestnuts best. Some like walnuts best. Be good in your sphere, and you will be sure to find some to like you. But mongrels all reject, for the mongrel is the eunuch of cultivation. It is not a native-born plant; nature perfects her own fruit on a self-reliant base. It is a bad cultivation that makes nature's prodigies. God made man a democrat; society makes him an aristocrat. Let not the aristocracy of the Presbyterian church boast of their being God's workmanship. No! aristocracy is the fruit of Calvinism, not Christianity. It is the true man, the true woman, which God makes. And those only are good men and good women who are *natural*—who bring forth the fruits of righteousness. "He that feareth God, and worketh righteousness, is accepted of him," whether Jew or Gentile, bond or free.

Be a good slave, and try to wait as patiently as you can for your free-

dom, for it is certain *God* will free us before long if the *government* do n't.
Be a good slaveholder, if God's providence has made you one; but
do n't trust to Providencé to be responsible for your continuing to be one ;
for to be a good slaveholder *now*, you must and will emancipate your
slaves forthwith : for God says you must do it, or he will do it for
you. Be a good Catholic, if God has made you a Catholic : and to be
a good Catholic you must not believe that Protestants are all heretics,
for they are not all heretics. It is only the bigoted Calvinist that
is a heretic — a tyrant — a despot. It is the Calvinist alone who re-
flects your image ; or rather, it is you that reflect his image.

Be generous to your impulses. Be a free, independent thinker,
standing on the self-reliant base of a whole true man. Be equally
generous to others. Let them be as true to themselves as you are
to yourself, and all will be harmony and peace.

It is the Christians, the *practical* Christians, who are alike — not the
creeds or sects. In every man behold a brother and a friend — one
endued with equal rights and privileges with yourselves.

Remember, there is a well in every rock. Moses does not well to
be impatient to see the waters of humanity gush out at the first
drill stroke. The drill of perseverance does wonders in tunneling the
rock.

Remember, too, that iron is smelted by the furnace of affliction.
Remember too, that God thought that one Niagara was enough for one
world. But not so with the verdant rill, the babbling brook, the
heavy moving stream, the pond, the lake, the sea. Each has his
own office to fill, and none can fill another's. The foaming cataract is
the world's wonder — but the mountain spring is the world's blessing.

One judgment-day — many days of probation. One revelation —
many revelations. " One Lord, one Faith, one Baptism."

ANALOGY

BETWEEN THE REBELLION IN OUR FAMILY AND IN OUR COUNTRY.

1. WE have been looked upon by outsiders as a most peaceable and happy family. So has our country been regarded, by other nations, as a model government.

2. It has been my pride of character which has kept me back from asserting my rights as a woman, before my husband cast me off. So our pride of country, and love of notoriety and popular esteem, has kept my country back from asserting their rights to be ruled with justice and equality, before we were cast out of the Union.

3. I bore with my husband long after forbearance ceased to be a virtue. So my country has borne with the insolent, intolerant spirit of the South, long after forbearance ceased to be a virtue.

4. My sin has been, in forgiving my husband, regardless of the terms of the gospel — practical repentance. So my country has long forgiven the usurpation and aggression upon the constitutional rights of its citizens, without their repenting of it, or giving any assurance that they will not so continue to do in future.

5. I can never return to my husband without *practical repentance* on his part, because my own self-defense forbids it. We cannot restore the South to our confidence without repentance on their part, because they might cause us another and more fatal rebellion next year, if we did.

6. My husband is the one to repent, for he is the one who has done wrong — not me — for I have never given him the first cause to regard or treat me as an insane person. So the South have rebelled without having had one cause for doing so.

7. I have suffered the most, because I am innocently sensitive to abuse, having never retaliated an injury in my life. But he is speechlessly guilty, for inflicting upon me the most unmerited abuse so long, that he has now become *conscientiously wrong*, in persecuting me. So the North are the greatest sufferers in the spiritual plane, for they are

keenly alive to justice and humanity, and love of country and kindred. But the South have hardened their sensibility by injustice and inhumanity so long, that they feel conscientiously right in persecuting the innocent North without cause.

8.   I have, by my *mildness* and *forbearance* in resisting his ruling my will   indirectly *encouraged him* in his usurpation and wrong doing.   So the North, by their forbearance with the insults of the South, have encouraged them to hope to entirely subdue and conquer the gentle North to their terms.

9.   My husband has found, or is destined to find, that the "wrath of a lamb" is an awfully implacable foe to contend with.   So the South will find that the North mean to defend themselves, and uphold a free government, even at the price of their best blood and ample treasure.

10.   My husband has aimed to remove from me every influence, or source of help or deliverance from imprisonment, except *through him ;* so that I may be driven to sue for pardon for doing right, and beg him to let me train up my own children, on terms of his own dictation — such as yielding up to his entire control my personal identity of being, by consenting not to do, say or *think* only as he shall permit me to do. So the South intends to hold the North, where their interests will compel them to compromise on their own terms, to restore the Union to its former basis.

11.   My husband's persecution of me, whom he solemnly promised, by his marriage vow, to *protect,* has, by this act of perjury, entirely abrogated the marriage obligation on my part, — so that his claims upon me are now only the claims of humanity.   So the South, by this act of high treason against the government, have entirely cast themselves off from any claims to its protection, except the claims of justice.

12.   My husband having robbed me, under the sham refuge of legalized right, of my children, my home, my clothes, my personal liberty, and all my constitutional rights as an American citizen, now asks me if I want them ; — evidently seeking to compel me to thank him for restoring them to me.   So the South, having robbed us of our treasury and our defenses, now seem to desire us to thank them for restoring them, as a condition of being thus admitted again to our Union.

13.   My husband has sought to prejudice my own father against his only daughter ; and he has succeeded in doing so, so far as to lead him to stand entirely aloof from me, during my persecutions, and give his influence in favor of my husband's wickedness towards me.   So the South has so misrepresented the North, to our mother country, as to

lead her not only to stand aloof from us, but decidedly to encourage the South in their rebellion.

14. I intend that my father shall see that his daughter is of age, and capable of assuming a self-reliant position, and of standing, too, independent of her father's patrimony and influence. So the North do n't intend to be beholden, again, to the mother country, for their liberty ; nor is their patronage essential to their life or prosperity.

15. My husband has sworn either to rule or ruin me — and I have determined he shall do neither. The South and North have alike sworn to God and to each other.

16. My husband is prosecuting his rebellion, in stolen or borrowed colors, borrowed from my own popularity, in which his own is reflected. It is so with the South. It is the weight of Northern influence with which they have been associated, which has given them power to injure us as much as they have already done.

17. I have always been my husband's voluntary slave, because 1 could not live with him without. So the North has been the tool of the South, because we could not live with them unless we let them rule us.

18. Since voluntary slavery is the cause of the family rebellion, so voluntary emancipation is the only cure. So the South must emancipate the North from its servitude, and voluntarily consent to be its subject, or companion, or partner, on equal terms, or there can be no reunion.

19. I have truth, justice and forbearance, and God. on my side. He has falsehood, injustice, persecution and Satan, on his side ; and time will decide which is the strongest party. It is so with the North and South.

20. For twenty-one years he has sought "to heal the hurt of the daughter of my people, slightly," and now God has undertaken the case, and he will remove the gangrene, since our vitality depends upon its complete removal from the system. It is so with our country, for their conscience was to be brought under subjection to human dictation, and thus the case had become one of life and death.

21. My husband claims that the wife has no inalienable rights which the husband is bound to respect. So the South claims that a portion of American citizens have no rights which they are bound to respect. The government ought to respect and protect my rights, and those of the slave too.

22. Both rebellions are the result of oppressing the defenseless. Both must be healed by protecting the defenseless, by the destruction of the oppressor's power to oppress. God demands it, and God must be obeyed.

23. My husband believes a lie, and is therefore conscientiously

wrong in his practice of treating me as an insane person, when I am not. He is insanely conscientious, and is thus beyond the reach of moral influence — thus no law but force can move him. So is the South, in relation to the North, believing a lie, and under this delusion are working out their own destruction. Evil slays the wicked, not God. No law but force can move them.

24. I have been under the strictest censorship. So has my country been. I have been three years entirely in the power of my enemies, and no deliverance from any quarter has been offered me, and I have seemed to be utterly uncared for, except by my enemies; no friendly aid has offered me succor. I hope my country will not be in the power of her enemies at all. But I fear she is fast approaching that awful vortex!

25. Having waited in vain for a leader, and finding none, I accepted God as my Leader, and sought my own deliverance by following the dictates of my own conscience — and time, alone, will prove whether I be successful or not. So my country must deliver itself. I am still imprisoned — but I confidently expect the government will deliver me out of the power of my persecutors, because I ask it of them on the ground of truth and justice. May my country present their appeal to the court of heaven, on the same immovable basis, and with as strong a faith of meeting as favorable a response, as I have. For I do believe they will hear my prayer and deliver me, and on this ground God will hear their prayer, and deliver them, for "with what measure ye mete it shall be measured to you again."

26. He persecutes my children, because they want mother and father, both, should be protected in their inalienable rights. The South persecutes the North, because the North wants its own rights, as well as the South has had theirs.

27. He is answerable for our family troubles. The South is responsible for the disasters of the American Republic.

28. I cannot thank him for my inalienable rights, neither can I recover my children, at the price of my identity. So our country cannot destroy themselves, to save the South, nor can they thank them for letting us be a nation!

29. My husband and I have grown apart — he conservative, and I radical — he Calvinistic, and I Christian. So the South and North have grown apart, instead of together — slavery and freedom — oppression and human rights.

30. I have outgrown the Calvinistic law of marriage. Our country has outgrown the Calvinistic side of its constitutional creed. We both want the liberty of the gospel. Calvinistic principles are the cause of

our family rebellion. Slavery, the germ of Calvinism, is the cause of our country's rebellion. It is these Calvinistic spectacles which so dis turb the mental and moral vision.

31. My husband has seceded from one of the best governed families in the world, so far as the maternal influence is concerned. So the South has seceded from one of the best governments in the world, so far as the Northern portion is concerned.

32. Every attempt to appease the insolent South, by a guilty com promise of principle, has always been preceded by a similar attempt, on my part, to prevent an outbreak in our family government, by a compromise of my inalienable rights to his arbitrary, despotic dictation. Thus the family within the government has been the "wheel within the wheel," both revolving on the same axle.

33. Satan seceded first. The South followed hard after! Can Satan and God be united?—Yes. How?—By restoring the original relation, and Satan taking his proper place as subject, and not as sovereign of God's government. Goodness must rule over evil, with love and kindness — and this love and kindness must be based on truth and justice, and truth and justice must be based on fear or force, the soul's lowest crank or handle.

There is a God and a devil in every human soul—in every family —in every government; and God must rule over the devil; for this is an unchangeable law of God's universal government.

Can liberty and freedom be united by agitation? — No. No more than oil and water can, by being shaken together. Can oil and water be united?—Yes. How?—In one way alone, and that is God's way; which is, to put in a third ingredient, for which both have an affinity. The pearlash of emancipation will alone unite them, by forming a new union of soap, or free labor — a much more useful article than washing machines!

CONCLUSION

As is my fate, so will be that of my country. Since our family rebellion has, thus far, been the counterpart of our country's drama, so I infer it may continue to be.

Therefore, it is my most fervent prayer, that my appeal to my country for protection against unmerited abuse, may be most cheerfully and promptly responded to, thereby securing to them a good claim, at the court of heaven, for protection in their time of need. And thus may they know, by their own blissful experience, what the Lord's deliverance, in times of trouble, signifies.

TRANSMIGRATION OF SOULS.

I FULLY believe in this doctrine or truth, because it is a demonstrable fact, that souls do inhabit different bodies, at different periods of their existence, as really as vegetable and animal life exist in different forms or bodies. The oak once existed in the acorn—the butterfly in the chrysalis.

The Archangel was once a female infant—the Seraph once was a human being—the God, Christ, once was a male infant in a cow's manger.

There may be more truth than poetry or fancy in the statement, I have seen in the "Independent" since I have been here, in this Asylum, quoting from an English publication, under the heading of "The Lunacy of Literature," that Mrs. Harriet Beecher Stowe had once been the wife of Cain, and once Voltaire, and many other different personages, existing at various periods, from before the flood, until the present time; and that Henry Ward Beecher was, in one of his bodies, Paul or Peter, I don't remember which, and it is no matter which, so far as the argument is concerned. It also traced the genealogies of many of the distinguished individuals of the present age back to the ante-deluvian age.

So can we all be traced; for there are no *new creations*, since God made the world and peopled it. "There is nothing new under the sun." Matter and mind always existed, although under different forms or bodies. At length, when our bodies become perfected, by this long transplanting process, so as to become entirely regenerated, or spiritualized, as Christ's ascended body was, we shall never die any more, or sink into a state of oblivion or forgetfulness of our past existences, as we now do.

There are many in this Asylum who are living witnesses to this truth. They can remember having lived in different bodies, as distinctly, as I can remember having lived in Massachusetts; and some can even trace themselves back to mother Eve herself. They have been fathers, brothers, sons, as well as mothers, wives, sisters and daughters! Sometimes in exchanging bodies, they have made a change for the better;

and sometimes for the worse, being resurrected to life or death just as their deserts, or the use, or abuse, of the old body designated. I fully believe, yea, even know, this to be the case, from observations made in this Asylum, and from the testimony of my own experience, and that of the Bible. I cannot boast of having had but one trance or vision in all my life, unless my whole life has been a trance or a vision; and that was, when I was eighteen years of age, when my father put me into the insane asylum, at Worcester, Mass., as an insane person for it; and I do believe, his degeneracy as a man, may be distinctly traced back to *that misguided act*, when Beelzebub first triumphed, completely, over the father in him. How long his punishment of *judicial blindness* will continue, God only knows. I was then no more insane than hundreds are here, who are simply spiritually illuminated, and dare to be true to the inspirations of the divinity within them. But these American inquisitions for the persecution of *this trait of Christianity*, have sadly interfered with this *heavenly light*, and have done their utmost to extinguish it from the earth!!

These spiritual gifts, including second sight, "discerning of spirits gifts of prophecy, gifts of healing, the word of wisdom, the word of knowledge, interpretation of tongues," etc., are the *phases of Christianity* which the American government seem fully determined to exterminate, by its insane asylums or inquisitions. It is Christianity, or *vital godliness*, which is so insanely persecuted by our government, as insanity, and punished as a crime, to which the awful penalty of *hopeless imprisonment* is attached, unless they recant and deny the vision!!

O! my God! do remove these scales from our Government's eyes, that they may see, as Saul did, that it is hard for them thus to kick against the pricks! O! may they see that it is Jesus himself, that they are thus persecuting in their nominally insane subjects! And as Saul was converted from the bloody persecutor of the Christians, into their most zealous protector and defender; so may our American Government be speedily converted from these damning heresies, and become the *protector* of Christianity, instead of being, as it now is, *its persecutor!*

There are no governments in the world where vital godliness, or *natural piety* meets such satanic persecution as under the insane laws of our nominally Christian governments! O how often have I sighed for the red man's privileges—*freedom to be natural!*

At no distant day, the purblind world will invoke in its prayers, this holy army of the "Martyrs of Thought" of the nineteenth century,

now in the inquisitions of this nominally free government! "Sacred are these fools—God understandeth them;" and our government ought to protect in them *freedom of thought!* Let it no longer be as it has been—"Come, let us garnish the sepulchre of one immured, because his stupid age could not understand;" and then go forth to stone the seer, on whose tongue lies the noblest secret of the universe for that day!

"Each clear idea that ascendeth the vault of human reason, is a Bethlehem star—be sure a Messiah is born for it on the earth"—a new power is set in motion among men. O! my Government! Protect these powers! *Protect these thinkers!* Let thought be no longer strangled at its birth, from the inquisitorial ignorance of the age which gave it birth."

I have no more doubt but that Shakespere and Washington, and I do n't know how many more of earth's noblest thinkers, have dictated portions of my book, then I have that my own mind is used as their medium of thought. It would be impious in me to boast of having written my book, unaided by the most *superior minds* of the universe. Its contents designate its heavenly origin. And if the pearls of thought it contains, are seized by swine, and trampled under foot, as insanity, let this swinish or devilish race of humanity, be alone responsible, at Heaven's court, for this act of heaven-daring impiety!

"Be not forgetful to entertain strangers, for thereby some have entertained angels unawares." Reject no stranger Thought! Reject no personified Diety in human form! Give Jeremiah, Daniel, Solomon, Judas, Jude, Job, Moses, Esther, Ruth, Sarah, Mary, Martha, Christ, God, all a welcome—for every human form has buried, somewhere beneath its rough exterior, its folded angel wings, waiting to bear its heaven-born, aspiring soul, back to its parent stock—the bosom of its God!

Where is Cromwell, the usurper? Where is Calvin, the persecuting bigot? Where is Packard, the murderer? Where is the subject's loyalty, due to his king, in Cromwell's murderous plot to usurp the kingly honors of Charles I? Where is the brother's love, due to Christian Servetus, in Calvin's roasting him at the stake? Where is the honor due the Christian wife, in Packard's murdering her personal identity? Where are these triune friends personified, in one and the same individual, if not, in the red-headed dragon of the Revelations? And if that great red-headed dragon, is not the *serpent-headed Packard,* of the nineteenth century, his wife do n't know where it is to be found! And if the three murderers—Cromwell, Calvin and Packard—are not

all waiting in Packard's form to be bound with the chains of their own forging, in the bottomless pit of destruction, where are they?

And brother Charles, and brother Servetus, if your martyr spirits have not been personified in your sister Elizabeth's form, for the twenty-one years of her spirit martyrdom, she has endured while under the absolute power of this "great red dragon," I know not where you can be found. But let God himself, with his own hands, place the crown of martyrdom upon the head of that individual, in whom he sees to centre the martyrdom of ages.

LETTER TO MISS DIX.

THE following is a copy of a letter which I wrote to Miss Dix
after her visit to this asylum, where I had several pleasant interviews
with her. I do not know whether it was ever sent; but I do
know I never got a reply; neither have I got but one reply from
my twenty-one clandestine letters, which I have sent out, since I have
been here, by the "Under-ground Express." I suppose they are yet
to come at a future day. Rev. Aaron Foster's, of East Charlemont,
Mass., was duly received with many thanks. A copy of these clandestine letters is preserved, with my other asylum documents.

JACKSONVILLE, MARCH 4, 1860.

MISS DIX:

Insane Asylums! O, they are the curse of the age! They are
the devil's best devised plan to delude, distress, and destroy God's
noblest work — man. Many are now in despair, sent there by their
influence alone. They are a terror to the good, and a shield to the
wicked. Mrs. De Le Hay, our attendant, confessed to me last night,
that she dare not express her honest convictions of truth lest she be
called insane, simply because others, more powerful on the natural plane,
might imprison her for her opinion's sake; because, differing from them,
it might be insanity! So that the powerful of earth are the sane
party! — the despised, weak, helpless, holy few, the insane party!!

O when, when will the eyes of the world be opened to see this
subject in its true light?

Our Insane Asylums must be destroyed, to be constructed anew on
a righteous basis. No friend who has the means, should be allowed to
put off an insane friend upon the tender mercies of strangers. Of all
others, this unfortunate should demand his first care and effort; and no
one should be admitted to this institution who has one friend who can
protect them. It is cruelty and inhumanity to do otherwise; for to
put off a friend because they have become troublesome, is to take a
course to become inhuman towards them — for, whom we will not care
for we insensibly despise.

But to love an insane friend, we must do for them and suffer for them, as we would wish to be done by; and it is an indispensable requisite for the cure of insanity, that the only remedy be employed, viz., love and sympathy. And who but the relative and friend can better apply this sovereign remedy or antidote?

An institution like this has caused a thousand fold more misery, agony and suffering, than it has alleviated.

O, Miss Dix, did you but know the untold agonies your benefactions have been indirectly the occasion of, you might well fear the curse Mrs. Lovel, pronounced upon you as you entered our ward. Said Mrs. Lovel, "Are you the woman who has given so much money to keep up such houses as this?" "I do something toward it." "Well, you ought to be God damned to hell for it, and all the men who won't God damn you ought to be God damned themselves for it!" Oh, Miss Dix, you don't know what misery, sin and guilt, the devil has made you accessory to, in the course you have been pursuing under the specious color of benevolence! Dear woman—deceived, deluded and Satan bound! O may your eyes be opened to see your true position and repent before it is too late, or you will be taken in Satan's trap also, and be imprisoned for life in one of your humane institutions! It will only be your just due for causing so many others, alike innocent ones, thus to be deprived of a natural life, in this world. And God has pronounced your sentence, "for with what measure ye mete, it shall be measured to you again," unless you avert the doom by timely repentance. Justice, stern justice, reigns, and will reign to all eternity. And O, do you wish for happiness, prepare for it, ere it is too late!

I know what you can never know, unless you can see from my stand-point. God grant that you may be ever ignorant of this knowledge—sad, experimental knowledge!

Please read my only apology for writing you this note, in the thirty-third chapter of Ezekiel, and also believe me your true friend,

E. P. W. PACKARD.

DEFENSE OF MISS DIX.

I regard Miss Dix as a Christian, although honestly and conscientiously wrong, in sustaining our present system of Insane Asylums.

I regard Paul as a Christian, when he was persecuting the church, although honestly and conscientiously wrong in doing so. He considered the national religion the true religion, and any influence which tended to undermine its power over men, he, a zealous church.

defender, "verily thought he ought to do many things contrary to the name of Jesus of Nazareth." He could not support this illiterate imposture! No, not he, one of Gamaliel's theological graduates! He had his creed to defend, and all innovation upon its sanctity must be put down at once! So, the unassuming Christ fared hard under this bigoted spirit. But God opened his eyes, without putting him through the school of martyrdom to which he had sent the Christians, until his faith had become strong enough to bear it.

So I hope Miss Dix may be converted without being called insane, and shut up in an Insane Asylum to be cured.

I think Cromwell was conscientiously wrong when he thought he could govern England so much better than Charles Stuart could, that it was right to usurp his kingly honors to do it in!

I think the slaveholders are conscientiously wrong when they think that because they can take so much better care of the slaves than they can of themselves, that it is right to enslave them, to do it for them!

I think he who returns the fugitive is conscientiously wrong, although the human law of a Christian government defends him in breaking the divine.

I think the Orphan Asylum is conscientiously wrong, when it robs the poor, defenseless parent of their offspring, under the specious subterfuge, that the good of the child justifies this abuse of the maternal instinct!

I think our professedly Christian government is conscientiously wrong, when it leaves its faithful subjects so exposed to insults and abuse as to make them insane, by abuse, alone, and then enacts laws by which the afflicted, innocent and abused individual can be punished with hopeless imprisonment, while the abuser is protected in these outrages!

I think the Jews were conscientiously wrong when they persecuted Christ, although the laws of their government upheld them in so doing!

And, although God overrules the sins of men to praise him, yet he does by no means clear the guilty — for "there is a way which seemeth right to a man, but the end thereof are the ways of death." "Thou thoughtest I was altogether such an one as thyself, nevertheless I will reprove thee."

"NOT A PRISON."

Dr. McFarland does not like to have me to call this place a prison—for he says, it is not a prison. But I say, it is. And it is my right to have my say in my own book.

When he writes his book from his prison, he may call it, his visiting place, if he chooses! I have no disposition to dictate his book: he is able to dictate it himself.

If he has a mind to look out of his strong, iron-grated windows, and go to the door and say to his keeper, "Please unlock the door, and just let me go out and pick a flower; I will come right back, if you will let me go alone—I will not run away. But if you are afraid I shall, I can wait until you get the work done, and then you can go with me, and can watch me." And when he comes back, stop at the bars and knock, and say, "Please to unlock the door, and let me in again," and then call his place a visiting place, he may; but I shall not, for I did not come to visit. I came just because I could not help coming. I did not come to scrape acquaintance with him, neither, if he wants you to think I did; for I did not know that there was such a man in the world as Dr. McFarland, until Calvin introduced us; and although I liked his looks well enough, yet I assure you I should not have stayed to make him so long a visit, if I could have got away from him!

But he has been pretty good to Calvin, and tried pretty hard to keep on the right side of him, so he need not complain of his keeping me too long! I think they cannot be far from coming to some sort of a settlement between them; for Theophilus told me, when he visited me last month, that his father had written to him since his last visit to the Doctor, saying, "that he feared he should not be able to keep his mother much longer in the Asylum." He need have no fears about my troubling him to keep me any more, for there is no danger of that, since Mrs. Packard believes the world is large enough for two such people as she and her husband to live in, without ever coming into proximity with each other.

Indeed, I have sometimes thought they might yet strike a bargain by which he would try to make a life-long visit of it, at Calvin's request. I am expecting he will pop the question one of these days to me, the third party in the case! I am watching his movements pretty closely these days to see which way the wind blows. For, if he should let me have my own way entirely, about my book, I think he would be in some danger of my gratitude growing into a stronger feeling!

For it is such a novel position for me — a woman of America — to be allowed to think and speak and even write as I please, I cannot tell what I should not be willing to do for the man who thus secured to me my spiritual freedom. I do not know but I should make choice of such an anomaly as a protector for my defenseless children!

But so far, I have just stayed because I could not get away, knowing, what could not be cured must be endured. I have endured him for a long time, and I do not know but it will be a hard thing to get cured of him.

There is a maxim, I do not know how true it is, that in relation to evil, we first endure, then pity, then embrace. I have endured and pitied Dr. McFarland, but whether I shall ever embrace him depends altogether upon circumstances! So you can see for yourselves how I have baited my hook to catch my spiritual freedom with!

A RECORD OF INCIDENTS

On the afternoon of Oct. 16th, as I was preparing to copy my first volume for the press, Dr. McFarland came to my room to inspect the business.

I saw by the eye of my instinct, rather than by the eye of my natural vision, that he had not come alone, as usual, but brought that most unwelcome guest, the *bad* Dr. McFarland, or the "old Adam," rather, with him.

I knew I must now be as wise as a serpent, in dealing with the serpent, or I should be bit by it. So I put on my "charming" powers to quiet his asperities and control his reason. And choosing, as I thought, the most unexceptionable manuscript, my "Dedication," I offered to read it to him, for him to offer his criticism upon, before copying it for the press. I had read about two-thirds of it, with rather a palpitating heart, when he suddenly interrupted me by saying, "I should like to remark here, that I do n't like your calling this place a *prison*, so much; for it is n't so. And as I 'm to superintend these manuscripts for the press, I 'm not willing you should call it a prison. You may call it a place of *confinement*, if you choose, but not a prison. It is only a notion you have taken up, to call it a prison, by your choosing voluntarily to confine yourself to it, as if it were a prison. But you have no occasion for so doing. I am just as willing you should have your liberty, as I am to let Mrs. Chapman have hers. And she goes about just where she pleases; and so could you, if you chose to."

Here he paused for a reply. A silence ensued. I saw he was in the possession of his "evil spirit," and I dared not to contradict him, or even to assert my rights of opinion, lest, by so doing, I tempt him to commit himself still more strongly on the wrong or Calvinistic side of truth; for I have found that opposition is apt to give the "old man" strength.

But at length, I, with the innocent fearlessness and composure of truth, took part in the discussion, hitherto so unsatisfactory to me, by remarking, "It is a prison *to me*, and I have based all my book upon this truth. I do not intend to exaggerate or overstep the bounds of truth in what I say; but I intend to clothe truth in its own drapery,

and to call things by their true names, as I apprehend them.   I profess
to report no one's opinions but my own ; and I do say, that Mrs. Chapman is as much a prisoner as Mrs. Packard is ; and Mrs. Packard is no
more a prisoner *now* than she was when she first came, when she
used her parole of honor as Mrs. Chapman now does.   When I took
the patients to ride fourteen times, and took a dollar from your own
hands, and went up town and expended it alone or according to my
own judgment, I was as much the State's prisoner as I have been for
the last eighteen months, though I have not stepped my foot out of this
house.   I am not your prisoner, nor the trustees' prisoner, but the
State's or the *Government's* prisoner."

He replied, "You will acknowledge that the penitentiary inmates are
on a different plane, as prisoners, from what you are."

I replied, "As to our both being prisoners, we are on one and
the same plane.   The inmates in each institution are alike prisoners
under keepers, who hold our personal liberty entirely under subjection to bolts, grates, bars and keys.   Those in each, whom their
keepers can trust, are allowed their paroles of honor, extending from
the liberty of the yard, to the furlough of a conditional absence upon
mutual terms of agreement.   But should either prisoners use their fur-
loughs or paroles of honor as a means of escape from their place of
involuntary confinement, each are alike sought as a fugitive from
justice, and the laws uphold the keepers in pursuing the fugitive, and
forcing his return to his place of "involuntary confinement," which expression, according to Webster, means *a prison*.

"In these respects we are alike, but in another respect we are unlike.
The convicts are imprisoned in the penitentiary for doing wrong; the
afflicted, persecuted, oppressed and innocent, are here imprisoned for
doing right.

"The penitentiary is our government's place of punishing the guilty ;
insane asylums are our government's place of punishing the innocent—
for to me 't is capital punishment to be thus hopelessly imprisoned.

"This general rule has its exceptions.   Some innocent ones are punished there ; some guilty ones are punished here.   Insane Asylums
are the *"Inquisitions"* of the American government.   My imprisonment is as hopeless as is my sinning to escape from it.

"I report opinions from the stand-point of a patient—a victim of this
inquisition ; and not from the stand-point of a governmental officer,
appointed as guardian of this institution.   'T is the government, not its
officers, who are responsible for the basis on which our institutions are
placed.

"I, for one, should altogether prefer to be a penitentiary prisoner, to an insane prisoner; for there, my *accountability* is recognized, but here it is not, by the laws of the institution. It is in defiance of these laws, that you recognize it in me. And besides, my sense of justice would not be so outraged by a false imprisonment there, as here. And as to treatment, no criminals ought to be treated *worse* than the insane are treated here, and it would not hurt them to be treated even better! *

"For to be lost to reason, is a greater misfortune than to be lost to virtue; and the contumely and scorn which the world attaches to it are greater; just in proportion as the slander is more deadly to the moral influence of the injured party."

He remarked, "You would not, in writing a dictionary, describe each as alike, would you?"

"I should say they are one and the same thing, as to being *prisoners*," replied I.

Another pause ensued. "Shall I read on?" said I.

"Yes."

I finished it, and he remarked, "It is very good." I responded to this opinion. On this point we agreed as strongly as we differed on the point under discussion!

The subject was not again alluded to.

I felt, after he left, that something was wrong. I could not put up with this interference, or dictation of the contents of my book. But what could be done that would not make the matter worse? I knew too well, that to *beg* of Dr. McFarland was not the way to succeed. For he is almost as hard to be entreated as Father Abraham. Not quite, though. But although our President dictated to his slaves, instead of giving them their freedom, yet it was n't a *woman* who pleaded with him! Possibly he 'll yet eclipse Dr. McFarland's magnanimity, after all, by his disposal of my appeal to him for help!

To beg for my liberty to write my thoughts, is not right for me to do. It will degrade my self-respect to do so. But to reprove him, and assert my rights, might so exasperate him as to rashly lead to the destruction of my labored manuscripts. I cannot conscientiously submit to dictation — I therefore will not.

So I must either suspend my project indefinitely, or seek a settlement of the thing on the basis of justice.

---

* This sentence was not in the manuscript when Dr. McFarland read it, simply because I did not think of it until afterwards. Dr. McFarland and his wife are together making this a model State's Prison for our new republic. The Godhead must be respected in the criminal.

I concluded to *dare to do right*, and risk the consequences to the overruling providence of God. For I have always found this to be the only safe and expedient course for me to pursue.

I claim that it is always expedient to do right, and always inexpedient to do wrong.

So after having sought the moral courage and wisdom needed, for the discharge of this responsible duty, I penciled the following note and sent it to Dr. McFarland, by my attendant, Miss Trion.

A PETITION FOR THE DISCHARGE OF AN EMPLOYEE.

(CONFIDENTIAL.)

To the GOOD *Dr. McFarland :*

My best friend, I deem it my painful duty to report to you, my spiritual protector, the insulting conduct I received from one of your employees, in this institution, yesterday afternoon. It was from a man, an old, and almost superannuated man; although I think he has sense enough left to be responsible for his own actions. He came, unbidden, to my room, and having seated himself, began to upbraid me about my book—my pet—my pride, and, if you believe me, he even threatened, in spite of your proffered protection, to intercept its appearance in print, unless I heeded his suggestions in relation to it!

Now, I appeal to you to say if it is not too bad to be thus trifled with. Ought not this old, bad man (whose name looks so much like your own that I don't like to write it!) to be discharged, and never again to be allowed to enter my presence?

Dr. McFarland, if you don't discharge him I shall report you to the trustees; and if that don't answer, I shall report you to the synod; and, if that don't answer, I shall report you up higher. I shall tell no lies to God, for you, nor about you.

God is preparing to summon you to his tribunal, to settle matters with you, and I'm a sworn witness, to testify, on trust to my integrity, candor, truthfulness and loyalty. I shoot evil, whether found in friend or foe, as God's enemy. And I trust to God's providence, alone, for my protection, in fighting these his spiritual battles.

Dr. McFarland, have not I a right to write my own thoughts, as well as to think them, under our constitution, even if I am a woman? And, has any man a right to interfere with this right? Did not you say it was *my* book, not *our* book? It is *our* country, *our* government, but it is *my* book. And can I claim it as my own book unless I indorse its contents? Can I indorse what, to me, are lies, and expect

the blessing of a truthful God upon it? Are not my reason and my conscience to be the sole agents in dictating my book? My conscience is 'God's secretary within me, and I shall not insult its dictations, by a proffered compromise with falsehood or error. My opinions and my conscience are my personal capital, which I can, by no means, consent on any terms, to barter away.

If I cannot be protected in these rights under your guardianship, I must defer the publication of my book until God raises up for me a protector, who will not dare to trample upon the sacred, inalienable rights of my God-given nature.

I ask you, kind friend, will you be the protector of the inalienable rights of my womanly nature? Or, must I suspend my contemplated project until God's providence prepares the way for my spiritual freedom to be so secured to me, that I can write a book true to God, and also true to my own truthful nature?

God offers you the honor of being my protector in this act, and he longs to confer it upon you. So do I. But there is one, and only one, condition, on which it can be conferred upon you; and that is, to dare to trust your interests, and the interests of this institution, and the interests of the country, on the immovable principles of truth and justice.

I shall venture to take my stand on the immutable rock of eternal truth, regardless of the foaming billows which dash at its base, and here shall I wield the sword of justice, regardless of my own interests, and those of all others. I stand or fall with God alone. God and Mrs. Packard's interests are eternally identified.

Your true friend,

E. P. W. P.

In about one hour after the above note was delivered, Dr. McFarland came to the door of my room, with a face radiant with smiles, and at the same time giving my hand a most perceptible grasp, inquired, "Who is that old man who has ventured to insult you so about that precious book? He shall not be tolerated here, on any account. You tell me his name, and he shall be discharged forthwith. The name of that old, bad, superannuated man, you just give me, and I shall see to his insulting you any more!"

I replied, "The good, new, Dr. McFarland is always welcome to my room — most welcome! But that old, bad man, I do not want to see any more."

"No, he shan't disturb you any more. Just give me his name, and I 'll see to his discharge," was his reply.

"You are doing right, Dr. McFarland! You are treating the old man as he deserves to be treated," said I.

Soon after, Mrs. McFarland came to my room, with a tumbler of her jelly, the second red (not bloody!) sacrifice she had presented me, for an atonement for her husband's sins! and gave me a pleasant visit besides.

I read to her my "Dedication," and she very sensibly remarked, "It is so very strange and mysterious why your friends should have all deserted you so. I cannot understand it—how friends can treat their friends in this manner. They put them in here, and then seem to desert them, as if they were not worth caring for afterwards. I am sure I could not desert my friends in this manner."

"No, Mrs. McFarland, I don't think you could, for you are too true to your womanly nature, to do such an unnatural act. But, Mrs. McFarland, this is a perverted age. Christianity is almost totally eclipsed by Calvinism. The sun, moon and stars are all under this eclipse. Men, women and children are all more or less perverted by it. This is the culminating age of Calvinism. Its deadly principles must be exposed and abandoned, before Christianity can exert its benign and legitimate influence over the character and destiny of the present age. Mrs. McFarland, we are now passing through the very nadir of the eclipse. It is not midnight. It is a noon-day eclipse of the world's luminary, and when this awful shadow shall have once passed across its disk, it is forever descending to its no distant tomb: while Christianity, dismantled of its false habiliments will shine out with meridian splendor, and the natural and spiritual reign of Christ will have fully commenced. Until then, we must grope our way in darkness, not knowing at what we stumble."

Mrs. McFarland is a very kind woman; none could fill her place, as our matron, better than she does. She has repeatedly remarked to me, "We should be glad to cure you all of your diseases, if we could." But, alas! mine is one of their "hopeless cases!" My Christianity is incurable! And all the treatment of this American inquisition cannot induce me to abandon it for Calvinism.

I told her how her husband was going to let me have my book all my own way, and how he should be upheld as the world's pattern, for so doing—for allowing an American woman her right of opinion during the great eclipse. For he should stand on his *own actions*, and if they exalted and promoted him, no influence could dethrone him. And he has as good a right to plume his cap with his own, well-earned feathers, as Mrs. Packard has her bonnet—for the fortitude of Honesty, in en-

during his chastisement, so martyr-like, is as truly his rightful claim as the innocent fearlessness of Truth in inflicting the chastisement is Mrs. Packard's rightful claim.

It is my private opinion, that Dr. McFarland's conscience dictated to him the fate which he assigned to the old man of sin: and that the wife of "Nathan" had exerted her share of influence in convincing this modern king, that the pet book of the pauper ought not to be sacrificed to the cupidity of the rich man.

It is also my fondly cherished opinion, that the good Dr. McFarland will never let the bad man crowd his ewe lamb again; since he has found, that a lamb can even crowd a lion, if self-defense demands the pressure of truth upon the lion's conscience, to quicken it into healthful action! He may, too, be compelled to admit the truth, however unwelcome, of Mrs. Timmons' compliment, viz. :—"That two hard heads meet when Mrs. Packard and Dr. McFarland meet," on the arena of discussion; and it is by no means certain which head would be the most exposed by a collision!

I have volunteered both my manuscripts and myself to Dr. McFarland as a burnt offering, on condition that he can detect a single lie in all my manuscripts. I shrink not on this condition, to be burnt alive, as God's appointed portion for the liar; for whether I choose it or not, I know it is God's invincible purpose, to make me stand on my own deserts: and if I am a liar, I know hell is my portion.

I make no claim to infallibility. I am finite in knowledge and intelligence, and liable to prejudices, prepossessions, and springs of error from educational influences; yet not from an imperfect organization: since God has endowed me with a model female development, and I am true to my own convictions of truth and duty — and I am no "respector of persons" in dealing with wrong, or evil, in any form. I always have been, and God grant I always may be, loyal to God's government, and disloyal to every other government which interferes with this; and the test of my loyalty is found in my being *true to my conscience* — God's secretary within me.

I am not a standard for any human being, except myself. I grant every human being an equal right to differ from me in opinion, that I have to differ from them, in relation to my views of truth and duty. God is the only dictator of my inalienable rights: and whoever dares to trespass upon them, does it at their own peril, not mine.

Dr. McFarland is most affectionately chosen as the scholastic critic of these manuscripts, in relation to their chirography, etymology, syntax and prosody. And, now, since he is allowed to superintend

5

these four great wheels of my engine, I think I ought to be allowed the entire charge of the single, little wheel of *truth!*

But he has no right guaranteed to him, from any intelligence in God's universe, to dictate to, or interfere with, the utterance of a single truth, or a single expression found in my book. And if *he* dares to attempt it, he dares to trespass on God's authority, not mine — and God, not I, will be his judge of the act.

Mrs. Packard is the writing medium of this book. Dr. McFarland is her chosen scholastic critic. But, God, alone, is the dictator of tne contents of the book — my book — God's book — our book.

QUESTIONS

FOR DR. McFARLAND'S CONSIDERATION.

SUPPOSE Mr. Bailey should find, on setting the types of my manuscripts, that he is thus being accessory to the destruction of the *printing offices* of the land, should the representations of the book, written by one whom the public has been made to regard as an *insane person*, be credited as the truth, by the public mind?

1. Would Mr. Bailey be doing right, thus to aid in the destruction of his own and other's interests?

2. Does not the law of *self-defense* demand, that he put a veto upon the book, and peremptorily refuse to publish such denunciatory misrepresentations of a *public blessing?*

3. Can he conscientiously allow his press to be thus employed, even while he knows that other *free presses* in the land will get the avails of the job, if he does not?

4. Can he throw the responsibility of the book entirely upon the writer, and pocket the avails of the job, as honestly earned wages?

5. Cannot the printing office stand on its own intrinsic merits — and can the private opinion of a *single woman* endanger its interests?

6. Is it right to put down *free speech*, or *free printing* to save our institutions, which cannot stand on their own merits?

7. Can our insane asylums stand on their own merits, or will the opinion of a single woman put them in jeopardy?

8. Can you, sir, be thus accessory to the destruction of the insane asylums of our land — (*these public blessings!*) — and be guiltless in God's sight?

9. Cannot goodness and virtue bear the light — or is it evil alone, which dreads exposure?

10. Cannot our government institutions stand the light of one single torch of truth, reflected from a central stand point, by a victim's own experience and observation?

O, do n't wrong your conscience, Dr. McFarland, to favor even me!

No act can be right, which conscience condemns.

I utterly refuse to be accessory to such a heaven-daring act, on your part.

Let me pass out of this Asylum, under the due forms of law as I came in, and let me stand alone on my own unsupported acts, for public or divine favor — trusting to God's providence alone to introduce me to my husband or protector, in issuing my contemplated book.

The gains of godliness, Dr. McFarland, are not always dollars and cents *at first;* but in due order these will arrive, with its other benignant fruits; for, "righteousness exalteth a nation," and continuance in well doing is sure to end in "eternal life."

A DREAM,

WITH ITS INTERPRETATION, DECEMBER, 1860.

THE following dream and its interpretation, may serve a valuable purpose, as an illustration of several important principles.

Mrs. Hosmer, who helped me to its interpretation, has superintended the sewing room here for three years or more, and was discharged about one year since. She has one of the most striking peculiarities of temperament I ever met with — in that her eccentric nature combines the extremes of good and evil, in their most glaring features. This trait she exhibited in being to me here, for about one year and a half, my *best friend*, and also, my *worst enemy* — in that she was the medium of some of my *choicest social blessings*, as well as the source of my *keenest sorrows* — in that she repeatedly told me that she regarded me as an insane person.

I dreamed that it was put upon me to draw a stage coach across a bridge spanning a broad, deep river, and that in order to get the coach up on to the bridge, I was compelled to draw it up five stone steps about five inches high each.

I looked upon my appointment *at first* as an impossibility; but recollecting that "I'll try" has done wonders, I determined to see what I could do by trying.

The stage was prepared for me by substituting a rope, instead of the neap or thills, which encircled my body, so that the greatest pressure came across my stomach and breast. Thus prepared I put forth a most herculean effort, when, to my great surprise and joy, the stage came up upon the bridge. Stimulated by my seemingly miraculous success, I started at full speed across the bridge; and found, to my joy, that by the momentum acquired by the velocity, the effort to draw it along became correspondingly diminished. Thus running at the top of my speed with my head down, I found, to my surprise, that before I was aware of it, I had run off from the bridge on to a piece of slitwork about four inches wide; which was the only medium of communication between the termination of the bridge, and the opposite shore — the dis-

tance being two tiers and a half. The termination of each tier was marked by a high beam extending from the water, up many feet above the level of the string-piece across the river. The half-tier was nearest the bridge, so that the first support to lean upon was not far distant from my present stand-point. I stopped and considered what was to be done. I thought that to draw the stage on to this narrow slitwork, and balance it exactly, so as to drag it over in this way, would plainly be an impossibility; and that the capsizing of the stage into the river, would necessarily drag me with it, by the rope around my body. I there-fore determined to drop the rope and step out of the traces; and, thus disentangled, walk on to the standing support. I did so, and then con-sidered, what to do. To return seemed impossible: for the stage presented an insuperable barrier to my getting on to the bridge. To go forward seemed too hazardous, for the two remaining reaches seemed very long, when looking at the deep river far below me; and the very narrow path I had to walk upon, appeared still more precarious as it neared the opposite shore — for the extreme end of the last string-piece was so raised on one side of the mortice, as to render the upper surface quite an inclined plane. On this I should not dare to expose myself, for fear I should slip off, and besides, I saw it would be likely to slip down into the mortice by my weight upon it; and the jar would be very likely to cause me to fall off.

I looked about for help. But no one was within speaking distance. On the shore I had left, far down below the bridge, I could see one man standing, solitary and alone, looking with a vacant stare upon the broad, bridgeless, boatless stream before him. I saw distinctly it was my husband, apparently cogitating his own means of crossing the fathomless deep, regardless of my perilous, exposed condition. Cold, selfish indifference, marked his appearance. I knew he cared not for me, or my deliverence, or safety. I turned from this granite statue, and cast a look upon the opposite bank. My courage revived at the prospect. I could distinctly see a company of men, who seemed to be consulting what to do for me, for I could see they had a rope in their hands. Life, motion, interest, the *most intense*, marked their energetic movements. But I considered—how can the rope be extended to me, and if it were, how could it help me in sustaining my footing, on the narrow string-piece I had to pass over upon? To look down, my head would swim. To look up, it was clear. Still, then I could not see where to place my feet. I concluded to hold on to my standing beam, and wait awhile, thinking, there will be doubtless some amongst the bystanding witnesses whose gallantry will prompt them to even

expose their own lives, to rescue a defenseless female from her hazardous position.

I therefore, for a time, trusted my deliverance, with all the trustful confidence of my womanly nature, to the care of manhood, whose God-like development instinctively volunteers help to the helpless — protection to the unprotected.

But upon a reconsideration of the difficulties in the case, I found a new one, which had before escaped my notice. I saw that the river below me was covered with *empty chairs* — large armed *office chairs* — all upright, but empty! These chairs so obstructed the passage that boats could not be sent to my aid from beneath. I thought, O! that the public officers had not vacated these chairs, and I would venture to drop into their arms! But no — instead of these officers being at their post to help the helpless, their fixtures only serve as an impediment, to obstruct other sources of help.

I therefore concluded, that since I was out of the reach of all human help, the only alternative left me, was to run the risk of saving myself by my own unaided exertions, by going forward, risking all the hazards of a progressive movement. I concluded my way must be to look constantly upward, and move my feet forward, with most careful, cautious steps.

Having fully settled upon this course, I stooped down to remove my shoes, and drop them into the stream, so that being thus disencumbered, I might with stocking feet move forward, with less danger of slipping off.

While in the act of removing my shoes, I awoke, happy to find myself in a dormitory bed in an insane asylum, instead of being a fifth of the way across the string-piece.

The next day I told Mrs. Hosmer of my dream; and the interpretation she put upon it, was, in her own *laconic style*, as follows:

"Mrs. Packard, you must leave *public opinion behind you*, until the bridge is built. You must just go on alone. You are now called to walk through Gethsemane's garden alone, as your Master did, depending upon no *human sympathy* for support. You may expect God's angel will be sent to sustain you, when your accumulated sorrows become too great for human fortitude to endure. Mrs. Packard, we must all pass to heaven in the *same steps* our Master trod — like him, we must all pass through Gethsemane's garden — and like his, the path leading to the consummation of our sanctification, is constantly narrowing, and attended with increasing difficulties, as we approach its termination. It is then, *too narrow*, for two to go abreast. Alone! alone!! we

must tread the wine-press of *God's wrath*, even while under the eclipse of God's countenance — for so God appoints. No other road terminates in eternal day.

"This promise must sustain you: 'If ye *suffer* with me, ye sha'l *reign* with me.'"

O, thanks! ten thousand thanks, Mrs. Hosmer, for these words of comfort to my sorrowing soul!

After being strengthened by this angel-visitant, my sinking soul could say with my Master, Yes, the cup which my Father in Heaven hath given me, I will drink, uncomplainingly. Yes, "Not my will but thine, O God, be done" concerning me. Henceforth, my purpose shall be not to get out of this asylum to be with my precious children — not to convince the world, that I am not an insane person — but it shall henceforth be my undivided purpose to become a perfect person in *Christ Jesus'* estimation, regardless of the estimation of perverted humanity.

Yes, God is my witness that hitherto this purpose in me has not been broken.

But O! the persecution — the sorrows — the agony my spiritual, sensitive nature has endured in carrying out this purpose into a practical on God only knows. For he only knows who has been misunderstood, misrepresented, maligned and persecuted unto death, how to feel for those who are. Yes, when I think how good and kind my Saviour was to all — how innocent he was of the least trespass upon other's rights — and then think how no cruel tyrant was ever hated with a more deadly hate than was my loving Master, I feel like saying, "it is enough for the servant that he be as his master."

Yes, alone! single handed and alone, I have dared to expose and condemn, as guilty, those laws and those practices which treat insanity as a crime! To imprison a person for being insane — to cut them off from all communication with outside influences that they may thus punish these helpless, innocent sufferers, with less danger of interference from abroad — thus to expose the most helpless, dependent creatures of God's government, to unmerited abuse, is a heaven-daring crime, which well merits the indignation of an incensed God, sure to follow such outrages, bestowed upon his children — upon himself, personified in human form.

Alone have I stood between the laws of my country and my God, and been a single-handed defender of the Divine code, in defiance of the human.

I have dared to be thus true to Jesus, even while in the absolute power of despotism — legalized despotism.

I have, too, felt this despotic power in full force to crush me beneath its iron foot. May God only know the multitude of sins which Dr. McFarland's repentance has covered !

I knew this despotic power could destroy all my earthly joys — hopes — rights — privileges — interests — my papers — my witnesses and my natural life ! And I knew too, full well, that he could be protected by the laws of our government in so doing !

I knew too, that he had power to destroy himself — but I knew it was as certain as the decrees of God, that he could not destroy *me*, or the mind which dictated these papers. Therefore in my spiritual might I have moved forward with a dauntless, inflexible purpose, that Christ's cause should not suffer here, for want of one faithful advocate — one loyal witness in defense of truth and righteousness.

The bloodless but terribly painful conflict has ended. The strong man, armed with all the burnished armory of the American statutes, could not defend himself against a stronger than he — personified in the form of a legally or constitutionally insane female pauper !

The rule of despotism is forever vanquished from this palace of hell, and the reign of righteousness has commenced, by means of which, it is to be converted into an asylum of rest for God's wearied, afflicted, suffering ones.

The repentant Dr. McFarland, with his gentle, amiable wife, are God's chosen instruments for the accomplishment of this glorious work. May Heaven defend them ! May Heaven protect them ! May an asylum of heavenly, eternal rest, be their welcome home — and as they have given rest to the weary here, so may they find rest to their weary souls there.

And let that individual or that government who has been guiltless of wronging me, be the one to cast the "first stone" at the *penitent* Dr. McFarland for his abuse of me.

O, how does my forgiving heart yearn to exalt the man whom God will delight to honor, as the sole and only protector of his utterly defenseless female advocate !

Again — My position on the string-piece illustrates another point. I have been alone in my position relative to never again returning to my husband. The advocates of my so doing, have argued, that the laws placed me there — that no place of refuge from his legal claims upon me could be found, outside of this asylum — that here, amongst maniacs as my almost sole companions, I must linger out a most hopeless, wretched existence; excluded from all communication with my children, or any other earthly friends, except through the strictest

censorship—that my active habits of body and mind would here be so restricted and limited, that the inevitable consequence must ultimately be loss of both health and spirits, however elastic at present—and therefore it was wholly a suicidal act on my part, to refuse to go to my husband, as the only alternative allowed me by individual or legal favor.

I have felt the full force of this logic, O, how keenly! Still, a higher logic has prevailed over my decisions. A simple "Thus saith the Lord," has forbid it. My conscience dictated, with unquestioning distinctness, it is morally wrong for you to trust yourself again in the legal, absolutely despotic power of one, who has proved himself to be, to me, a most unrelenting persecutor. Self-defense forbids it. It is for me to obey conscience. It is for God to work out the consequences or results of obedience.

Helpless and alone, I have thus moved my frail bark on the tempestuous sea of human destiny—with God alone for my pilot. My frail bark has not yet foundered, even amidst the dashing breakers of cruelly disappointed hopes, of insults heaped on abuses; by the cold and chilling gusts of ridicule, scorn, derision, contumely and contempt. No, all, all combined, have not overmatched the skill of my faithful Pilot, who has moved my frail bark safely through them all, to a haven of rest. Thanks! thanks! to Thee, alone, my Pilot, for thy superior skill and restraining power. Peacefully I now lie in this haven of rest, trustfully waiting my Captain's orders for the next voyage.

It is due to two human minds alone, to testify at this period of my sad drama, that they did not oppose my decision. These are, a Mr. George Lyons, of Georgetown, Illinois, who brought his sister to this asylum as a patient; who, after hearing of the facts relating to my being brought here, from my own lips, remarked, "Don't you go back to your husband; the country will not always suffer you to remain thus unprotected from injury and abuse." May his cheering assurance prove prophetic of the truth!

The other was, Miss Mary McFarland, the youngest daughter of my patron. A most kind-hearted, natural girl; her mother's child, in this respect. She remarked to me before I had been here six months, and she in her fifteenth year, "If I had a husband, and he put me into an insane asylum, when I was not insane, I would not have anything to do with him afterwards!" No, Mary, neither will I. And I warn the future husband of Mary not to trample upon her inalienable rights, for she is too true a woman to bear it with impunity! Would that such Marys were multiplied in the same ratio with the increase of female forms.

Again — I was alone in protesting against my illegal imprisonment. Scarcely a single individual has given me the shadow of approval of this stand — but, instead, I have been sneered at, ridiculed, and my "tyrant conscience" has been reproached as being an usurper! But after more than nineteen long months of self-immolated, unsympathizing imprisonment, Miss Martha Mills, my intelligent and strong-minded attendant, has, within a few days, assured me that "she should have done just so herself, under similar circumstances." O, how grateful is such a response from a human tongue, to one whose love of approbation is so very large as my own. O! it is this love of approbation which has led me to suffer so cheerfully the loss of all things to secure the approval of my final Judge at last. And when I plainly saw that I must either sacrifice his approbation or that of perverted humanity; I unhesitatingly chose to lose the latter — for I esteem it no great honor to be popular amongst devils and fallen angels!

Again — I seemed to be alone upon the connecting link between the natural and spiritual worlds. The bridge connecting them is nearly completed. But who dares to step out beyond the limits of popular opinion and sentiment, and let himself be cut loose from all things tangible, to gain the hidden treasures of knowledge laid up in God's vast storehouse ready for distribution to any applicant? Who dares to stand *alone* in his opinion, and face a frowning world? Mrs. Packard dares to do it; for she has done it; and she dares to do it again, in spite of all the locks, bolts, bars, and keys of all the insane asylums of Christendom.

Where do you find courage? Where do you find dauntless perseverance? Where do you find God-like forgiveness? Where do you find holy resentment? Where do you find the "wrath of the Lamb"? Where do you find *self-sacrificing benevolence?* In woman! in true woman! in spiritual women! In God's angels!

Can man, whom God has made a little lower than the angels, be expected to equal them?

Can a man excel a woman?

Nay, verily, for God has made them to differ in excellence, as he has made one star to differ from another in glory.

Woman is God's crowning work of creation.

Again — The length of my imprisonment and my supports, find here an illustration.

I had been in prison six months, when I had my dream, and I was then, at my first post, six months from the bridge. The remaining two

whole reaches, being each double in length to the space already passed over, would make two years more of prison life assigned me. I now expect to be discharged at the trustees' next meeting, in December, when the two years and a half will have just expired. What scene in this long drama will next open upon me, God only knows. *God reigns!* This truth has been, still is, and God grant it may ever be, the downy pillow of rest, where my anxious, troubled soul loses all its sorrows, cares, doubts, forebodings, and retains its only heritage and its unfailing portion —*peace.*

The support, upon which I was leaning at that half-tier post, was, the hope that the appeal which I had made to my father for *protection,* would be responded to by a father's heart. But no. A fond hope was most cruelly blasted, by the return to my long, kind, and affectionate letter to him — being only a letter to Dr. McFarland, assuring him that I was an insane person, and most earnestly soliciting the charities of this institution to be extended to his insane daughter, since he considered this place as the most appropriate place for me for the present!

He plead this claim out of pity to my husband, and from a regard to my children's interests; fearing my influence over their susceptible minds might be ruinous to them, if I was where I could hold any communication with them!!

This claim was backed up by both my brothers!

Justice and truth demand that I here state, that neither my father nor my brother, Austin Ware, have seen me for more than ten years, and their knowledge of me was almost entirely derived from my husband's representations, by means of his clandestine correspondence with them; while at the same time my own was intercepted, or secretly undermined in its legitimate influence upon their minds by his *artful strategy.* For he well knew he could not complete his nefarious plot, unless their eyes were blinded to the truth.

Another fact. My father is a rich man, and I am one of only three children, his lawful heirs to his great possessions. He is a Congregational clergyman, retired from the ministry, and living at his ease on his interest money. And so is my husband far from being a poor man, if having $4,000, or more, invested in money speculations, besides plenty of money to freight out thirteen thousand pounds of portable possessions to Mount Pleasant, Iowa, does not disqualify him from claiming this title which he seems so exceedingly anxious to covet! He has also insured his life for my benefit, for $4,000, at the life insurance company in Hartford, Ct.

But in spite of the truth, he has so successfully dusted the trustees'

eyes, as well as my father's, as to lead them to believe his lies: and under the influence of this strong delusion, they have placed me, as an indigent, incapacitated pauper — and, as such, a just and suitable claim-ant — upon the charities of Illinois tax payers! !

Tax-payers of Illinois! Resent this base imposition upon your legal rights!! For I *am* capable of supporting myself, independently of husband's or father's patrimonies — if there is a woman in America that can do it — on my own self-reliant strength and health, both of body and of mind!

My father's letter to Dr. McFarland did not contain one word of sympathy or regard for me, except as a lunatic pauper! (Dr. McFar-land kindly read me the entire contents of the letter, but refused to let me have a copy of it. I have a copy of all mine to my father.) It contained no message of love or affection for me — not even the slight-est, in return for my loving, kind, intelligent, filial letter to him. Silence — *mute silence*, was its only response.

So was silence the only response to another equally kind letter which I sent him soon after — pleading with all a daughter's eloquence, that he would *come and see me*, for himself, or send a messenger to take me to him on a visit, assuring him I would then return willingly again to my prison, if he *then* thought that was the proper place for his daughter, instead of being the mother of her own offspring! !

I told him, moreover, that I would pay the expenses of the experi-ment, in either case, from a sum which the Manteno sane party had volunteered for my benefit.

O! my Calvinistic father! have the doctrines of devils, which you have so long advocated, both in your preaching and practice, so per-verted your manly nature, as to lead you to become entirely devoid of human feelings? Are you so debased as to be entirely without natural affection, implacable, unmerciful? Are you hopelessly lost to the last *form* of godliness, *apparent* love for your own offspring? Calvinistic selfishness! Calvinistic deviltry! !

My next post or support was, the hope that my appeal to the trustees for a discharge, on the ground of my intrinsic merits, as devel-oped by my *own actions,* independent of testimony, might meet the claims it justly demanded. The following is a copy of the petition which I handed to the trustees, as they passed through our wards, at their September meeting, 1861. Dr. McFarland politely introduced me to them, when I, in a kind of hollow square, bounded on all sides by the trustees, held a short, intelligent conversation with them, upon the intrinsic merits of this institution.

PETITION TO THE TRUSTEES OF THE ILLINOIS STATE LUNATIC ASYLUM.

Messrs : — I, Mrs. Elizabeth P. W. Packard, wife of Rev. Theophilus Packard, of Manteno, Kankakee county, Ill., do most respectfully play your honorable body to discharge me from this Asylum, and place me on a self-reliant position forthwith — for the following reasons :

1. I am illegally imprisoned here on the false charge of insanity. That the charge *is* a false one can be demonstrated, by allowing my own words and actions, truthfully represented, as proof of my real condition. And does not reason and justice demand, that a state or act, which exposes an individual to a life-long imprisonment, should be supported by the stubborn argument of facts, founded in truth; not merely on opinions, founded on an untenable basis?

2. This my imprisonment, being a false imprisonment, eminently imperils the vital interests of this institution, which you are sacredly bound to protect; and delay in this matter is only enhancing this danger, by the just indignation which is rapidly accumulating, in view of the wrongs which I, and my dear children, are suffering by this illegal act. The mere forms of the law, without the spirit or intent of the law, will be found to be a *bogus* protection to the institution. A petition to the legislature is already drawn up, to solicit investigation.

3. I am entirely capable of assuming a self-reliant position in community, being in the full possession of all my mental and physical faculties — and having always been a healthy and practical woman, I possess more than common capacities, for sustaining a self-reliant position, independent of all pecuniary aid whatever.

4. My long, dreary imprisonment among maniacs is of a kind, to a person of my intelligence, and my peculiarly sensitive nature, extremely wearisome and tedious.

5. It was only for the lawful exercise of my rights of opinion, and my rights of conscience, that the charge of insanity was instituted against me; and it is the same cause which perpetuates my imprisonment. When the storm of persecution in Manteno arose against me, in consequence of advancing opinions conflicting with those of my classmates, my husband, instead of protecting me in my inalienable right to my opinion, as his marriage vows required him to do, became my worst persecutor, demanding the subjection of these inalienable rights of opinion and conscience to his arbitrary will, or imprisonment in an insane asylum !! My conscience forbade my yielding to this despotic demand; and therefore I have deliberately and intelligently suffered the loss of all things for conscience sake.

Dr. McFarland offered me my liberty, after I had been here about three weeks, on condition that I would return to my husband, as my protector. But my conscience forbade my doing so, as an act of self-defense, until the question was legally settled, whether a virtuous, peaceable, useful, Christian wife, *could* be protected in her right of opinion and conscience, under the constitution of free America?

6. I think it would hasten this matter to a crisis to allow me my *personal liberty*, which I have never forfeited; and thus sooner secure to those six precious, motherless children, the care of their God-given guardian, which they so much need in their now dependent, infantile years.

For a confirmation of the above reasons I would respectfully ask you to read my "Defense," a document now in Dr. McFarland's possession, on which I have bestowed much labor, hoping and trusting it might defend me from that most unjust, false and cruel slander, which represents me as lost to reason, when I am not:—or, allow me to speak for myself. This most base and cruel defamation of my fair and unblemished character, God requires me to expose, that this flagrant crime may secure its condign punishment by the laws of my country. (Here follows a series of questions, which are not at hand for me to copy. They are safe, however, and so are my other asylum records and documents, journal, etc., in all amounting to a volume quadruple the size of this.)

This house in some instances has been perverted from its original object, as a retreat for the insane—and has been employed as a penitentiary, a house of correction, a hospital for the sick, a poor-house, and an inquisition. When the truth becomes known, as it at length will, it is as certain as the decrees of God, that it will then appear, that one intelligent, consistent, practical Christian was sent here to be tortured—spiritually agonized—to induce her to yield the supremacy of her conscience to human dictation.

Indeed, it is true, all that human ingenuity could devise, has been most skillfully employed, to *make* me a maniac! But by God's help alone I have survived, unharmed, the horrors of this American inquisition, and reason still maintains its throne, and demands justice at your hands, or at the bar of my country.

You, Gentlemen, as guardians of this charitable institution, are now required to do what you can to redeem this institution from the curse of an insulted God, which now hangs over its destiny, threatening its destruction.

May divine wisdom guide you in the disposal of this petition of a persecuted follower of Jesus,   E. P. W. PACKARD.

The following protest I added to the above petition :

PROTEST.

Dr. McFarland informs me that I am soon to be liberated and returned to my husband !　Christian gentlemen, I do hereby enter my most solemn protest against being returned to my husband.　This shall never be done with my consent : if done at all, it must be done as an act of mere brute force on your part.

I shall never surrender my conscience to the rebel traitors of Christ's government.　His law says, " Judge ye not of your own selves what is right."　I shall obey this law of my Sovereign, and shall judge for myself what is right for me to do.

I shall always yield to intelligence — to argument based in truth — but to despotism, *never*.

I shall hold no sort of fellowship with this unfruitful worker of darkness — my husband.　"So help me God ! "

A follower of Jesus,

E. P. W. P.

The result of this effort, Dr. McFarland told me, was to perpetuate my imprisonment, indefinitely, on the ground that I refused to return to my husband!

He assured me, there was no place which they could legally offer me, but the county poor-house, or my husband's home, outside of this asylum !

Again was my long-deferred hope blasted — without sympathy from humanity, to cheer or comfort me, lest I be strengthened in my foolish, insane notion, that I could not conscientiously go to my husband!　The long, cheerless, dreary reaches between these supports, was bounded only by the rayless prospect of hopeless imprisonment for life !

I have now, I fondly hope, passed the *jar of danger*, when the slanting string-piece slipped down into the mortice.　Dr. McFarland's scare, when he threatened to intercept the publication of my book, unless I listened to his dictation, must be the jar.　But the brave man finds that a braver than he holds my destiny upon the decisions of my *own* conscience.

Indeed, God has so wonted me to my self-reliant position, and he has taught me how to so exactly balance dangers, by the poise of truth, that I can now as fearlessly walk the narrow line of duty, as can Blondin walk the rope suspended from Niagara's banks.　And although I would not, like him, like to risk a cook-stove on my back — yet a

child, one of my jewels, should be cheerfully packed over by his mother, rather than be thus separated from her own flesh and blood.

December arrived — but no discharge from this institution, by the trustees, at their December meeting — as I had fondly expected Hope so long deferred, sickened within me. I burst into tears when Dr. McFarland informed me that the trustees had again indefinitely postponed my imprisonment; and thus I sat before him *silently weeping*, *waiting in vain* for some apology, or some explanation of the reasons which induced them thus, again, to blast my fond hopes of liberty, after they had had such unanswering proof of my real sanity, both from my written and spoken communications; and also the evidence, so constantly accumulating, that all the charges which had been brought against me, were *false!*

I broke the silence, by exclaiming, " O, Dr. McFarland, the trustees have forsaken me ! Won't you stand by me? You will not leave me, will you?" He simply replied, " No, I will not." Said I, "I feel like saying to you in my agony, as Christ said to his Father, when all forsook him and fled, 'My God! My God! wilt thou forsake me?' May I go on writing my book?" He answered; "Yes, you may."

Thus I saw that the end of the string-piece was not the end of my imprisonment, as I had fondly hoped; but merely the end of my exemption from human sympathy. Now I had something tangible to stand upon, viz., the hope that my *book* might bring me succor. So, while this was left me, I was not in a state of rayless, hopeless imprisonment as I had been, while on the string-piece; except while leaning on my two supports.

And I find, too, that just in the ratio that the Doctor defends me, just in the same ratio is the sympathy of the house extended to me. So that my all of earthly hope lies in the decisions of Dr. McFarland's single mind concerning me.

Thus God's Providence compels me to trust in Dr. McFarland as the God of my earthly destiny; and as "the hearts of men are in God's hands and he turneth them whithersoever he will," I must learn to trust this his agent as my God.

My real feelings while passing under this cloud of disappointment, may be best described by a letter I wrote to my son Isaac, about this time. The following is a copy of the letter.

LETTER TO MY SON ISAAC.

JACKSONVILLE, DECEMBER, 1862.

My Dear Son Isaac:—

Yours of November 24th is received. I rejoice to find your health s so good. May your improved health and strength be all expended in the cause of truth and righteousness. May you be wise to do good, but to do evil may you have no knowledge. My confidence in your integrity is almost unbounded. I do feel that you will follow out your honest convictions of truth and duty, in spite of all opposition. Therefore my heart is at rest respecting you. But, Isaac, dear, what is in store for your mother, God only knows!

When I wrote you last, the bow of hope spanned my horizon. I hoped, then, to be liberated at the next meeting of the trustees; because I expected that the principles of integrity would rule their decisions respecting me.

But, Isaac, I am disappointed — sadly disappointed in them as Christian men.

They have dared to wink at oppression, and shut their ears to the cry of the oppressed. They have coolly and deliberately dared to perpetuate my imprisonment indefinitely, in open defiance of reason, truth and justice, and conscience.

They know that I am not an insane person; and they know that am enduring a most unjust and cruel imprisonment and persecution, merely for opinion's and conscience sake, and their own consciences are my advocates.

Still, they have sold themselves to do iniquity. They have dared to forsake God and serve tables. Satan now has them in his power; and there is no hope of my ever receiving justice at their hands.

Where! O where! shall I now look, Isaac, for protection or mercy?

Is there no man who cares for my soul? Has justice died on earth? Can the innocent find no protection from injustice?

O, Isaac, I do feel that I am utterly forsaken of all men, except Dr. McFarland. He has promised not to leave me desolate. He has promised me the right of self-defense, and I do believe he will be true to his promise and protect me in this right — that right, which all governments on earth allow to even their worst criminals, except the American government, which does not allow a wife to defend herself against the most cruel of all charges — the charge of insanity, from a wicked husband !!

I say, should I be allowed this inalienable right, it is all I ask of my fellow citizens, or friends, if I have any on earth.

Isaac, I wrote to Mr. Haslet many weeks since, and told him of this magnanimous act of the Doctor's, and asked his aid in carrying it out. But I have not heard a syllable in response.

What does this indicate?

Has the letter miscarried? or, has he become "weary in well-doing," and decided, like the priest and the Levite, to "pass by on the other side"?

Please call on Mr. Haslet and ascertain whether he has received the letter or not; and inform me immediately; for, if I have no true friends in Manteno, to rely upon for help in this time of my greatest need, I must look elsewhere for pecuniary aid in getting my book into print.

I have written to Theophilus to send me $100, but can get no reply from him, either. If you can get any response from him, do write on my account, and inform me your result, as soon as possible: for I am in a state of most painful suspense.

I never felt so much like despairing of all human help as I do now. I feel desolate and forsaken.

But, O, my God! thou hast sustained my soul in trouble, hitherto; and I still hope and pray thou wilt not leave me to sink into despair in this my hour of midnight darkness.

Perhaps I am to die a prisoner in my cell—forgotten—unknowing and unknown. If so, may I have grace to say, "God's will be done" —not mine. For it is my will to have my personal liberty, and the other inalienable rights of my being on earth secured to me, inviolate.

O, my dear Isaac—do all you can for me; and then trust God with the result of right action.

Kiss the precious children for me, and tell them not to forget their mother, although we may never meet again on earth.

My heart is almost broken and crushed from hope of seeing them once more, so long deferred, and now all so cruelly blasted—and if grief can kill, it seems as if I should be killed of overmuch sorrow.

I feel very much grieved that Dr. McFarland did not publish my first volume, which he promised to do, before the trustees met; for then I should have been liberated now. The trustees would not then have dared to perpetuate my imprisonment as they now have done.

Isaac, I ask no grace or favor of any man. I ask for justice at the bar of my country.

If our Christian government will imprison for opinion's sake, it is

time the world knew of the fact, that our government may be destroyed from off the face of the earth !

O, Isaac, let us trust God, knowing that the "triumph of the wicked is short." Truth and justice will prevail—for God reigns—not the trustees of an insane asylum.

Your loving mother,

E. P. W. PACKARD.

It is now May, 1863, and I have as yet had no response from this letter whatever. Darkness—doubt—suspense—uncertainty—is all the nourishment my hope is permitted to receive of ever having justice done me, even so far as to be permitted to tell my own simple—but to me and my children most sad—story of our wrongs.

But the brightest ray of hope from any mundane source, now lies in the fact contained in the following letter to my son Theophilus ; whom I am daily expecting will again visit me, and whom I hope to be able to influence to act as my agent in getting my first volume through the press forthwith.

The writer of this letter—Mrs. Sophia N. B. Olsen—has been an occupant of this institution for the last nine months, and an intimate acquaintance of mine for the last seven ; and she, like Mrs. Chapman and myself, and a host of others here, are enduring the tortures of this American inquisition, with all the fortitude and patience of angel martyrs for the truth, as God has revealed it to us through our organization. And daring to be true to these inspirations of the Divinity within us, we have, as a consequence, been made living sacrifices on this altar of Moloch, for the sins of our government, which will not protect us in our rights of opinion and rights of conscience.

It is now our most fondly cherished hope, that the publication of my twelve books, may so open the eyes of my countrymen, that they may see the truth as it is, and also have the moral courage to dare to destroy these hells from off this American continent.

Behold as you read the record of my wrongs, a mirror, in which thousands of the choicest specimens of humanity on this American continent, can see reflected their own most bitter experience.

Deliver me on the principles of truth, humanity and justice, and then the way will be fully prepared to lead forth this whole glorious host of living martyrs from their prison house, of worse than any Egyptian bondage, to bask in the liberty wherewith Christ makes his people free—free to sit under their own vine and fig tree, with none to molest or make them any more afraid of being called insane, simply

because they dare to be true to themselves, and true to God. May Moses' God thus lead forth his elect, chosen people, from their captivity in this American wilderness, into the promised land of American freedom. The prison captive as well as the slave must both be completely emancipated, ere this jubilee of American freedom can be consummated.

MRS. OLSEN'S LETTER TO THEOPHILUS.

JACKSONVILLE, APRIL 30, 1863.

My Dear Young Friend :

Your most estimable mother last winter introduced me to yourself, by showing me one of your letters to her. You will therefore pardon a brief letter from me to yourself. It is written principally for the sake of the book she is now writing here, and secondly for the sake of the writer of the book — your long-suffering — most patiently enduring — and deeply afflicted mother.

Respecting her, it would be superfluous and foolish in the extreme for me to inform you that she is not insane, since I do not know a single person base or ignorant enough to say that she is so.

I do rejoice that you, my young friend, are, as I believe, a true son to her; and permit me to add also my hope, that all your brothers, with no exception, will unite with your amiable sister and yourself in every exertion suggested by your mother herself, for her emancipation from this Insane Asylum, and for her restoration to all the liberty, of which her well known, excellent and Christian character has proved her worthy.

Permit me also, in bidding you adieu, to add my wish, that all those six children whose happiness it is to call her " my mother," may find in their progressive lives all the rich blessings, physical, mental and moral, which cannot fail to be the sure accompaniment of all who follow her example.

I could add much more — and it is my wish to describe on paper some of the many obligations she has conferred on myself, by acts of kindness; but I have not at my present disposal twenty quires of paper, and twice as many days, for such a pleasing task!

I will only add, sir, that when her book is printed, which I hope will be very soon indeed, that I will purchase one hundred copies.

Permit me to subscribe myself,

Yours, in true friendship and love,

SOPHIA N. B. OLSEN.

The fact which radiates so brightly from the bow of hope wh'ch now spans my horizon, is, that one hundred copies of my book are already solicited, as a voluntary, free-will offering, to cause this star of hope to rise above the horizon, and send it into the zenith of power—into the homes and hearts of the common people of this great American republic.

If I could have a few more such demonstrations of sympathy, I might have thus the most pleasing kind of tangible proof, that Mrs. Packard is not the friendless being it has so often been intimated I must in reality be, to be so long neglected, deserted and forsaken as I have been for the last three years.

Mrs. Olsen had not the most distant idea of the above letter ever appearing in print when it was written.

The writer of the following poetry, Mrs. Olsen, of Chicago, a patient in this Asylum, could not sleep on the night of January 26th, until she had obeyed an impulse which seemed almost irresistible, to rise, and write the images upon her brain. She did so as best she could, and wrote the following by moonlight on a leaf of a book. In the morning she could only recall the first line from memory.

THE BOOK OF 1863.

LINES suggested by the perusal of the book written by MRS. ELIZABETH P. W. PACKARD, *entitled "The Great Drama; or, The Millennial Harbinger."*

Affectionately and respectfully presented to the 'World's Friend,' MRS. F. P. W. PACKARD, *by her Friend,*

MRS. SOPHIA N. B. OLSEN.

Go, little book, go seek the world ;
With banner new, with flag unfurled ;
Go, teach mankind aspirings high,
By *human* immortality !

Thou canst not blush ; thine open page
Will all our higher powers engage ;
Thy name on every soul shall be,
Defender of humanity !

The poor, the sad, the sorrowing heart,
Shall joy to see thy book impart
Solace, to every tear-dimmed eye,
That's wept, till all its tears are dry.

The pallid sufferer on the bed
Of sickness, shall erect the head
And cry, "Life yet hath charms for me
When Packard's books shall scattered be."

Each prison victim of despair
Shall, in thy book, see written there
Another gospel to thy race,
Of sweet "Requiescat in pace."

The time-worn wigs, with error gray,
Their dusty locks with pale dismay,
Shall shake in vain in wild despair,
To see their prostrate castles, where?

No mourner's tear shall weep their doom,
No bard shall linger o'er their tomb,
No poet sing, but howl a strain
Farewell, thou doom'd, live not again.

Yes, oh, poor Ichabod must lay,
Deep buried in Aceldama!
His lost Consuelo shall rise
No more, to cheer his death-sealed eyes.

Then speed thy book, oh, sister, speed,
The waiting world thy works must read;
Bless'd be the man who cries, "Go on,"
"Hinder it not, it shall be gone."

Go, little book, thy destiny
Excelsior shall ever be;
A fadeless wreath shall crown thy brow,
O writer of that book! e'en now.

The wise shall laugh—the foolish cry—
Both wise and foolish virgins, why?
Because the first will wiser grow,
The foolish ones some wisdom show.

The midnight cry is coming soon,
The midnight lamp will shine at noon;
I fear for some, who snoring lie,
Then rise, ye dead, to judgment fly.

The stars shall fade away—the sun
Himself grow dim with age when done
Shining upon our frigid earth;
But Packard's book shall yet have birth,
But never death, on this our earth.

JACKSONVILLE LUNATIC ASYLUM, Jan. 27, 1863.

68 THE GREAT DRAMA.

The following letter to the trustees was written at the time it bears date; but like Miss Dix's letter, did not go through our post office, since my postmaster, Dr. McFarland, concluded not to forward it.

LETTER TO MR. BROWN.

JACKSONVILLE, DECEMBER 16, 1862.

MR. BROWN,
Chairman of Board of Trustees of Insane Asylum,

Sir :—I am most grievously disappointed that you did not discharge me at your last meeting.

I did not think it possible that a man of your intelligence and development, would dare, under our government, to imprison for opinion's sake! But you have done the deed, and on your own individual act you must stand or fall in the judgment of the intelligent world of the nineteenth century.

This deed will yet be looked upon as one of the foulest blots on the page of American history; and the notoriety you have secured to yourself, and your descendants, will not be enviable.

You must defend yourself as best you can, from the indignant response, which all the true men and all the true women of America will feel, as expressed by a most intelligent gentleman, Mr. Chedister, to me, when I told him of your action—"I hope the trustees will get justice done them!"

Yes, it is the response of all true Americans, if our public officers will imprison for opinion's sake, and the government uphold them in so doing, the government is not worth sustaining! The Christian world ought to know of it, and the government ought to be destroyed from off the face of the earth! Yes, Mr. Brown, you have imprisoned me for opinion's sake, and such opinions as large and influential bodies of Christians have embraced in all ages of the world. And if I am insane, then all these different classes of God's chosen ones are so also, and, in your judgment, ought to be imprisoned — and you would do it, if they happened to be defenseless, like me, and it cost you any effort to defend your Saviour, in these his persecuted ones! Will Christ defend you in your time of need?

You know me to be an intelligent, accountable moral agent; for you have seen me for yourself, and whatever causes may have operated to warp or control your private judgment, you, alone, are responsible for the act. For, as Mr. Jones, our farmer, says, "No one need but to converse with Mrs. Packard, a few moments, to be convinced she is

not an insane person;" and, as Mrs. Hosmer remarked to Dr. Eddy, "You see Mrs. Packard once, you see her always."

There is not one about this building who recognizes me as an insane person, except Mrs. McFarland, and she did not until *her husband became my protector!* And Miss Mills, my educated attendant, remarked, "If the Dr. attempts to prove you to be an insane person, he will have to prove a lie."

Mr. Brown, you cannot defend yourself on the delusion that I am insane, before any intelligent jury in the land. It is a moral impossibility.

Mr. Brown, I feel conscience-bound to report you at head-quarters, and seek satisfaction at the bar of my country. You must be made an example of to the world, both as a lesson and a warning to those Calvinists who dare to impede the car of progress, by the arm of the law. Justice and truth will triumph, and I shall triumph with it; but "though the wicked join hand in hand, they shall not go unpunished."

Your sister in bonds,

E. P. W. PACKARD.

A DREAM,

WITHOUT AN INTERPRETATION, SEPTEMBER, 1862.

LAST night I dreamed another dream, which has left such ineffaceable impressions upon my mind, as leads me to feel that it has some significance.

I dreamed that I was attending anniversary meetings of national benevolent institutions, in company with my husband, as I had been wont to do, while living in Massachusetts.

My husband was called upon to perform some important service on the occasion, which required him to take a conspicuous seat upon the platform.

I was seated in a front slip nearest the platform, fronting the pulpit.

My husband seemed to attract a great deal of notice to himself, from those immediately about him, as well as the congregation generally, by his peculiar maneuvers, which he seemed strangely determined to practice. I became embarrassed, and concerned for his reputation; and this, added to the unaccountable fact that I was bonnetless, and with disheveled hair, with not even a net to confine the straggling locks, combined to render my situation, in so conspicuous a seat, anything but comfortable or desirable.

Still, my fortitude and self-control never left me; knowing that "what could not be cured, must be endured," with Christian fortitude and meekness.

At length, my husband became so strangely eccentric in his movements, that the bystanders undertook to, gently, interfere, and to give him some gentle hints, that he was disturbing the audience. But all to no purpose. He even seemed determined to defy interference; plainly intimating that he could tend to his own business, without their help — when he wanted their help, and asked for it, it was soon enough for them to bestow it!

Finally, his time came to perform his part, which he chose to execute in the high pulpit, far above them, which was reached by two long, steep flights of stairs, on each side of the pulpit.

But he, instead of going directly up the stairs, when summoned to his post, began to circumambulate the platform, and walk down, first the front aisle, then the side aisles, and so on. No one could control him, not even the Moderator.

I felt that it was time for me to interfere, and try my power over him. I accordingly arose, and passing out of the slip, followed him down the side aisle, and joining arms with him, said, in a very pleasant, confiding tone, "Come, husband, let us go together, and I will help you find the platform — you seem confused, as though you had lost your way. Come, go with me, and I will set you all straight and right." The work was done. This voluntary surrender of himself to my control, seemed to set him all right again, and he, like a man, went about his duties, and all was quiet again.

As I sat, with my head down, striving to compose my agitated feelings, suddenly I was aroused, by his whispering in my ear, "I am going to wash my face!"

Looking up, I saw him just stepping upon the platform, to wash him in the baptismal bowl, entirely stripped of every article of clothing, except his shirt, which, to my extreme mortification, I saw was an old torn one, which I had laid by for sickness!

The shirt being a torn one, so distressed me, as to wholly absorb every other thought respecting him, in the extreme mortification which I experienced, when I considered, what will be thought of me, that I let him wear such an old, worn-out shirt to the anniversaries!

But this feeling was soon supplanted by a stronger fear, that he might disgracefully expose his own person.

Still, no one interposed.

I next prayed, most fervently, that he would put on his pants, at least, before ascending the high, steep, pulpit stairs! But my silent ejaculations availed not, to prevent this awful catastrophe.

Seeing him rushing for the stairs, I, instinctively, together with the other true women of the house, covered our faces, or turned our backs, in disgust, from the horrid spectacle of seeing him ascend those high, steep stairs, pantless!

The male part of the house uttered one general shout of merriment.

I then looked up, and beckoned to a gentleman who occupied the pulpit with my husband, to come to me. He did so.

I then whispered in his ear, "My husband is crazy — he must be taken care of — I think it must have been coming on for some time; for, some thought he was crazy when he put me in the asylum."

I awoke — to find myself still an occupant of that dreadful asylum.

As this dream has found no interpreter, (since "Joseph" has left), I present it to the astrologers and soothsayers, of the infallible Calvinistic church, for interpretation — only asking you, not to blame me too severely for neglecting to patch up the Calvinistic shirt; but to bear in mind, that I did not leave it unmended, for the purpose of exposing the person of Calvin, but simply because I did not think it worth mending!

NOTICE.

The succeeding "Defense" was presented after I had been here about four months.

I here present it, that the public may see and judge for themselves, of the facts as they exist. And also, that it may serve as a certificate of my sanity, when I entered as a patient into this institution.

I maintain, that I *entered* this institution as *sane* a person as I *left* it.

A SELF-DEFENSE.

The following plea was presented to Dr. McFarland, Superintendent of the State Lunatic Asylum, Illinois, by his sane patient, E. P. W. Packard, October 26, 1860, in defense of the following

PETITION.

Dr. McFarland — *Sir :*

I, your sane patient, E. P. W. Packard, wife of Rev. Theophilus Packard, of Manteno, Kankakee county, Ill., do hereby respectfully request that you forthwith give me an honorable discharge from this Asylum, upon your own responsibility — that is, without consulting my husband in the matter, for the following

REASONS.

1. I have a legal and constitutional claim to my liberty as a citizen of the United States, having never said or done anything justly to forfeit it.

2. Since the first few weeks, I remained at my own request, that you might have a reasonable time and opportunity to see for yourself that I had been placed here on a *false* charge of insanity.

3. My conscience forbids any further extension of this merely bogus claim to my support, since I know that I have capacities which render me self-reliant, with God's providence as my only protector.

4. I know, too, sir, that to hold me from this date, as a patient, you are exposing yourself to a just condemnation at the bar of public opinion, at the legal bar, at the bar of God, for having intelligently and knowingly broken your solemn " oath of office," by retaining a *sane* person as a patient, after having had all reasonable time to judge for yourself in the matter.

5. I am fully determined never to return to my husband again, of my own free-will, for he has forever forfeited all claim to my love and confidence ; having proved himself to be an enemy to righteousness — an "apostate from the faith "— an "arch deceiver "—with whom I shall henceforth hold no fellowship whatever.

6. I do desire that you make no consultation with him in this matter, since I fully believe that instead of consenting to any such plan, he would rather desire your aid to incarcerate me in an insane asylum *for life*, on the plea of hopeless insanity. And I assure you it is dangerous for you to cope with this my arch-enemy. You are putting in jeopardy the interests of your precious soul to do it. He may tempt you to do a deed which to all eternity you may have occasion to regret having done. O, Dr. McFarland, I entreat you to take the warning so kindly intended, and escape the snare unharmed.

7. I feel now fully prepared to risk the consequences of uttering opinions without "respect of persons," and I am determined fearlessly and boldly to advocate the *truth*, as it respects my husband, or you — my kind protector; and all the combined power of earth will not tempt me to recant what I conscientiously believe to be the truth, even should its utterance expose me to the insane's dungeon for life. For in truth is my trust — in God's providence is my protection — in his promises, my support.

8. I do hereby pledge myself that when you grant me my liberty, which I claim is already legally mine, I will pay up all my dues here, amounting to $10.35 — making it the first payment out of wages received.

QUESTIONS.

1. Since I have been illegally retained, can I not be illegally discharged, as a case of exception to the general rule?

2. Will your humanity or Christianity allow you to return the fugitive to his master, notwithstanding the law requires it? and will your honor allow you to return a poor, defenseless suppliant to that sorest of all bondage, that of a married slave to a tyrannical, arbitrary, unfeeling man?

3. Will you not do by me as the golden rule directs you to desire to have your dear daughter, Hattie, dealt by, in exchange of circumstances, when you remember that God is just?

4. Is there not now offered you one of those rare instances for the display of that most noble, magnanimous trait of true manliness, by venturing to espouse the cause of injured virtue and helpless innocence, even in defiance of a strong, popular tide of feeling, believing that an approving conscience far transcends all we may gain or lose from a fickle public sentiment, which one day cries 'Hosanna!' and the next, 'Crucify'?

5. Have you not abundant evidence at hand showing that the time

has already arrived, when a man's foes shall be those of his own household; and also when there is nothing covered which shall not be revealed and made manifest, by the effulgent light which is now dawning upon the world?

6. Have you not reason to fear that my case fairly represents a class of oppressed women, who have been unjustly imprisoned here, by unnatural men; who, because they had the power to oppress an unprotected wife, secretly rejoice in the aid which this institution furnishes them for doing it, and thus escape detection and deserved justice at the bar of their country's law — as, for example, Mr. Tucker, Mr. Miller, Mr. Wood, and perhaps Mr. Hart?

7. Would it not be an exhibition of true moral courage on your part to promptly discharge such patients as Mrs. Kenney, as soon as you find that the decision of an ignorant quack respecting her, (whose acts indicate that he lives in the light of the past century,) are not founded in truth?

8. Dr. McFarland, are you not, like me, working out your own destiny for this enlightened age, as well as for eternity, by your own acts?

9. Have you not reason to hope that what you in reality do for me, and other oppressed victims of a husband's cruelty, your Saviour will accept as done unto himself? And will not your reward be glorious?

10. Will you not dare to do right, and espouse the cause of injured innocence, and be our protector, instead of our husbands' abettor in crime; for on the part of our oppressors there is power, and we do need a comforter?

11. Will you not make such a decision as you will delight to have legally investigated —publicly known; such as may add another gem to your character for manly honor and Christian integrity?

12. But should you deny me my petition, will you please to give me your reasons in writing, for regarding and treating me as insane? Or, in other words, what irrational or unreasonable conduct have you observed in me within the four months time I have been under your intelligent inspection?

13. Will your developed manliness allow you to uphold a man who will place such a person as you find me to be, by your own personal knowledge, in an insane asylum, as a fit patient, simply for maintaining the supremacy of conscience over the arbitrary will of a husband — I say, will you uphold a man whose real character is truthfully indicated by this act, when another true gentleman of Jacksonville, upon a short acquaintance of a few hours, has had the boldness to

pronounce me as not insane—and has said, " The man who will regard and treat that woman as insane, is too mean a man to live, and is also too mean a man to die, except to go to the bad place, where he deserves to go " ?

14. Will not the keeper of Washington jail be condemned by the Christian sentiment of the whole world, as it is in 1860 ; and by God himself, when it is ascertained that he has knowingly and voluntarily retained Mr. Hyatt, as a prisoner, after he has had ample testimony to believe that he was illegally and unconstitutionally placed there ; and by retaining him, is he not really conniving at the doings of a corrupt body, who, in defiance of law and justice, had ventured to do an abominable, cruel, and wicked deed, trusting to the frail refuge of *position* to sustain them in it — and will not *you*, Dr. McFarland, be condemned by the same tribunals, and for the same reasons, should you venture or dare to retain me as a prisoner from this date ?

15. Have the laws of our country entrusted the will of the Senate, and the will of the husband, with power to imprison a citizen without judge or jury ?

16. Will you not prayerfully consider this point before you cast your influence into the scales of despotism ?

In view of the above Petition, Reasons, and Questions, I wish to make an appeal to your understanding, to your conscience, and to your heart.

1. *An Appeal to your Understanding.*

Dr. McFarland, the state of our family has for a long time been aptly illustrated by the figure my son Isaac, a very intelligent lad of sixteen, often uses to describe his father's position. He is like a man struggling, as in a death-grapple, to smother and keep out of view the pent-up fires of an immense volcano, the darting of whose flames he is anxiously fearing and expecting at every quarter. He is in reality a smothered volcano — the raging fires of an accusing conscience have long been consuming all except the exterior man, and he himself has now opened the crater by publicly imprisoning his wife, for her simply choosing to obey God rather than man. Yes, through this open crater are now leaping up the long-pent-up fires of despotism, and it is now past his power to stem the fiery current that is fast consuming, not only the mountain itself, but also all who come near its fiery gorge, or within the course of its devastating stream.

For my own part I dare not come again within the influence of this man, as I know him to be an arch deceiver, whose power I know only to dread, fear, and avoid. And as your Christian sister, I warn you of this enemy of Christ, who, for wise reasons, has the use of a power to deceive if possible the very elect.

O, Dr. McFarland, your pure heart cannot conceive the mighty power — the psychological power — this man possesses to deceive. All the wealth of the universe would not tempt me to exchange places with him.

I regard him as the "son of perdition," for whom there is not found a ransom. He is an object of pity, but past hope. He himself is the most perfect practical specimen of his own favorite text and doctrine, viz., "the heart of man is deceitful above all things, and desperately wicked, who can know it?

I know now and fully believe that the heart of *one man* is so, and that man is my husband. And this belief is henceforth to become a practical one; for "faith without works is dead," you know!

Yes, Dr. McFarland, my future life is to be a standing proof, by God's help, of my utter withdrawal of all fellowship from this arch foe of my espoused Master's unpopular cause — the cause of truth.

Again — in coming to this conclusion, my children's interests are not, nor ever have been, forgotten by me, a true Christian mother. I have done for them all I can do or shall attempt to do, under the dictatorship of their tyrant father. They must now contend with this their tyrant foe alone. For them I fear not. My faith assures me they will, like their mother, come off victorious at last. But like all other spiritual victors, they must fight before they can reign. And I fully believe that my absence will only serve to drive them the sooner to their only refuge — the Saviour's bosom.

Yes, I am sustained by the sweet hope that the pledge which my daughter of ten years voluntarily gave me a short time before I left home, may become the practical language of them all. The remark was this : "Mother, if you are ever compelled to leave us, I shall always remember to do in my troubles as I know you to do in yours; instead of returning evil for evil, you go and tell Jesus and get help to be patient, and return good for evil." She testified truthfully of her mother.

Another fact. I have given my pledge to my husband, two years since, in the presence of his sister as witness, that I never should live with him a day, if I could help it, after I had become fully convinced that he regarded me as insane.

7

This pledge I have thus far redeemed, and by God's help I intend always to follow God's directions as found in this verse to which my attention was particularly directed, when, upon the reception of my husband's letter, I looked to my only counselor for direction by asking him to direct me to open the Bible to some text or portion that I might regard as an exponent of his will. I opened to the following verse -- "Lord, remember David and all his afflictions, how he sware unto the Lord, and vowed unto the mighty God of Jacob, surely I will not come into the tabernacle of my house, nor go up into my bed."

Again — I freely take the entire responsibility of this pledge upon myself alone. No one shares it with me as an adviser. My only counsel is God.

And does not God in his providence sometimes call his children to the exercise of that kind or degree of faith that transcends our reason?

Could Abraham's *reason* have approved of that act which faith demanded — the murder of his only son? How long think you would he have been obliged to defer this act of obedience to Heaven's mandate, had he waited to test his duty by popular opinion?

Would he not have been regarded as a lunatic, and treated as one, had he lived in our day? I think I might have had the pleasure of his company in this Asylum had he chanced to have been my cotemporary in Illinois!!

Now, Dr. McFarland, by the exercise of the same kind of faith I am prepared to bear meekly and silently the taunts and sneers which an unfeeling world may delight to heap upon me for so doing, confident that I am entirely safe under Heaven's protection. Indeed, I much prefer to beg my bread from door to door, and die in a poor-house, than to trust to my husband for protection or help.

I ask no favor at his hands. No — not even my own children, my clothes, my money, my life insurance policy of $4,000.

I ask for no passports, no testimonials from him, from yourself, or from any other human tribunal or arbitration.

I only ask my *liberty* as a citizen of these United States. *Freedom* to serve the present age according to the dictates of my *own conscience*, depending only upon my own words and actions as my only passport to the confidence of an enlightened Christian public, and as my only title through grace to my heavenly inheritance.

To God's honor I make my boast of being endowed with treasures of rare bestowment, viz., a sound mind in a comparatively sound body Possessed with these gifts I deem it no act of presumption on my part, to assume a self-reliant position in society.

Another fact. I am *not insane* as my husband would have the world believe me to be. Hon. Gerrit Smith's physician, to whom I made a free representation of our internal condition as a family, a few years since, testified, that my husband was the insane party. Said he, "Mrs. Packard, your husband is a monomaniac on the treatment of a wife — he is insane on his amativeness."

I do not regard him insane to that extent as to excuse him from being an entirely responsible agent.

The wrongs he has heaped upon me, his wife, I regard as having been committed in defiance of reason, knowledge and conscience. I believe his wrong treatment of me commenced in ignorance — was pursued in willful wrong doing — and ended in conscientiously wrong doing. And this third degree of wrong doing I regard as beyond the power of human influence to restrain or correct. And the degree of light and love that he has resisted to reach that point, renders him, in my opinion, past hope from all good influences. All his promises and pledges of future amendment will henceforth be regarded by me as mere idle tales.

I know these opinions respecting an husband may seem uncharitably severe from one who claims a title to the capacities of a true wife.

But, O, Dr. McFarland, the saddest truth remains yet to be uttered, viz., these terrible opinions are supported by the most stubborn of all arguments — facts — dreadful facts. God grant that self-defense may never render it incumbent on me to prove these my honestly cherished opinions, by being obliged to bring these arguments before the public for proof.

I trust to God's providence to develop the fact that these opinions are no fancy sketch — the pictures of an overheated imagination.

This same physician testified of me that it was impossible for me to become an insane person, on the ground that I knew too much in connection with the conscience I had, which would compel me to make a practical use of this knowledge and thus prevent the cause.

It is my opinion that, since insanity is an unnatural state of being, it must always be induced by ignorantly or willfully infringing some law, either natural or moral, or both ; and that as the knowledge of these laws has been given to me by God in an unusual degree, by both instinct and science, I really believe it would be a sin for me to become insane.

Again — Mr. O. S. Fowler testified of me, "you not only have the ability to do the very best, but you cannot do otherwise, since con-

science commands such sovereign sway in your organization. You would die a martyr for the truth, and your instincts render you a true prophet. Your organization is purely womanly to an extent beyond any I have ever found." "Indeed," he added, "you ought to have gone to the 'World's Fair' at New York, as a specimen of the purest womanly organization the world ever saw!"

He closed the examination by remarking, very significantly, to my husband, "you ought to be appreciated."

I apprehend he believed I was not appreciated by my husband, by the development of the sad truths he told of my husband's organization.

One fact my argument requires me to present, viz. : "Your mind," said he to my husband, "works like an old worn-out horse in a tread-mill, and unless you can break up these monotonous habits by some change of mental action, you will soon lose all your faculties, so that in a few years you will not know even your own name."

Now, Dr. McFarland, cannot our differences in opinion be here accounted for on scientific principles ? Here we see his sluggish, conserative temperament rejecting light, which costs any effort to obtain or use — clinging, serf-like, to the old paths as with a death-grasp; while my active, radical temperament calls for light to bear me onward and upward, never satisfied until all available means are faithfully used to reach a more progressive state.

Now I ask, can hope and fear, sloth and action, truth and falsehood, light and darkness, liberty and despotism, see subjects in just the same light ? Or, in Christ's expressive language, can Christ and Belial hold fellowship together ?

Another fact. A few years since, I noticed an article in the New Englander on spiritualism, showing, in a very candid and intelligent light, that these developments might be the incipient developments of a new spiritual science, by the aid of which, the spiritual history of this planet was to be developed — that it might be but the dawning light by which Christ's spiritual reign upon the earth was to be ushered in. This article led me to desire to look into the subject myself. But I was obliged to encounter a most strenuous opposition in attempting to carry out this desire, from both my husband and his conservative church.

As usual, I sought my counsel for direction, and as the result, I regarded it to be the will of God, that out of regard to the consciences of my weaker brothers and sisters in Christ, I might be justified in yielding a personal, inalienable right for the sake of peace. I then

gave them a voluntary pledge that I would not then investigate the subject any further. Hitherto that pledge has been redeemed.

But when this recent storm of persecution commenced, I began to fear it was a just rebuke from the Lord upon me, for having thus attempted to seek peace at the expense of purity.

I mentioned it to my husband, and he, instead of allowing this interpretation to be put upon it, said, that he regarded that act as the wisest and the best act of my life.

His approbation can only be secured to me at the expense of light and truth.

There is one way, and only one way in which I can live with him in peace—and that is, by choosing darkness and a guilty conscience. This I cannot do, even to secure the approbation of that person whose esteem I have desired to possess above all others in the world.

But all these giant efforts to crush out and to destroy the rights of true womanhood, have been fruitless.

He has not prevailed against me. Paul's motto is still mine. "This one thing I do, forgetting those things which are behind, and reaching forth unto those which are before, I press toward the mark for the prize of the high calling of God in Christ Jesus."

Through the atoning blood of the Lamb I have conquered; and by faith I expect to be completely released from this loathsome body of sin and death, to which I have been bound lo! these twenty-two weary years almost.

Who shall deliver me? My God replies, "I will deliver thee."

Will not you who have been to me a most noble, kind protector, receive the honor which awaits Heaven's appointed agent in this work?

Another fact. Mr. Blessing, of Manteno, who called upon me with his wife, and Dr. Shirley, a short time since, confirmed the description I was giving them of our diverse dispositions, by exclaiming, "It is just as she says—you may rely upon all Mrs. Packard says as true, for she is a woman worthy of trust and confidence."

Again—in speaking to them of my present situation, I remarked, that all I had suffered here, arising from treatment received, did not begin to equal what I endured in one day's time at home from my husband. He replied, "Yes, I believe it to be true, for," said he, turning to Dr. Shirley, "that woman endured enough every day of her life for weeks before she left home, to ——

Here I was interrupted, and lost the remainder of the sentence.

Indeed, Dr. McFarland, this asylum has been to me a refuge for the oppressed, a covert from the storm of severe persecution. Mr. Blessing

inquired if I wished to return to my family. I replied, "Indeed I do. I long to be within the embrace of my precious children—but I must be protected from my husband."

"Yes, I supposed it was so," he replied; and turning to Dr. Shirley, he remarked, "I must see Dr. McFarland to-night."

Dr. McFarland, instead of being an insane woman, I am a persecuted woman—persecuted, because I dared to speak the truth in face of mighty opposition. Yes, supported by no human sympathy—with no counselor but God, I dared to utter such words of truth and soberness, as made both the church and pulpit quake and tremble—and lest the little stone of truth cut out of the mountain without hands, and wielded by the sling of faith, should enter the understanding, and discomfit Goliah and all his vaunted hosts—and lest this stone should fall on them, and grind them to powder, they agreed to trample under foot, and place on a level with the beasts, the weak, defenseless, unprotected medium whom God had employed to use these potent weapons of truth and love to their overthrow.

The opinions which I uttered, and which caused such convulsive throes in the social and moral elements of that community, are all in black and white, and in a form such as I should delight to have presented for the criticism and inspection of the whole enlightened world of 1860. I ask no better passport to the confidence of enlightened Christianity than these documents, and no better evidence than these, that the mind which dictated them was in the full exercise of all its mental faculties.

My husband, well aware of this fact, employed the most adroit and efficient measures to prevent my having them to use as testimonials. Alas! They are in the hands of my arch-enemy. He may destroy the records—but he cannot destroy the truths which they contain, or the mind that dictated them—which mind he has long vainly striven to obliterate.

This thing is not done in a corner. It is no ordinary event. The momentous results of this event remain yet to be developed in the providence of the All-Wise Governor of the universe.

The part you are to take, my kind protector, remains yet to be known.

But if I must remain here until I am willing to return to my husband, (as some assure me I must), I assure you my term of imprisonment must not only be life-long, but eternity-long.

Am I under laws which compel those wives who cannot live with their husbands to spend their days in an insane asylum?

Again—God's purposes are accomplished by the use of means, such means as our own free agency chooses to employ. I expect God to help me only as I help myself. Since the day of miracles is past, and since God works only by immutable laws, I look for deliverance only by the use of means appropriate to the end.

I feel confident that I am following God's directions by trying to protect myself—by skilfully using the sword he has placed in my hands to use—the sword of truth. I expect God's blessing only by doing right. I fear his curse only by doing wrong.

To protract my stay here after this document has been candidly considered by you, would be a sin, as I view it.

Again—by making me an example of one who has dared to break the fetters of married servitude; chosing by far, a self-reliant position in society, rather than the subjection of her womanly rights to the demands of an unnatural man, who claims to be her protector! is there not reason to hope that you will be regarded as a Moses to lead forth a host of bond-women who have been called to serve a most rigorous servitude—because these unnatural men claim the law of marriage to be the subjection of the weaker vessel to the arbitrary will of the stronger, rather than the protection of the true womanly rights of the weak, defenseless being who claims such protection from the man whom of all others she chooses to obey?

Do not despise the honor which awaits you as my deliverer. I know I shall be delivered out of the hands of that cruel, unreasonable man, and by some human instrumentality; and as Christ said of himself, so I, as his follower, say of myself, as a witness for the truth, "They that honor me (the truth) I will honor, but they that despise me shall be lightly esteemed."

Another fact. Testimony is being obtained from eye and ear witnesses of my conduct, since I was put under your care, whether I have given them any evidence of being an insane person.

The first individual is yet to be found who dares to testify against me. One is dead who dared to do it. "There is a sin unto death," that is, a sin which God punishes with the death of the body. Yes, Mrs. Hart testified that she regarded me as a monomaniac, in that I carried my religion into every thing!

I promptly acknowledge this charge to be just: for I do aim both by word and deed, by spirit and conduct, to be a living witness of that true, practical godliness which is "perfect and entire, wanting nothing." I strive to be guilty of no act or emotion which is not pervaded by the religious element.

I have reason to believe that Mrs. Hosmer and Miss Eagle regard me as a liar in that which I say of my husband, and they may probably say of me that I am insane on that point.

But these individuals believe a lie if they believe I do not speak the truth of my husband.

I do hate and abhor lying, and I do not and I will not practice it to secure the favor of the highest earthly potentate.

The transparency of my frank, honest, truthful nature my husband has tried hard to destroy, by persecuting me to compel me to act the hypocrite.

For example. In order to prevent our extending the rights of hospitality to friends and strangers, he has tried to induce me to belie my nature, and give them a cold reception, that he may in this way save the food he has provided only for his family !

But I have dared to defy his power, by extending to our guests that hearty, cordial welcome which my nature prompts me to exercise ; and as a result, our happy and delighted guests have gone away extolling the hospitable home of that good (?) minister, who is thus following Christ's directions, " to use hospitality without grudging " — while I, his wife, am left silently and alone to suffer persecution from him, for doing that for which he is thus being extolled !

Yes, it is true that I and my dear children have actually gone hungry, and deprived ourselves of needed, suitable nourishment, to appease his wrath towards me for so doing.

I do feel morally bound to testify truthfully against my husband under the circumstances in which I am now placed, not only on the ground of my own self-defense, but also on the ground of your defense also — my kind protector.

For I am well aware of the mighty opposing surge you will have to contend with in granting my petition ; and I deemed this stubborn argument of facts might be necessary for your defense at the bar of public opinion and at the legal bar.

Do not, my kind, humane protector, believe that I regarded this argument as necessary to induce you to do the thing so simple, upright and just as my petition asks you to do. Indeed, I do expect you will do the thing that is right, although this argument may in itself seem to imply that I believed it was necessary as a means to secure my request.

Again — You well know that a giant evil must be met by a giant force — the force of truth.

The weapon of truth should be well prepared to wield if necessary

in our defense; and with this, well prepared and used in love, we have nothing to fear.

Might does not make right. But right makes might; for truth is mighty and will prevail.

You may be persecuted as I have been, for doing right. But from my own experience I can testify that "gold loses nothing by the furnace but its dross."

And your righteous Judge may deem it necessary for you to pass the trying ordeal of fiery persecution to fit you for the place he designs you shall occupy, as a king or a priest unto himself, in this dawning of his blessed reign upon the earth. Particularly may you need it in order to fit you for sympathizing with, and to pity and feel for and treat with tender compassion those poor despised objects of persecution, who have been and still are and probably will be placed under your care, regarded by some as insane; when all they need is sympathy to help them to bear with Christian fortitude the wrongs which have been and still are heaped upon them. Solomon says that "oppression makes the wise man mad," and a very little increase of it on your part may make maniacs of them.

Do be careful that you add not, even ignorantly, to the burdens of the already overburdened and oppressed victims of persecution.

Discriminate wisely between the insane and the persecuted, and act accordingly. Then when your noble work of administering to Christ in one of his afflicted tender ones, is done, your plaudit is secure.

The "well done" will not be forgotten. Then can we rejoice and be exceeding glad, as by faith we contemplate the prize to which persecution for Christ's sake alone gives us a title.

2. *Appeal to your Conscience.*

Can it be right for you to give your influence to support such a man as my husband? Can a hypocrite be justified in God's sight?

He is a hypocrite — a deceiver. He is as "wise as a serpent," and he "honors God with his lips."

This is the highest praise his character merits. Like Christ's whited sepulchres, he appears outwardly righteous unto men, but within is full of hypocrisy and iniquity.

I think the testimony of Dr. Pettigue, of Mt. Pleasant, Iowa, a man who rented a house of him there, is too true. Said he, "Mr. Packard, you are doing more to damn souls, than all your preaching does to save them!"

It is a fact, that so far as my knowledge extends, I do not know of a single soul that he has been the direct instrument of bringing to Christ, either by his preaching or by his direct personal efforts. He has great power to bring souls into bondage, but no power to bring them into the liberty wherewith Christ makes his people free.

He can preach depravity from personal experience; but repentance, faith and obedience, he cannot teach from experience. In attempting to bring souls to Christ, he is like the blind leading the blind.

I know of no man whom I have reason to fear will be responsible for the ruin of more souls than I think my husband will be responsible for.

Now, Dr. McFarland, will your conscience uphold you in sustaining one whom you have so much reason to fear is a foe to your Master's cause?

Can you reasonably expect the approval of a God of justice in so doing?

In the language of Solomon I would say, "He that sayeth to the wicked, thou art righteous, him shall the people curse, nations shall abhor him; but to them that rebuke him shall be delight, and a good blessing shall come upon him."

To consult with him before you liberate me, would be giving him your countenance.

Again — Will your conscience allow you to lend your influence to sustain such bogus legislation — such mock administration of justice and law, as my case develops?

Indeed, it was nothing but the arbitrary will of my husband that placed me here.

True, some of the mock forms of law were passed through with; but the spirit of them was utterly rejected and despised by him. For example:

His jury, (if it may be so called,) was entirely of his own selection, composed mostly of his own church and people, and he himself assumed the two-fold office of advocate and judge; and I think he must be a poor lawyer who would not get his case under such circumstances, with no opposition!

No one uttered a word in my defense, I was told (I was not present) except my son, Isaac, who ventured to correct some of his father's gross mistakes in his plea, which he made out, that I was an insane person. Isaac told me that his father did not bring one charge against me but what I could have refuted entirely as a false representation. His testimony was all founded on *perverted truth* — which weapon he is peculiarly adapted to wield, both by nature and practice.

He is a perverted and unnatural man, and has long preached perverted truths.

After having completely psychologized his jury into his own sentiments and opinions, by his arch, cunning, artful plea, he called upon those present, who regarded me as an insane person, to rise. Isaac thought they all arose — he could hardly tell, as our parlor was crowded by perhaps thirty or forty people.

I have reason to think some arose who did not regard me as insane, but felt that it was better for me to be put here, than be longer exposed to my husband's persecuting power, fearing it might make me insane in reality.

But these weaker brothers and sisters in Christ did not realize the potent influence of the antidote by which I was being sustained. From sweet experience I can testify that the antidote of faith — a calm and holy trust in God — is a sovereign quietus to the nerves, such as can carry the soul safely through even the severest of all trials — the persecution of a bosom companion — unharmed.

Probably this company comprised the greater part of the forty signers to my husband's petition to get me put in here, although I was told there were signers there who had never seen me! All were in about the same condition as to personal evidence of insanity on my part, since his own sister, Mrs. Dole, who was at our house more, and saw me more than any one else outside of the family, wrote to my son, Theophilus, at Mt. Pleasant, Iowa, that she had never seen any insanity in me herself, but if she must credit the testimony of her brother — his father — she must believe I was.

Another fact. I had a good, kind, faithful hired girl, a few weeks before I left home, whom my husband abruptly sent away from me, greatly to my own and my family's discomfort and inconvenience, for the only offense of giving the following testimony in my favor, viz. :

"I see no reason in Mrs. Packard's own conduct, why she should be regarded and treated as insane. She is one of the kindest and best women I ever knew — I never worked for so kind a mistress."

I do not think the community would have treated me as they did, had my husband protected me in my rights of opinion, instead of trying to subject them to his will.

That arch deceiver had power so to blind their eyes that they could not see the truth. Therefore, he who delivered me up to them had the greater sin.

Father in Heaven! O, forgive that community for the treatment they have bestowed upon me, for they know not what they do.

Isaac, my son, wept at the thought of so many witnessing against his dear mother, whom he knew was not insane. Esquire Labrie, who was present at the trial, tried to comfort him, by assuring him there could be no dependence placed upon such testimony, adding, "This is wholly a one-sided affair."

But as my son then feared it would be, it was the only kind of jury trial I had.

This was on Saturday afternoon. Early the following morning, as I arose from my bed, preparing to take my morning bath, I saw my husband approaching my door with our two physicians, both members of his church. Fearing exposure, I hastily locked my door, and proceeded, with the greatest dispatch, to dress myself; but before I had hardly commenced, my husband forced an entrance into my room through the window with an axe! And I, for shelter and protection, against an exposure in a state of almost entire nudity, sprang into bed, just in time to receive my unexpected guests.

The trio approached my bed, and each doctor felt my pulse, and both pronounced me insane. I think they asked me no questions. Of course my pulse indicated a very excited state of feeling under these circumstances: for what woman, with the least degree of true womanly delicacy and refinement, would not be petrified, almost, with such an unexpected, untimely, unreasonable, unmanly, and even outrageous entrance into her private sleeping room!

Ought not these skilful doctors, Dr. Newkirk and Dr. Merrick, who can detect insanity by the feeling of the pulse under such circumstances, to be required to publish, for the world's enlightenment, the wonderful secret by which insanity can be detected by the pulse!!

My husband then informed me that the "forms of law" were all complied with; and he therefore requested me to dress myself for a ride to Jacksonville, to enter the Insane Asylum as an inmate. I obeyed, and was soon in the hands of the sheriff, who forced me from my home, by ordering two men to carry me to the wagon, which took me to the depot.

I was carried from the depot to the cars in the arms of two strong men, whom my husband appointed for this purpose, amid the silent and almost speechless gaze of the crowd of citizens who had assembled to witness the novel scene, of a husband *forcing* a sane, an intelligent and amiable wife into an Insane Asylum, for simply uttering opinions different from his own!

I was not allowed even a parting kiss, a word, or a look from those five precious children, who, could they have had the opportunity,

would have clung to me with a death-like grasp, to prevent my separation from them. Only one was allowed to witness the scene, and he, with streaming eyes, was pleading in vain for his mother's parting kiss and blessing.

This son, Samuel, twelve years of age, Judas-like, had sold himself for money, to sustain the false accusations of his father against me, his mother.

Now, Dr. McFarland, is this justice, properly and lawfully administered? Is this doing what is right in the sight of high Heaven?

My husband has had every advantage which position could secure to him, for counteracting the influence of what he might regard my erroneous opinions, by meeting me on the common plane of argument, and there testing our different opinions in the scales of free discussion; or he might have preached against them from his pulpit.

But neither of these would he do.

He chose what he regarded as the most feasible plan for him to accomplish his object, viz., to put down my *opinions* by putting *me* down.

In reply to my question, " Why do you try to injure and destroy my character rather than my opinions ?" He replied, " That your opinions may not be believed ! "

Now, I ask, is this a fair, a right way to treat an opponent in argu ment? And although the opponent be a wife, does the law of mar riage justify *such* a protection of the rights of opinion of the weakei vessel, on the part of the stronger one — the one who has sworn forever to be the protector of his wife? No. No law justifies such treatment of an opponent in argument.

This is only the exercise of the despot's power over his helpless, uncomplaining, innocent victim.

It is not that I am unwilling that my husband should cling to his long-cherished opinions, that I solicited a fair course of treatment towards me, his opponent in argument; but only that I claimed equality with him, in my individual right to my private opinion.

And I say it is persecution of the foulest kind to imprison a person for simply maintaining this right.

I am a martyr for the rights of opinion in woman, in the year 1860, n this boasted, free America!

Shall I be driven to seek protection under the government of the British Queen, in order that I, a minister's wife, may be allowed to think independently of my husband?

Am I driven to choose one of two evils, either the subjection of my

womanly rights, or imprisonment in an insane asylum? If so, I resist the powers that be, knowing that they are not ordained of God, who never allows us to choose any evil, but rather good.

I resist all the evils of slavery and oppression, and choose all the good of liberty — and freedom to serve the present age according to the dictates of my own conscience; and I shall pursue this object until this blessed boon is obtained.

My Advocate and sworn Counsel will work out my deliverance, because he has pledged himself to "break every yoke, and let the oppressed go free" — and woe to that power who shall dare to oppose Omnipotence.

Again — can your conscience approve of the wrongs you will be inflicting upon me by denying my petition?

I am unjustly imprisoned here; and I am morally bound not to return to my husband; and you, sir, by not releasing me except on condition that I return to my husband, are attempting to lord it over the conscience of a weak sister.

Can you be in any sense guilty by granting my request? Can you be guiltless in not granting it?

To return me to my husband or to retain me as a prisoner, will be, henceforth, as I view it, a sinful act, by which your title to Heaven's protection will be forfeited.

If my husband wishes to kidnap me, let him do it alone, without your help or countenance in any form or shape.

I ask no help from you or any one else to defend me against him, except *liberty* to defend and protect myself. I know and feel the need of deliverance from his power better than any one else; for I am the agrieved party — the sufferer.

I ask no one to share the responsibility of the act with me — it is my own act, and to God alone am I responsible for it, as a moral act.

Now for you to deny me my liberty under these circumstances would be doing me a willful wrong.

In attempting to maintain a conscience void of offense towards God, I have offended my husband, and I shall never allow any compromise of principle to make up with him. The hurt of the daughter of my people has too often already been attempted to be healed slightly, by crying "peace! peace!" at the expense of purity. I compromise with evil no more.

I henceforth acknowledge no protector but Omnipotence. With such a protector, I now boldly and undauntingly espouse the cause of truth — and I fear nothing.

Although I boast of no carnal weapons in its defense, yet I use mighty ones, such as will prostrate all the combined powers which men or personified devils may bring against me.

The dungeon, or the rack, or the stake, I defy.

I have borne with that man until forbearance ceases to be a virtue. I have bowed in subjection to his despotic will for the last time. I now henceforth resist it. I give this giant foe to my spiritual interests, henceforth. no quarter. With the pledged help of Omnipotence I shall surmount every obstacle which impedes the achievement of a complete victory : which is, entire deliverance from his power.

He has forced me from home as insane, when I am not insane. I shall not be guilty of the insane act of returning to such a protector.

It may be God will make use of the laws of my country to protect me against such a protector.

I do not refuse to return to him because I wish to marry another. I shall never marry another while my lawful husband lives.

I believe God forbids it.

I only keep from him that I may not die the second death. I am only safe in trusting God by doing right ; and for me it would be a sin to hold any sort of fellowship with my lawful husband. And that confidence is misplaced, insecure, groundless, which expects the protection of Omnipotence in doing wrong.

Again — as a follower of Christ, are you not bound to throw your influence wholly against despotism, tyranny and oppression, in all its forms?

Indeed, brother, your covenant obligations forbid you from turning a deaf ear to the prayers of an oppressed sister — denying her the boon of liberty, when it is in your power to bestow it.

3. *Appeal to your Heart.*

Dr. McFarland, I beg and entreat you to have pity upon me. Now that I have just tasted the sweets of spiritual freedom, under your kind protective care, the galling yoke of spiritual bondage seems more and more unendurable.

O, I do struggle and pant to be free — free from this man's power.

He is my worst, and, so far as my knowledge extends, my only, enemy. And is there not room enough in this wide world for me to live separate from him ? For light and darkness can no longer dwell together.

The light of 1860 is too great for the darkness of the past to eclipse.

O, I had rather die many natural deaths than to return to that man. He has done all he can do to dethrone my reason. But all in vain. Reason still maintains its throne, and claims justice at your hands.

As the cork which is kept under water only by the pressure which holds it down, rises, when the pressure is removed; so I, when removed from the mighty pressure of his crushing power, shall naturally and instinctively rise to that position in society which my character justly merits.

Once more, I entreat you, my kind friend, to secure Heaven's smiles and approbation, by espousing the cause of a weak, despised, down-trodden follower of Christ, whose only offense has been to indorse Truthism, instead of Calvinism, as her creed, and the life of Christ as her only pattern in its application. In other words, to extend Christian fellowship to the good and true of all denominations, and to withhold fellowship from the evil and false of all denominations.

I have also ventured to make use of my own reason in applying the only infallible tests of truth to my educated belief, viz., the tests of facts — the revelation of God's works and word — of providence and the Bible.

I have also ventured to express the opinion that that universal common religion which is designated by the "One Lord, one faith, one baptism," was a religion which could be tested on the common plane of common sense.

Now, Dr. McFarland, granting these opinions to be errors, is a difference of opinion to be accounted insanity, when the actions of the individual are consistent and correct? If so, have not I as good right to imprison you because you are insane, as you have to imprison me; for do you not differ from me just as much as I do from you?

I am imprisoned here for simply maintaining that I, though a woman, have just as good a right to my opinion, as my husband has to his, although he is a professed minister of Christ.

Now, Dr. McFarland, would you not be doing the same thing he has done, to claim that I was insane on all those points wherein I may differ from you in opinion? Would you feel that you were treated with that charity which Christ both taught and practiced, to have all those who differed from you in opinion on a certain point, agree to treat you as insane, because you honestly cherished an opinion opposite from them, and on that account imprison you as an insane person, and you being the minority, had no power to resist their will?

My husband claims of me that my rights of property — my parental rights — my rights of opinion — my rights of conscience, are all to be subject to his will, as being head over me.

I claim a right to my identity of being, although bound by the law of marriage to obey my husband in all things, such as the law of love — the true law of marriage — requires.

But when the perverted law of marriage requires me to subject these inalienable rights of womanhood, the claims of a moral, accountable agent under God's government, forbid my doing it. I feel that my husband may, with equal justice, require me to subject my ability to breathe, to sneeze, or to cough, to his dictation, as to require the subjugation of my inalienable, womanly rights to think and act as my own conscience dictates.

I have suffered spiritual martyrdom at my husband's hands, for maintaining inviolate these inalienable rights of womanhood. For what is it but spiritual death to the world, to be placed in their estimation on a level with the beasts, when deprived of the only faculty, *reason*, which distinguishes man from the beast? This he has done by placing me here, and making the world believe me to be an insane person.

Again — am I to be regarded as insane, because alone in my opinion? Because the law of love in my nature forbids my condemning as evil that which I do not understand, shall I be charged as insane — because I will not follow the multitude to do evil? I do not say it is wrong for others to do this — I only say, it is wrong for me to do it.

Others have the same right to judge of their duty as they please, just as much as I have of mine ; being all alike accountable to God alone for our personal acts.

For example — suppose I had been the only one whose conscience would not allow me to condemn Mr. Morse ten years since, as an insane person, because he saw he could send a message from New York to Chicago in two seconds of time, ought the multitude to deprive me of my personal liberty on the plea of insanity, for cherishing my inalienable right to my private opinion?

Shall you, because my conscience will not allow me to condemn Mrs. Minard as insane, simply because I cannot understand her, say that in this thing I am insane, because all others believe her to be insane? I acknowledge that in many things she appears to me to be insane : but shall I judge from appearances, or shall I judge righteous judgment? I do not understand the new science of spiritualism well enough to pass any judgment upon it.

O, my God and Guide ! keep me from obstructing, even ignorantly, any ray of light sent by Thee to ameliorate man's fallen condition.

8

CONCLUSION.

In view of the facts and principles on which this argument is based, I feel sure that the array of sophisms which my husband may attempt to marshall against it, will only be like arguing the sun out of the heavens at noon day.

My husband is the only one who dares to bring personal evidence of insanity against me, so far as my knowledge extends. Others believe me to be insane, but it is on the ground of his *testimony*, not from personal proof, by my own words and actions, independent of the coloring *he* has put upon them.

You, sir, now have a fair opportunity to judge for yourself, independent of testimony. But if you can conscientiously say that I have given you proof, from my own words and actions, of being insane, I wish you to say so, and take upon yourself the entire responsibility of this decision.

I stand boldly upon my own words and actions, honestly and fairly represented, before any tribunal in the world, in 1860, except a Presbyterian Church jury, and willingly abide their decision.

Another fact. There is one door, and only one, through which I can return to my husband, and that is by his repentance — *practical repentance.* The following proof I require, contained in these six conditions, which I left with my husband in writing, as I penned them, after I told him that I should never live with him again, now that I had evidence that he regarded me as insane :

1. He should give me in writing a promise, that he would ever grant to me the proper exercise of my rights of opinion and conscience.

2. He should publish to the world as extensively as he had the slander, that I was not insane, and that he had placed me in Jacksonville Insane Asylum, on a false charge of insanity.

3. He should, in the same manner, testify that his wife was a woman of unimpeachable virtue.

4. He should also promise me in writing, that I should have hired help whenever I felt that I needed it, and that I should be allowed to be her mistress.

5. He should put the $600 he has of my money into my own hands for me to do as I please with, independent of his dictation.

6. He must give a written agreement that I should regard a breach of either of the above conditions, as a certificate of leave of absence from him for life.

Another fact. In reply to my husband's last letter, in which he solicited my advice in relation to certain family matters, I wrote to him as follows:

" Since you solicit me so earnestly for advice, as your counselor, I venture to give you the only counsel which my conscience will allow me to give, viz., that you repent of the wrongs done to your wife, by openly and publicly confessing that you placed her in an insane asylum on a false charge — that she never, either by word or deed, has given you any just cause for regarding or treating her as insane. But, on the contrary, by a prompt and faithful discharge of the many and varied duties incumbent on the wife of a minister — a mother, a nurse, a housekeeper, a teacher, a friend to all — I have given you full evidence that I have ever been in the full and constant exercise of all my mental faculties, and that all these duties were discharged by me, up to the last hour I was permitted to remain with my family, so far as my health would admit. And I regard it as your imperative and solemn duty to reinstate me into these various offices, and there protect me, until my own acts shall prove me incompetent thereto."

My husband has been faithfully warned of what he has now brought upon himself — the loss of his wife Elizabeth.

I know that the greatest earthly trial that can befall him, is separation from me. But the deed is done.

I plead in vain for him to protect me in my rights of womanhood. He has turned a deaf ear to my crying, and my tears of anguish have failed to move his obdurate heart into compassion for his bleeding victim.

Now has come his turn to plead in vain. God has begun his work of merited punishment. And I must stand where God has put me, and act the part he has assigned me in this great drama.

I came here, Dr. McFarland, pleading with God, that, if it were possible, he would allow me to suffer in my husband's stead, so that, by my sufferings, atonement could be made for his sins against me, and he be forgiven on this ground by his Judge at last.

I am still willing to suffer any punishment short of the second death, to save his soul. But this I cannot do, to save even a husband. He has had an opportunity given him to repent. But he has sinned it away, and now he must suffer the reward of his own evil deeds. My sensitive heart melts in pity for him — yes, many a bitter tear of real anguish have I shed for him, in pity for his sad fate. But O, it is just! — a God of justice has poised the scales, and he is found wanting.

I honestly believe that if there is any case in God's universe where

it is impossible to renew again unto repentance, and for whom there is not found a ransom, it is my husband.

So, Dr. McFarland, you see I am entirely faithless in expectation of any light from this source, for *I know the man.* And I utterly disclaim ever having designedly given you any encouragement of expectations of a contrary nature which you may cherish.

Another fact. Since last Sabbath night—the 14th of October, 1860—David's prayer for his persecutors, has become my prayer for mine: "He remembered not to show mercy, but persecuted the poor and needy man, that he might even slay the broken in heart. As he loved cursing, so let it come upon him; as he delighted not in blessing, so let it be far from him. As he clothed himself with cursing like as with a garment, so let it come into his bowels like water. Let mine adversaries be clothed with shame. Let them curse, but bless thou. Let his net that he hath hid, catch himself: into that very destruction let him fall."

Yes, Dr. McFarland, if you desire to look into the secret recesses of my heart, in its present stage of Christian experience and development, I can give no more lucid or truthful representation of it, than you can find in the 35th Psalm of David. If it is not asking of you too much, I should like to have you pause here and read it over attentively. In every particular it is truly applicable to me.

Now, my kind brother in Christ, as Paul said to his keeper, so I say to you, "Do thyself no harm." Me you cannot harm. Decide as you will, you are the most concerned in the results of your own individual acts.

You have got to be developed to the world as well as all your patients, by your own acts—and by your own acts your character is to stand or fall before the coming light, by which all characters are to be revealed, and made to stand on this one common footing of their own acts—not their reputation or position.

The day for such false standards of true merit or real worth is forever past. *Now* Christ asks each and all his accountable agents, "Judge ye not of yourselves what is right?" Not what others think I ought to do, is my duty, but what my conscience says I ought to do.

At this tribunal of conscience we are all to stand or fall.

O, my friend, do not disappoint my high, very high expectations of you as a man—one who respects his conscience more than his popularity—one who dares to risk his reputation on doing right even in face of a frowning world.

Dr. McFarland, I have been your advocate and defender since I

became acquainted with you, because I thought you deserved it, as really a humane man; although I own that appearances have sometimes been against you.

But since my charitable nature prompts me to err on the side of that charity which "thinketh no evil," I know I may have tried to excuse you when I ought not to have done so. But being ignorant of all the light by which your actions have been guided, I forbore a harsh judgment.

But now in my case I know what light you have had to guide you in your decision, and I therefore shall take your decision in my case as casting the die in my opinion of your real character. And I here feel bound to add, that should this document fail to accomplish the end which it is designed and expected it will accomplish, you may look for another document from the same source, entitled "Friendly warning and advice," such as I feel fully competent to give, in view of what I have hitherto for the most part been a silent eye and ear witness of, since I entered this institution.

Dr. McFarland, my nature prompts me to practically overcome evil with good—that is, to praise and extol the virtues of another, rather than to expose and reprove their faults. But God in his Providence may compel me to bear this cross, and lift up my voice like a trumpet—to cry aloud—and spare not, and "show my people their iniquities, and the house of Jacob their sins."

"Lord, what wilt thou have me to do?" is now the prevailing desire of my heart; knowing that duties are mine, and events God's.

The issue of this "woman's rights" struggle, and the turn which Providence gives to this affair, my kind friend, depends greatly upon the decision you make upon this petition.

Therefore, as your sister in Christ, I entreat you, in view of my appeal to your understanding, to act honorably, manly, intelligently. In its relation to your conscience, to act justly, charitably. And to your heart, act kindly, humanely, mercifully.

In other words, "do justly, love mercy, and walk humbly with thy God;" and it shall be well with thee and thy seed after thee.

Both God and man look to thee, and are intently watching thy decision.

Be true to man. Be true to God. O stand! stand firmly on the rock of Eternal Truth, undaunted by the raging surge around it. Your time has come to be weighed in the evenly-poised balances of justice. God grant that you be not found wanting!

Finally. — I now, as a free citizen, and as one who desires to serve the present age according to the dictates of her own conscience, present to you my first application for lucrative employment, by which I can support myself, independent of aid from any quarter. I am willing to fill any post of usefulness you may offer me, either in your own family or in this institution. I consider myself competent to fill any position in this institution filled by a woman, except that of washerwoman. A physical weakness incapacitates me for that employment.

But do not incommode yourself or suffer any one to be incommoded by me, for I do not think I shall be entirely dependent upon you to provide me with a situation.

I hope Dr. Sturtevant, or Dr. Shirley, or Mr. Day, will be willing to befriend me, as a sister in need: and perhaps they can find me employment in some family in Jacksonville as hired help.

Duty and interest both compel me to seek employment for the present under your protective care; for I desire still to be allowed the privilege of seeking you as my counselor and guide, and under God a protector — as one in whom I have unbounded confidence, as a true man.

And I fear a powerful protector on the natural plane may be needed, as God's agent, to protect me against the snares which may be laid for me.

I am in my nature artless, truthful and confiding, and in some need of the sagacity of the serpent, to fully capacitate me alone to carry out my plans efficiently and successfully. This needed sagacity, I beg you, my noble friend, to supply, as you may see I need such aid.

In short, I am simply a true woman who feels her need of an earthly protector.

In the expressive language of my favorite motto I close my argument.

> "With cheerful feet thy path of duty run ;
> God nothing does nor suffers to be done
> But what thou would'st thyself, could'st thou but see
> Through all events of things as well as he."

Now, Dr. McFarland, my duty is done. Yours remains to be done. Choose for yourself whom you will serve. Choose evil or good, light or darkness, joy or sorrow, God's blessing or his curse, and God will accept the act as a testimony of your real character.

That you, sir, and all others who favor my righteous cause, may soon have occasion to shout for joy and be glad, has been, still is, and shall continue to be, the sincere prayer of

Your sane patient,

E. P. W. PACKARD.

JACKSONVILLE, OCT. 26, 1860.

P. S. — Copies of all communications from me to you are carefully kept, as well as your replies. Copies of this document are already in circulation, so that your decision is eagerly and anxiously expected by many others besides myself.   E. P. W. P.

A NOTE OF EXPLANATION.

THE reader will have noticed this idea several times repeated in the foregoing defense — viz., that I should never return to my husband, until he had repented, and made suitable satisfaction for the wrongs he had done me, in treating me as an insane person when I was not; and had never given him the first cause for doing so.

And now I have returned to him, and he is not a penitent. This seeming contradiction is thus explained.

I was taken from the Asylum against my will by my husband, at the demand of the trustees — they giving as their reason for removing me, that the house was not designed for such cases. Mr. Packard placed me in Granville, Putnam county, Illinois, in the family of Mr. David Field, who married my adopted sister. This family had strict orders given them not to let me have one dollar of money, lest I use it in going to see my own dear children, then with him in Manteno. He assured them that should I return to them he would be compelled to put me back into an Asylum, to save their souls!

He took me from the Asylum, June 18, 1863, and I remained in Granville until the middle of October, when my desire to see my six dear children became so strong that I ventured to visit them, in defiance of my husband's threat that he would send me back again to my prison if I ever came to my own dear home, to see my own dear children.

Self-defense prompted me to make this vow, and the spirit of it has not been violated by returning home when and *as* I did.

I knew that while in his present deluded state of mind, I should have no ground to expect but that he would send me directly back to the Asylum; and I knew also, from Dr. McFarland's practice, that he would admit me, although he knew and fully believed in his heart that I was truly a sane person. Yet his policy, regardless of the principles of justice and humanity, allows him to give full license to the strongest power, hoping thus to secure that power to his support, as is the case at present.

But since the devil's license has nearly run out, when Oppression is

to be buried in the very grave it has dug for the Republic; or, in other words, the "wolf in sheep's clothing" having so far developed his real character, that the wool of office no longer conceals the "spiritual wickedness" enthroned in it, from the gaze of *unperverted* humanity, I felt confident, that these representatives of Christ in America would not suffer a second kidnapping to take place, without a "jury trial" of my case.

And furthermore, Granville community had volunteered to me their pledge, that, should Mr. Packard attempt to imprison me again without a trial, they would use their influence to get *him* imprisoned in the penitentiary, where they thought the laws of this Commonwealth would place him. And as proof of their sincerity, they furnished me an ample purse to return home with, and money besides, to commence a prosecution, should self-defense require it.

Thus fortified and protected, I felt that the spirit of my vow was not violated, by returning to my home as I did, to see and care for my children, but *not* to fellowship my husband in his present state of mind towards me.

I have withdrawn all fellowship from him and all the insane party, and do not so much as speak to them, as I believe Christ requires me to do, so long as they repent not of their blasphemy against me. But I hold myself in readiness to forgive every practical penitent on the gospel terms. And I shall not forgive any blasphemer of my fair name, until he has given me reason for believing him to be a penitent; because Christ says, if thy brother *repent*, forgive him; which, to me, signifies, that I am not allowed to forgive him unless he does repent.

The following Trial was the result of this return home, and although it is, in the order of events in this "Great Drama," the Supplement to my twelve volumes, yet, since the public ought to know what evidence of insanity the writer of this Great Drama exhibited, before they buy the Drama, it is due the public that the Trial be introduced in the *first* rather than in the *last* volume.

THE GREAT TRIAL

O F

MRS. ELIZABETH P. W. PACKARD,

WHO WAS CONFINED FOR THREE YEARS IN THE STATE ASYLUM, OF ILLINOIS,
CHARGED BY HER HUSBAND, REV. THEOPHILUS PACKARD, WITH BEING
INSANE. HER DISCHARGE FROM THE ASYLUM, AND SUBSE-
QUENT IMPRISONMENT AT HER OWN HOUSE BY HER
HUSBAND. HER RELEASE ON A WRIT OF
Habeas Corpus, AND THE QUESTION
OF HER SANITY TRIED
BY A JURY.
HER SANITY FULLY ESTABLISHED.

A FULL REPORT OF THE TRIAL, INCIDENTS, ETC.

BY STEPHEN R. MOORE, ATTORNEY AT LAW.

IN preparing a report of this trial, the writer has had but one object in view, namely, to present a faithful history of the case as narrated by the witnesses upon the stand, who gave their testimony under the solemnity of an oath. The exact language employed by the witnesses, has been used, and the written testimony given in full, with the exception of a letter, written by Dr. McFarland, to Rev. Theophilus Packard, which letter was retained by Mr. Packard, and the writer was unable to obtain a copy. The substance of the letter is found in the body of the report, and has been submitted to the examination of Mr. Packard's counsel, who agree that it is correctly stated.

This case was on trial before the Hon. Charles R. Starr, at Kankakee City, Illinois, from Monday, January 11th, 1864, to Tuesday the 19th, and came up on an application made by Mrs. Packard, under the *Habeas Corpus Act*, to be discharged from imprisonment by her husband in their own house.

The case has disclosed a state of facts most wonderful and startling. Reverend Theophilus Packard came to Manteno, in Kankakee county, Illinois, seven years since, and has remained in charge of the Presbyterian Church of that place until the past two years.

In the winter of 1859 and 1860, there were differences of opinion

between Mr. Packard and Mrs. Packard, upon matters of religion, which resulted in prolonged and vigorous debate in the home circle. The heresies maintained by Mrs. Packard were carried by the husband from the fireside to the pulpit, and made a matter of inquiry by the church, and which soon resulted in open warfare; and her views and propositions were misrepresented and animadverted upon, from the pulpit, and herself made the subject of unjust criticism. In the Bible Class and in the Sabbath School, she maintained her religious tenets, and among her kindred and friends, defended herself from the obloquy of her husband.

To make the case fully understood, I will here remark, that Mr. Packard was educated in the Calvinistic faith, and for twenty-nine years has been a preacher of that creed, and would in no wise depart from the religion of his fathers. He is cold, selfish and illiberal in his views, possessed of but little talent, and a physiognomy innocent of expression. He has large self-will, and his stubbornness is only exceeded by his bigotry.

Mrs. Packard is a lady of fine mental endowments, and blest with a liberal education. She is an original, vigorous, masculine thinker, and were it not for her superior judgment, combined with native modesty, she would rank as a "strong-minded woman." As it is, her conduct comports strictly with the sphere usually occupied by woman. She dislikes parade or show of any kind. Her confidence that Right will prevail, leads her to too tamely submit to wrongs. She was educated in the same religious belief with her husband, and during the first twenty years of married life, his labors in the parish and in the pulpit were greatly relieved by the willing hand and able intellect of his wife.

Phrenologists would also say of her, that her self-will was large, and her married life tended in no wise to diminish this phrenological bump. They have been married twenty-five years, and have six children, the issue of their intermarriage, the youngest of whom was eighteen months old when she was kidnapped and transferred to Jacksonville. The older children have maintained a firm position against the abuse and persecutions of their father toward their mother, but were of too tender age to render her any material assistance.

Her views of religion are more in accordance with the liberal views of the age in which we live. She scouts the Calvinistic doctrine of man's total depravity, and that God has foreordained some to be saved and others to be damned. She stands fully on the platform of man's free agency and accountability to God for his actions. She believes

that man, and nations, are progressive; and that in his own good time, and in accordance with His great purposes, Right will prevail over Wrong, and the oppressed will be freed from the oppressor. She believes slavery to be a national sin, and the church and the pulpit a proper place to combat this sin. These, in brief, are the points in her religious creed which were combatted by Mr. Packard, and were denominated by him as "emanations from the devil," or "the vagaries of a crazed brain."

For maintaining such ideas as above indicated, Mr. Packard denounced her from the pulpit, denied her the privilege of family prayer in the home circle, expelled her from the Bible Class, and refused to let her be heard in the Sabbath School. He excluded her from her friends, and made her a prisoner in her own house.

Her reasonings and her logic appeared to him as the ravings of a mad woman — her religion was the religion of the devil. To justify his conduct, he gave out that she was insane, and found a few willing believers, among his family connections.

This case was commenced by filing a petition in the words following, to wit:

STATE OF ILLINOIS, } ss.
    KANKAKEE COUNTY. }

To the Honorable CHARLES R. STARR, Judge of the 20th Judicial Circuit in the State of Illinois.

William Haslet, Daniel Beedy, Zalmon Hanford, and Joseph Younglove, of said county, on behalf of Elizabeth P. W. Packard, wife of Theophilus Packard, of said county, respectfully represent unto your Honor, that said Elizabeth P. W. Packard is unlawfully restrained of her liberty, at Manteno, in the county of Kankakee, by her husband, Rev. Theophilus Packard, being forcibly confined and imprisoned in a close room of the dwelling-house of her said husband, for a long time, to wit, for the space of four weeks, her said husband refusing to let her visit her neighbors and refusing her neighbors to visit her; that they believe her said husband is about to forcibly convey her from out the State; that they believe there is no just cause or ground for restraining said wife of her liberty; that they believe that said wife is a mild and amiable woman. And they are advised and believe, that said husband cruelly abuses and misuses said wife, by depriving her of her winter's clothing, this cold and inclement weather, and that there is no necessity for such cruelty on the part of said husband to said

wife; and they are advised and believe, that said wife desires to come to Kankakee City, to make application to your Honor for a writ of *habeas corpus*, to liberate herself from said confinement or imprisonment, and that said husband refused and refuses to allow said wife to come to Kankakee City for said purpose; and that these petitioners make application for a writ of *habeas corpus* in her behalf, at her request. These petitioners therefore pray that a writ of *habeas corpus* may forthwith issue, commanding said Theophilus Packard to produce the body of said wife, before your Honor, according to law, and that said wife may be discharged from said imprisonment.

        (Signed)   WILLIAM HASLET.
                           DANIEL BEEDY.
J. W. ORR,   } *Petitioners' Attorney.*   ZALMON HANFORD.
H. LORING, }   J. YOUNGLOVE.
      STEPHEN R. MOORE, *Counsel.*

STATE OF ILLINOIS, } *ss.*
KANKAKEE COUNTY. }

    William Haslet, Daniel Beedy, Zalmon Hanford, and Joseph Younglove, whose names are subscribed to the above petition, being duly sworn, severally depose and say, that the matters and facts set forth in the above petition are true in substance and fact, to the best of their knowledge and belief.

                        WILLIAM HASLET.
                        DANIEL BEEDY.
                        ZALMON HANFORD.
                        J. YOUNGLOVE.

Sworn to and subscribed before me, this }
    11th day of January, A. D. 1864. }
          MASON B. LOOMIS, *J. P.*

    Upon the above petition, the Honorable C. R. Starr, Judge as aforesaid, issued a writ of *habeas corpus*, as follows:

STATE OF ILLINOIS, } *ss.*
KANKAKEE COUNTY. }

The People of the State of Illinois, To THEOPHILUS PACKARD:

    WE COMMAND YOU, That the body of Elizabeth P. W. Packard, in your custody detained and imprisoned, as it is said, together with the day and cause of caption and detention, by whatsoever name the same may be called, you safely have before Charles R. Starr, Judge of the Twentieth Judicial Circuit, State of Illinois, at his chambers, at Kankakee City in the said county, on the 12th instant, at one o'clock,

P. M., and to do and receive all and singular those things which the said Judge shall then and there consider of her in this behalf, and have you then and there this writ.

Witness, Charles R. Starr, Judge aforesaid, this 11th day of January, A. D. 1864.

CHARLES R. STARR,   [SEAL.]

[*Revenue Stamp.*]   *Judge of the 20th Judicial Circuit of the State of Illinois.*

Indorsed: "By the *Habeas Corpus* Act."

To said writ, the Rev. Theophilus Packard made the following return :

The within named Theophilus Packard does hereby certify, to the within named, the Honorable Charles R. Starr, Judge of the 20th Judicial Circuit of the State of Illinois, that the within named Elizabeth P. W. Packard is now in my custody, before your Honor. That the said Elizabeth is the wife of the undersigned, and is and has been for more than three years past insane, and for about three years of that time was in the Insane Asylum of the State of Illinois, under treatment, as an insane person. That she was discharged from said Asylum, without being cured, and is incurably insane, on or about the 18th day of June, A. D. 1862, and that since the 23rd day of October, the undersigned has kept the said Elizabeth with him in Manteno, in this county, and while he has faithfully and anxiously watched, cared for, and guarded the said Elizabeth, yet he has not unlawfully restrained her of her liberty ; and has not confined and imprisoned her in a close room, in the dwelling-house of the undersigned, or in any other place or way, but, on the contrary, the undersigned has allowed her all the liberty compatible with her welfare and safety. That the undersigned is about to remove his residence from Manteno, in this State, to the town of Deerfield, in the county of Franklin, in the State of Massachusetts, and designs and intends to take his said wife Elizabeth with him. That the undersigned has never misused or abused the said Elizabeth, by depriving her of her winter's clothing, but, on the contrary, the undersigned has always treated the said Elizabeth with kindness and affection, and has provided her with a sufficient quantity of winter clothing and other clothing ; and that the said Elizabeth has never made any request of the undersigned, for liberty to come to Kankakee City, for the purpose of suing out a writ of *habeas corpus*. The undersigned hereby presents a letter from Andrew McFarland, Superintendent of the Illinois State Hospital, at Jacksonville, in this State,

showing her discharge, and reasons of discharge, from said institution, which is marked " A," and is made a part of this return. And also presents a certificate from the said Andrew McFarland, under the seal of said hospital, marked " C," refusing to re-admit the said Elizabeth again into said hospital, on the ground of her being incurably insane, which is also hereby made a part of this return.

THEOPHILUS PACKARD.

Dated *January* 12, 1864.

The Court, upon its own motion, ordered an issue to be formed, as to the sanity or insanity of Mrs. E. P. W. Packard, and ordered a venire of twelve men, to aid the court in the investigation of said issue. And thereupon a venire was issued.

The counsel for the respondent, Thomas P. Bonfield, Mason B. Loomis, and Hon. C. A. Lake, moved the court to quash the venire, on the ground that the court had no right to call a jury to determine the question, on an application to be discharged on a writ of *habeas corpus*. The court overruled the motion ; and thereupon the following jury was selected :

John Stiles, Daniel G. Bean, V. H. Young, F. G. Hutchinson, Thomas Muncey, H. Hirshberg, Nelson Jarvais, William Hyer, Geo. H. Andrews, J. F. Mafet, Lemuel Milk, G. M. Lyons.

CHRISTOPHER W. KNOTT was the first witness sworn by the respondent, to maintain the issue on his part, that she was insane ; who being sworn, deposed and said :

I am a practicing physician in Kankakee City. Have been in practice fifteen years. Have seen Mrs. Packard ; saw her three or four years ago. Am not much acquainted with her. Had never seen her until I was called to see her at that time. I was called to visit her by Theophilus Packard. I thought her partially deranged on religious matters, and gave a certificate to that effect. I certified that she was insane upon the subject of religion. I have never seen her since.

Cross-examination.—This visit I made her was three or four years ago. I was there twice — one-half hour each time. I visited her on request of Mr. Packard, to determine if she was insane. I learned from him that he designed to convey her to the State Asylum. Do not know whether she was aware of my object, or not. Her mind appeared to be excited on the subject of religion ; on all other subjects she was perfectly rational. It was probably caused by overtaxing the mental faculties. She was what might be called a monomaniac. Monomania

is insanity on one subject. Three-fourths of the religious community are insane in the same manner, in my opinion. Her insanity was such that with a little rest she would readily have recovered from it. The female mind is more excitable than the male. I saw her perhaps one-half hour each time I visited her. I formed my judgment as to her insanity wholly from conversing with her. I could see nothing except an unusual zealousness and warmth upon religious topics. Nothing was said, in my conversation with her, about disagreeing with Mr. Packard on religious topics. Mr. Packard introduced the subject of religion the first time I was there : the second time, I introduced the subject. Mr. Packard and Mr. Comstock were present. The subject was pressed on her for the purpose of drawing her out. Mrs. Packard would manifest more zeal than most of people upon any subject that interested her. I take her to be a lady of fine mental abilities, possessing more ability than ordinarily found. She is possessed of a nervous temperament, easily excited, and has a strong will. I would say that she was insane, the same as I would say Henry Ward Beecher, Spurgeon, Horace Greely, and like persons, are insane. Probably three weeks intervened between the visits I made Mrs. Packard. This was in June, 1860.

Re-examined.—She is a woman of large, active brain, and nervous temperament. I take her to be a woman of good intellect. There is no subject which excites people so much as religion. Insanity produces, oftentimes, ill-feelings towards the best friends, and particularly the family, or those more nearly related to the insane person — but not so with monomania. She told me, in the conversation, that the Calvinistic doctrines were wrong, and that she had been compelled to withdraw from the church. She said that Mr. Packard was more insane than she was, and that people would find it out. I had no doubt that she was insane. I only considered her insane on that subject, and she was not bad at that. I could not judge whether it was hereditary. I thought if she was withdrawn from conversation and excitement, she could have got well in a short time. Confinement in any shape, or restraint, would have made her worse. I did not think it was a bad case ; it only required rest.

J. W. BROWN, being sworn, said :

I am a physician ; live in this city ; have no extensive acquaintance with Mrs. Packard. Saw her three or four weeks ago. I examined her as to her sanity or insanity. I was requested to make a visit, and had an extended conference with her : I spent some three hours with her.

I-had no difficulty in arriving at the conclusion, in my mind, that she was insane.

Cross-examination. — I visited her by request of Mr. Packard, at her house. The children were in and out of the room ; no one else was present. I concealed my object in visiting her. She asked me if I was a physician, and I told her no; that I was an agent, selling sewing machines, and had come there to sell her one.

The first subject we conversed about was sewing machines. She showed no signs of insanity on that subject.

The next subject discussed, was the social condition of the female sex. She exhibited no special marks of insanity on that subject, although she had many ideas quite at variance with mine, on the subject.

The subject of politics was introduced. She spoke of the condition of the North and the South. She illustrated her difficulties with Mr. Packard, by the difficulties between the North and the South. She said the South was wrong, and was waging war for two wicked purposes : first, to overthrow a good government, and second, to establish a despotism on the inhuman principle of human slavery. But that the North, having right on their side, would prevail. So Mr. Packard was opposing her, to overthrow free thought in woman; that the despotism of man may prevail over the wife; but that she had right and truth on her side, and that she would prevail.

During this conversation I did not fully conclude that she was insane.

I brought up the subject of religion. We discussed that subject for a long time, and then I had not the slightest difficulty in concluding that she was hopelessly insane.

Question. Dr., what particular idea did she advance on the subject of religion that led you to the conclusion that she was hopelessly insane?

Answer. She advanced many of them. I formed my opinion not so much on any one idea advanced, as upon her whole conversation. She then said that she was the "Personification of the Holy Ghost." I did not know what she meant by that.

Ques. Was not this the idea conveyed to you in that conversation : — That there are three attributes of the Deity — the Father, the Son, and the Holy Ghost? Now, did she not say, that the attributes of the Father were represented in mankind, in man ; that the attributes of the Holy Ghost were represented in woman; and that the Son was the fruit of these two attributes of the Deity ?

Ans. Well, I am not sure but that was the idea conveyed, though I did not fully get her idea at the time.

9

Ques. Was not that a new idea to you in theology?

Ans. It was.

Ques. Are you much of a theologian?

Ans. No.

Ques. Then because the idea was a novel one to you, you pronounced her insane.

Ans. Well, I pronounced her insane on that and other things that exhibited themselves in this conversation.

Ques. Did she not show more familiarity with the subject of religion and the questions of theology, than you had with these subjects?

Ans. I do not pretend much knowledge on these subjects.

Ques. What else did she say or do there, that showed marks of insanity?

Ans. She claimed to be better than her husband — that she was right—and that he was wrong—and that all she did was good, and all he did was bad; that she was farther advanced than other people, and more nearly perfection. She found fault particularly that Mr. Packard would not discuss their points of difference on religion in an open, manly way, instead of going around and denouncing her as crazy to her friends and to the church.

She had a great aversion to being called insane. Before I got through the conversation she exhibited a great dislike to me, and almost treated me in a contemptuous manner. She appeared quite lady-like. She had a great reverence for God, and a regard for religious and pious people.

Re-examined. — *Ques.* Dr., you may now state all the reasons you have for pronouncing her insane.

Ans. I have written down, in order, the reasons which I had, to found my opinion on, that she was insane. I will read them.

1. That she claimed to be in advance of the age thirty or forty years.

2. That she disliked to be called insane.

3. That she pronounced me a copperhead, and did not prove the fact.

4. An incoherency of thought. That she failed to illuminate me and fill me with light.

5. Her aversion to the doctrine of the total depravity of man.

6. Her claim to perfection or nearer perfection in action and conduct.

7. Her aversion to being called insane.

8. Her feelings towards her husband.

9. Her belief that to call her insane and abuse her, was blasphemy against the Holy Ghost.

10. Her explanation of this idea.

11. Incoherency of thought and ideas.

12. Her extreme aversion to the doctrine of the total depravity of mankind, and in the same conversation, saying her husband was a specimen of man's total depravity.

13. The general history of the case.

14. Her belief that some calamity would befall her, owing to my being there, and her refusal to shake hands with me when I went away.

15. Her viewing the subject of religion from the osteric stand-point of Christian exegetical analysis, and agglutinating the polsyn-thetical ectoblasts of homogeneous asceticism.

The witness left the stand amid roars of laughter; and it required some moments to restore order in the court-room.

JOSEPH H. WAY, sworn, and said:

I am a practicing physician in Kankakee City, Illinois. I made a medical examination of Mrs. Packard a few weeks since, at her house; was there perhaps two hours. On most subjects she was quite sane. On the subject of religion I thought she had some ideas that are not generally entertained. At that time I thought her to be somewhat deranged or excited on that subject; since that time I have thought perhaps I was not a proper judge, for I am not much posted on disputed points in theology, and I find that other people entertain similar ideas. They are not in accord-ance with my views, but that is no evidence that she is insane.

Cross-examined. —I made this visit at her house, or his house, per-haps, at Manteno. I conversed on various subjects. She was per-fectly sane on every subject except religion, and I would not swear now that she was insane. She seemed to have been laboring under an undue excitement on that subject. She has a nervous temperament, and is easily excited. She said she liked her children, and that it was hard to be torn from them. That none but a mother could feel the anguish she had suffered ; that while she was confined in the Asylum, the children had been educated by their father to call her insane. She said she would have them punished if they called their own mother insane, for it was not right.

ABIJAH DOLE, sworn, and says:

I know Mrs. Packard ; have known her twenty-five or thirty years. I am her brother-in-law. Lived in Manteno seven years. Mrs.

Packard has 'lived there six years. I have been sent for several times by her and Mr. Packard, and found her in an excited state of mind. I was there frequently ; we were very familiar. One morning early, I was sent for : she was in the west room; she was in her night clothes. She took me by the hand and led me to the bed. Libby was lying in bed, moaning and moving her head. Mrs. Packard now spoke and said, "How pure we are." "I am one of the children of heaven ; Libby is one of the branches." "The woman shall bruise the serpent's head." She called Mr. Packard a devil. She said, Brother Dole, these are serious matters. If Brother Haslet will help me, we will crush the body. She said, Christ had come into the world to save men, and that she had come to save woman. Her hair was disheveled. Her face looked wild. This was over three years ago.

I was there again one morning after this. She came to me. She pitied me for marrying my wife, who is a sister to Mr. Packard ; said I might find an agreeable companion. She said if she had cultivated amativeness, she would have made a more agreeable companion. She took me to another room and talked about going away ; this was in June before t..ey took her to the State Hospital. She sent for me again ; she was in the east room ; she was very cordial. She wanted me to intercede for Theophilus, who was at Marshall, Michigan ; she wanted him to stay there, and it was thought not advisable for him to stay. We wished him to come away, but did not tell her the reasons. He was with a Swedenborgian.

After this I was called there once in the night. She said she could not live with Mr. Packard, and she thought she had better go away. One time she was in the Bible class. The question came up in regard to Moses smiting the Egyptian ; she thought Moses had acted too hasty, but that all things worked for the glory of God. I requested her to keep quiet, and she agreed to do it.

I have had no conversation with Mrs. Packard since her return from the Hospital ; she will not talk with me because she thinks I think she is insane. Her brother came to see her ; he said he had not seen her for four or five years. I tried to have Mrs. Packard talk with him, and she would not have anything to do with him because he said she was a crazy woman. She generally was in the kitchen when I was there, overseeing her household affairs.

I was superintendent of the Sabbath School. One Sabbath, just at the close of the school, I was behind the desk, and almost like a vision she appeared before me, and requested to deliver or read an address to

the school. I was much surprised ; I felt so bad, I did not know what to do. (At this juncture the witness became very much affected, and choked up so that he could not proceed, and cried so loud that he could be heard in any part of the court-room. When he became calm, he went on and said), I was willing to gratify her all I could, for I knew she was crazy, but I did not want to take the responsibility myself, so I put it to a vote of the school, if she should be allowed to read it. She was allowed to read it. It occupied ten or fifteen minutes in reading.

I cannot state any of the particulars of that paper. It bore evidence of her insanity. She went on and condemned the church, all in all, and the individuals composing the church, because they did not agree with her. She looked very wild and very much excited. She seemed to be insane. She came to church one morning just as services commenced, and wished to have the church act upon her letter withdrawing from the church immediately. Mr. Packard was in the pulpit. She wanted to know if Brother Dole and Brother Merrick were in the church, and wanted them to have it acted upon. This was three years ago, just before she was taken away to the hospital.

Cross-examined. — I supposed when I first went into the room that her influence over the child had caused the child to become deranged. The child was nine years old. I believed that she had exerted some mesmeric or other influence over the child, that caused it to moan and toss its head. The child had been sick with brain fever ; I learned that after I got there. I suppose the mother had considerable anxiety over the child ; I suppose she had been watching over the child all night, and that would tend to excite her. The child got well. It was sick several days after this ; it was lying on the bed moaning and tossing its head ; the mother did not appear to be alarmed. Mr. Packard was not with her ; she was all alone ; she did not say that Mr. Packard did not show proper care for the sick child. I suppose she thought Libby would die.

Her ideas on religion did not agree with mine, nor with my view of the Bible.

I knew Mr. Packard thought her insane, and did not want her to discuss these questions in the Sabbath School. I knew he had opposed her more or less. This letter to the church was for the purpose of asking for a letter from the church.

Question. Was it an indication of insanity that she wanted to leave the Presbyterian Church ?

Answer. I think it strange that she should ask for letters from the church. She would not leave the church unless she was insane.

I am a member of the church — I believe the church is right. I believe everything the church does is right. I believe everything in the Bible.

Ques. Do you believe literally that Jonah was swallowed by a whale, and remained in its belly three days, and was then cast up?

Ans. I do.

Ques. Do you believe literally that Elijah went direct up to Heaven in a chariot of fire — that the chariot had wheels, and seats, and was drawn by horses?

Ans. I do — for with God all things are possible.

Ques. Do you believe Mrs. Packard was insane, and is insane?

Ans. I do.

I never read any of Swedenborg's works. I do not deem it proper for persons to investigate new doctrines or systems of theology.

Re-examined. — I became a Presbyterian eight years ago. I was formerly a Congregationalist; Mr. Packard was a Congregationalist.

Re-cross-examination. — *Ques.* Was it dangerous for you to examine the doctrines or theology embraced in the Presbyterian Church, when you left the Congregational Church, and joined it?

Ans. I will not answer so foolish a question.

Witness discharged.

JOSEPHUS B. SMITH, sworn, says:

Am aged fifty years; have known Mrs. Packard seven years. I cannot tell the first appearance of any abnormal condition of her mind. I first saw it at the Sabbath School. She came in and wished to read a communication. I do not recollect everything of the communication. She did not read the letter, but presented it to Brother Dole. She said something about her small children, and left. She seemed to be excited. There was nothing very unusual in her appearance. Her voice was rather excited; it could be heard nearly over the house. I merely recall the circumstance, but recollect scarce anything else. It was an unusual thing for any person to come in and read an address. I do not recollect anything unusual in her manner.

(At this stage of the trial, an incident occurred that for a time stopped all proceedings, and produced quite an excitement in the court-room; and this report would not be faithful if it were passed over unnoticed. Mrs. Dole, the sister of Mr. Packard, came in, leading

the little daughter of Mrs. Packard, and in passing by the table occupied by Mrs. Packard and her counsel, the child stopped, went up to her mother, kissed and hugged her, and was clinging to her with all child-like fervor, when it was observed by Mrs. Dole, who snatched the child up — and bid it "come away from that woman ; " adding, "She is not fit to take care of you — I have you in my charge; " and thereupon led her away. The court-room was crowded to its utmost, and not a mother's heart there but what was touched, and scarce a dry eye was seen. Quite a stir was made, but the sheriff soon restored order.)

Cross-examined. — I had charge of the Sunday School; am a member of Mr. Packard's church. I knew Mr. Packard had considered her insane; knew they had had difficulties. I was elected superintendent of the school in place of Brother Dole, for the special purpose of keeping Mrs. Packard straight.

SYBIL DOLE, sworn, and says —

I am Mr. Packard's sister; have known her twenty-five years. Her natural disposition is very kind and sweet. Her education is very good; her morals without a stain or blemish. I first observed a change in her after we came to Manteno. I had a conversation with her, when she talked an hour without interruption ; she talked in a wild, excited manner; the subject was partly religion. She spoke of her own attainments ; she said she had advanced in spiritual affairs. This was two or three years before she went to the Asylum.

The next time was when she was preparing to go to York State. She was weeping and sick. Her trunk was packed and ready to go, but Mr. Packard was sick. From her voice, and the manner she talked, I formed an opinion of her insanity. She talked on various points; the conversation distressed me very much; I could not sleep. She was going alone ; we tried to persuade her not to go alone. She accused Mr. Packard very strangely of depriving her of her rights of conscience — that he would not allow her to think for herself on religious questions, because they disagreed on these topics. She made her visit to New York. The first time I met her after her return, her health was much improved; she appeared much better. In the course of a few weeks, she visited at my house.

At another time, one of the children came up, and wanted me to go down; I did so. She was very much excited about her son remaining at Marshall. She was wild. She thought it was very wrong and tyrannical for Mr. Packard not to permit her son to remain there. She

said very many things which seemed unnatural. Her voice, manner and ways, all showed she was insane.

I was there when Mr. Baker came there, to see about Theophilus remaining at Marshall with him. She was calmer than she was the day before. She said that she should spend the day in fasting and prayer. She said he had came in unexpectedly, and they were not prepared to entertain strangers. She was out of bread, and had to make biscuit for dinner. (One gentleman in the crowd turned to his wife and said, "Wife, were you ever out of bread, and had to make biscuit for dinner? I must put you into an Insane Asylum! No mistake!") I occupied the same room and bed with her. She went to Mr. Packard's room, and when she returned, she said, that if her son was not permitted to remain at Marshall, it would result in a divorce. She got up several times during the night. She told me how much she enjoyed the family circle. She spoke very highly of Mr. Packard's kindness to her. She spoke particularly of the tenderness which had once existed between them. I did not notice anything very remarkable in her conduct toward Mr. Packard, until just before she was sent to the Hospital.

One morning afterward, I went to her house with a lady; we wanted to go in, and were admitted. She seemed much excited. She said, "You regard me insane. I will thank you to leave my room." This was two or three months before she was sent to Jacksonville. Mr. Packard went out. She put her hand on my shoulder, and said she would thank me to go out too. I went out.

I afterward wanted to take the baby home. One morning I went down to see her, and prepared breakfast for her. She appeared thankful, and complimented me on my kindness. She consented for me to take the child; I did so. In a short time, about ten days after, the other children came up, and said, that she wanted to take her own child. I took the child down. Her appearance was very wild. She was filled with spite toward Mr. Packard. She defied me to take the child again, and said that she would evoke the strong arm of the law to help her keep it.

At another time, at the table, she was talking about religion, when Mr. Packard remonstrated with her; she became angry, and told him she would talk what and when she had a mind to. She rose up from the table, and took her tea-cup, and left the room in great violence.

Cross-examined. — I am a member of Mr. Packard's church, and am his sister. He and I have often consulted together about Mrs. Packard. Mr. Packard was the first to ever suggest that she was insane; after

that, I would more carefully watch her actions to find out if she was insane. The religious doctrines she advanced were at variance with those entertained by our church. She was a good, neat, thrifty and careful housekeeper. She was economical; kept the children clean and neatly dressed. She was sane on all subjects except religion. I do not think she would have entertained these ideas, if she had not been insane. I do not think she would have wanted to have withdrawn from our church, and unite with another church, if she had not been insane. She said she would worship with the Methodists. They were the only other Protestant denomination that held service at Manteno at the time. I knew when she was taken to Jacksonville Hospital. She was taken away in the morning. She did not want to go; we thought it advisable for her to go.

SARAH RUMSEY, sworn, and says:

Have lived one week in Mrs. Packard's house. I was present at the interview when Mrs. Packard ordered us to leave the room. Mrs. Packard was very pale and angry. She was in an undress, and her hair was down over her face. It was 11 o'clock in the forenoon — I staid at the house; Mrs. Packard came out to the kitchen. She was dressed then. She said she had come to reveal to me what Mr. Packard was. She talked very rapidly; she would not talk calm. She said Mr. Packard was an arch deceiver; that he and the members of his church had made a conspiracy to put her into the Insane Asylum; she wanted me to leave the conspirators. Soon after dinner she said, "Come with me, I have something to tell you." She said she had a new revelation; it would soon be here; and that she had been chosen by God for a particular mission. She said that all who decided with her, and remained true to her, would be rewarded by the millennium, and if I would side with her, that I would be a chief apostle in the millennium. She wanted to go to Batavia, but that Mr. Packard would give her no money to take her there; that Mr. Packard called her insane. She started to go out, and Mr. Packard made her return; took her into Mr. Comstock's, and Mr. Comstock made her go home.

I saw her again when Libby had the brain fever. She was disturbed because the family called her insane. She and Libby were crying together; they cried together a long time. This was Tuesday. She would not let me into the room. The next morning while at breakfast Mr. Labrie passed the window and came in. He said that Georgie had been over for him, and said that they were killing his mother. She acted very strangely all the time; was wild and excited.

Cross-examined. — Knew Mr. Packard two years before I went there to live. He was the pastor of our church. I am a member of the church. I did not attend the Bible class. Brother Dole came to me and said somebody of the church should go there, and stay at the house, and assist in packing her clothes and getting her ready to take off to the Hospital, and stay and take care of the children. I consented to go; I heard that Brother Packard requested Brother Dole to come for me. I never worked out before. They had a French servant, before I went there; Mr. Packard turned her off when I came, the same day. I did not want to take Mrs. Packard away. I did not think she exhibited any very unusual excitement, when the men came here to take her away. Doctors Merrick and Newkirk were the physicians who came there with Sheriff Burgess. She did not manifest as much excitement, when being taken away, as I would have done, under the same circumstances; any person would have naturally been opposed to being carried away.

The church had opposed her, in disseminating her ideas in the church: I was opposed to her promulgating her religious ideas in the church; I thought them wrong, and injurious. I was present at the Sabbath School when she read the paper to the school; I thought that bore evidence of insanity. It was a refutation of what Mrs. Dixon had written; I cannot give the contents of the paper now.

I was present when she read a confession of her conduct to the church; she had had her views changed partially, from a sermon preached upon the subject of the sovereignty and immutability of God. I did not think it strange conduct that she changed her views; and never said so. This was in the spring before the June when they took her away.

The article she read in the school was by the permission of the school.

I was present when she presented a protest against the church for refusing to let her be heard; I have only an indistinct recollection of it; it was a protest because they refused to listen to her.

Mr. Dole was the only person who came to the house when she was taken away, except the men with Burgess.

She said that Mr. Packard had deprived her of the liberty of conscience in charging her to be insane, when she only entertained ideas new to him.

I thought it was an evidence of insanity, because she maintained these ideas. I do not know that many people entertain similar ideas; I suppose a good many do not think the Calvinistic doctrine is right; they are not necessarily insane because they think so.

When she found I was going to stay in the house, and that the French servant had been discharged, she ordered me into the kitchen; before that, she had treated me kindly as a visitor.

I thought it was an evidence of insanity for her to order me into the kitchen; she ought to have known that I was not an ordinary servant. The proper place for the servant is in the kitchen at work, and not in the parlor; I took the place of the servant girl for a short time.

She wanted the flower beds in the front yard cleaned out, and tried to get Mr. Packard to do it; he would not do it. She went and put on an old dress and went to work, and cleaned the weeds out, and worked herself into a great heat. It was a warm day; she staid out until she was almost melted down with the heat.

Question. What did she do then?

Answer. She went to her room and took a bath, and dressed herself, and then lay down exhausted. She did not come down to dinner.

Ques. And did you think that was an evidence of insanity?

Ans. I did — the way it was done.

Ques. What would you have done under similar circumstances? Would you have set down in the clothes you had worked in?

Ans. No.

Ques. Probably you would have taken a bath and changed your clothes too. And so would any lady, would they not?

Ans. Yes.

Ques. Then would you call yourself insane?

Ans. No. But she was angry and excited, and showed ill-will. She was very tidy in her habits; liked to keep the house clean, and have her yard and flowers look well. She took considerable pains with these things.

I remained there until she was taken away; I approved taking her away; I deemed her dangerous to the church; her ideas were contrary to the church, and were wrong.

The baby was eighteen months old when she was taken away. She was very fond of her children, and treated them very kindly. Never saw her misuse them. Never heard that she had misused them. Never heard that she was dangerous to herself or to her family. Never heard that she had threatened or offered to destroy anything, or injure any person.

JUDGE BARTLETT was next called to the stand.

Am acquainted with Mrs. Packard. Had a conversation with her on religious topics. We agreed very well in most things. She did not say

she believed in the transmigration of souls; she said, some persons had expressed that idea to her, but she did not believe it. It was spoken of lightly. She did not say ever to me, that Mr. Packard's soul would go into an ox. She did not say anything about her being related to the Holy Ghost. I thought then, and said it, that religious subjects were her study, and that she would easily be excited on that subject. I could not see that she was insane. I would go no stronger than to say, that her mind dwelt on religious subjects. She could not be called insane, for thousands of people believe as she does, on religion.

Mrs. Sybil Dole, recalled.

At the time she got up from the table she went out. She said, "I will have no fellowship with the unfruitful works of darkness. No! not so much as to eat with them."

Re-cross-examined. — *Question.* Did you deem that an evidence of insanity?

Answer. I did.

Ques. She called Mr. Packard the unfruitful works of darkness?

Ans. I suppose so.

Ques. Did she also include you?

Ans. She might have done so.

Ques. This was about the time that her husband was plotting to kidnap her, was it not?

Ans. It was just before she was removed to the Asylum.

Ques. He had been charging her with insanity, had he not, at the table?

Ans. He had.

The prosecution now wished to adjourn the court for ten days, to enable them to get Dr. McFarland, Superintendent of the State Hospital, who, they claimed, would testify that she was insane. Counsel stated, he had been telegraphed to come, and a reply was received, that he was in Zanesville, Ohio, and would return in about ten days. They claimed his testimony would be very important. This motion the counsel of Mrs. Packard opposed, as it was an unheard-of proceeding to continue a cause after the hearing was commenced, to enable a party to hunt up testimony.

The matter was discussed on each side for a considerable length of time, when the court held that the defense should go on with their testimony, and after that was heard, then the court would determine about continuing the case to get Dr. McFarland, and perhaps he could

be got before the defense was through, and if so, he might be sworn; and held that the defense should go on now.

The counsel of Mrs. Packard withdrew for consultation, and in a brief time returned, and announced to the court that they would submit the case without introducing any testimony, and were willing to submit it without argument. The counsel for Mr. Packard objected to this, and renewed the motion for a continuance; which the court refused.

The counsel for Mr. Packard then offered to read to the jury a letter from Dr. McFarland, dated in the month of December, 1863, written to Rev. Theophilus Packard; and also a certificate, under the seal of the State Hospital at Jacksonville, certifying that Mrs. Packard was discharged from the institution in June, 1863, and was incurably insane, which certificate was signed by Dr. McFarland, the Superintendent. To the introduction of this to the jury, the counsel for Mrs. Packard objected, as being incompetent testimony, and debarred the defense of the benefit of a cross-examination. The court permitted the letter and certificate to be read to the jury.

These documents were retained by Rev. Theophilus Packard, and the reporter has been unable to obtain copies of them. The letter is dated in December, 1863, at the State Hospital, Jacksonville, Illinois, and written to Rev. Theophilus Packard, wherein Dr. McFarland writes him that Mrs. Packard is hopelessly insane, and that no possible good could result by having her returned to the Hospital; that the officers of the institution had done everything in their power to effect a cure, and were satisfied she could not be cured, and refused to receive her into the institution.

The certificate, under the seal of the Hospital, was a statement, dated in June, 1863, at Jacksonville, Illinois, setting forth the time (three years) that Mrs. Packard had been under treatment, and that she had been discharged, as beyond a possibility of being cured.

The above is the import of these documents, which the reporter regrets he cannot lay before the public in full.

The prosecution now announced that they closed their case.

DEFENSE.

J. L. SIMINGTON was the first witness called for the defense. Being sworn, he said:

I live in Manteno; lived there since 1859, early in the spring. Knew Rev. Mr. Packard and Mrs. Packard. First became acquainted

with them in 1858; I was then engaged in the ministry of the Methodist Church. I have practiced medicine eleven years.

I was consulted as a family physician by Mrs. Packard in 1860. Was quite well acquainted with Mrs. Packard, and with the family. Lived fifty or sixty rods from their house. Saw her and the family almost daily. I did not see anything unusual in her, in regard to her mind. I never saw anything I thought insanity with her. So far as I know she was a sane woman. I have seen her since she came from the Hospital; have seen nothing since to indicate she was insane. My opinion is, she is a sane woman.

No cross-examination was made.

Dr. J. D. MANN, sworn, and says:

I live in Manteno ; have lived there nine years. Practiced medicine there six years. I am not very intimately acquainted with either Mr. or Mrs. Packard. Mr. Packard invited me to go to his house to have an interview with Mrs. Packard. I went at his request. He requested me to make a second examination, which I did. There had been a physician there before I went. The last time, he wanted me to meet Dr. Brown, of this city, there. This was late in November last. He introduced me to Mrs. Packard. I had known her before she was taken to the Hospital, and this was the first time I had seen her since she had returned. I was there from one to two hours. I then made up my mind, as I had made up my mind from the first interview, that I could find nothing that indicated insanity. I did not go when Dr. Brown was there. Mr. Packard had told me she was insane, and my prejudices were, that she was insane. He wanted a certificate of her insanity, to take East with him. I would not give it.

The witness was not cross-examined.

JOSEPH E. LABRIE, sworn, and says:

Have known Mrs. Packard six years; lived fifteen or twenty rods from their house. Knew her in spring of 1860. Saw her nearly every day — sometimes two or three times a day. I belong to the Catholic Church. Have seen her since her return from Jacksonville. I have seen nothing that could make me think her insane. I always said she was a sane woman, and say so yet.

Cross-examined.—I am not a physician. I am not an expert. She might be insane, but no common-sense man could find it out.

Re-examined.—I am a Justice of the Peace, and Notary Public. Mr. Packard requested me to go to his house and take an acknowledg-

ment of a deed fr&m her. I went there, and she signed and acknowledged the deed. This was within the past two months.

Re-cross-examined.—I was sent for to go to the house in the spring
of 1860. My wife was with me. It was about taking her to Jacksonville. Mrs. Packard would not come to the room where I was. I
stayed there only about twenty minutes.

Have been there since she returned from the Hospital. The door
to her room was locked on the outside. Mr. Packard said, he had
made up his mind to let no one into her room.

The counsel for Mrs. Packard offered to read to the jury the following paper, which had been referred to by the witnesses, as evidence of
Mrs. Packard's insanity, and which Deacon Smith refused to hear read.
The counsel for Mr. Packard examined the paper, and admitted it was
the same paper.

The counsel for Mrs. Packard then requested permission of the court
for Mrs. Packard to read it to the jury, which was most strenuously
opposed. The court permitted Mrs. Packard to read it to the jury.
Mrs. Packard arose, and read in a distinct tone of voice, so that every
word was heard all over the court-room.

HOW GODLINESS IS PROFITABLE

DEACON SMITH—A question was proposed to this class, the last Sabbath
Brother Dole taught us, and it was requested that the class consider and report
the result of their investigations at a future session. May I now bring it up?
The question was this :

" Have we any reason to expect that a Christian farmer, *as a Christian*, will
be any more successful in his farming operations, than an impenitent sinner—
and if *not*, how is it that godliness is profitable unto all things? Or, in other
words, does the *motive* with which one prosecutes his secular business, other
things being equal, make any difference in the *pecuniary* results?"

Mrs. Dixon gave it as her opinion, at the time, that the motive *did* affect the
pecuniary results.

Now the *practical* result to which this conclusion leads, is such as will justify
us in our judging of Mrs. Dixon's true *moral* character, next fall, by her *success*
in her farming operations this summer.

My opinion differs from hers on this point ; and my *reasons* are here given in
writing, since I deem it necessary for *me*, under the existing state of feeling
toward me, to put into a written form *all* I have to say, in the class, to prevent
misrepresentation.

Should I be appropriating an unreasonable share of time, as a pupil. Mr.

Smith, to occupy four minutes of your time in reading them? I should like very much to read them, that the class may pass their honest criticisms upon them.

AN ANSWER TO THE QUESTION.

I think we have no *intelligent* reason for believing that the motives with which we prosecute our secular business, have any influence in the *pecuniary* results.

My reasons are *common sense* reasons, rather than strictly Bible proofs, viz. : I regard man as existing in three distinct departments of being, viz., his physical or animal, his mental or intellectual, his moral or spiritual ; and each of these three distinct departments are under the control of *laws*, peculiar to itself ; and these different laws do not interchange with, or affect each other's department.

For instance, a very *immoral* man may be a very *healthy*, long-lived man ; for, notwithstanding he violates the *moral* department, he may live in conformity to the *physical* laws of his animal nature, which secure to him his physical health. And, on the other hand, a very moral man may suffer greatly from a diseased body, and be cut off in the very midst of his usefulness by an early death, in consequence of having violated the physical laws of his animal constitution. But on the moral plane he is the *gainer*, and the immoral man is the *loser*.

So our success in business depends upon our conformity to *those laws* on which success depends—*not* upon the *motives* which act *only* on the moral plane.

On *this* ground, the Christian farmer has no more *reason* to expect success in his farming operations, than the impenitent sinner. In either case, the foundation for success must depend upon the degree of *fidelity* with which the *natural laws* are applied, which cause the natural result—*not* upon the *motives* of the operator ; since these moral acts receive their penalty and reward on an entirely different plane of his being.

Now comes in the question, how then is it true, that "godliness is *profitable* unto all things," if godliness is no guarantee to success in business pursuits?

I reply, that the profits of godliness cannot mean, simply, *pecuniary* profits, because this would limit the gain of godliness to this world. alone ; whereas, it is profitable not only for *this life*, but also for the *life to come*. Gain and loss, dollars and cents, are not the coins current in the spiritual world.

But happiness and misery are coins which are current in *both* worlds. Therefore, it appears to me, that happiness is the profit attendant upon godliness, and for this reason, a *practically godly* person, who lives in conformity to all the various laws of his entire being, may expect to secure to himself, as a natural result, a greater amount of happiness than the ungodly person.

So that, in this sense, " Godliness is profitable unto all things," to every department of our being.

MANTENO, March 22, 1860.   E. P. W. PACKARD.

Mrs. Packard then stated that the above was presented to the class, the 15th day of the following April, and was *rejected* by the teacner Deacon Smith, on the ground of its being irrelevant to the subject, since she had not confined herself to the Bible alone for proof of ner position.

As she took her seat, a murmur of applause arose from every part, of the room, which was promptly suppressed by the sheriff.

DANIEL BEEDY, sworn, and says:

I live in Manteno. Have known Mrs. Packard six years; knew her in the spring of 1860. I lived a mile and a half from them. Have seen her very frequently since her return from Jacksonville. Had many conversations with her before she was taken away, and since ner return. She always appeared to me like a sane woman. I heard she was insane, and my wife and I went to satisfy ourselves. I went there soon after the difficulties in the Bible class.

She is not insane. We talked about religion, politics, and various matters, such as a grey-haired old farmer could talk about, and I saw nothing insane about her.

Mr. BLESSING, sworn, and says:

I live in Manteno; have known Mrs. Packard six years; knew her in the spring of 1860; lived eighty rods from their house. She visited at my house. I have seen her at church. She attended the Methodist church for a while after the difficulties commenced, and then I saw her every Sunday. I never thought her insane.

After the word was given out by her husband that she was insane, she claimed my particular protection, and wanted me to obtain a trial for her by the laws of the land, and such an investigation she said she was willing to stand by. She claimed Mr. Packard was insane, if any one was. She begged for a trial. I did not then do anything, because I did not like to interfere between man and wife. I never saw anything that indicated insanity. She was always rational Had conversations with her since her return. She first came to my house. She claimed a right to live with her family. She considered herself more capable of taking care of her family than any other person.

I saw her at Jacksonville. I took Dr. Shirley with me to test her insanity. Dr. Shirley told me she was not insane.

Cross-examination waived.

10

Mrs. BLESSING, sworn, and says:

Have known Mrs. Packard seven years; knew her in 1860. Lived near them; we visited each other as neighbors. She first came to our house when she returned from Jacksonville. I did not see anything that indicated that she was insane. I saw her at Jacksonville. She had the keys, and showed me around. I heard the conversation there with Dr. Shirley; they talked about religion; did not think she talked unnatural. When I first went in, she was at work on a dress for Dr. McFarland's wife. I saw her after she returned home last fall, quite often, until she was locked in her room. On Monday after she got home, I called on her; she was at work; she was cleaning up the feather beds; they needed cleaning badly. I went there afterward; her daughter let me in. On Saturday before the trial commenced, I was let into her room by Mr. Packard; she had no fire in it; we sat there in the cold. Mr. Packard had a handful of keys, and unlocked the door and let me in. Mrs. Hanford was with me. Before this, Mrs. Hanford and myself went there to see her; he would not let us see her; he shook his hand at me, and threatened to put me out.

Mrs. HASLET, sworn, and said:

Know Mrs. Packard very well; have known her since they lived in Manteno; knew her in the spring of 1860; and since she returned from Jacksonville, we have been on intimate terms. I never saw any signs of insanity with her. I called often before she was kidnapped and carried to Jacksonville, and since her return.

I recollect the time Miss Rumsey was there; I did not see anything that showed insanity. I called to see her in a few days after she returned from Jacksonville; she was in the yard, cleaning feather beds. I called again in a few days; she was still cleaning house. The house needed cleaning; and when I again called, it looked as if the mistress of the house was at home. She had no hired girl. I went again, and was not admitted. I conversed with her through the window; the window was fastened down. The son refused me admission. The window was fastened with nails on the inside, and by two screws, passing through the lower part of the upper sash and the upper part of the lower sash, from the outside. I did not see Mr. Packard this time.

Cross-examination.—She talked about getting released from her imprisonment. She asked if filing a bill of complaint would lead to a divorce. She said she did not want a divorce; she only wanted protection from Mr. Packard's cruelty. I advised her to not stand it quietly, but get a divorce.

Dr. DUNCANSON, sworn, and said:

I live here; am a physician; have been a clergyman; have been a practicing physician twenty-one years. Have known Mrs. Packard since this trial commenced. Have known her by general report for three years and upwards. I visited her at Mr. Orr's. I was requested to go there and have a conversation with her and determine if she was sane or insane. Talked three hours with her, on political, religious and scientific subjects, and on mental and moral philosophy. I was educated at and received diplomas from the University of Glasgow, and Anderson University of Glasgow. I went there to see her, and prove or disprove her insanity. I think not only that she is sane, but the most intelligent lady I have talked with in many years. We talked religion very thoroughly. I find her an expert in both departments, Old School and New School theology. There are thousands of persons who believe just as she does. Many of her ideas and doctrines are embraced in Swedenborgianism, and many are found only in the New School theology. The best and most learned men of both Europe and this country, are advocates of these doctrines, in one shape or the other; and some bigots and men with minds of small calibre may call these great minds insane; but that does not make them insane. An insane mind is a diseased mind. These minds are the perfection of intellectual powers, healthy, strong, vigorous, and just the reverse of diseased minds, or insane. Her explanation of woman representing the Holy Ghost, and man representing the male attributes of the Father, and that the Son is the fruit of the Father and the Holy Ghost, is a very ancient theological dogma. and entertained by many of our most eminent men. On every topic I introduced, she was perfectly familiar, aud discussed them with an intelligence that at once showed she was possessed of a good education, and a strong and vigorous mind. I did not agree with her in sentiment on many things, but I do not call people insane because they differ from me, nor from a majority, even, of people. Many persons called Swedenborg insane. That is true; but he had the largest brain of any person during the age in which he lived; and no one now dares call him insane. You might with as much propriety call Christ insane, because he taught the people many new and strange things; or Galileo; or Newton; or Luther; or Robert Fulton; or Morse, who electrified the world; or Watts or a thousand others I might name. Morse's best friends for a long time thought him mad; yet there was a magnificent mind, the embodiment of health and vigor.

So with Mrs. Packard; there is wanting every indication of insanity

that is laid down in the books. I pronounce her a sane woman, and wish we had a nation of such women.

This witness was cross-examined at some length, which elicited nothing new, when he retired

The defense now announced to the court that they had closed all the testimony they wished to introduce, and inasmuch as the case had occupied so much time, they would propose to submit it without argument. The prosecution would not consent to this arrangement.

The case was argued ably and at length, by Messrs. Loomis and Bonfield for the prosecution, and by Messrs. Orr and Loring on the part of the defense.

It would be impossible to give even a statement of the arguments made, and do the attorneys justice, in the space allotted to this report.

On the 18th day of January, 1864, at 10 o'clock, P. M., the jury retired for consultation, under the charge of the sheriff. After an absence of seven minutes, they returned into court, and gave the following verdict:

STATE OF ILLINOIS, } ss.
  KANKAKEE COUNTY,

We, the undersigned, Jurors in the case of Mrs. Elizabeth P. W. Packard, alleged to be insane, having heard the evidence in the case, are satisfied that said Elizabeth P. W. Packard is SANE.

JOHN STILES, *Foreman.*   H. HIRSHBERG,
DANIEL G. BEAN.   NELSON JERVAIS.
F. G. HUTCHINSON.   WILLIAM HYER.
V. H. YOUNG.   GEO. H. ANDREWS.
G. M. LYONS.   J. F. MAFIT.
THOMAS MUNCEY.   LEMUEL MILK.

Cheers rose from every part of the house; the ladies waved their handkerchiefs, and pressed around Mrs. Packard, and extended her their congratulations. It was sometime before the outburst of applause could be checked. When order was restored, the counsel for Mrs. Packard moved the court, that she be discharged. Thereupon the court ordered the clerk to enter the following order:

STATE OF ILLINOIS, } *ss.*
KANKAKEE COUNTY,

It is hereby ordered that Mrs. Elizabeth P. W. Packard be relieved from all restraint incompatible with her condition as a sane woman.

C. R. STARR,
Judge of the 20th Judicial Circuit of the State of Illinois

January 18, 1864.

Thus ended the trial of this remarkable case. During each day of the proceedings the court-room was crowded to excess by an anxious audience of ladies and gentlemen, who are seldom in our courts. The verdict of the jury was received with applause, and hosts of friends crowded upon Mrs. Packard to congratulate her upon her release.

During the past two months, Mr. Packard had locked her up in her own house, fastened the windows outside, and carried the key to the door, and made her a close prisoner. He was maturing a plan to immure her in an Asylum in Massachusetts, and for that purpose was ready to start on the Thursday before the writ was sued out, when his plan was disclosed to Mrs. Packard by a letter he accidentally dropped in her room, written by his sister in Massachusetts, telling him the route he should take, and that a carriage would be ready at the station to put her in and convey her to the Asylum.

Vigorous action became necessary, and she communicated this startling intelligence through her window to some ladies who had come to see her, and were refused admission into the house.

On Monday morning, and before the defense had rested their case, Mr. Packard left the State, bag and baggage, for parts unknown, having first mortgaged his property for all it is worth to his sister and other parties.

We cannot do better than close this report with the following editorial from the Kankakee Gazette, of January 21, 1864:

MRS. PACKARD.

The case of this lady, which has attracted so much attention and excited so much interest for ten days past, was decided on Monday evening last, and resulted, as almost every person thought it must, in a complete vindication of her sanity. The jury retired on Monday evening, after hearing the arguments of the counsel; and after a brief consultation, they brought in a verdict that Mrs. Packard is a *sane* woman.

Thus has resulted an investigation which Mrs. Packard has long and always desired should be had, but which her cruel husband has ever sternly refused her. She has always asked and earnestly pleaded for a jury trial of her case, but her relentless persecutor has ever turned a deaf ear to her entreaties, and flagrantly violated all the dictates of justice and humanity.

She has suffered the alienation of friends and relatives; the shock of a kidnapping by her husband and his posse when forcibly removed to the Asylum; has endured three years incarceration in that Asylum — upon the general treatment in which there is severe comment in the State, and which in her special case was aggravatingly unpleasant and ill-favored; returning to her home she found her husband's saintly blood still congealed, a winter of perpetual frown on his face, and the sad dull monotony of " insane, insane," escaping his lips in all his communications to and concerning her; her young family, the youngest of the four at home being less than four years of age, these children — over whose slumbers she had watched, and whose wailings she had hushed with all a mother's care and tenderness — had been taught to look upon her as insane, and they were not to respect the counsels or heed the voice of a maniac just loosed from the Asylum, doom scaled by official certificates.

Soon her aberration of mind led her to seek some of her better clothing carefully kept from her by her husband, which very woman-like act was seized by him as an excuse for confining her in her room, and depriving her of her apparel, and excluding her lady friends. Believing that he was about to again forcibly take her to an asylum, four responsible citizens of that village made affidavit of facts which caused the investigation as to her sanity or insanity. During the whole of the trial she was present, and counseled with her attorneys in the management of the case.

Notwithstanding the severe treatment she has received for nearly four years past, the outrages she has suffered, the wrong to her nature she has endured, she deported herself during the trial as one who is not only not insane, but as one possessing intellectual endowments of a high order, and an equipoise and control of mind far above the majority of human kind. Let the sapient Dr. Brown, who gave a certificate of insanity after a short conversation with her, and which certificate was to be used in aid of her incarceration for life — suffer as she has suffered, endure what she has endured, and the world would be deprived of future clinical revealings from his gigantic mind upon the subject of the spleen, and he would, to a still greater extent than in the past,

TRIAL OF MRS. PACKARD.

"fail to illuminate" the public as to the virtues and glories of the martyr who is "watching and waiting" in Canada.

The heroic motto: "suffer and be strong," is fairly illustrated in her case. While many would have opposed force to his force, displayed frantic emotions of displeasure at such treatment, or sat convulsed and "maddened with the passion of her part," she meekly submitted to the tortures of her bigoted tormentor, trusting and believing in God's Providence the hour of her vindication and her release from thraldom would come. And now the fruit of her suffering and persecution ha· all the autumn glory of perfection

> " One who walked
> From the throne's splendor to the bloody block,
> Said : ' This completes my glory' with a smile
> Which still illuminates men's thoughts of her.'

Feeling the accusations of his guilty conscience, seeing the meshes of the net with which he had kept her surrounded were broken, and a storm-cloud of indignation about to break over his head in pitiless fury, the intolerant Packard, after encumbering their property with trust-deeds, and despoiling her of her furniture and clothing, left the country. Let him wander! with the mark of infamy upon his brow, through far-off States, where distance and obscurity may diminish till the grave shall cover the wrongs it cannot heal.

It is to be hoped Mrs. Packard will make immediate application for a divorce, and thereby relieve herself of a repetition of the wrongs and outrages she has suffered by him who for the past four years has only used the marriage relation to persecute and torment her in a merciless and unfeeling manner.

NO DIVORCE.

As my case now stands, there is no sort of legal protection for my identity, in the statute book, short of a divorce. So my judge and counsel assure me since the insane laws do not allow the right of self-defense, from the charge of insanity, to a *married* woman.

Thus I must expose myself to another kidnapping process, cloaked under the insane laws of this State, or go out of the married state into a single state, where alone a woman's identity is recognized in the statute book of this Republic !

Again, in order to secure my children or my property, I must go into a single state, since our laws do not recognize the offspring of a married woman as her inalienable right ; nor is her right to her property recognized, unless this right is guaranteed to her before marriage. But the illegitimate offspring of a single woman is secured to the mother, as her right by nature ! !

Now, by the practical application of these laws, I must either do violence to my conscience by getting a divorce, without the sanction of the Higher Statute Book, or expose myself to a life-long imprisonment, and the loss of all my property and my children, and every other right as an American citizen !

I do not believe in the divorce, or *secession* principle, since it undermines the very vital principle of our Union, and saps the very foundation of our social and civil obligations. Therefore, I deliberately and intelligently maintain my *right to be a married woman*, with all the tenacity with which my husband maintains his right to divorce me, or secede from the marriage union.

I know he has the laws of his country to justify him in divorcing or putting me off, as he has done. And I know, too, that no law protects me, so long as I claim the right to be a married woman. Still, trusting to the overruling providence of a just God, I trust myself, as a married woman, to be put where the statute book of this State assigns a married woman — viz., in the *vortex of oblivion*, as an American citizen !

And if, for want of civil protection, I am immured in another insane asylum, for life, to die a prisoner, and a martyr for married women, I now go without a murmur, since I have told my case to our

Government, and have thus done all that is in my power, to secure the protection of my inalienable rights.

No — I cannot get a divorce, to save me from a life-long imprisonment, since no adultery exists to justify the separation. What I want is, not to live with my husband as his wife, since he has put me off so wantonly, without any cause; but to be protected in my own dear home, to love and care for my own dear children, as nature dictates. Or, because I have been so cruelly wronged and abused, must I *continue* to be thus trifled with, because a married woman is nothing and nobody in law !! O! will not our Government heed my prayer, and thus and there protect me in my home and family, so long as my virtuous, christian conduct claims such protection?

Citizens of Illinois : Will not the history of my persecutions in Illinois, be a foul blot on the page of our American history?

Our forefathers fled to this continent to escape persecution for uttering opinions in conflict with the established Church. Shall one of their children be driven back to that same crown for protection, to escape that *most cruel* of all kinds of persecution — that of being treated as an insane person for *opinion's sake alone ?* Christianity is at this age, in America, being persecuted as *Insanity*, instead of *Heresy*, as it used to be in England ; and the woes which were then inflicted upon the Heretic by the *Bigot*, are now inflicted upon the Insane by the Calvinist.

The Heretic and the Insane are the true Church — the *Christians ;* the Bigot and the Calvinist are the Heretic and the Madman ; and our Insane Asylums have degenerated into *Inquisitions !*

By your laws I am nothing but a *slave*, and have no refuge from the tyranny of the church, but a State's prison for life, simply because I struggle for the RIGHT — for *Liberty* to serve my day and generation according to the dictates of my *own* conscience, instead of the conscience of my tyrannical master.

No refuge ! did I say ? I *have* a refuge in the *manliness* of this Republic.

My faith assures me that the Christianity of Illinois will fly to my rescue, in *defiance* of the statute book.

God grant that the manliness of this Republic be not found wanting, when a True Woman — with her whole, warm, trusting heart — flies to it as her *only* refuge from the merciless storm of a husband's persecutions !

CHICAGO, May, 1864.

The following Appeal to the Government was written while in the Asylum.

AN APPEAL

TO THE GOVERNMENT FOR PROTECTION.

My Countrymen:

My case is now before you for action, and O, may God grant that your eyes may be opened to see, that the "Achan" in your camp is not confined to the abuse of the negro. No, never, never can a peace be established in righteousness, so long as these outrageous abuses to afflicted humanity remain unredressed. O, how many, many times has Christ been imprisoned in your Insane Asylums, to be most wantonly abused under your insane laws! And can such insults to God and his authority be bestowed upon Him with impunity? No, never. Self-defense demands that God arise to his own defense. And he is doing so. He has taken the sword as his avenger, and it will never be returned to its scabbard again, until his law of justice is established on earth. Yes, the red sea of blood lies between us and the promised land. He, himself, is leading out the oppressed captives from bondage, but we have forced him to do it by the spoiling of the Egyptians!

Would that none but slaveholders were among the Egyptians! that God's image had been oppressed in none but the negro — the less guilty than the oppressive husband. O, how many of our best citizens know, by sad experience, what it is to wear the galling yoke of bondage.

How many a sainted wife and mother has been ground down and trampled into the very dust — crushed by the arbitrary power of perverted manhood: thus degrading the high and noble relation of husband for the weak, into that of a blood-thirsty persecutor! How many inspirations of the Deity have thus been stifled, and strangled at their birth!

O, how many a nobly endowed woman, subjected to a tyrant's unlimited control, has been crushed, and been led to desire death, rather than such a life of cruel bondage! Yea, how many have sought death, as their only refuge from this never-dying death!

O, the long train of living martyrs that have gone to God's throne, and God's tribunal, to get their wrongs avenged on the earth — because they had no protection, no claims for justice at their country's tribunal!

Have they appealed to this higher court in vain? No — "Verily, the Judge of all the earth will do right," and no power can hinder it. Will not the claims of this host of martyred married slaves be exacted from the government, which would not protect their identity from the usurpation of perverted manhood? Yes, 'tis true this government has a great account to meet and settle, for protecting, by its laws, that most guilty of all oppressors — *an oppressive husband.*

Think you, my Countrymen, that God will compromise with these guilty men, by not bringing out each individual act of injustice to his wife, for investigation — to be singly weighed in the balances of eternal justice?

Can any guilty husband elude this test? Will any artful subterfuge avail to screen him from receiving the just sentence of his angry Judge? Did you, guilty man, seek to quiet your accusing conscience, by the fact, "that because sentence against an evil doer was not speedily executed," therefore it never would be executed? If so, your refuge of lies will be demolished. On the character of your own individual acts, you must stand or fall, in judgment.

O! my Countrymen, see to it that these oppressive fiends are no longer sheltered under the insane laws of your government — laws which obliterate the personal identity of the largest and best portion of our American citizens. Let married women's inalienable rights be protected by the laws of our country. Let no law or practice which conflicts with the law of *love to all,* receive your sanction any longer. O, protest, in the name of God, that these wicked, devilish influences shall exist no longer, so far as your individual practice extends.

Dare to stand up for Jesus, amid this evil and adulterous generation, as Abraham did, alone, with none but God for his defense — remembering that God says, "He that is ashamed of me and of my words, in this evil and adulterous generation,' of him shall the Son of man be ashamed, when he cometh to judge the world." "What you do, do quickly; for the end is at hand," and judgment has already "begun, at the house of God." Yes, God has, by his inscrutable Providence, presented my husband, a professed minister of Christ, before you, for judgment! God is now giving you an opportunity to manifest your real character, preparatory to the judgment; by seeing in which party you will be found — whether in the insane party, who protect the

oppressor, or in the sane party, who desire to protect the oppressed, and have, as yet, seen no way in which they could do it. Now is the crisis which is to mark your individual destiny. "If the Lord be God," uphold his government; "but if Baal," then uphold him. The decision will develope to which kingdom you belong.

Will you, my Countrymen, protect the weak, on the principles of God's government, by the higher law; or will you, in defense of human laws, seek to maintain those laws of our government which conflict with this higher law?

As the ocean is made up of drops, so our government is made up of individual voters, and the sum of their votes will decide the individual, real character of this government.

To the Government of these United States of America, I now make my appeal for protection. Say, will you protect the inalienable rights of womanhood in me, or will you not? I wait a prisoner, among maniacs, for your answer!

Say, shall I remain, buried alive, in this living tomb, till the trumpet of the archangel summons us to judgment; or will you protect me, and allow me to come forth to the world, with my new, resurrected life, with which I will try to aid in moving on the triumphal car of universal liberty?

Let the votes of the people for the higher and the lower law be speedily tested — for as is *my fate*, so will be that of *my country*.

Will you restore to me my personal liberty? Will you secure to me my rights as an American citizen?

Will you restore to me my family rights — my maternal rights — and my inalienable rights; and will you protect me in the lawful Christian exercise of these rights?

These rights have been all usurped, and wrested from me, by my husband, in consequence of my immovable determination to maintain, inviolate, my rights of conscience.

Must another American wife be liable to have to pay this enormous price for the lawful exercise of these God-given rights?

I do not ask you to redress my wrongs; I only ask you to protect me in my rights. God will be my avenger, in his own time and way. "Vengeance is mine, I will repay, saith the Lord." I do not believe in one sinner punishing another sinner. My conscience forbids my doing so; for the simple reason, that God tells me not to do so; and I, like a dutiful child, have only to trust his promise to do for me, what he strictly forbids my doing for myself.

But it is not my object in presenting this statement to the world, to

make out a logical argument, addressed to your understanding, my Countrymen, to enforce my appeal for protection; although such an invincible argument could be framed, based on the eternal principles of ethics and religion, both; but it is now my object to present that most stubborn of all arguments and appeals, viz., the argument of facts as they exist, leaving them to make their own mute appeal to your hearts and consciences. It is not *knowledge* of what is right, that you most need, but it is moral courage *to do right*, as your own consciences dictate, that is wanting.

Once more, only, I ask you, will you deliver me from the oppressive, usurping, persecuting, murderous power of my Calvinistic husband, *in spite* of the laws of this American Government, which protect him in his outrages?

Can you not enact laws by which a married woman can stand on the same platform as a married man — as an American citizens — that is, have an equal right, at least, to the protection of their inalienable rights? And is not this, our petition for protection, founded in justice and humanity? Is it just to leave the weakest and most defenseless of these two parties wholly without the shelter of law to shield her, while the strongest and most independent party has all the aid of the legal arm to strengthen his own? Nay, verily, it is not right or manly for our man government thus to usurp the whole legal power of self-protection and defense, and leave confiding, trusting woman, wholly at the mercy of this gigantic power. For perverted men will use this absolute power to abuse the defenseless, rather than protect them; and this abuse of power inevitably leads to the contempt of its victim. For example — a man who can trample on all the inalienable rights of his wife, will, by so doing, come to despise her, as an inevitable consequence of this wrong doing. For it is an immutable law of our moral nature that our feelings grow out of our actions. If we *do* right, we shall *feel* right — if we *do* wrong, we shall *feel* wrong. Let Calvinistic husbands, therefore, be *compelled* to treat their wives with decent respect, and they will then be made to feel a decent regard for them as their companions, whom the laws protect from their abuse.

My husband said to me when he was putting me into this Asylum, "I am putting you where the laws of your country put you, to protect you, as your protector!!" I replied, "I shall ask the Government to protect me against such a protector."

I have kept my word. My work is done. I have been weighed in the balances, and have not been found wanting. Your time to oe weighed has fully come. God grant that you be not found wanting!

Now is your time to choose, whether you will be a God fearing government, or a God-oppressing government. Remember, that in every human being is a personified Deity — that in every human being he creates, he multiplies himself.

Remember, too, that woman is a more spiritual being than a man, and is, therefore, a more sensitive being, and a more patient sufferer than a man. And O, forget not, that a spiritual woman is a living temple of the Holy Ghost. O! do not let her be any longer *blasphemed* by this American Government.

And, as she, more than any other being, needs protection, so may she find it, in *that* government which she has sacrificed so much to uphold and sustain. And, as you succor and protect her, in her necessities, so may you be succored and delivered out of your troubles.

Will you not, my Countrymen, recognize in every human being a brother or a sister, who has equal rights, as an independent sovereign, with yourselves — crowned with the same power, and subject to the same authority?

Say, will you respect God's authority, or Calvin's authority?

Will you be a Christian government, or a Calvinistic government?

END OF VOLUME I.

Women in America

FROM COLONIAL TIMES TO THE 20TH CENTURY

An Arno Press Collection

Andrews, John B. and W. D. P. Bliss. **History of Women in Trade Unions** (*Report on Conditions of Woman and Child Wage-Earners in the United States,* Vol. X; 61st Congress, 2nd Session, Senate Document No. 645). 1911

Anthony, Susan B. **An Account of the Proceedings on the Trial of Susan B. Anthony, on the Charge of Illegal Voting at the Presidential Election in November, 1872,** and on the Trial of Beverly W. Jones, Edwin T. Marsh and William B. Hall, the Inspectors of Election by Whom her Vote was Received. 1874

The Autobiography of a Happy Woman. 1915

Ayer, Harriet Hubbard. **Harriet Hubbard Ayer's Book:** A Complete and Authentic Treatise on the Laws of Health and Beauty. 1902

Barrett, Kate Waller. **Some Practical Suggestions on the Conduct of a Rescue Home.** *Including* **Life of Dr. Kate Waller Barrett** (Reprinted from *Fifty Years' Work With Girls* by Otto Wilson). [1903]

Bates, Mrs. D. B. **Incidents on Land and Water;** Or, Four Years on the Pacific Coast. 1858

Blumenthal, Walter Hart. **Women Camp Followers of the American Revolution.** 1952

Boothe, Viva B., editor. **Women in the Modern World** (*The Annals of the American Academy of Political and Social Science,* Vol. CXLIII, May 1929). 1929

Bowne, Eliza Southgate. **A Girl's Life Eighty Years Ago:** Selections from the Letters of Eliza Southgate Bowne. 1888

Brooks, Geraldine. **Dames and Daughters of Colonial Days.** 1900

Carola Woerishoffer: Her Life and Work. 1912

Clement, J[esse], editor. **Noble Deeds of American Women;** With Biographical Sketches of Some of the More Prominent. 1851

Crow, Martha Foote. **The American Country Girl.** 1915

De Leon, T[homas] C. **Belles, Beaux and Brains of the 60's.** 1909

de Wolfe, Elsie (Lady Mendl). **After All.** 1935

Dix, Dorothy (Elizabeth Meriwether Gilmer). **How to Win and Hold a Husband.** 1939

Donovan, Frances R. **The Saleslady.** 1929

Donovan, Frances R. **The Schoolma'am.** 1938

Donovan, Frances R. **The Woman Who Waits.** 1920

Eagle, Mary Kavanaugh Oldham, editor. **The Congress of Women,** Held in the Woman's Building, World's Columbian Exposition, Chicago, U.S.A., 1893. 1894

Ellet, Elizabeth F. **The Eminent and Heroic Women of America.** 1873

Ellis, Anne. **The Life of an Ordinary Woman.** 1929

[Farrar, Eliza W. R.] **The Young Lady's Friend.** By a Lady. 1836

Filene, Catherine, editor. **Careers for Women.** 1920

Finley, Ruth E. **The Lady of Godey's:** Sarah Josepha Hale. 1931 **Fragments of Autobiography.** 1974

Frost, John. **Pioneer Mothers of the West;** Or, Daring and Heroic Deeds of American Women. 1869

[Gilman], Charlotte Perkins Stetson. **In This Our World.** 1899

Goldberg, Jacob A. and Rosamond W. Goldberg. **Girls on the City Streets:** A Study of 1400 Cases of Rape. 1935

Grace H. Dodge: Her Life and Work. 1974

Greenbie, Marjorie Barstow. **My Dear Lady:** The Story of Anna Ella Carroll, the "Great Unrecognized Member of Lincoln's Cabinet." 1940

Hourwich, Andria Taylor and Gladys L. Palmer, editors. **I Am a Woman Worker:** A Scrapbook of Autobiographies. 1936

Howe, M[ark] A. De Wolfe. **Memories of a Hostess:** A Chronicle of Friendships Drawn Chiefly from the Diaries of Mrs. James T. Fields. 1922

Irwin, Inez Haynes. **Angels and Amazons:** A Hundred Years of American Women. 1934

Laughlin, Clara E. **The Work-a-Day Girl:** A Study of Some Present-Day Conditions. 1913

Lewis, Dio. **Our Girls.** 1871

Liberating the Home. 1974

Livermore, Mary A. **The Story of My Life; Or,** The Sunshine and Shadow of Seventy Years . . . To Which is Added Six of Her Most Popular Lectures. 1899

Lives to Remember. 1974

Lobsenz, Johanna. **The Older Woman in Industry.** 1929

MacLean, Annie Marion. **Wage-Earning Women.** 1910

Meginness, John F. **Biography of Frances Slocum, the Lost Sister of Wyoming:** A Complete Narrative of her Captivity of Wanderings· Among the Indians. 1891

Nathan, Maud. **Once Upon a Time and Today.** 1933

[Packard, Elizabeth Parsons Ware]. **Great Disclosure of Spiritual Wickedness!!** In High Places. With an Appeal to the Government to Protect the Inalienable Rights of Married Women. 1865

Parsons, Alice Beal. **Woman's Dilemma.** 1926

Parton, James, et al. **Eminent Women of the Age:** Being Narratives of the Lives and Deeds of the Most Prominent Women of the Present Generation. 1869

Paton, Lucy Allen. **Elizabeth Cary Agassiz:** A Biography. 1919

Rayne, M[artha] L[ouise]. **What Can a Woman Do;** Or, Her Position in the Business and Literary World. 1893

Richmond, Mary E. and Fred S. Hall. **A Study of Nine Hundred and Eighty-Five Widows Known to Certain Charity Organization Societies in 1910.** 1913

Ross, Ishbel. **Ladies of the Press:** The Story of Women in Journalism by an Insider. 1936

Sex and Equality. 1974

Snyder, Charles McCool. **Dr. Mary Walker:** The Little Lady in Pants. 1962

Stow, Mrs. J. W. **Probate Confiscation:** Unjust Laws Which Govern Woman. 1878

Sumner, Helen L. **History of Women in Industry in the United**

States (*Report on Conditions of Woman and Child Wage-Earners in the United States,* Vol. IX; 61st Congress, 2nd Session, Senate Document No. 645). 1910

[Vorse, Mary H.] **Autobiography of an Elderly Woman.** 1911

Washburn, Charles. **Come into My Parlor:** A Biography of the Aristocratic Everleigh Sisters of Chicago. 1936

Women of Lowell. 1974

Woolson, Abba Gould. **Dress-Reform:** A Series of Lectures Delivered in Boston on Dress as it Affects the Health of Women. 1874

Working Girls of Cincinnati. 1974